Dr. STONE

STORY **RIICHIRO INAGAKI**
ART **BOICHI**

19

**CORN CITY:
POPULATION
ONE MILLION**

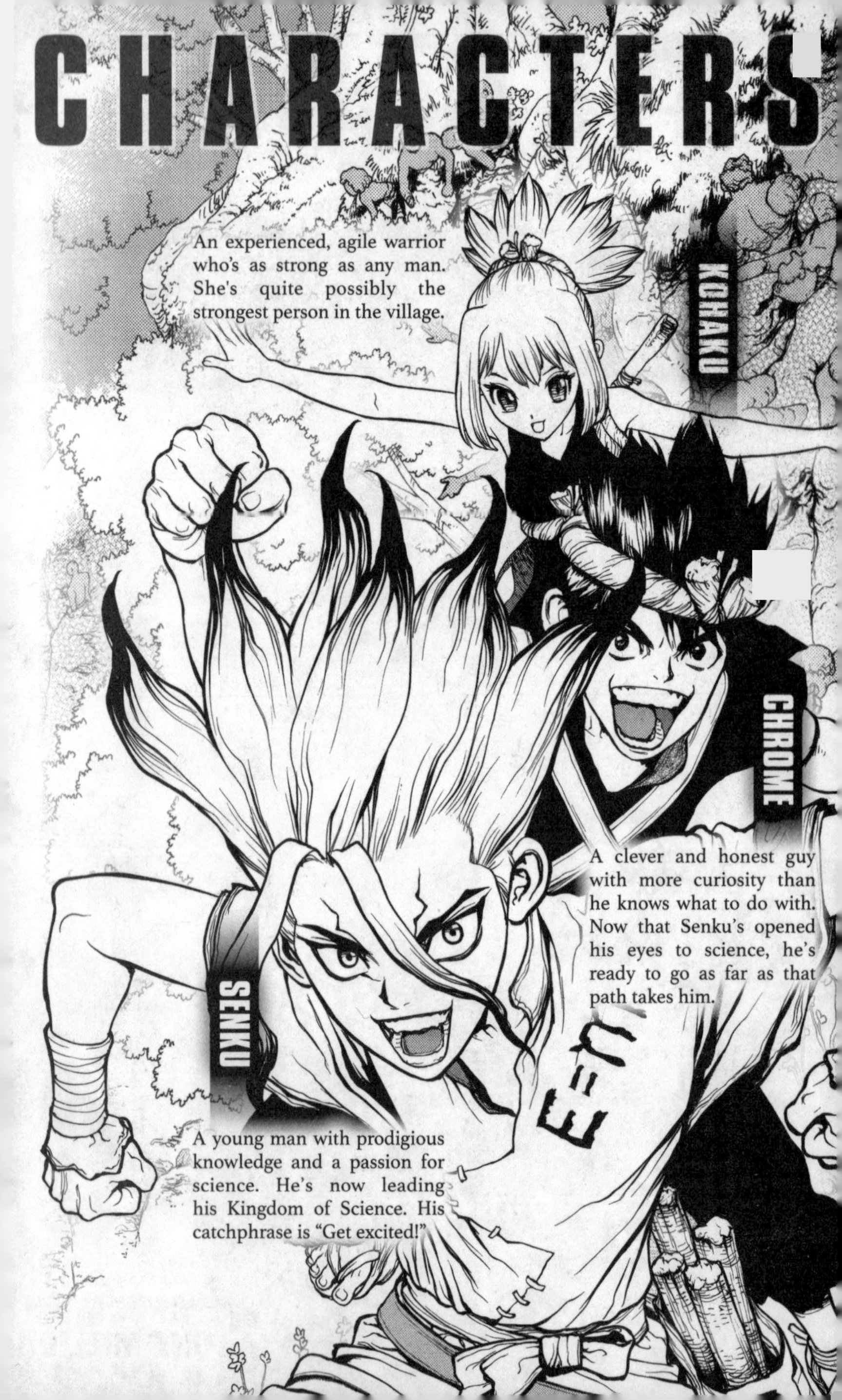
CHARACTERS
KOHAKU
An experienced, agile warrior who's as strong as any man. She's quite possibly the strongest person in the village.
CHROME
A clever and honest guy with more curiosity than he knows what to do with. Now that Senku's opened his eyes to science, he's ready to go as far as that path takes him.
SENKU
A young man with prodigious knowledge and a passion for science. He's now leading his Kingdom of Science. His catchphrase is "Get excited!"

Dr.STONE

STORY

Every human on earth is turned to stone by a mysterious phenomenon, including high school student Taiju. Nearly 3,700 years later, Taiju awakens and finds his friend Senku, who revived a bit earlier. Together, they vow to restore civilization, but Tsukasa, once considered the strongest high schooler alive, nearly kills Senku in order to put a stop to his scientific plans.

After being secretly revived by his friends, Senku arrives at Ishigami Village. But when word of Senku's survival gets back to Tsukasa, the war between the two forces begins! Eventually, the two factions make peace, but the traitorous Hyoga skewers Tsukasa. Senku cryogenically freezes Tsukasa's body. After acquiring the petrification device on Treasure Island, Senku revives Tsukasa.

Now, in the former U.S.A., it's science kingdom versus science kingdom, and each side is racing to take down the other's scientist leader! Senku and Dr. Xeno realize that they knew each other before the great petrification, but Xeno still orders Stanley to snipe Senku. Heavily wounded, Senku has to trust Chrome the scientist to get the job done!

LUNA   STANLEY   DR. XENO

TAIJU   RYUSUI   TSUKASA   GEN ASAGIRI

CONTENTS

19
CORN CITY: POPULATION ONE MILLION

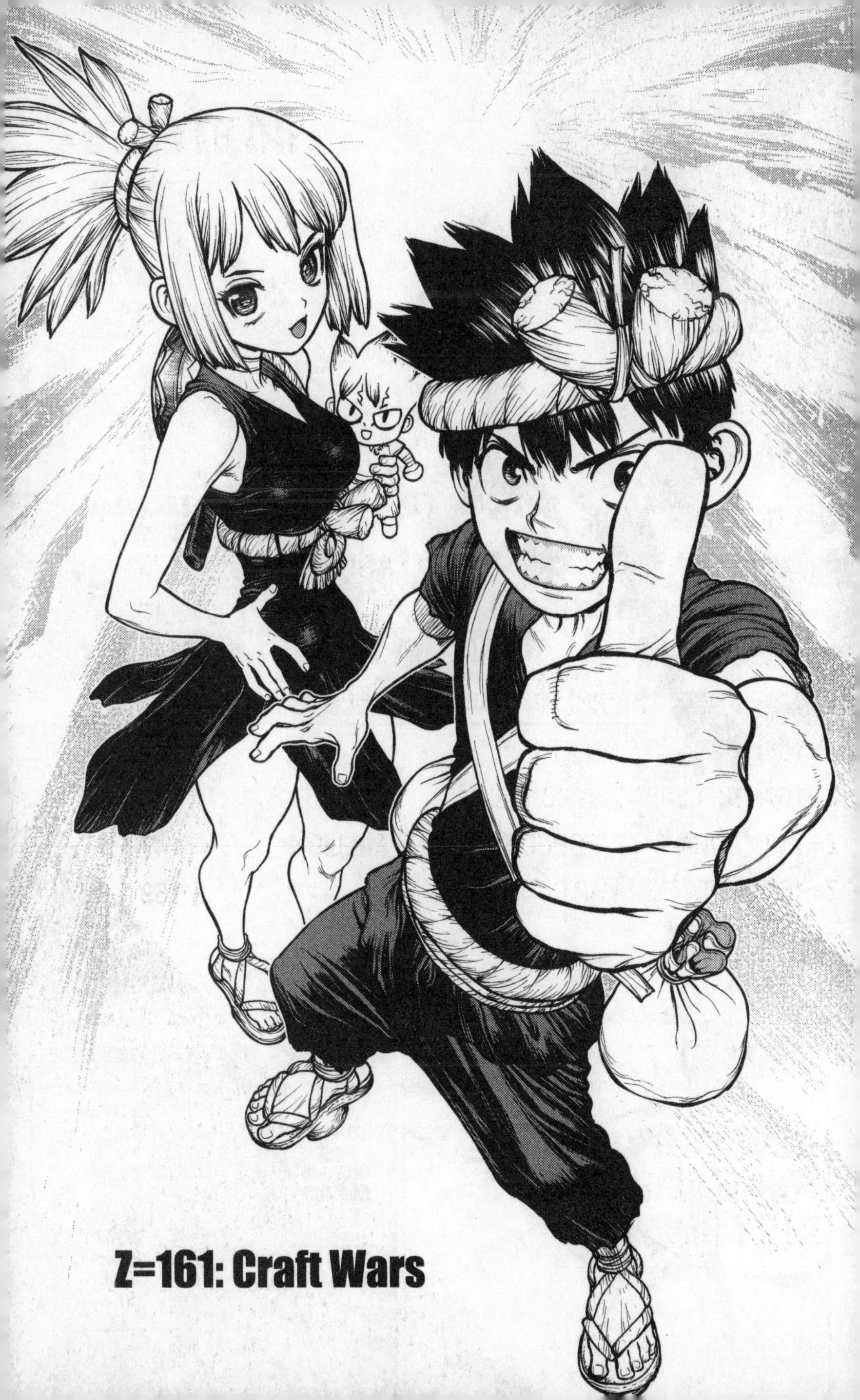

Z=161: Craft Wars

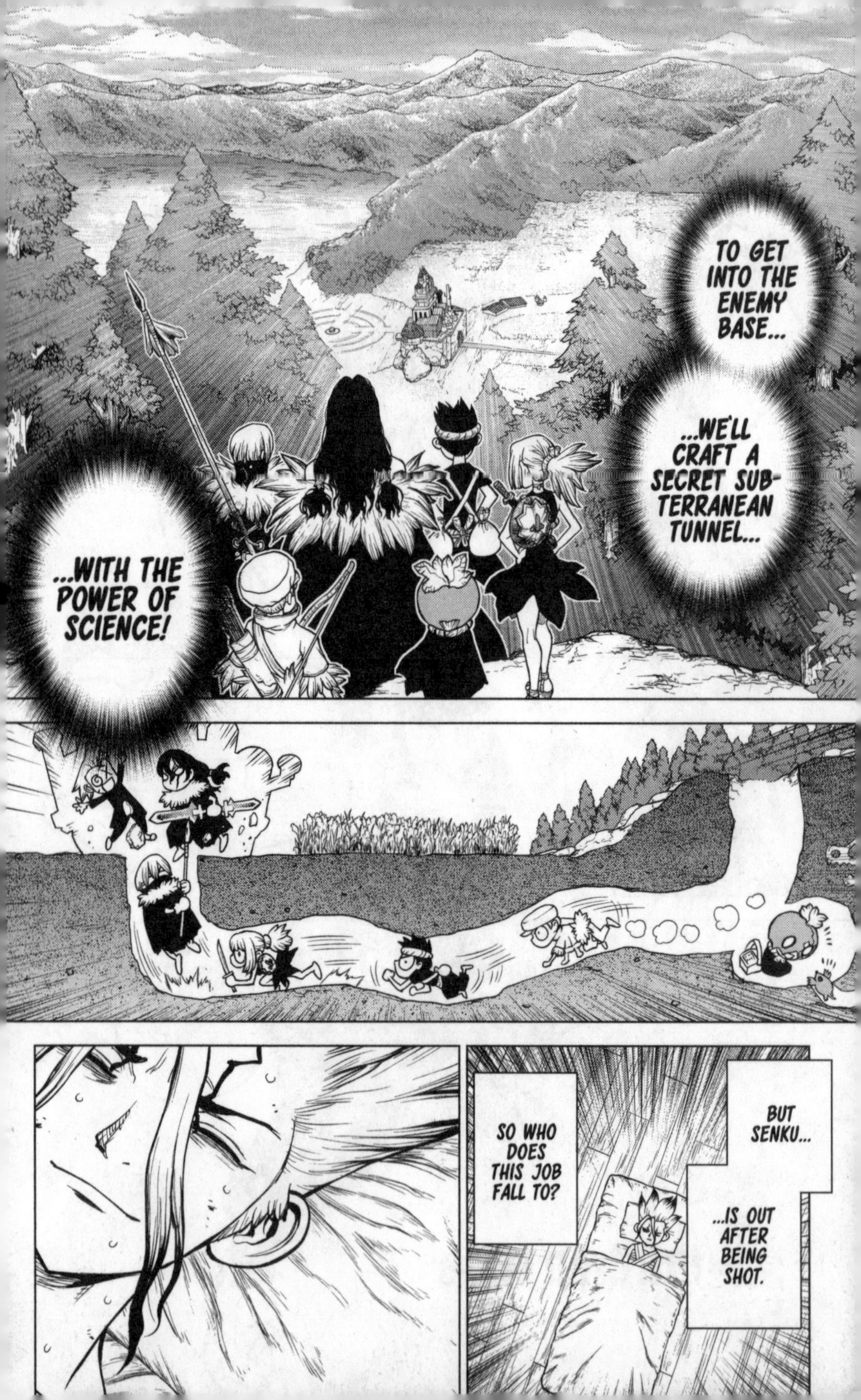
TO GET INTO THE ENEMY BASE...
...WE'LL CRAFT A SECRET SUB-TERRANEAN TUNNEL...
...WITH THE POWER OF SCIENCE!
BUT SENKU...
...IS OUT AFTER BEING SHOT.
SO WHO DOES THIS JOB FALL TO?

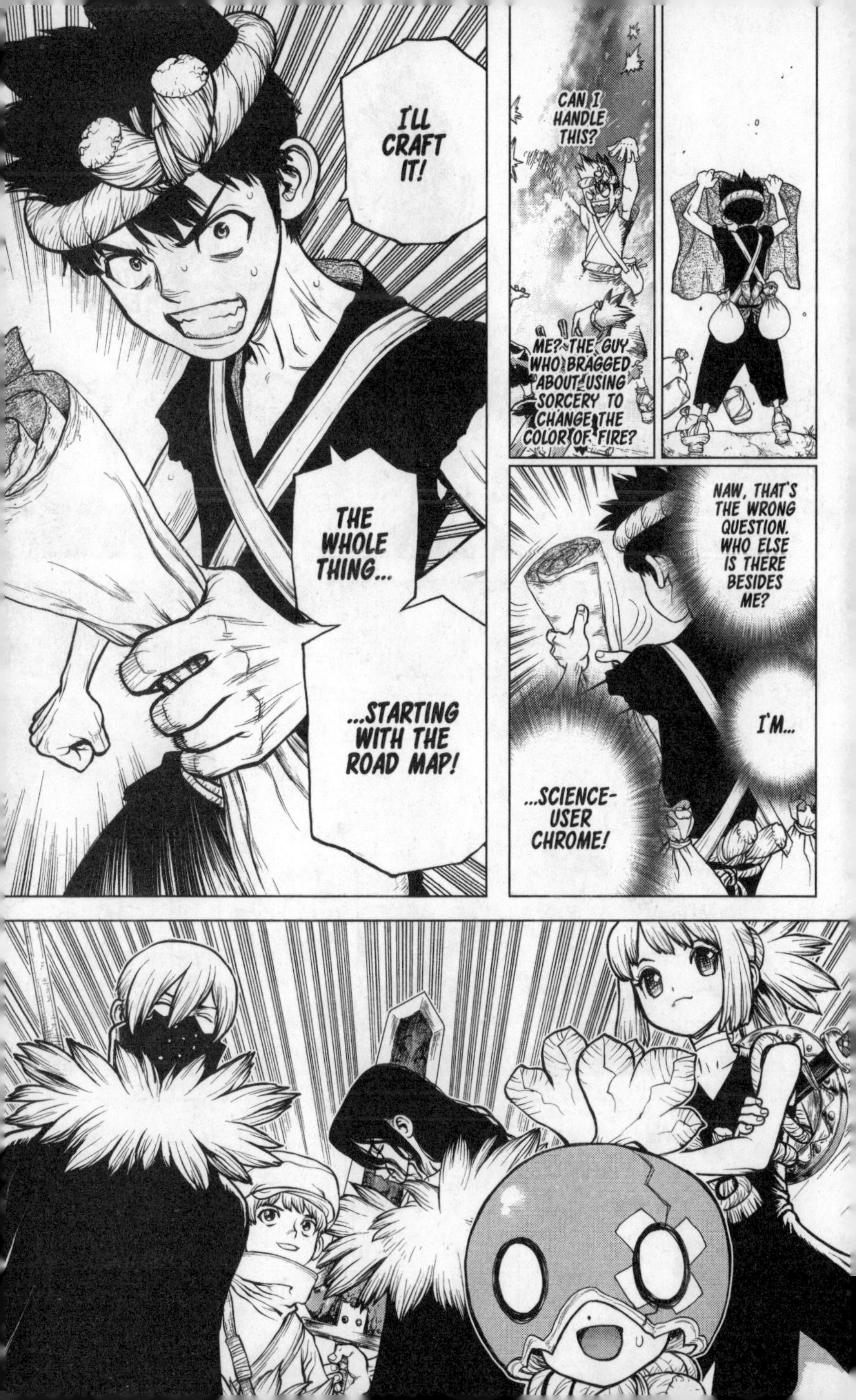
CAN I HANDLE THIS?
ME? THE GUY WHO BRAGGED ABOUT USING SORCERY TO CHANGE THE COLOR OF FIRE?
NAW, THAT'S THE WRONG QUESTION. WHO ELSE IS THERE BESIDES ME?
I'M...
...SCIENCE-USER CHROME!
I'LL CRAFT IT!
THE WHOLE THING...
...STARTING WITH THE ROAD MAP!

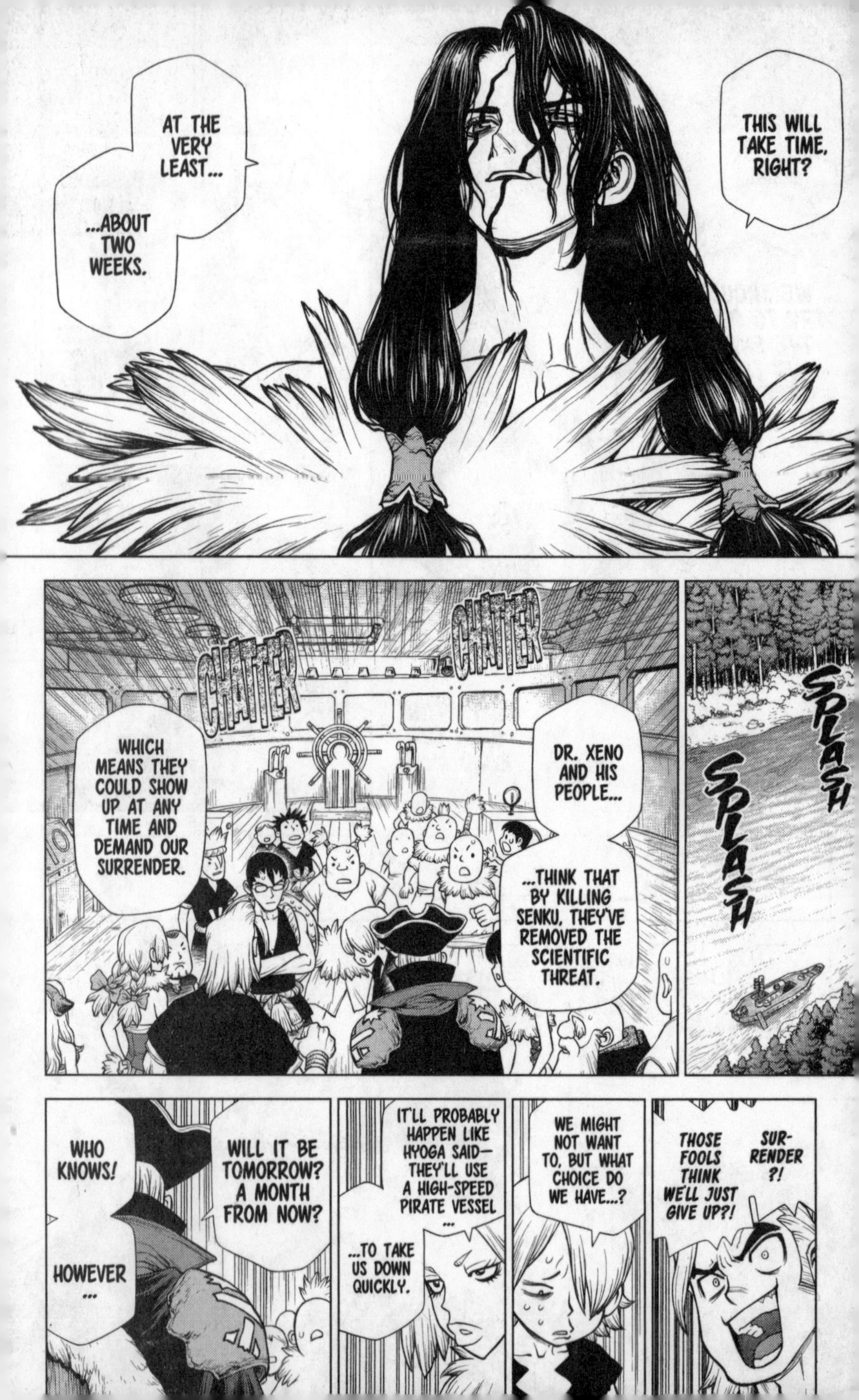
THIS WILL TAKE TIME, RIGHT?
AT THE VERY LEAST...
...ABOUT TWO WEEKS.
SPLASH
SPLASH
CHATTER
CHATTER
DR. XENO AND HIS PEOPLE...
...THINK THAT BY KILLING SENKU, THEY'VE REMOVED THE SCIENTIFIC THREAT.
WHICH MEANS THEY COULD SHOW UP AT ANY TIME AND DEMAND OUR SURRENDER.
SUR-RENDER?!
THOSE FOOLS THINK WE'LL JUST GIVE UP?!
WE MIGHT NOT WANT TO, BUT WHAT CHOICE DO WE HAVE...?
IT'LL PROBABLY HAPPEN LIKE HYOGA SAID—THEY'LL USE A HIGH-SPEED PIRATE VESSEL...
...TO TAKE US DOWN QUICKLY.
WILL IT BE TOMORROW? A MONTH FROM NOW?
WHO KNOWS!
HOWEVER...

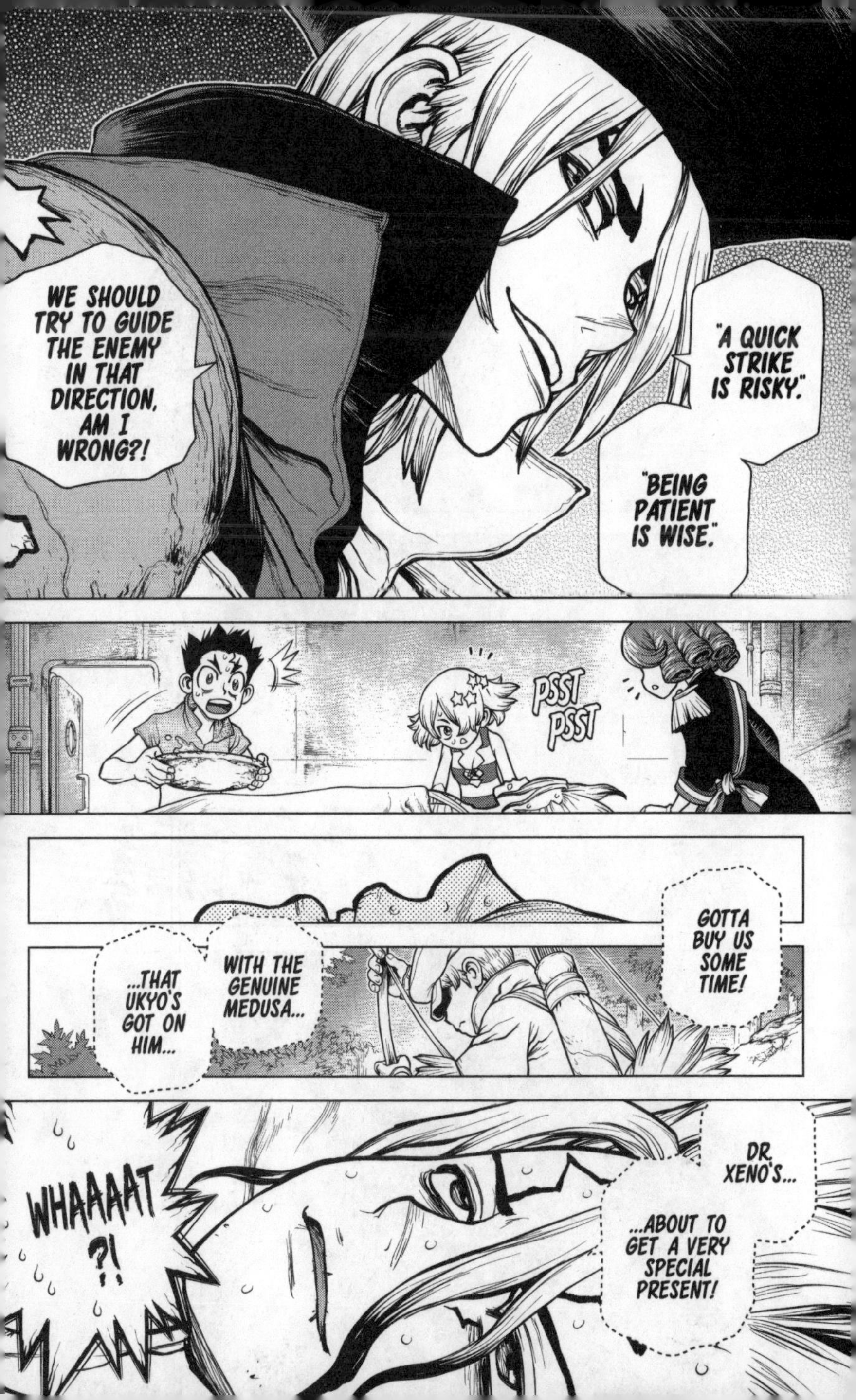
"A QUICK STRIKE IS RISKY."
"BEING PATIENT IS WISE."
WE SHOULD TRY TO GUIDE THE ENEMY IN THAT DIRECTION, AM I WRONG?!
PSST PSST
GOTTA BUY US SOME TIME!
WITH THE GENUINE MEDUSA...
...THAT UKYO'S GOT ON HIM...
DR. XENO'S...
...ABOUT TO GET A VERY SPECIAL PRESENT!
WHAAAAT?!

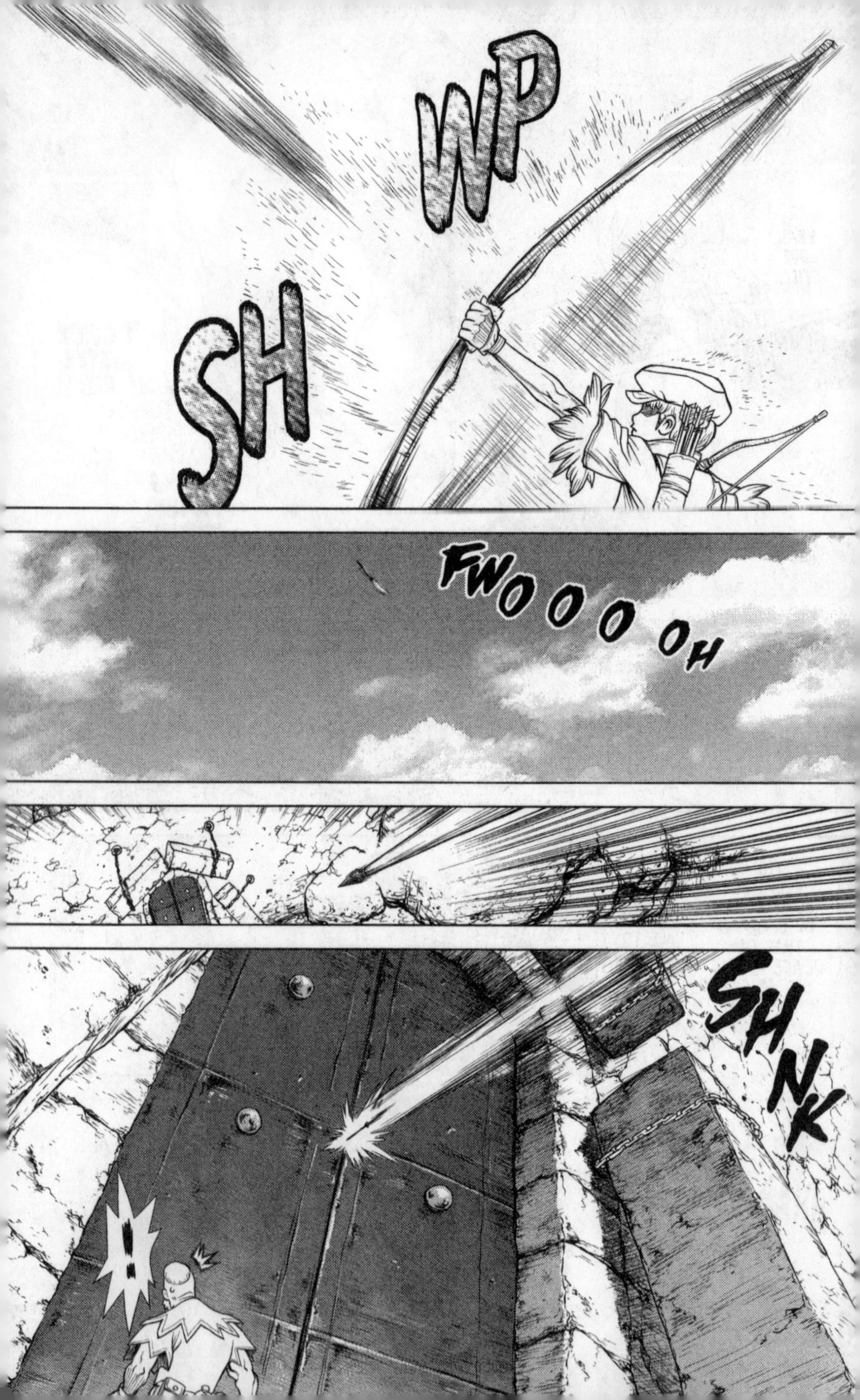
SHWP
FWOOOOH
SHNK
!

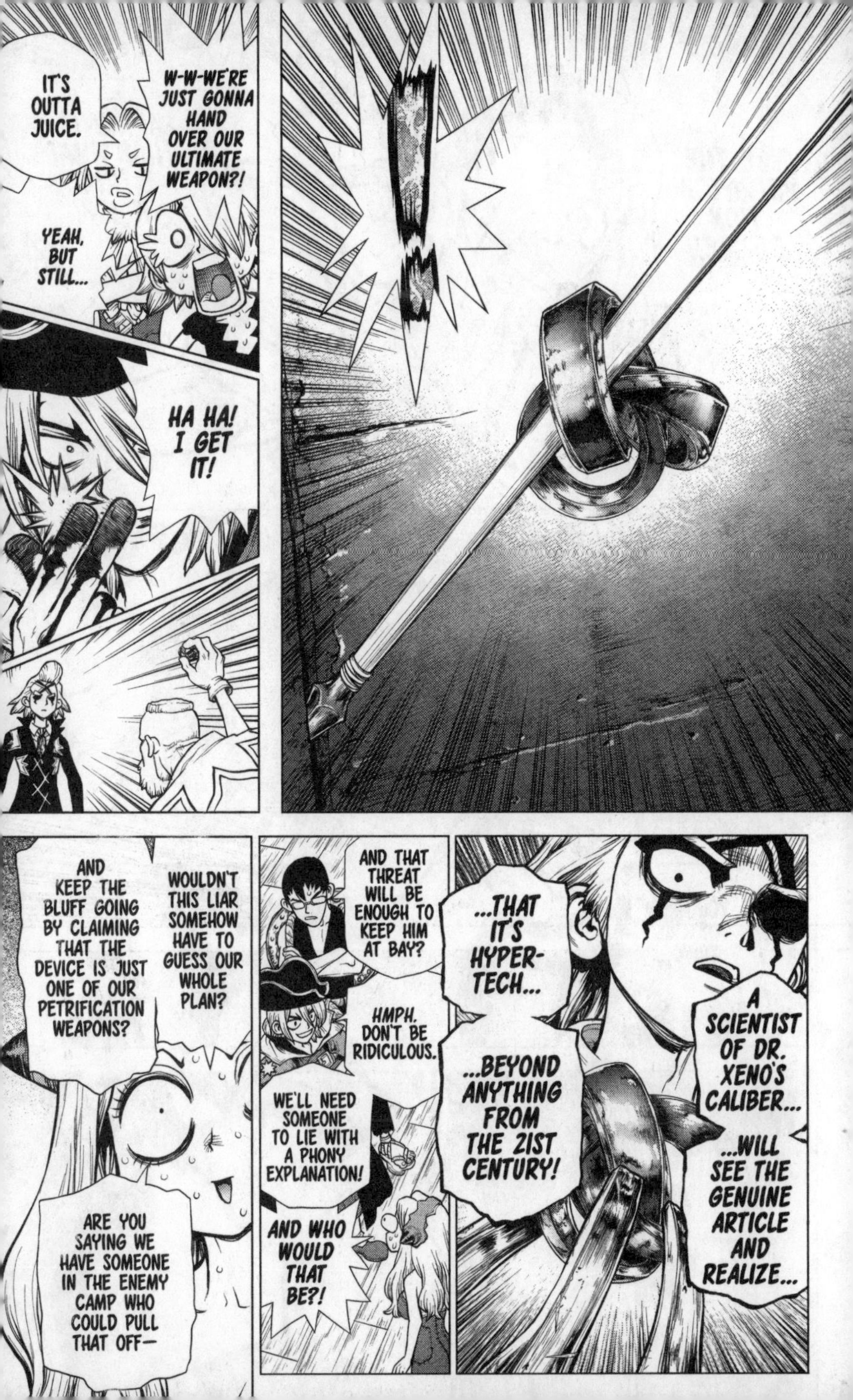
W-W-WE'RE JUST GONNA HAND OVER OUR ULTIMATE WEAPON?!
IT'S OUTTA JUICE.
YEAH, BUT STILL...
HA HA! I GET IT!
A SCIENTIST OF DR. XENO'S CALIBER...
...WILL SEE THE GENUINE ARTICLE AND REALIZE...
...THAT IT'S HYPER-TECH...
...BEYOND ANYTHING FROM THE 21ST CENTURY!
AND THAT THREAT WILL BE ENOUGH TO KEEP HIM AT BAY?
HMPH. DON'T BE RIDICULOUS.
WE'LL NEED SOMEONE TO LIE WITH A PHONY EXPLANATION!
AND WHO WOULD THAT BE?!
WOULDN'T THIS LIAR SOMEHOW HAVE TO GUESS OUR WHOLE PLAN?
AND KEEP THE BLUFF GOING BY CLAIMING THAT THE DEVICE IS JUST ONE OF OUR PETRIFICATION WEAPONS?
ARE YOU SAYING WE HAVE SOMEONE IN THE ENEMY CAMP WHO COULD PULL THAT OFF—

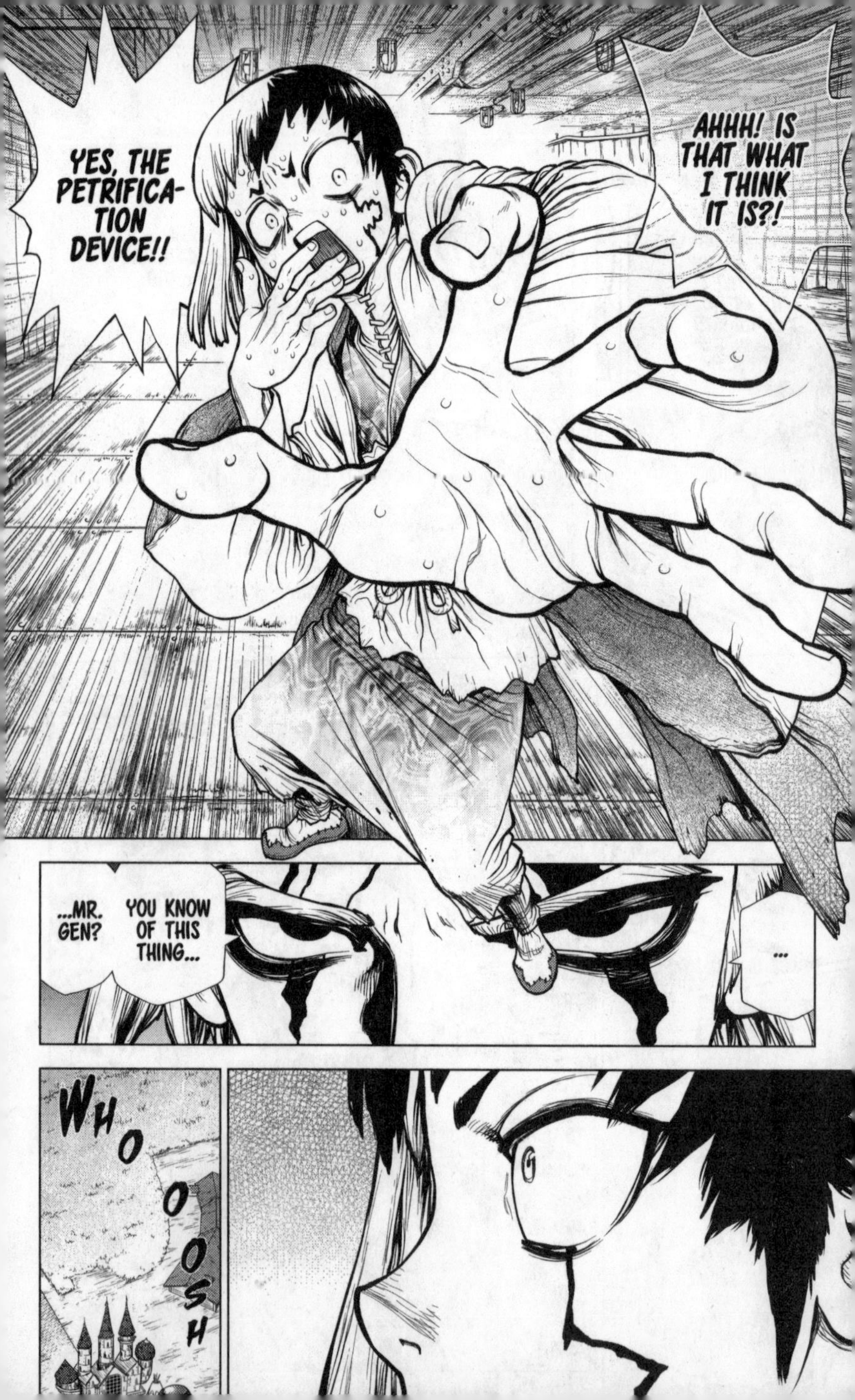
AHHH! IS THAT WHAT I THINK IT IS?!
YES, THE PETRIFICATION DEVICE!!
...
YOU KNOW OF THIS THING...
...MR. GEN?
WHOOOOSH

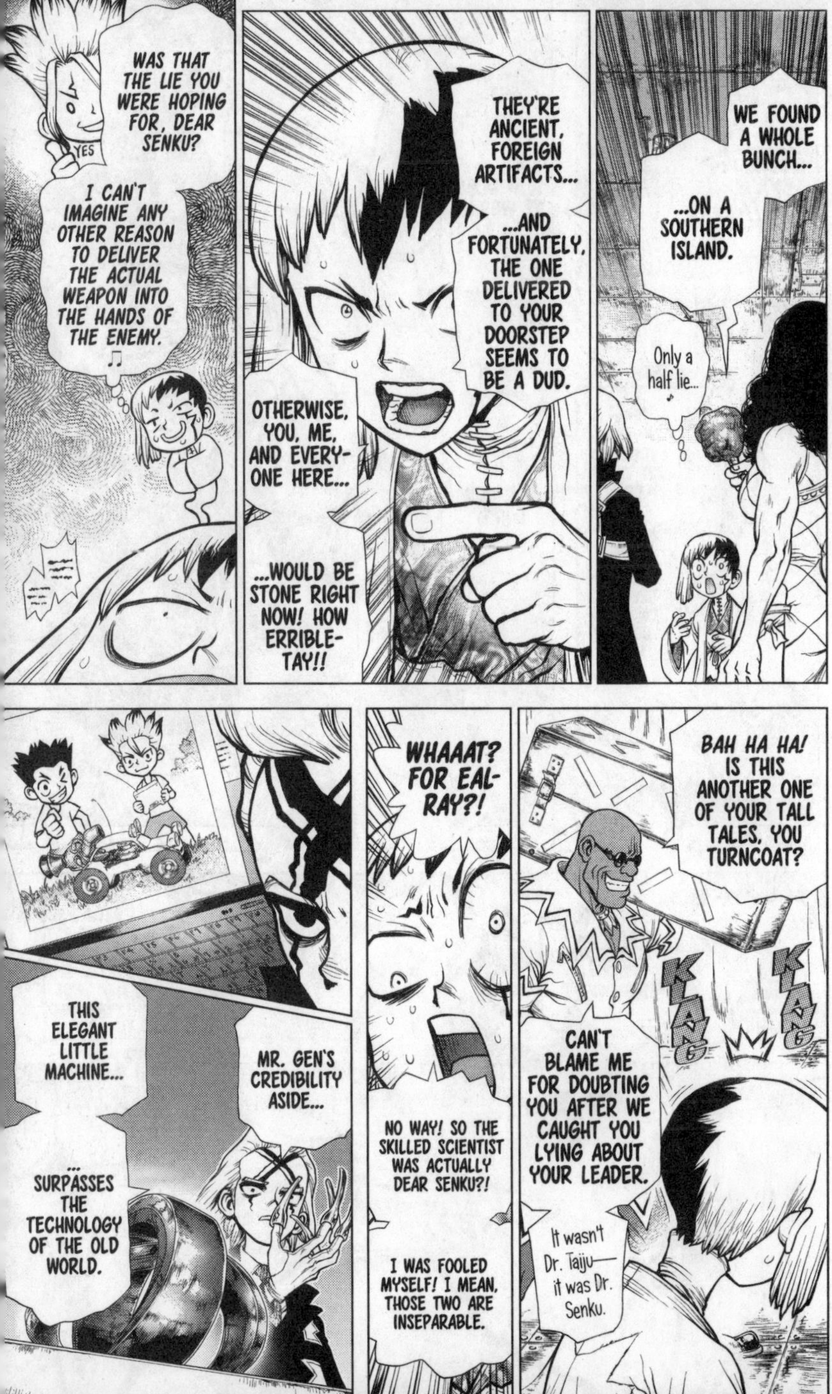
WE FOUND A WHOLE BUNCH...
...ON A SOUTHERN ISLAND.
Only a half lie... ♪
THEY'RE ANCIENT, FOREIGN ARTIFACTS...
...AND FORTUNATELY, THE ONE DELIVERED TO YOUR DOORSTEP SEEMS TO BE A DUD.
OTHERWISE, YOU, ME, AND EVERYONE HERE...
...WOULD BE STONE RIGHT NOW! HOW ERRIBLE-TAY!!
WAS THAT THE LIE YOU WERE HOPING FOR, DEAR SENKU?
YES
I CAN'T IMAGINE ANY OTHER REASON TO DELIVER THE ACTUAL WEAPON INTO THE HANDS OF THE ENEMY. ♫
BAH HA HA! IS THIS ANOTHER ONE OF YOUR TALL TALES, YOU TURNCOAT?
KLANG
KLANG
CAN'T BLAME ME FOR DOUBTING YOU AFTER WE CAUGHT YOU LYING ABOUT YOUR LEADER.
It wasn't Dr. Taiju— it was Dr. Senku.
WHAAAT? FOR EAL-RAY?!
NO WAY! SO THE SKILLED SCIENTIST WAS ACTUALLY DEAR SENKU?!
I WAS FOOLED MYSELF! I MEAN, THOSE TWO ARE INSEPARABLE.
MR. GEN'S CREDIBILITY ASIDE...
THIS ELEGANT LITTLE MACHINE...
...SURPASSES THE TECHNOLOGY OF THE OLD WORLD.

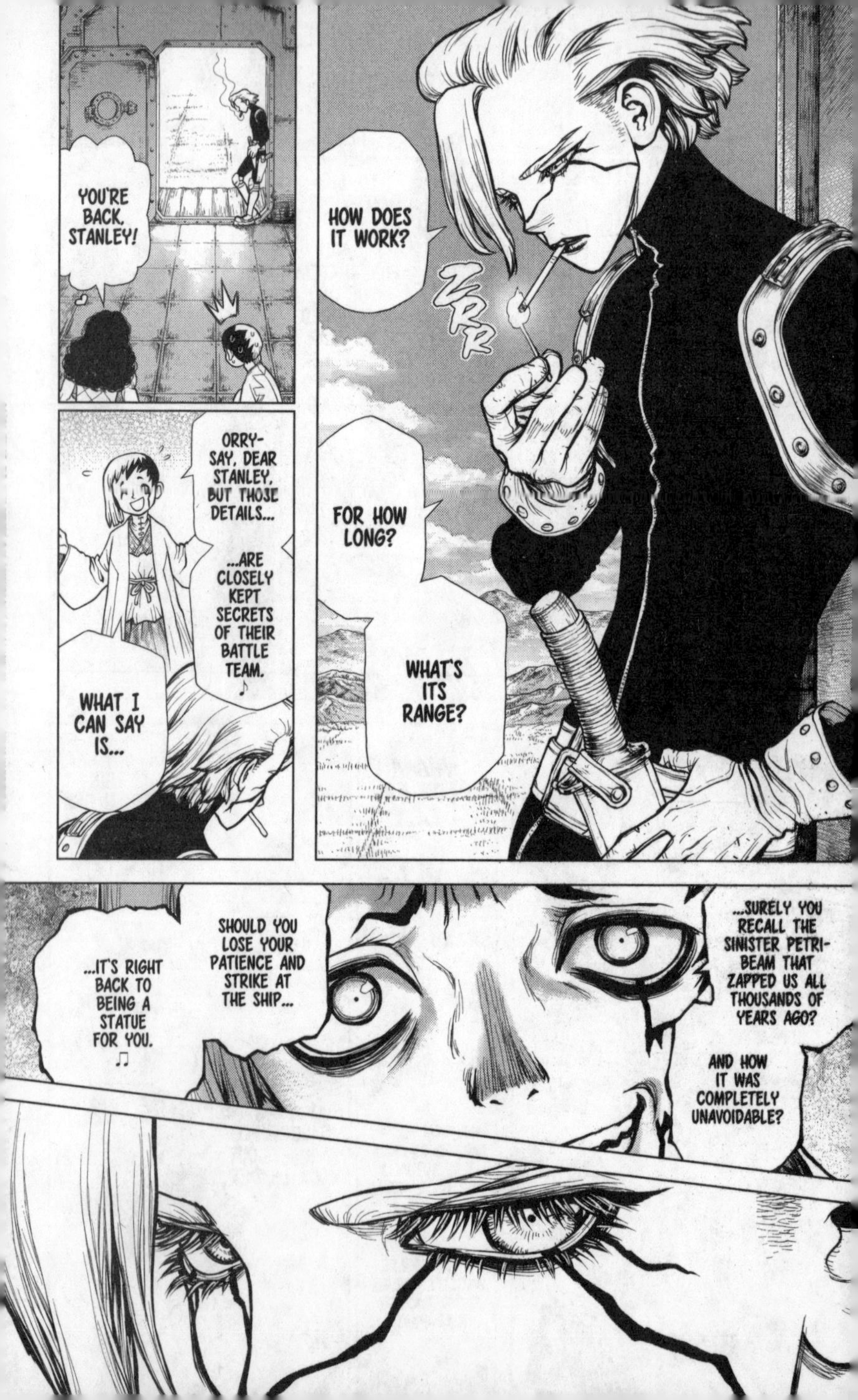
HOW DOES IT WORK?
ZRR
FOR HOW LONG?
WHAT'S ITS RANGE?
YOU'RE BACK, STANLEY!
ORRY-SAY, DEAR STANLEY, BUT THOSE DETAILS...
...ARE CLOSELY KEPT SECRETS OF THEIR BATTLE TEAM. ♪
WHAT I CAN SAY IS...
...SURELY YOU RECALL THE SINISTER PETRI-BEAM THAT ZAPPED US ALL THOUSANDS OF YEARS AGO?
AND HOW IT WAS COMPLETELY UNAVOIDABLE?
SHOULD YOU LOSE YOUR PATIENCE AND STRIKE AT THE SHIP...
...IT'S RIGHT BACK TO BEING A STATUE FOR YOU. ♫

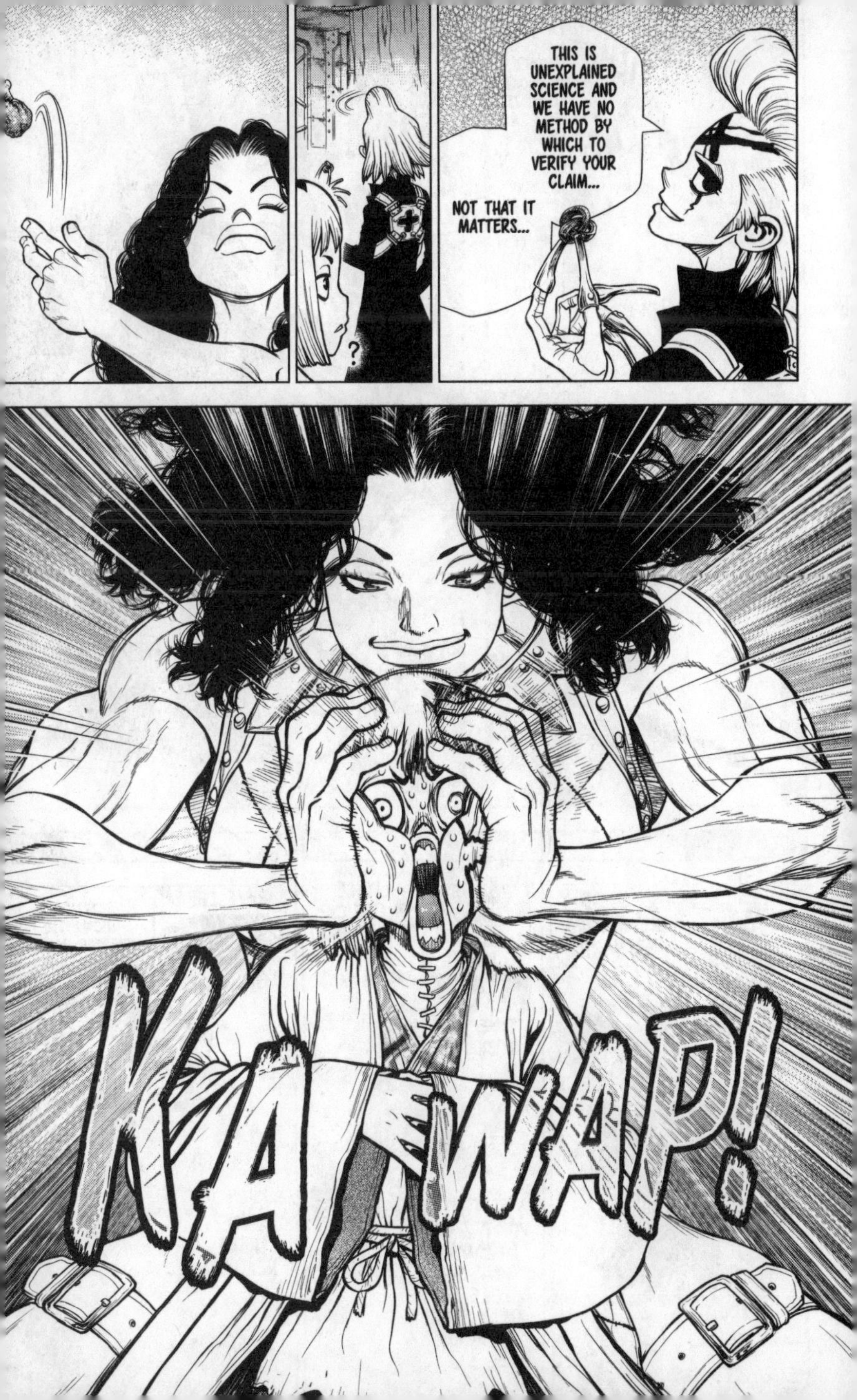
THIS IS UNEXPLAINED SCIENCE AND WE HAVE NO METHOD BY WHICH TO VERIFY YOUR CLAIM...
NOT THAT IT MATTERS...
?
KAWAP!

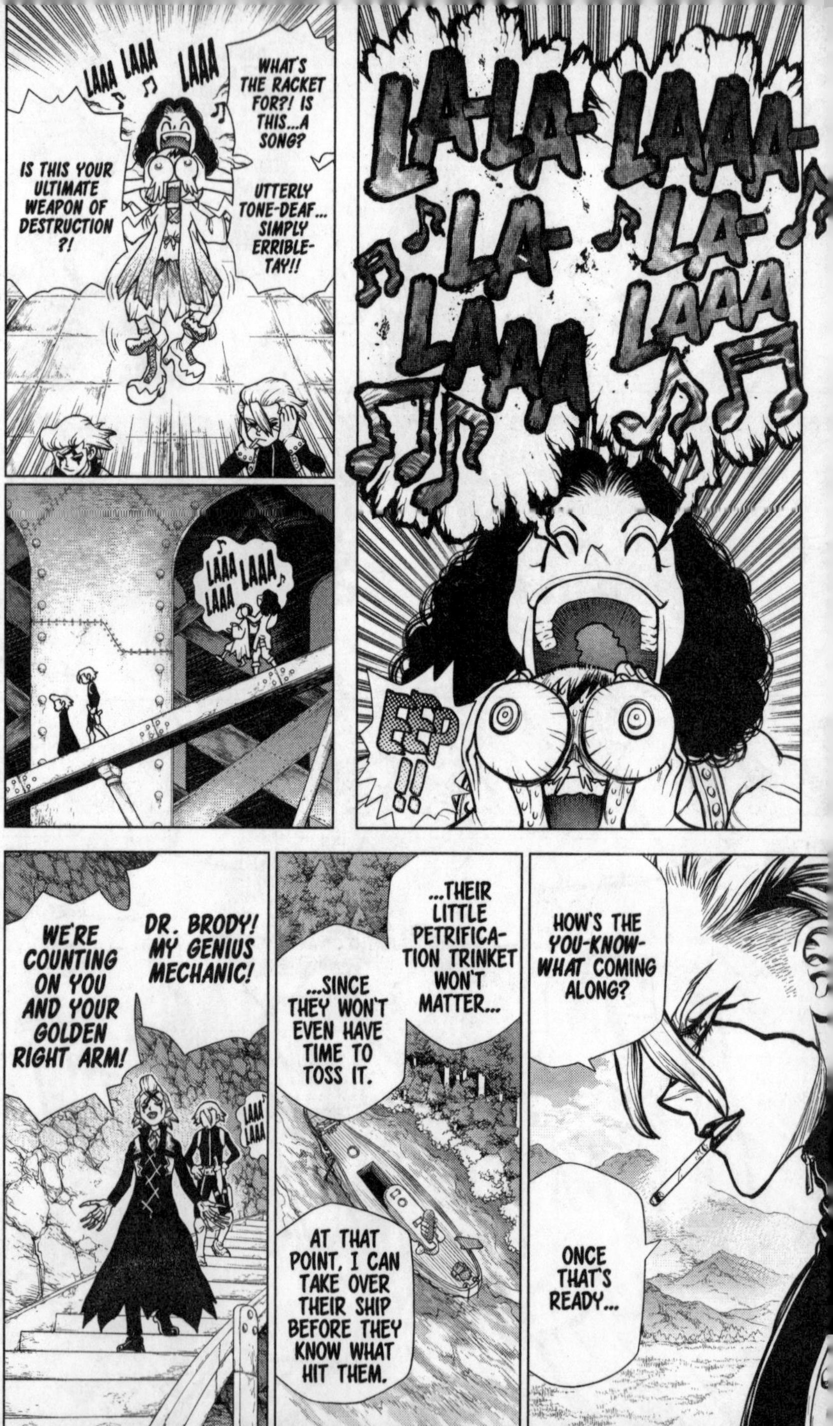
LA-LA-LAAA-
LA-LA-LAAA
LA-LA-LAAA
EEP!!
WHAT'S THE RACKET FOR?! IS THIS...A SONG?
LAAA LAAA LAAA
IS THIS YOUR ULTIMATE WEAPON OF DESTRUCTION?!
UTTERLY TONE-DEAF... SIMPLY ERRIBLE-TAY!!
LAAA LAAA LAAA LAAA
HOW'S THE YOU-KNOW-WHAT COMING ALONG?
ONCE THAT'S READY...
...THEIR LITTLE PETRIFICATION TRINKET WON'T MATTER...
...SINCE THEY WON'T EVEN HAVE TIME TO TOSS IT.
AT THAT POINT, I CAN TAKE OVER THEIR SHIP BEFORE THEY KNOW WHAT HIT THEM.
DR. BRODY! MY GENIUS MECHANIC!
WE'RE COUNTING ON YOU AND YOUR GOLDEN RIGHT ARM!
LAAA LAAA

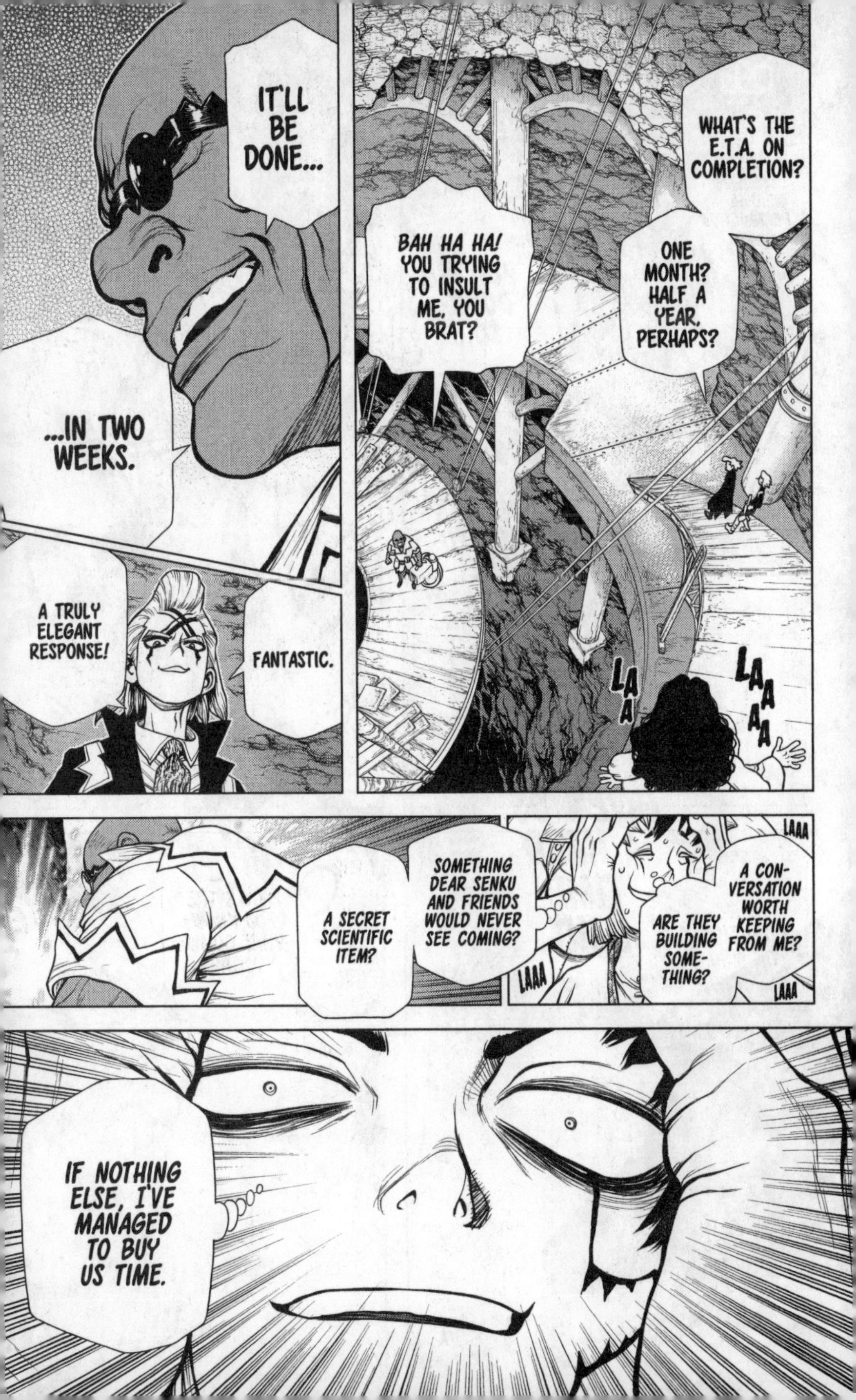
WHAT'S THE E.T.A. ON COMPLETION?
ONE MONTH? HALF A YEAR, PERHAPS?
BAH HA HA! YOU TRYING TO INSULT ME, YOU BRAT?
LAAAA
LAAA
IT'LL BE DONE...
...IN TWO WEEKS.
FANTASTIC.
A TRULY ELEGANT RESPONSE!
LAAA
A CON-VERSATION WORTH KEEPING FROM ME?
ARE THEY BUILDING SOME-THING?
LAAA
LAAA
SOMETHING DEAR SENKU AND FRIENDS WOULD NEVER SEE COMING?
A SECRET SCIENTIFIC ITEM?
IF NOTHING ELSE, I'VE MANAGED TO BUY US TIME.

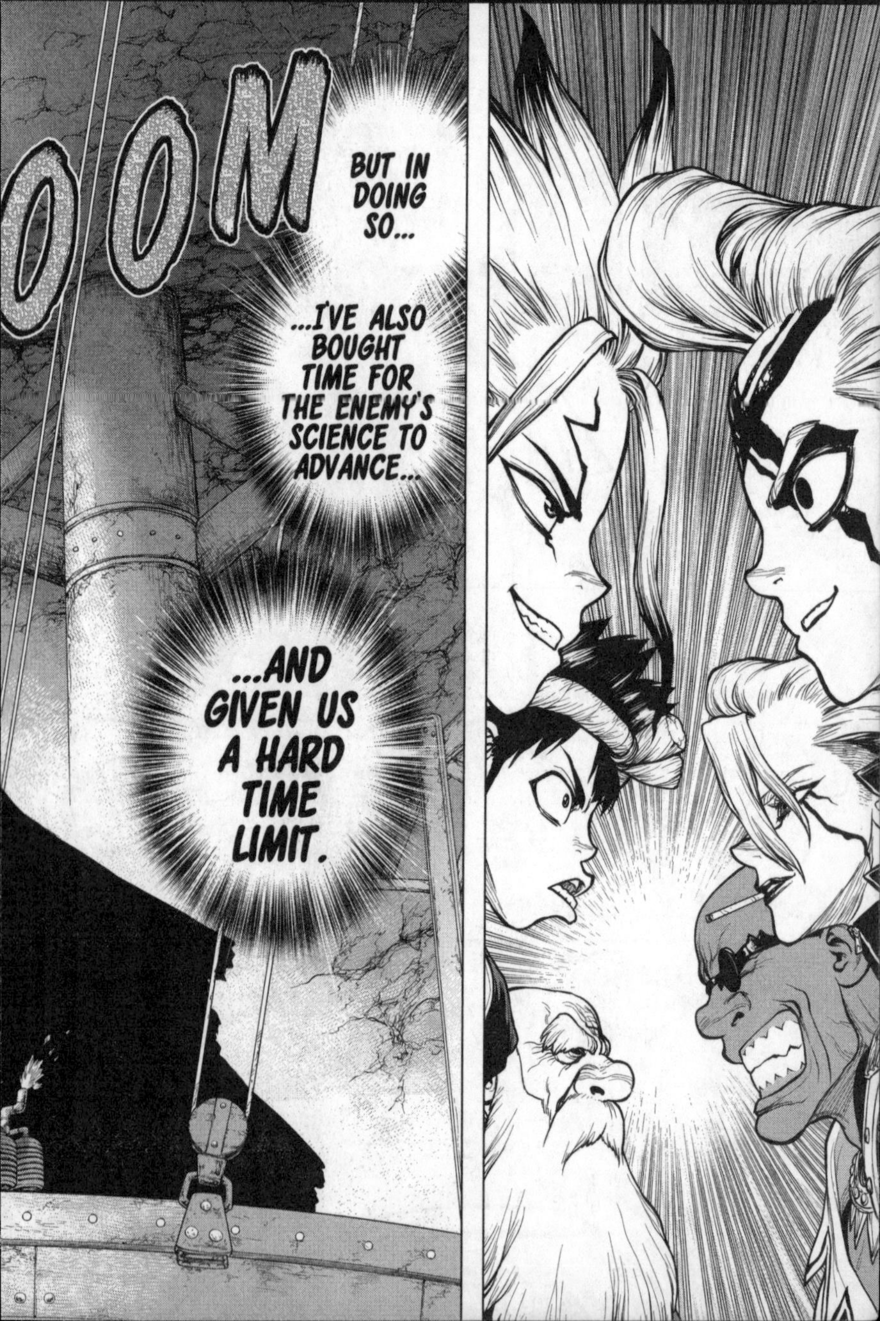
OOM
BUT IN DOING SO...
...I'VE ALSO BOUGHT TIME FOR THE ENEMY'S SCIENCE TO ADVANCE...
...AND GIVEN US A HARD TIME LIMIT.

SCIENCE V

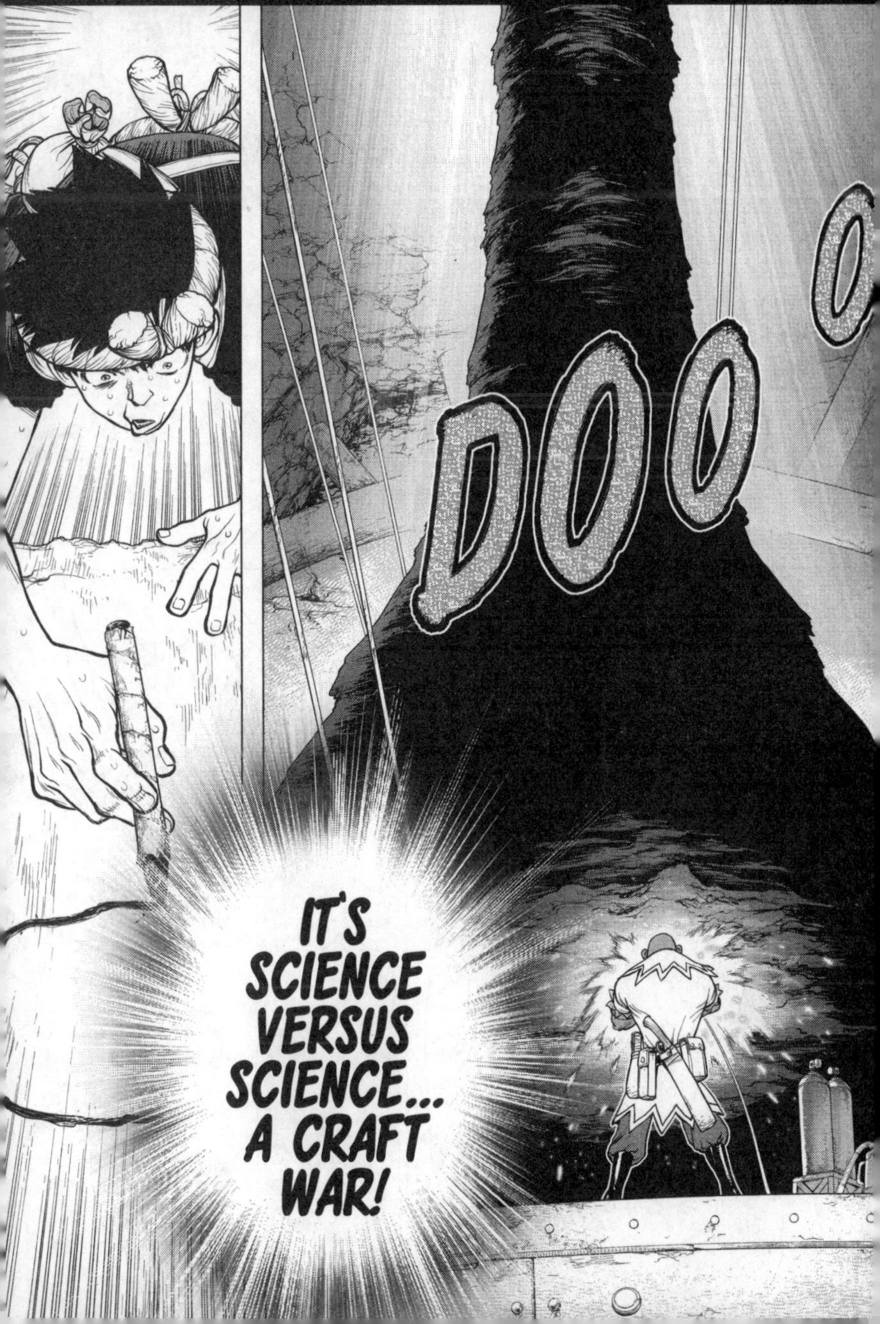
DOOOO
IT'S SCIENCE VERSUS SCIENCE... A CRAFT WAR!

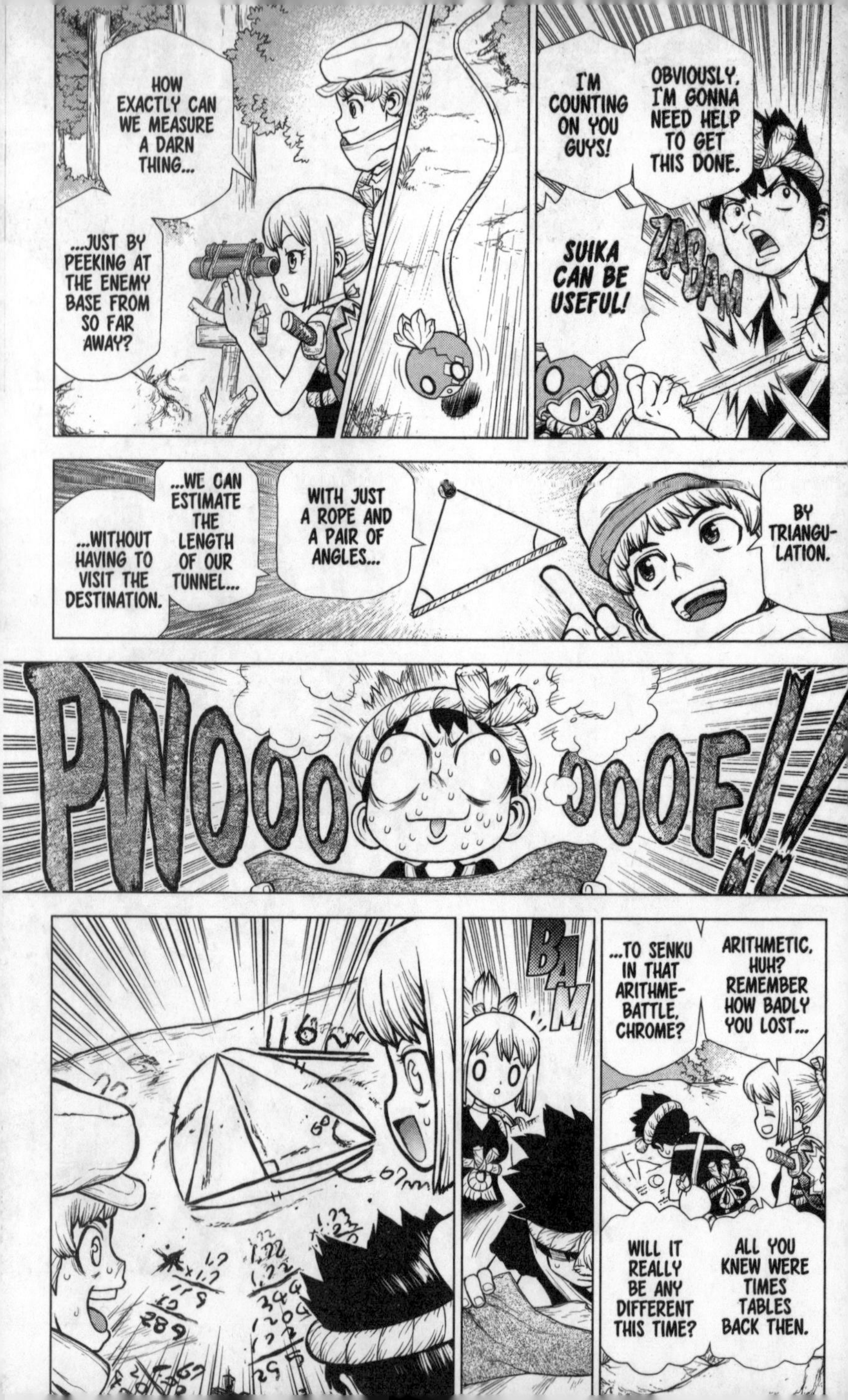
OBVIOUSLY, I'M GONNA NEED HELP TO GET THIS DONE.
I'M COUNTING ON YOU GUYS!
ZABAM
SUIKA CAN BE USEFUL!
HOW EXACTLY CAN WE MEASURE A DARN THING...
...JUST BY PEEKING AT THE ENEMY BASE FROM SO FAR AWAY?
BY TRIANGU-LATION.
WITH JUST A ROPE AND A PAIR OF ANGLES...
...WE CAN ESTIMATE THE LENGTH OF OUR TUNNEL...
...WITHOUT HAVING TO VISIT THE DESTINATION.
PWOOOOOOOF!!
ARITHMETIC, HUH? REMEMBER HOW BADLY YOU LOST...
...TO SENKU IN THAT ARITHME-BATTLE, CHROME?
ALL YOU KNEW WERE TIMES TABLES BACK THEN.
WILL IT REALLY BE ANY DIFFERENT THIS TIME?
BAM

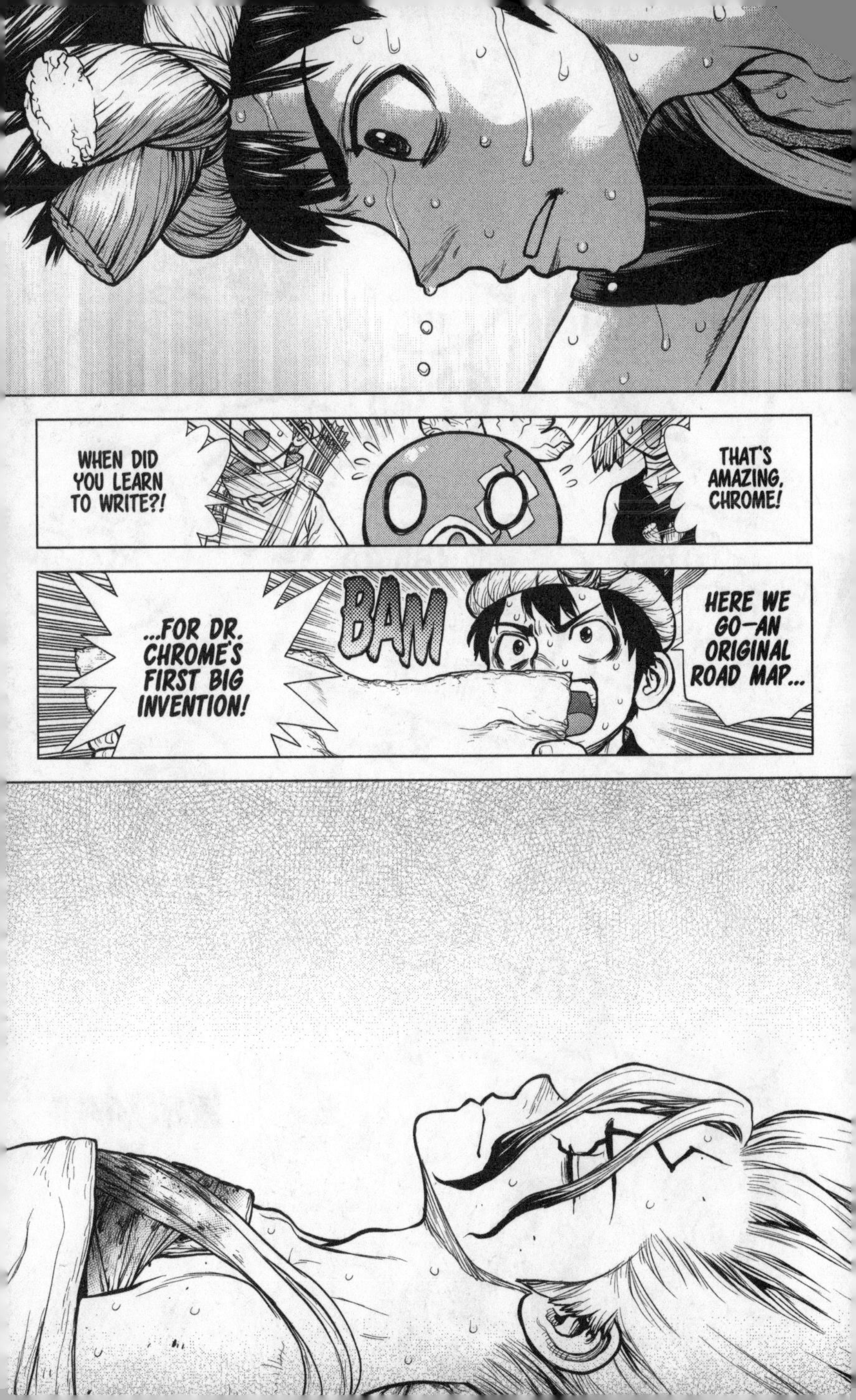
THAT'S AMAZING, CHROME!
WHEN DID YOU LEARN TO WRITE?!
HERE WE GO—AN ORIGINAL ROAD MAP...
BAM
...FOR DR. CHROME'S FIRST BIG INVENTION!

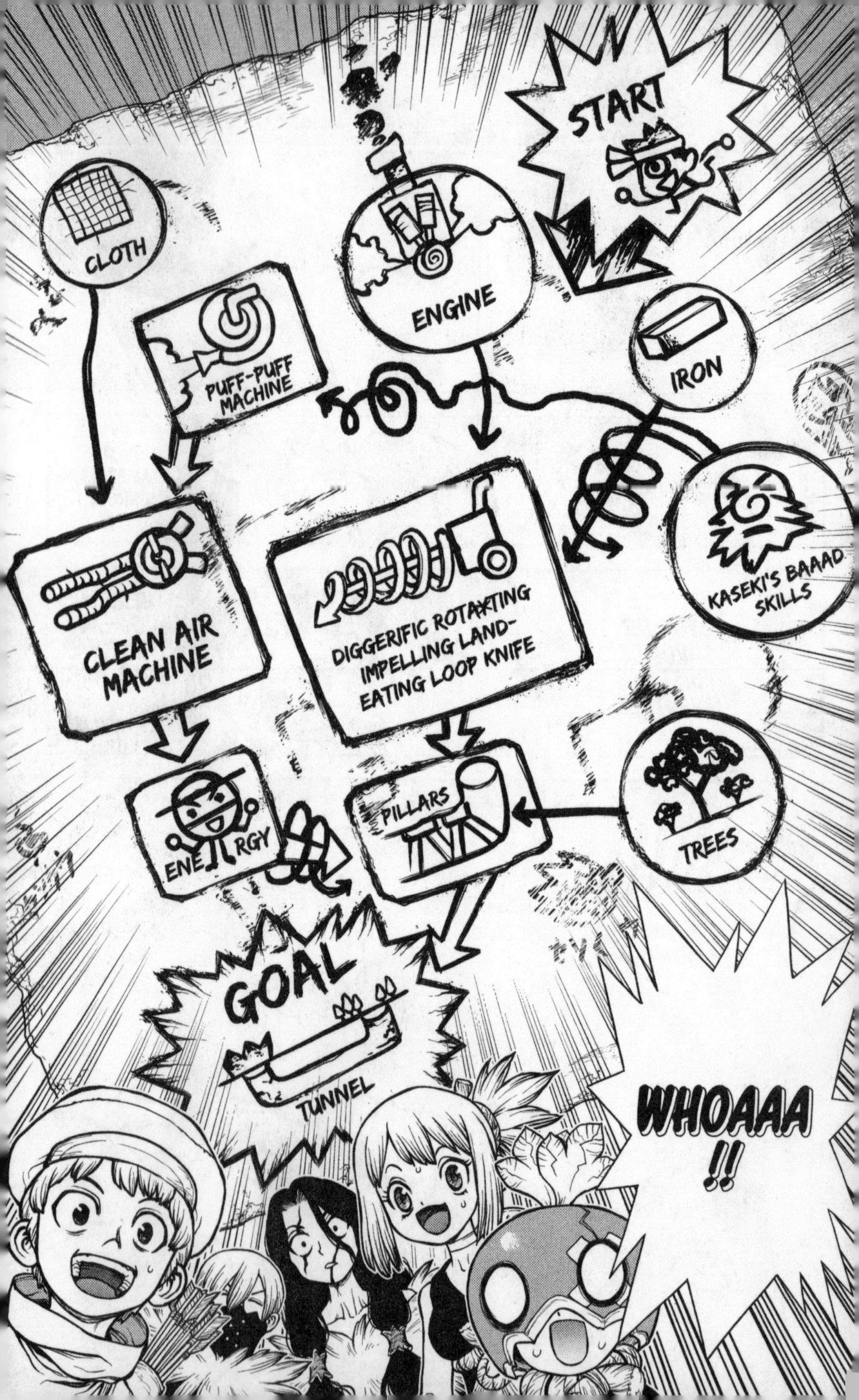
START
IRON
KASEKI'S BAAAD SKILLS
ENGINE
PUFF-PUFF MACHINE
CLOTH
DIGGERIFIC ROTAXTING IMPELLING LAND-EATING LOOP KNIFE
CLEAN AIR MACHINE
TREES
PILLARS
ENE RGY
GOAL
TUNNEL
WHOAAA!!

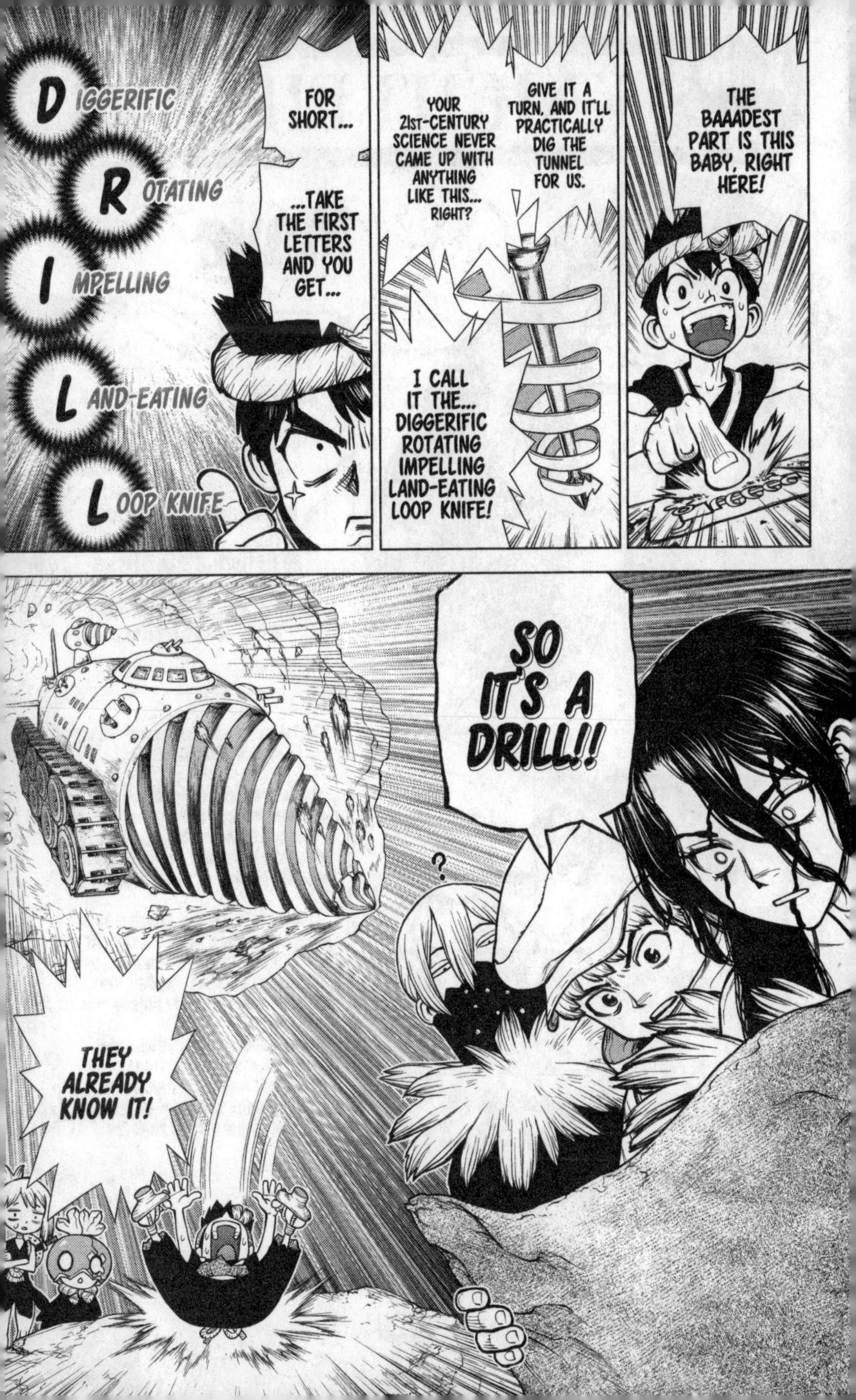
THE BAAADEST PART IS THIS BABY, RIGHT HERE!
GIVE IT A TURN, AND IT'LL PRACTICALLY DIG THE TUNNEL FOR US.
YOUR 21ST-CENTURY SCIENCE NEVER CAME UP WITH ANYTHING LIKE THIS... RIGHT?
I CALL IT THE... DIGGERIFIC ROTATING IMPELLING LAND-EATING LOOP KNIFE!
FOR SHORT...
...TAKE THE FIRST LETTERS AND YOU GET...
DIGGERIFIC
ROTATING
IMPELLING
LAND-EATING
LOOP KNIFE
SO IT'S A DRILL!!
?
THEY ALREADY KNOW IT!

Xeno's Science Kingdom

KNIGHT FILE 3

Maya

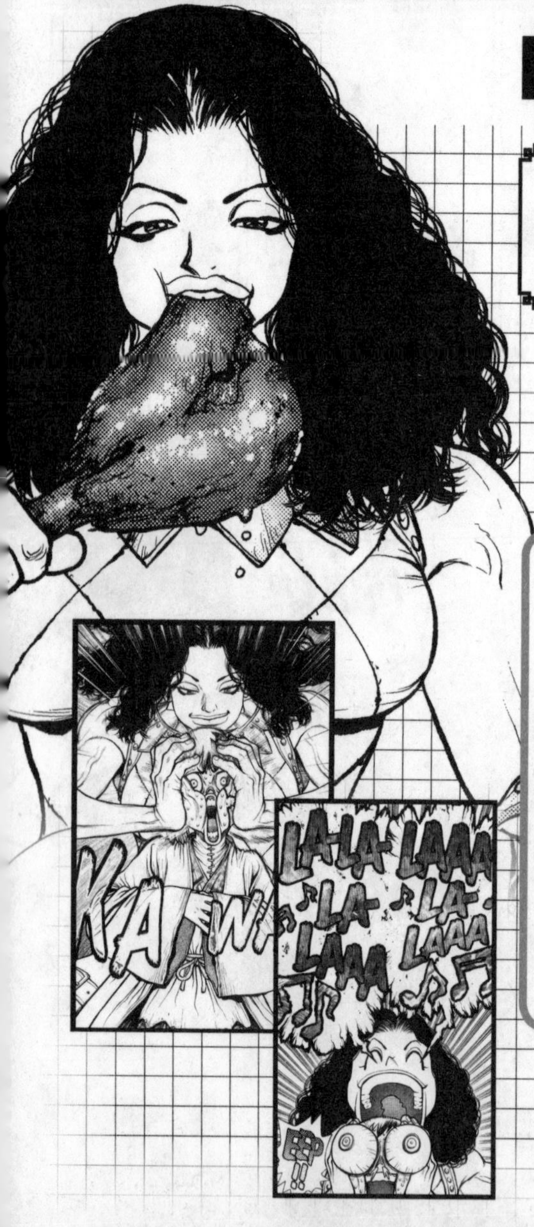

KAW
LA-LA-LAAA
LAAA LA- LAAA
EEP!!

Power	★★★★★
Appetite	★★★★★
Singing	★

■ Full Name: Maya Biggs

■ Height: 200 cm

■ Profession: Anything requiring strength

The former all-American women's division MMA champ!

Having suffered no losses, Maya earned enough money to retire young but eventually had to file for bankruptcy after her voracious appetite consumed all her savings.

That's when she was scouted by the special-ops unit. She accepted the job offer, saying, "As long as you keep me fed." In that sense, her career path was a rather unique one.

Don't be fooled by Maya's casual, congenial attitude. She won't harm others for no good reason, but as a professional, she'll show no mercy if that's what the job calls for.

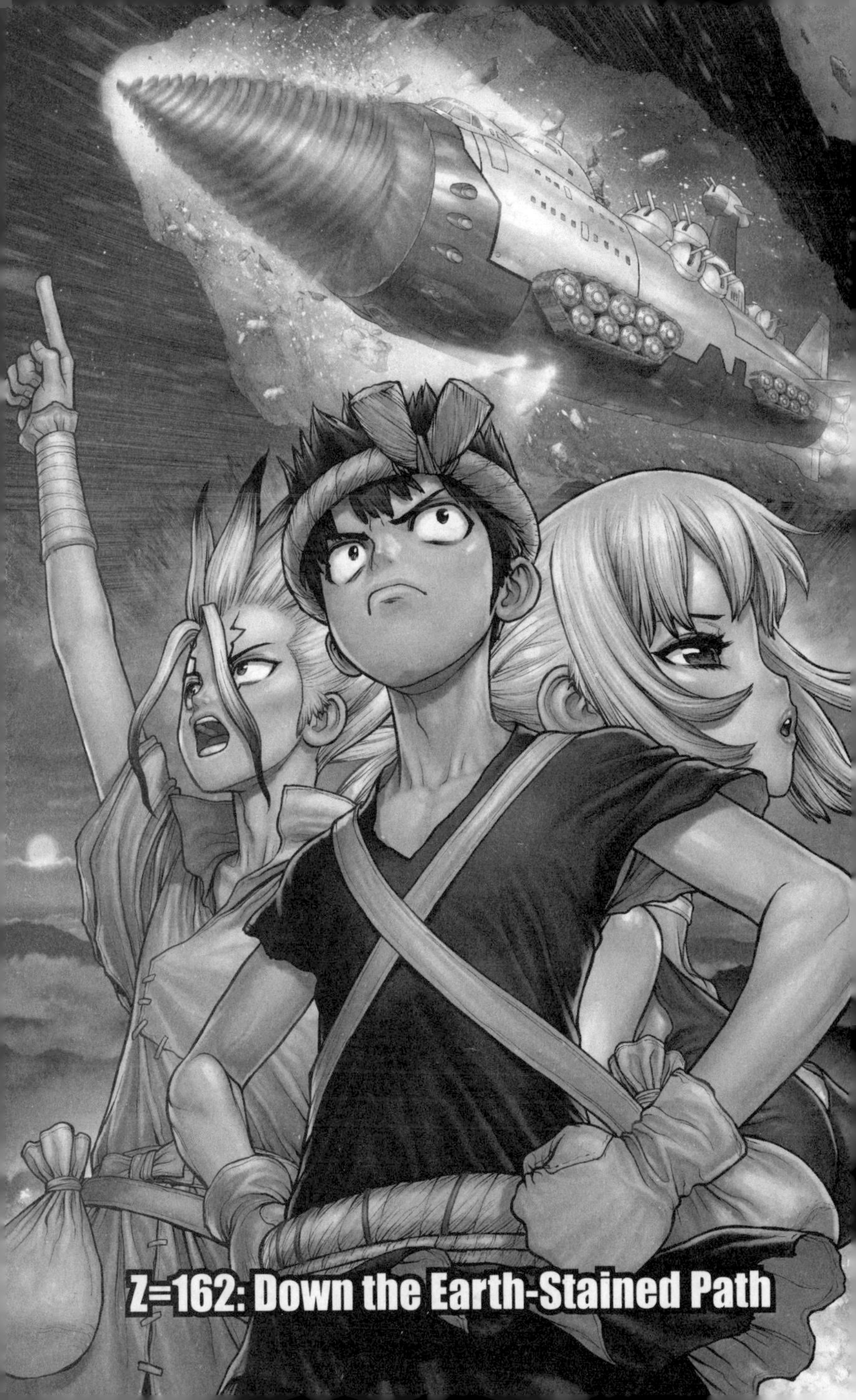
Z=162: Down the Earth-Stained Path

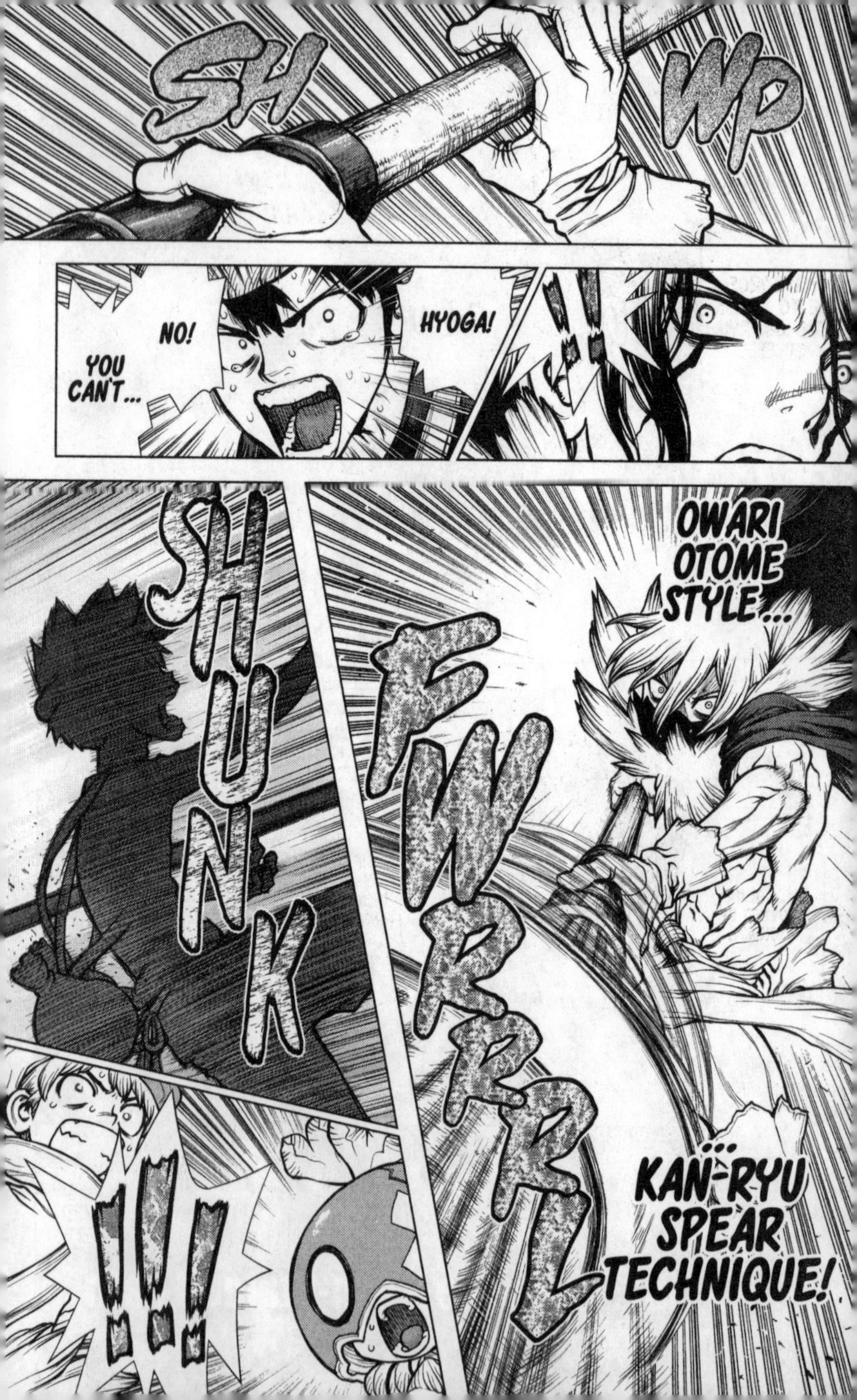
SH
WP
!!
HYOGA!
NO!
YOU CAN'T...
OWARI OTOME STYLE...
...KAN-RYU SPEAR TECHNIQUE!
FWRRRL
SHUNK
!!!

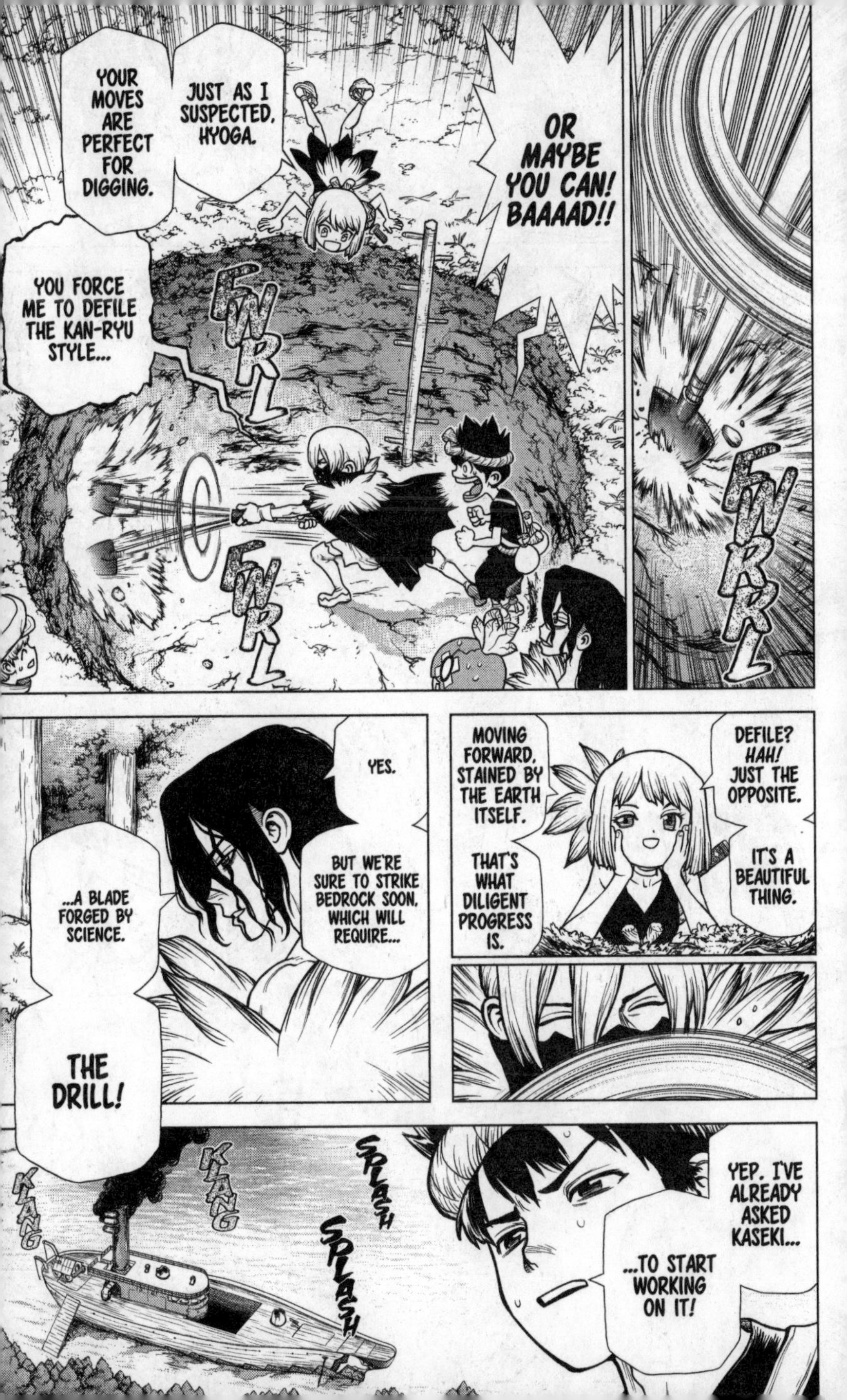
FWRRL
OR MAYBE YOU CAN! BAAAAD!!
JUST AS I SUSPECTED, HYOGA.
YOUR MOVES ARE PERFECT FOR DIGGING.
YOU FORCE ME TO DEFILE THE KAN-RYU STYLE...
FWRL
FWRL
DEFILE? HAH! JUST THE OPPOSITE.
IT'S A BEAUTIFUL THING.
MOVING FORWARD, STAINED BY THE EARTH ITSELF.
THAT'S WHAT DILIGENT PROGRESS IS.
YES.
BUT WE'RE SURE TO STRIKE BEDROCK SOON, WHICH WILL REQUIRE...
...A BLADE FORGED BY SCIENCE.
THE DRILL!
YEP. I'VE ALREADY ASKED KASEKI...
...TO START WORKING ON IT!
SPLASH
SPLASH
KLANG
KLANG

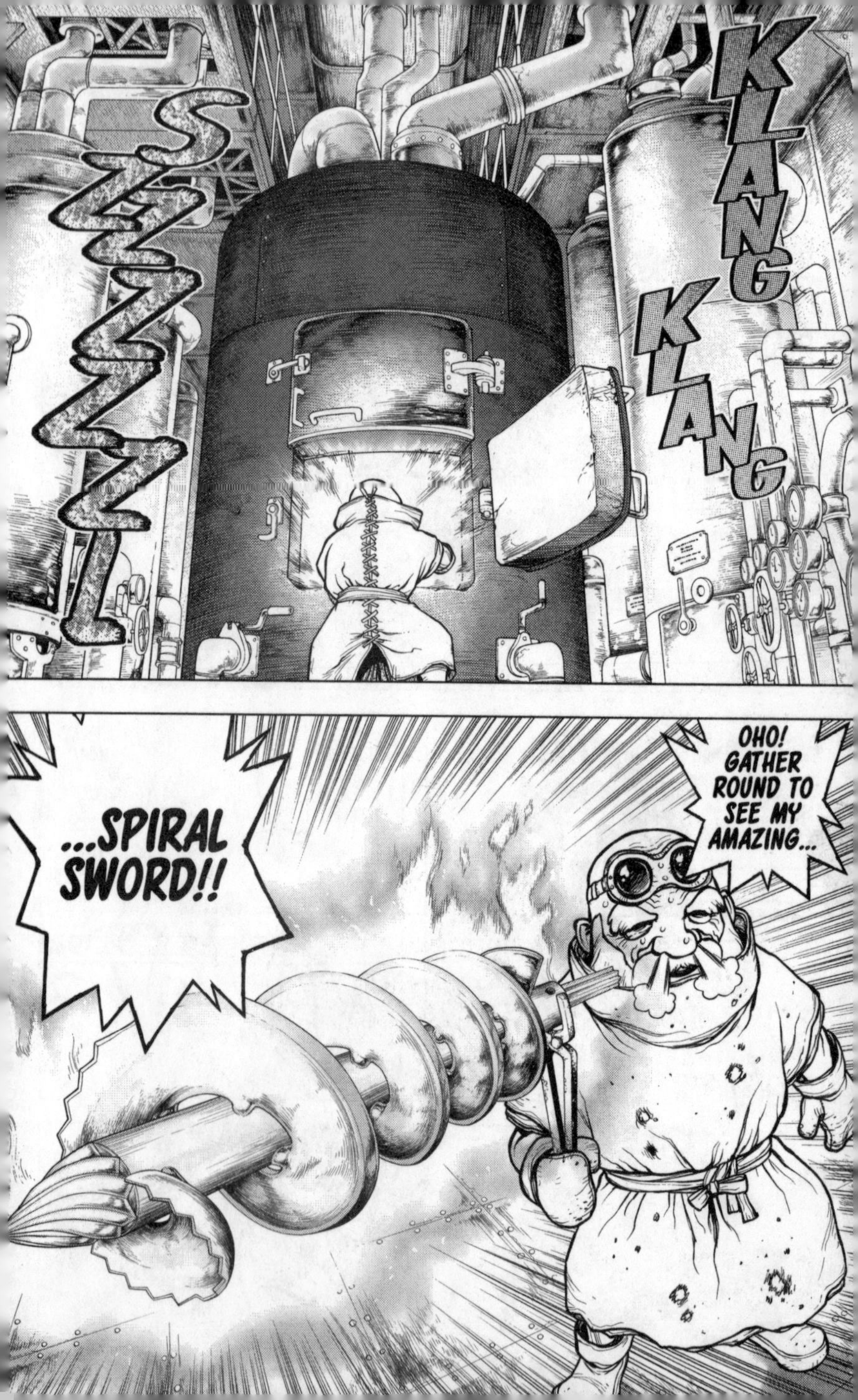
KLANG
KLANG
SZZZZZL
OHO! GATHER ROUND TO SEE MY AMAZING...
...SPIRAL SWORD!!

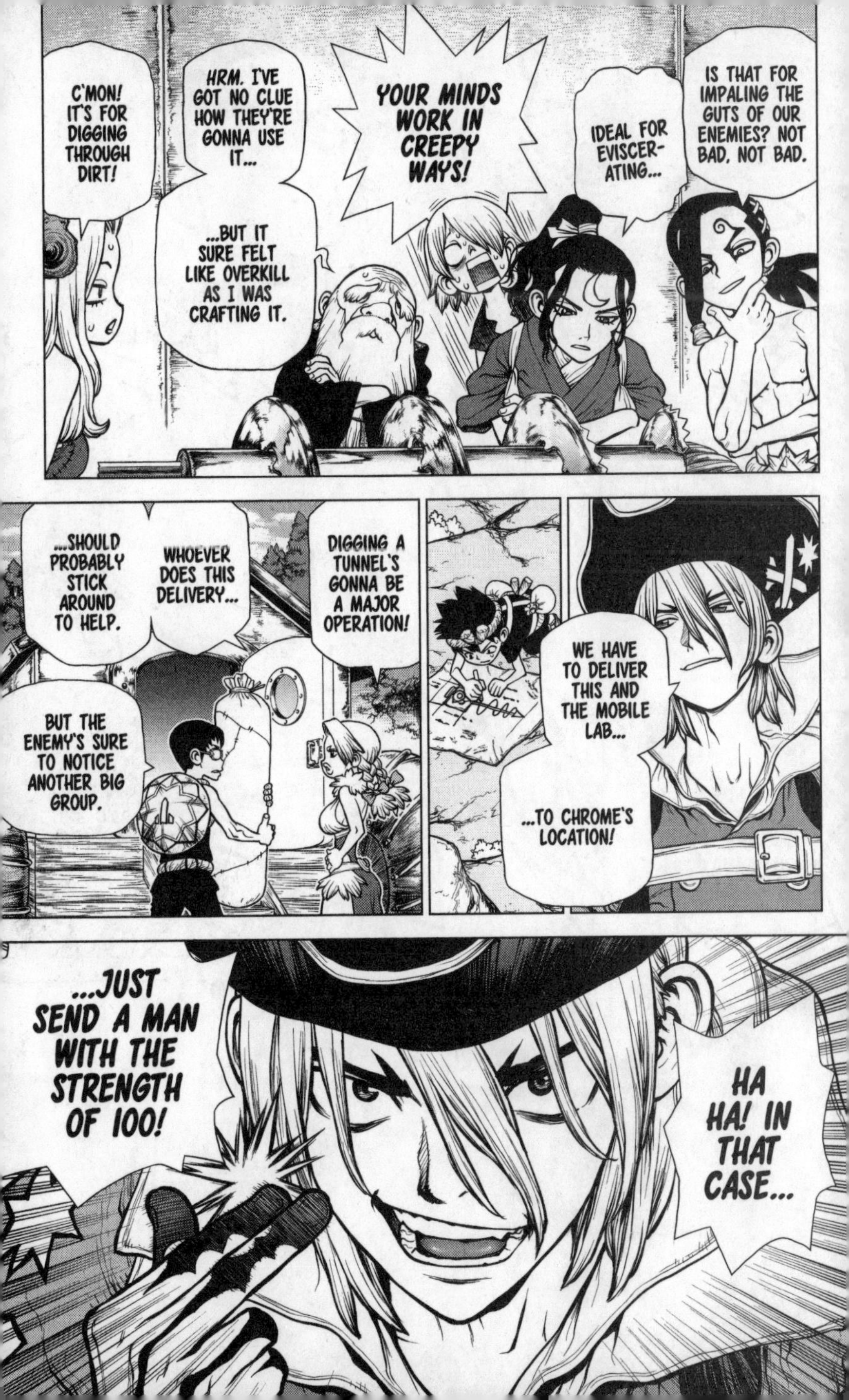
IS THAT FOR IMPALING THE GUTS OF OUR ENEMIES? NOT BAD, NOT BAD.
IDEAL FOR EVISCER-ATING...
YOUR MINDS WORK IN CREEPY WAYS!
HRM. I'VE GOT NO CLUE HOW THEY'RE GONNA USE IT...
...BUT IT SURE FELT LIKE OVERKILL AS I WAS CRAFTING IT.
C'MON! IT'S FOR DIGGING THROUGH DIRT!
WE HAVE TO DELIVER THIS AND THE MOBILE LAB...
...TO CHROME'S LOCATION!
DIGGING A TUNNEL'S GONNA BE A MAJOR OPERATION!
WHOEVER DOES THIS DELIVERY...
...SHOULD PROBABLY STICK AROUND TO HELP.
BUT THE ENEMY'S SURE TO NOTICE ANOTHER BIG GROUP.
HA HA! IN THAT CASE...
...JUST SEND A MAN WITH THE STRENGTH OF 100!

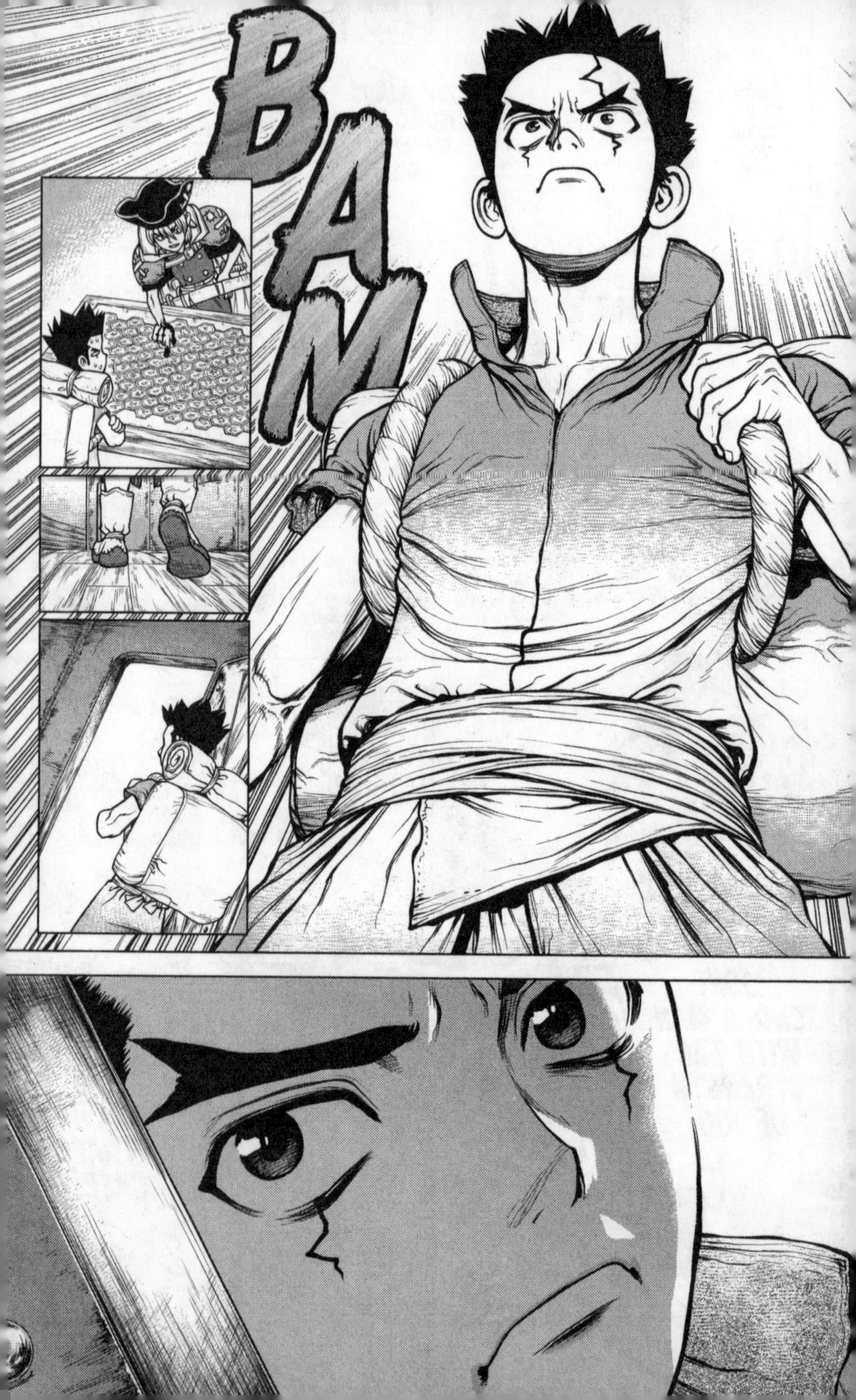
BAM

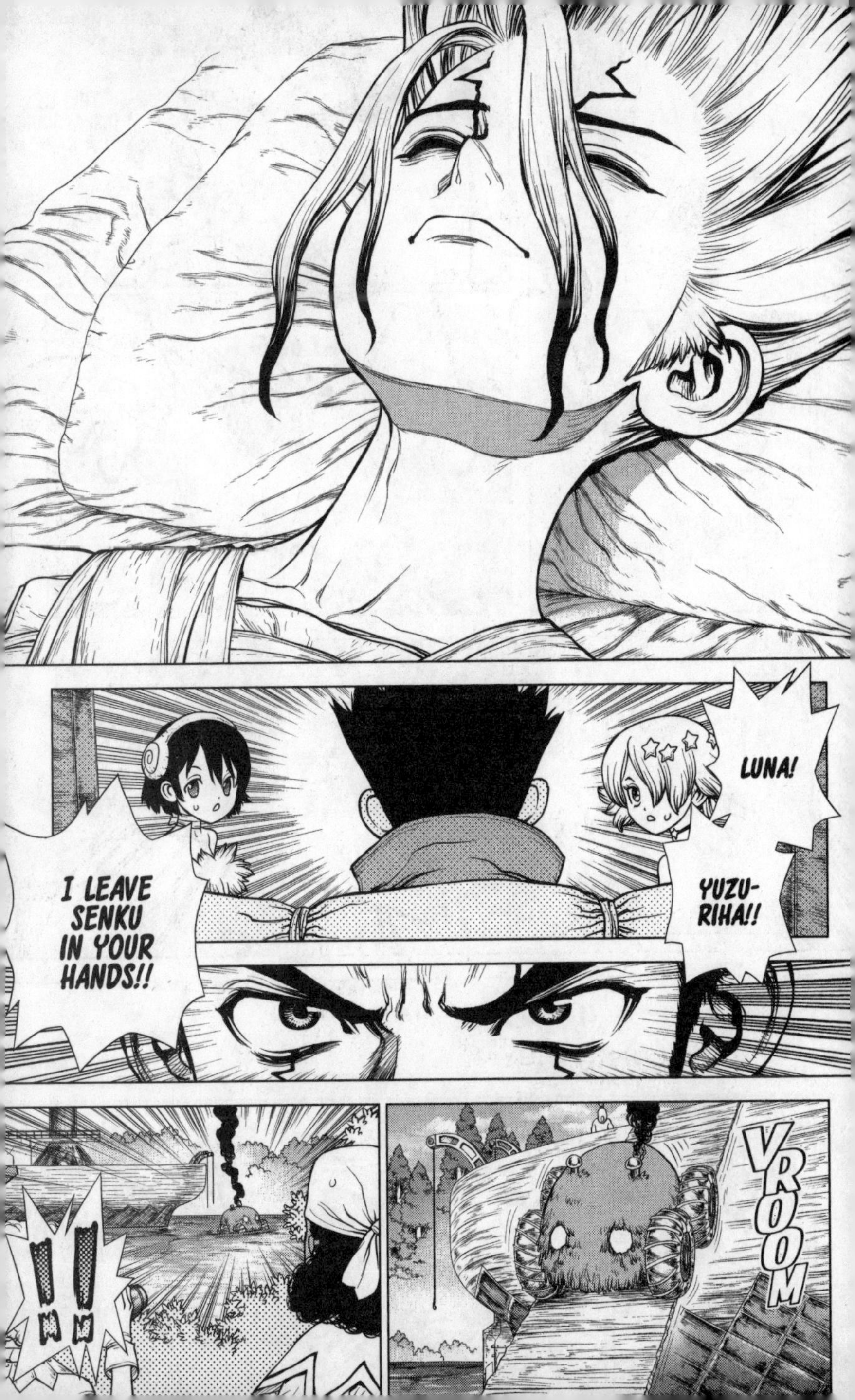
LUNA!
YUZU-RIHA!!
I LEAVE SENKU IN YOUR HANDS!!
VROOM
!!

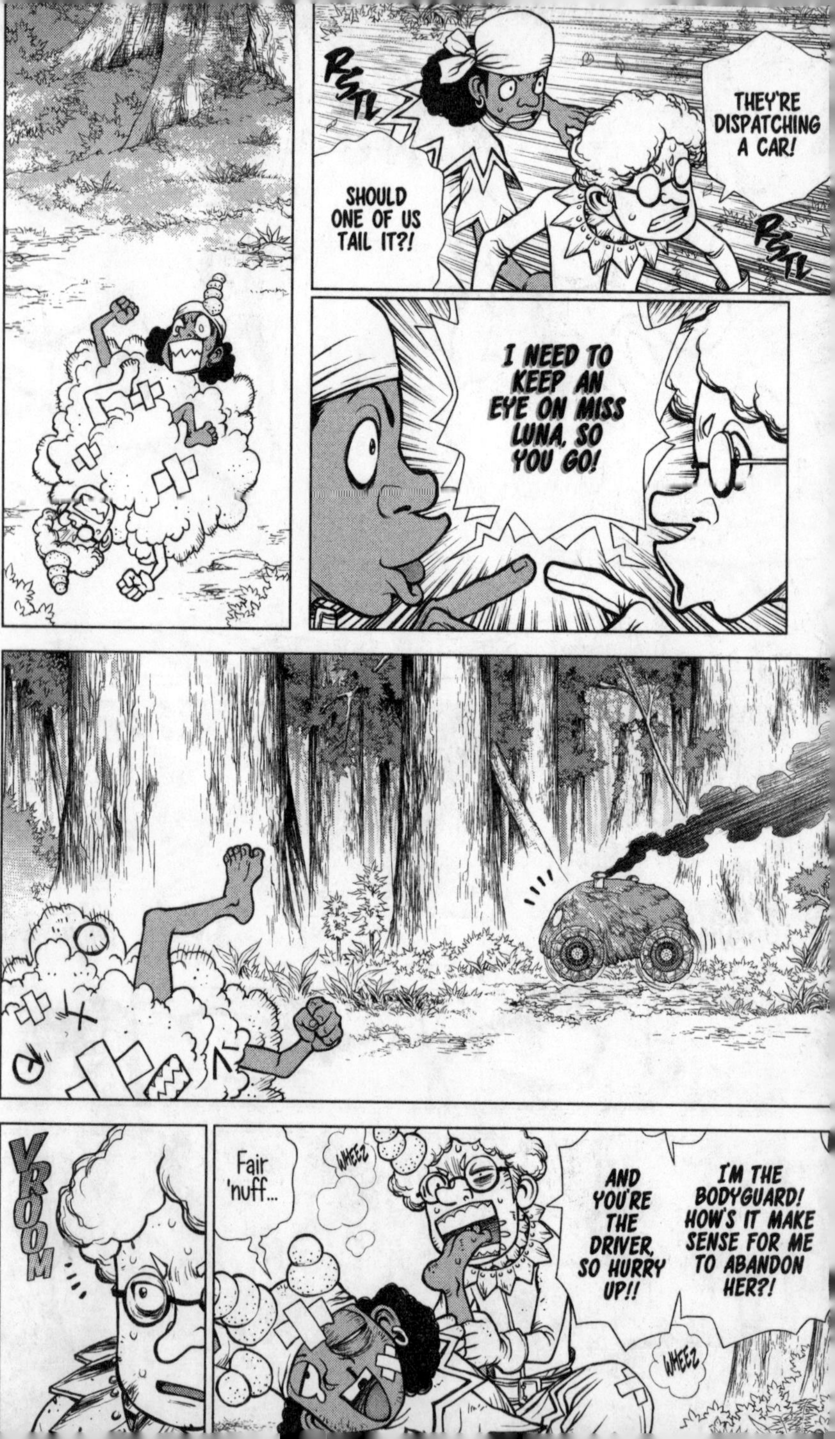
THEY'RE DISPATCHING A CAR!
RSTL
SHOULD ONE OF US TAIL IT?!
RSTL
I NEED TO KEEP AN EYE ON MISS LUNA, SO YOU GO!
I'M THE BODYGUARD! HOW'S IT MAKE SENSE FOR ME TO ABANDON HER?!
AND YOU'RE THE DRIVER, SO HURRY UP!!
WHEEZ
WHEEZ
Fair 'nuff...
VROOM

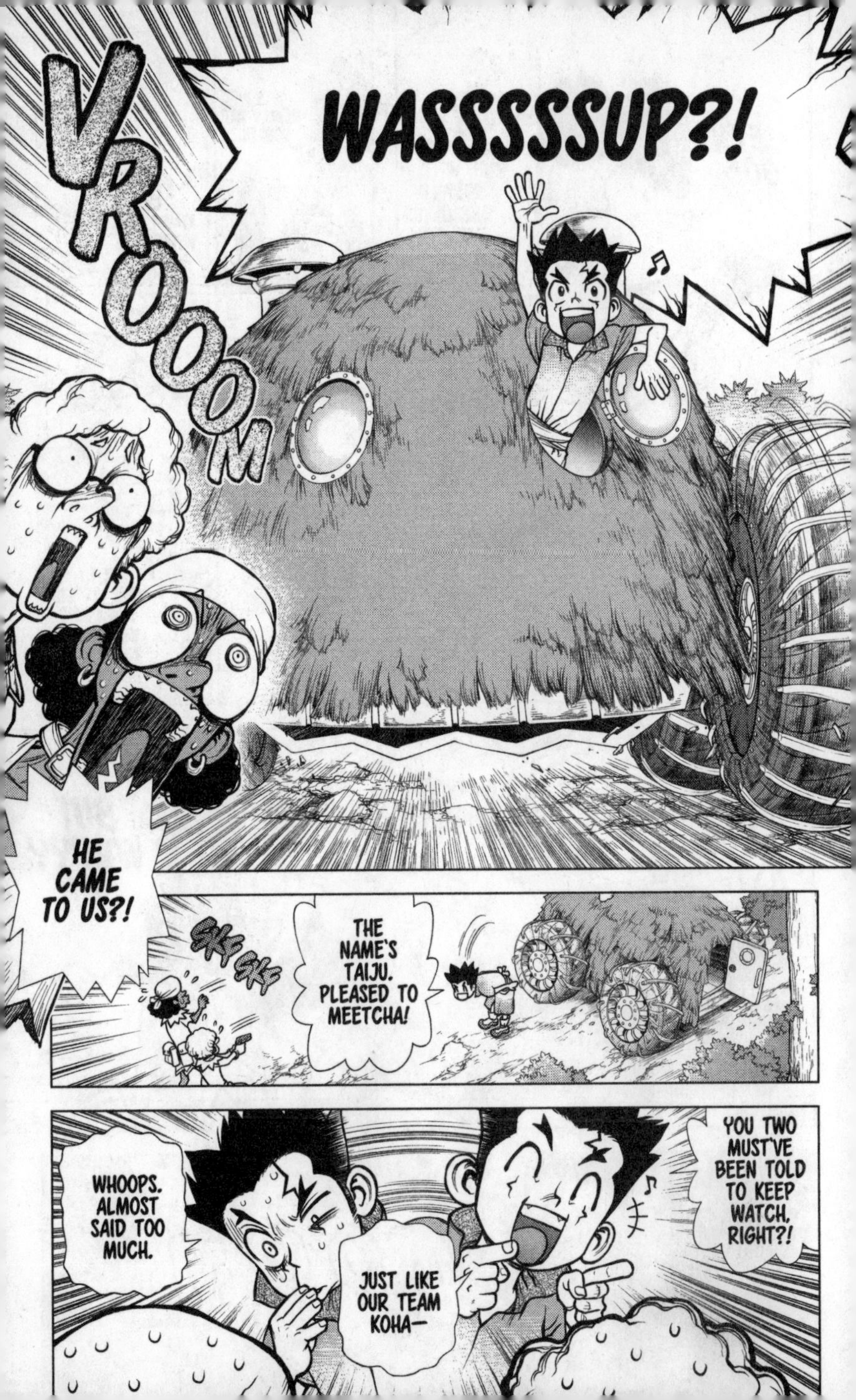
WASSSSSUP?!
VROOOOM
HE CAME TO US?!
THE NAME'S TAIJU. PLEASED TO MEETCHA!
SKF SKF
YOU TWO MUST'VE BEEN TOLD TO KEEP WATCH, RIGHT?!
JUST LIKE OUR TEAM KOHA—
WHOOPS. ALMOST SAID TOO MUCH.

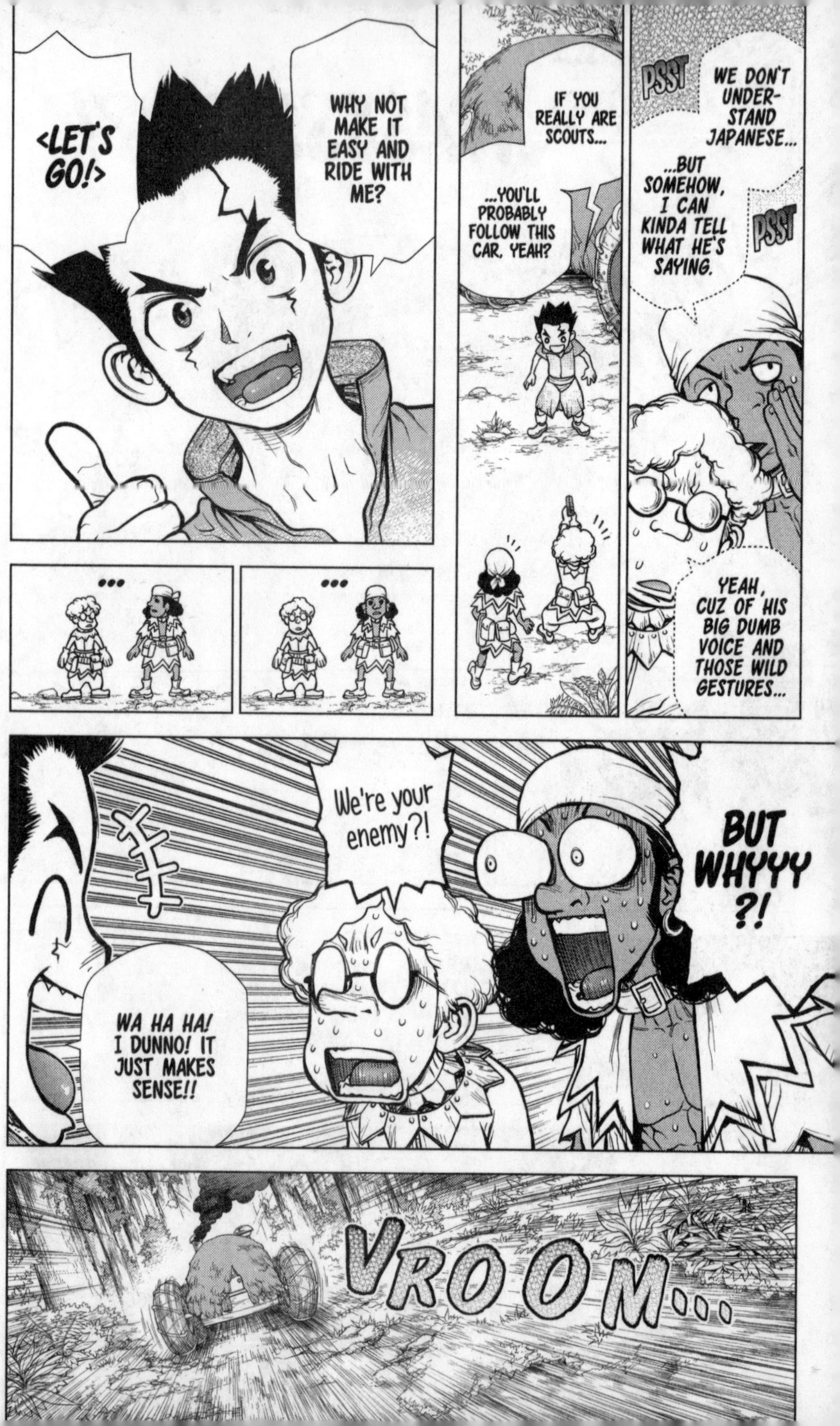
PSST
WE DON'T UNDER-STAND JAPANESE...
...BUT SOMEHOW, I CAN KINDA TELL WHAT HE'S SAYING.
PSST
YEAH, CUZ OF HIS BIG DUMB VOICE AND THOSE WILD GESTURES...
IF YOU REALLY ARE SCOUTS...
...YOU'LL PROBABLY FOLLOW THIS CAR, YEAH?
WHY NOT MAKE IT EASY AND RIDE WITH ME?
<LET'S GO!>
...
...
BUT WHYYY?!
We're your enemy?!
WA HA HA! I DUNNO! IT JUST MAKES SENSE!!
VROOM...

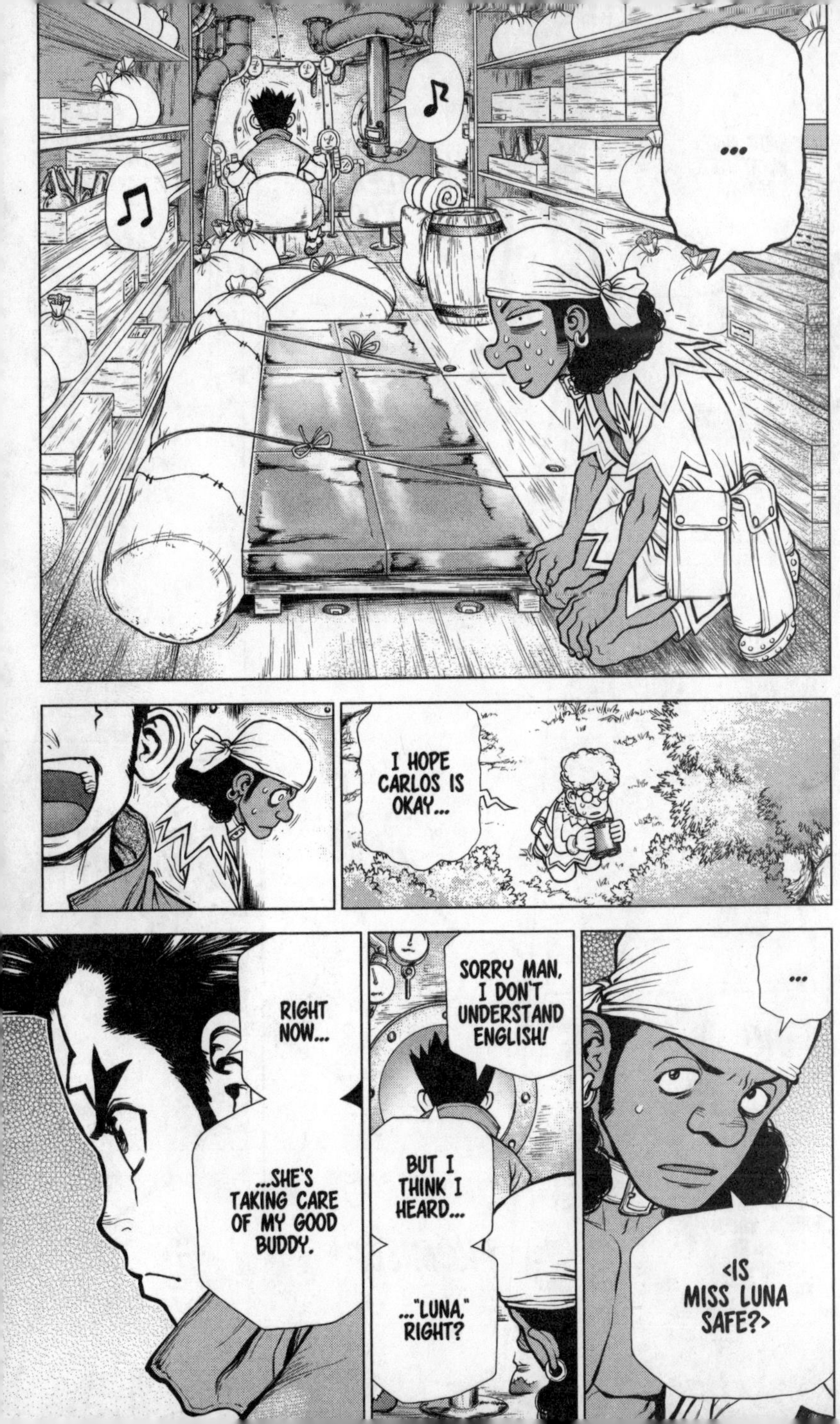
...
I HOPE CARLOS IS OKAY...
...
<IS MISS LUNA SAFE?>
SORRY MAN, I DON'T UNDERSTAND ENGLISH!
BUT I THINK I HEARD...
..."LUNA," RIGHT?
RIGHT NOW...
...SHE'S TAKING CARE OF MY GOOD BUDDY.

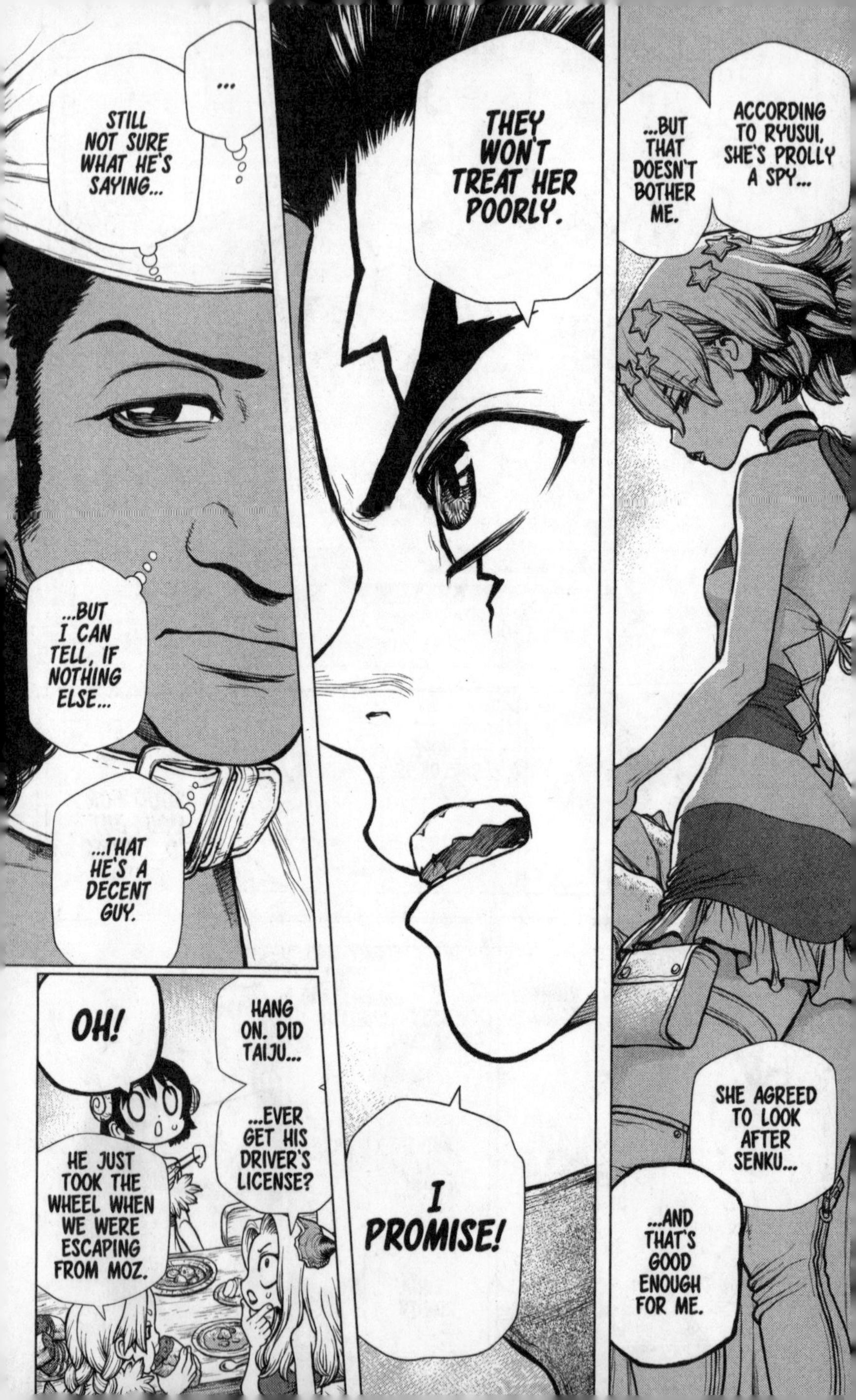
ACCORDING TO RYUSUI, SHE'S PROLLY A SPY...
...BUT THAT DOESN'T BOTHER ME.
SHE AGREED TO LOOK AFTER SENKU...
...AND THAT'S GOOD ENOUGH FOR ME.
THEY WON'T TREAT HER POORLY.
I PROMISE!
...
STILL NOT SURE WHAT HE'S SAYING...
...BUT I CAN TELL, IF NOTHING ELSE...
...THAT HE'S A DECENT GUY.
HANG ON. DID TAIJU...
...EVER GET HIS DRIVER'S LICENSE?
OH!
HE JUST TOOK THE WHEEL WHEN WE WERE ESCAPING FROM MOZ.

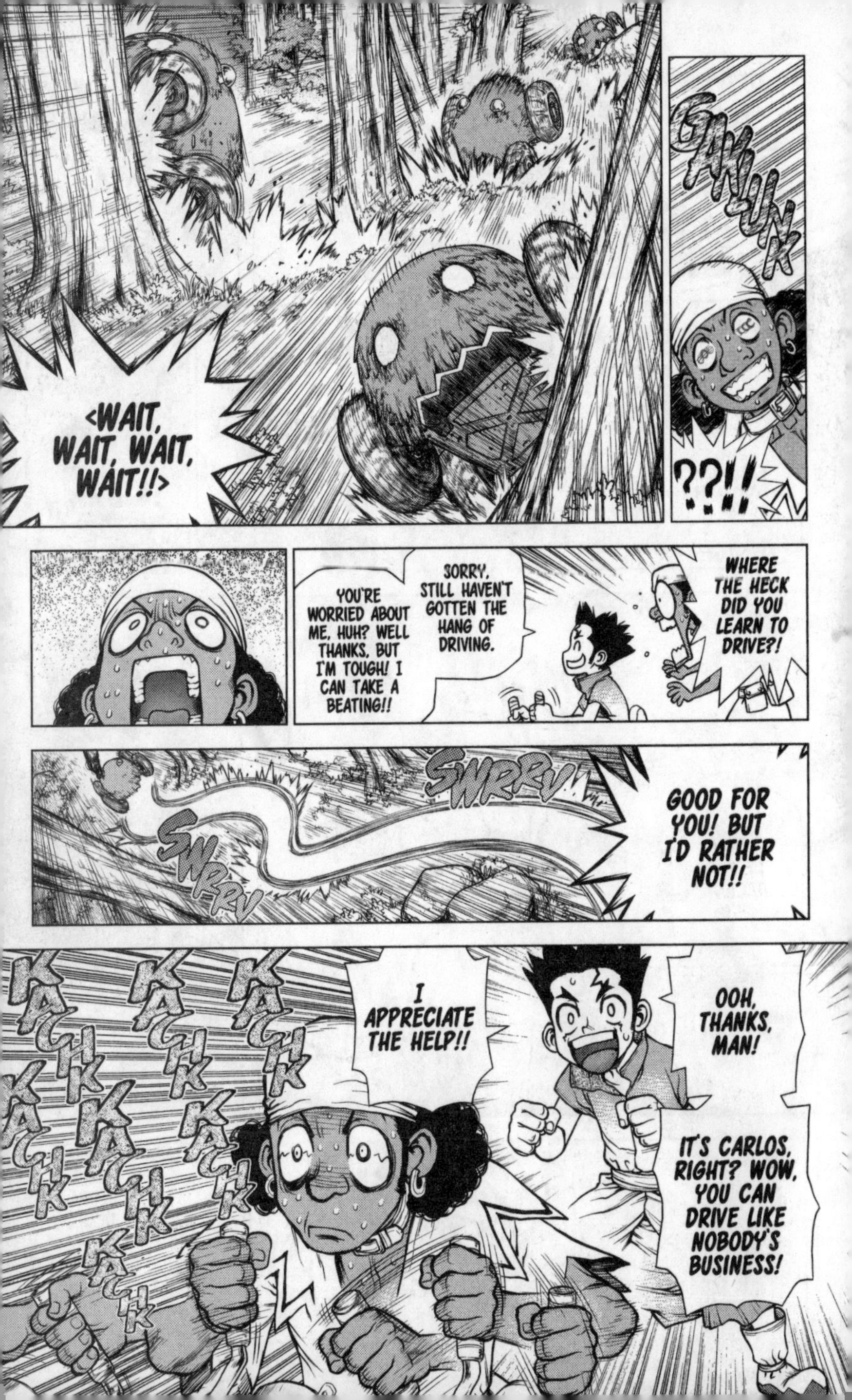

GAKUNK
??!!
<WAIT, WAIT, WAIT, WAIT!!>
WHERE THE HECK DID YOU LEARN TO DRIVE?!
SORRY, STILL HAVEN'T GOTTEN THE HANG OF DRIVING.
YOU'RE WORRIED ABOUT ME, HUH? WELL THANKS, BUT I'M TOUGH! I CAN TAKE A BEATING!!
GOOD FOR YOU! BUT I'D RATHER NOT!!
SWRRV
SWRRV
OOH, THANKS, MAN!
IT'S CARLOS, RIGHT? WOW, YOU CAN DRIVE LIKE NOBODY'S BUSINESS!
I APPRECIATE THE HELP!!
KACHK KACHK KACHK
KACHK KACHK KACHK KACHK

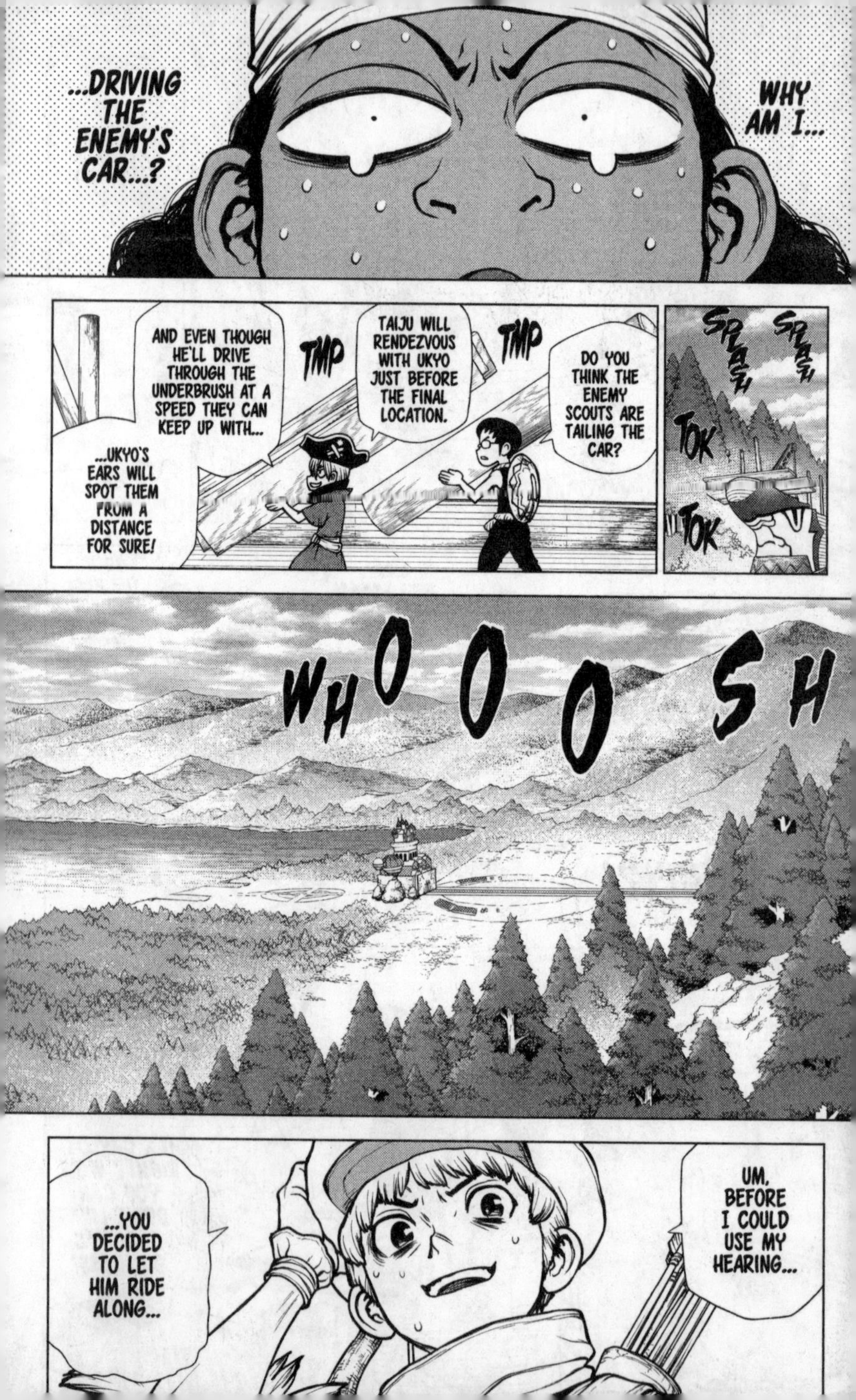
WHY AM I...
...DRIVING THE ENEMY'S CAR...?
SPLASH
SPLASH
TOK
TOK
DO YOU THINK THE ENEMY SCOUTS ARE TAILING THE CAR?
TMP
TAIJU WILL RENDEZVOUS WITH UKYO JUST BEFORE THE FINAL LOCATION.
TMP
AND EVEN THOUGH HE'LL DRIVE THROUGH THE UNDERBRUSH AT A SPEED THEY CAN KEEP UP WITH...
...UKYO'S EARS WILL SPOT THEM FROM A DISTANCE FOR SURE!
WHOOOOSH
UM, BEFORE I COULD USE MY HEARING...
...YOU DECIDED TO LET HIM RIDE ALONG...

CARE TO EXPLAIN?

...

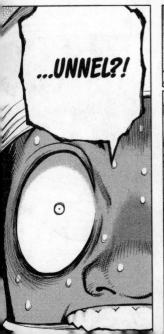

...UNNEL?!

...UNNEL?

WHY DIDJA TIE UP CARLOS LIKE THAT?!

HE'S THE COOL DUDE WHO DROVE ME HERE!

THE MOMENT WE UNTIE HIM, HE'LL RACE OFF TO XENO'S CASTLE.

AND BOOM— OUR WHOLE TUNNEL PLAN GETS OUTED.

DANG! OH... RIGHT.

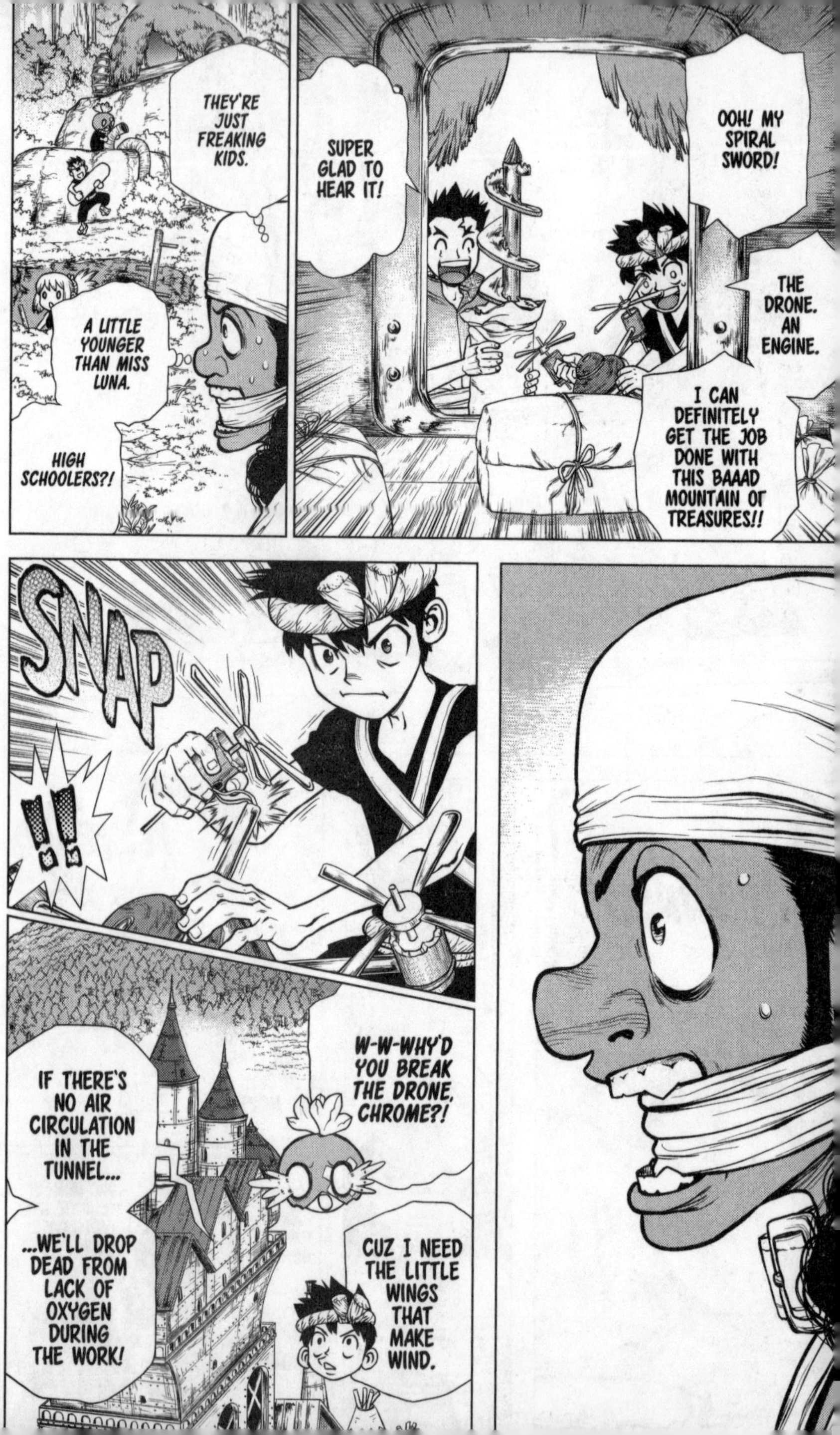
OOH! MY SPIRAL SWORD!
SUPER GLAD TO HEAR IT!
THE DRONE. AN ENGINE.
I CAN DEFINITELY GET THE JOB DONE WITH THIS BAAAD MOUNTAIN OF TREASURES!!
THEY'RE JUST FREAKING KIDS.
A LITTLE YOUNGER THAN MISS LUNA.
HIGH SCHOOLERS?!
SNAP
!!
W-W-WHY'D YOU BREAK THE DRONE, CHROME?!
CUZ I NEED THE LITTLE WINGS THAT MAKE WIND.
IF THERE'S NO AIR CIRCULATION IN THE TUNNEL...
...WE'LL DROP DEAD FROM LACK OF OXYGEN DURING THE WORK!

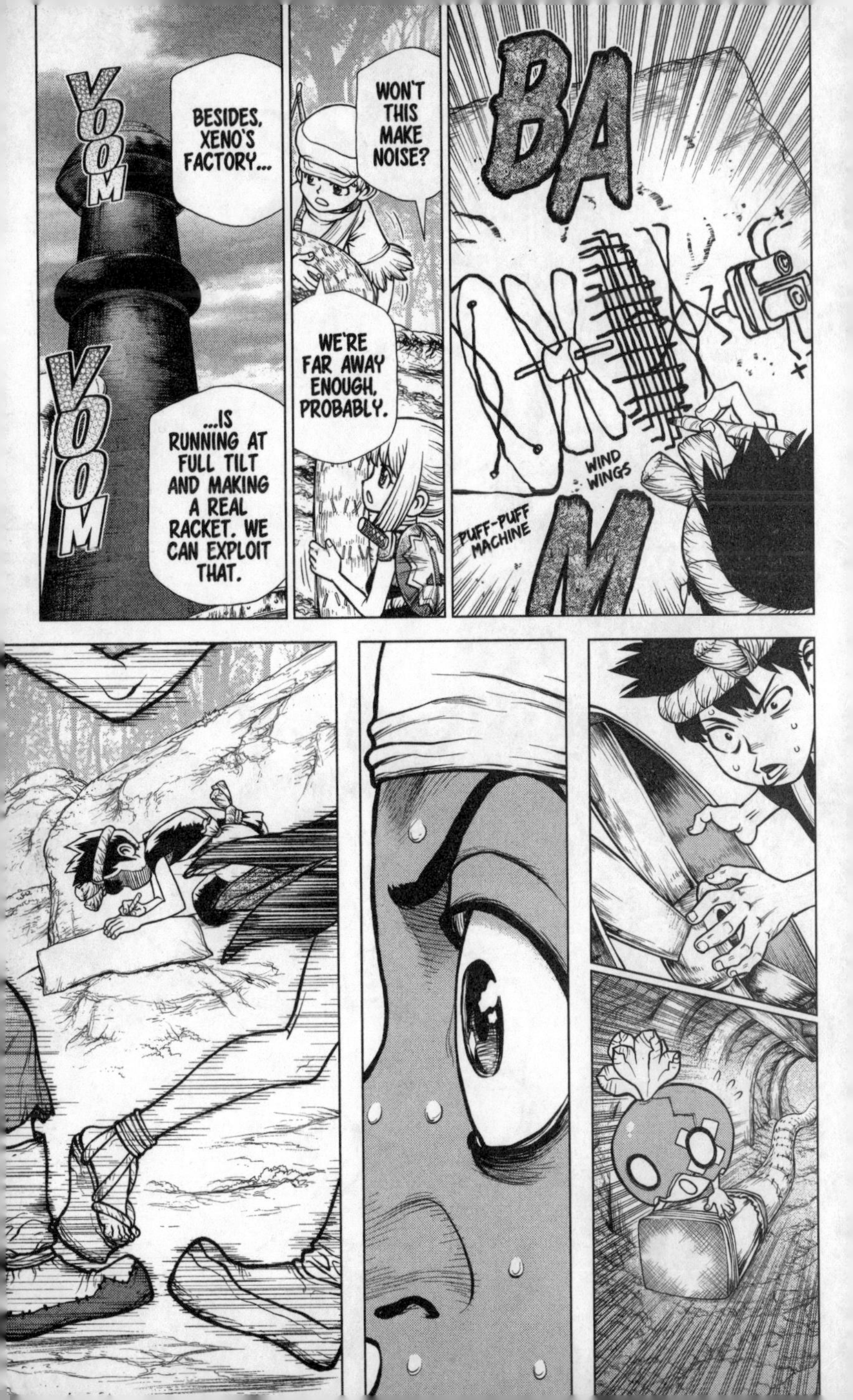
BAM
WIND WINGS
PUFF-PUFF MACHINE
WON'T THIS MAKE NOISE?
WE'RE FAR AWAY ENOUGH, PROBABLY.
BESIDES, XENO'S FACTORY...
VOOM
...IS RUNNING AT FULL TILT AND MAKING A REAL RACKET. WE CAN EXPLOIT THAT.
VOOM

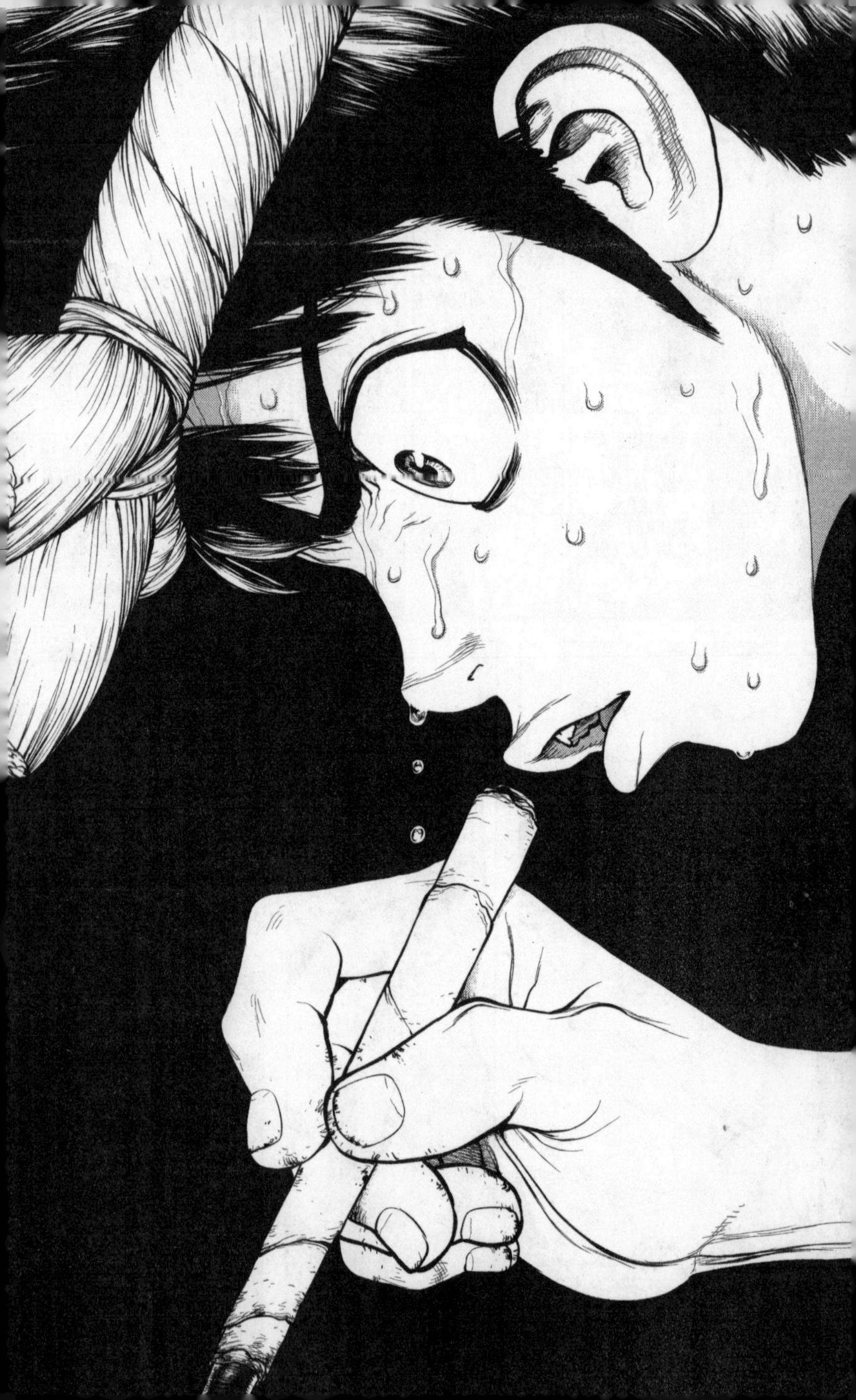

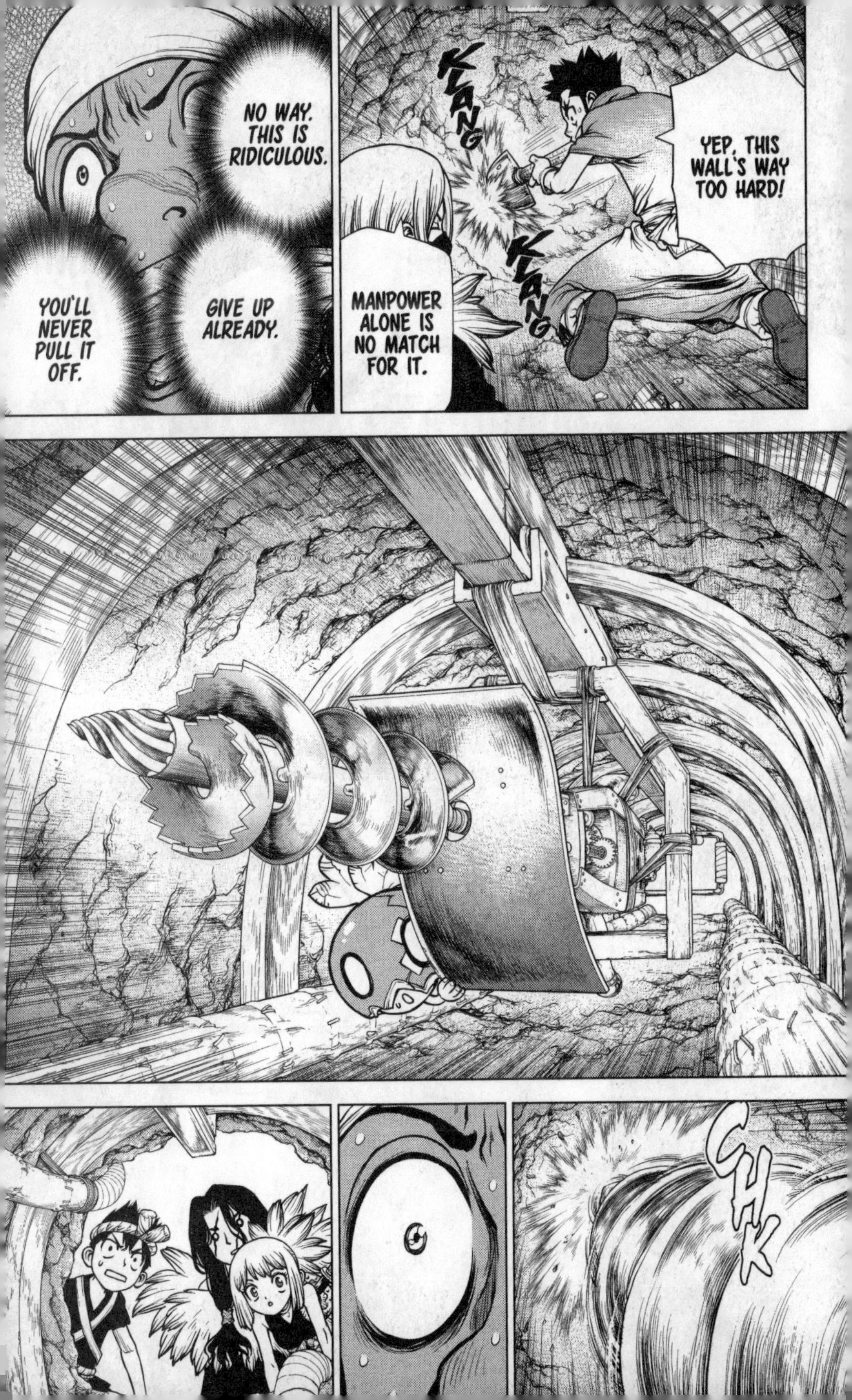
YEP, THIS WALL'S WAY TOO HARD!
KLANG
KLANG
MANPOWER ALONE IS NO MATCH FOR IT.
NO WAY. THIS IS RIDICULOUS.
GIVE UP ALREADY.
YOU'LL NEVER PULL IT OFF.
CHK

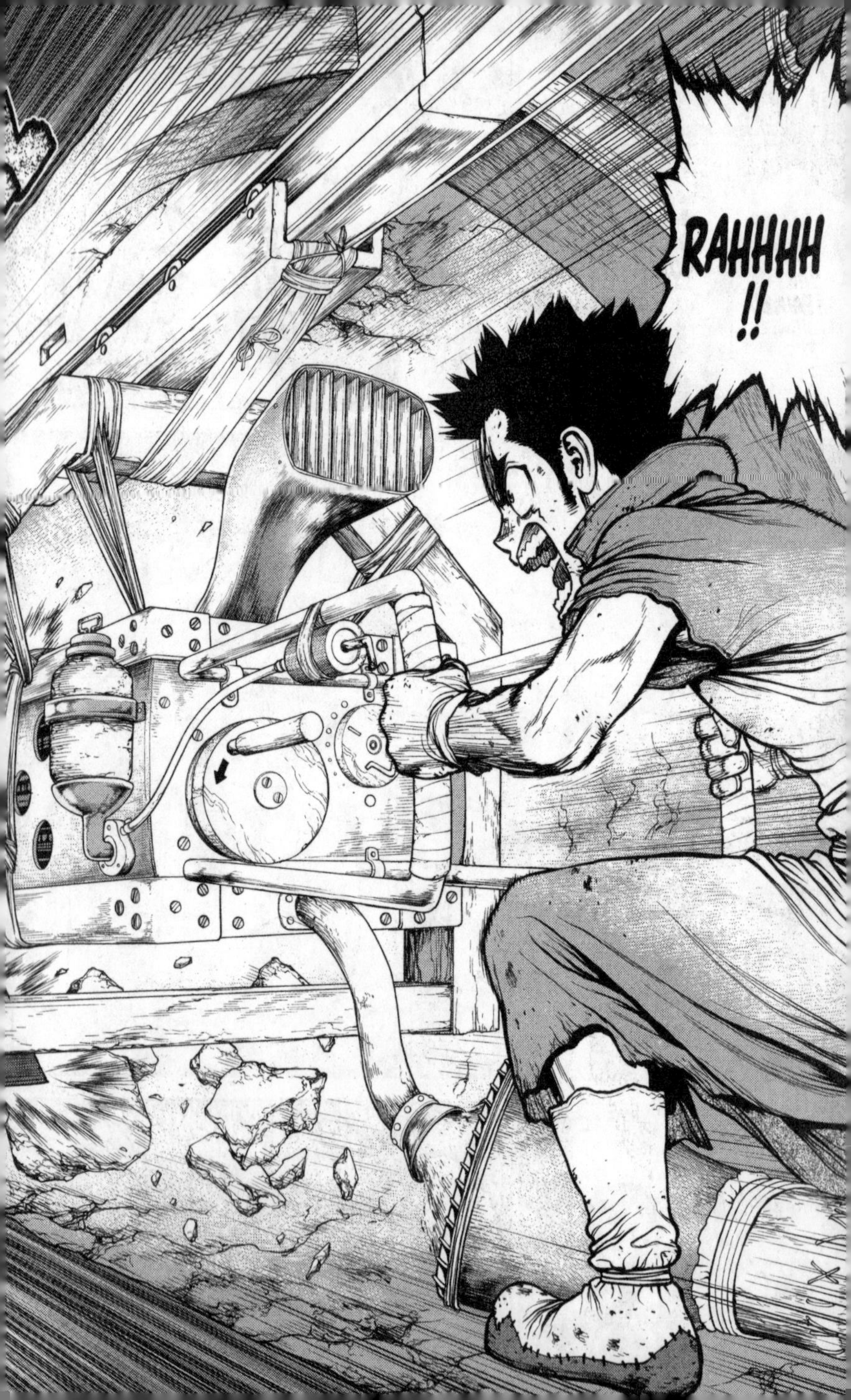
RAHHHH!!

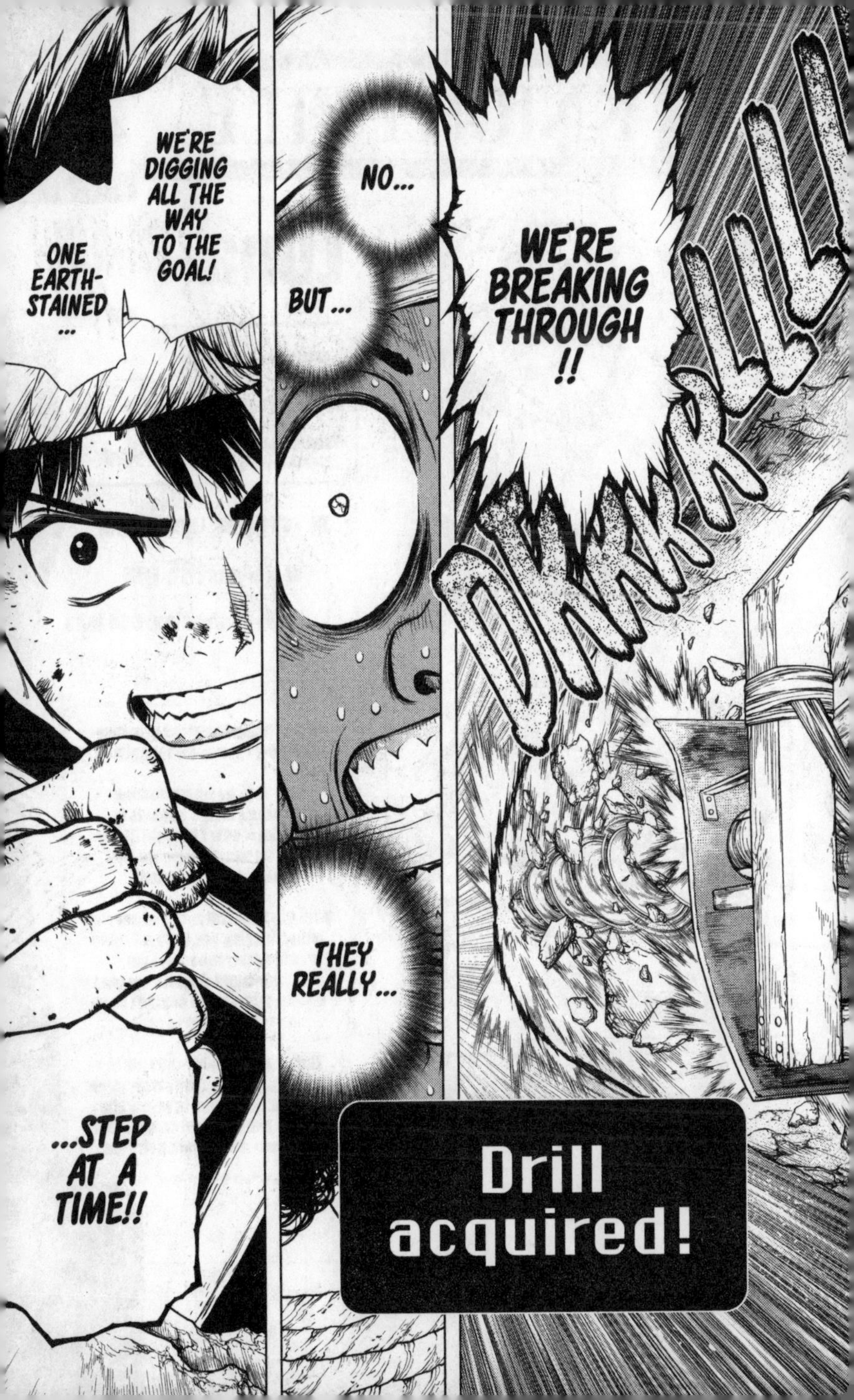
WE'RE BREAKING THROUGH!!
DRRRRILL
Drill acquired!
NO...
BUT...
THEY REALLY...
WE'RE DIGGING ALL THE WAY TO THE GOAL!
ONE EARTH-STAINED...
...STEP AT A TIME!!

Xeno's Science Kingdom

KNIGHT FILE 4

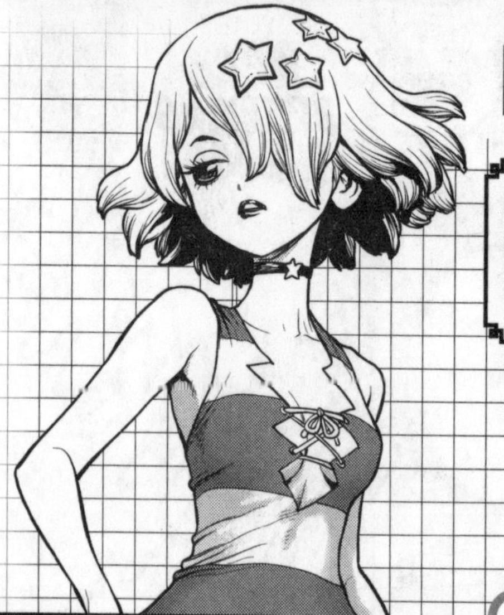

Luna

School Smarts	★★
Medical Skills	★★★★
Tendency to Fantasize	★★★★★

■ **Full Name:** Luna Wright

■ **Height:** 165 cm

■ **Profession:** Odd jobs

A privileged American princess who grew up wanting for nothing.

And yet, she wants nothing more than to be a capable gal who can fend for herself! Along with an equally capable and awesome boyfriend!

With the financial power of her rich father backing her, Luna was able to skip a few grades and get into medical school. Despite her best efforts, though, she couldn't keep up with the course load...

Then, she got a part-time job at a café (hoping for a random romantic encounter), which is where she and her two constant companions were when they were petrified.

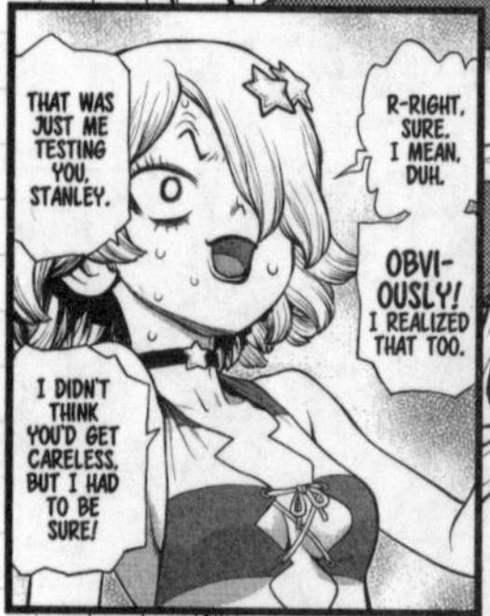
R-RIGHT, SURE. I MEAN, DUH.
THAT WAS JUST ME TESTING YOU, STANLEY.
OBVIOUSLY! I REALIZED THAT TOO.
I DIDN'T THINK YOU'D GET CARELESS, BUT I HAD TO BE SURE!

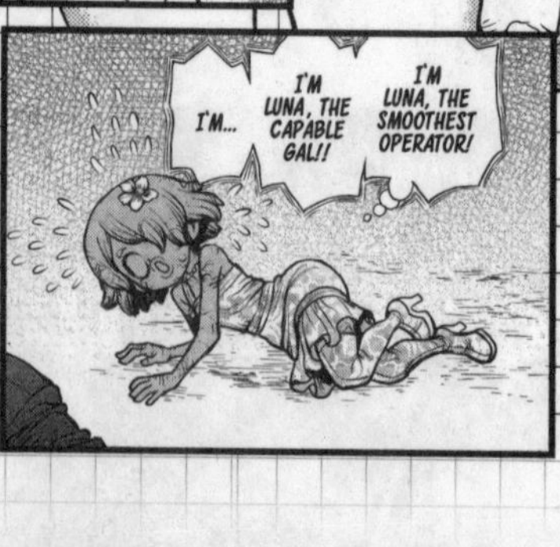
I'M LUNA, THE SMOOTHEST OPERATOR!
I'M LUNA, THE CAPABLE GAL!!
I'M...

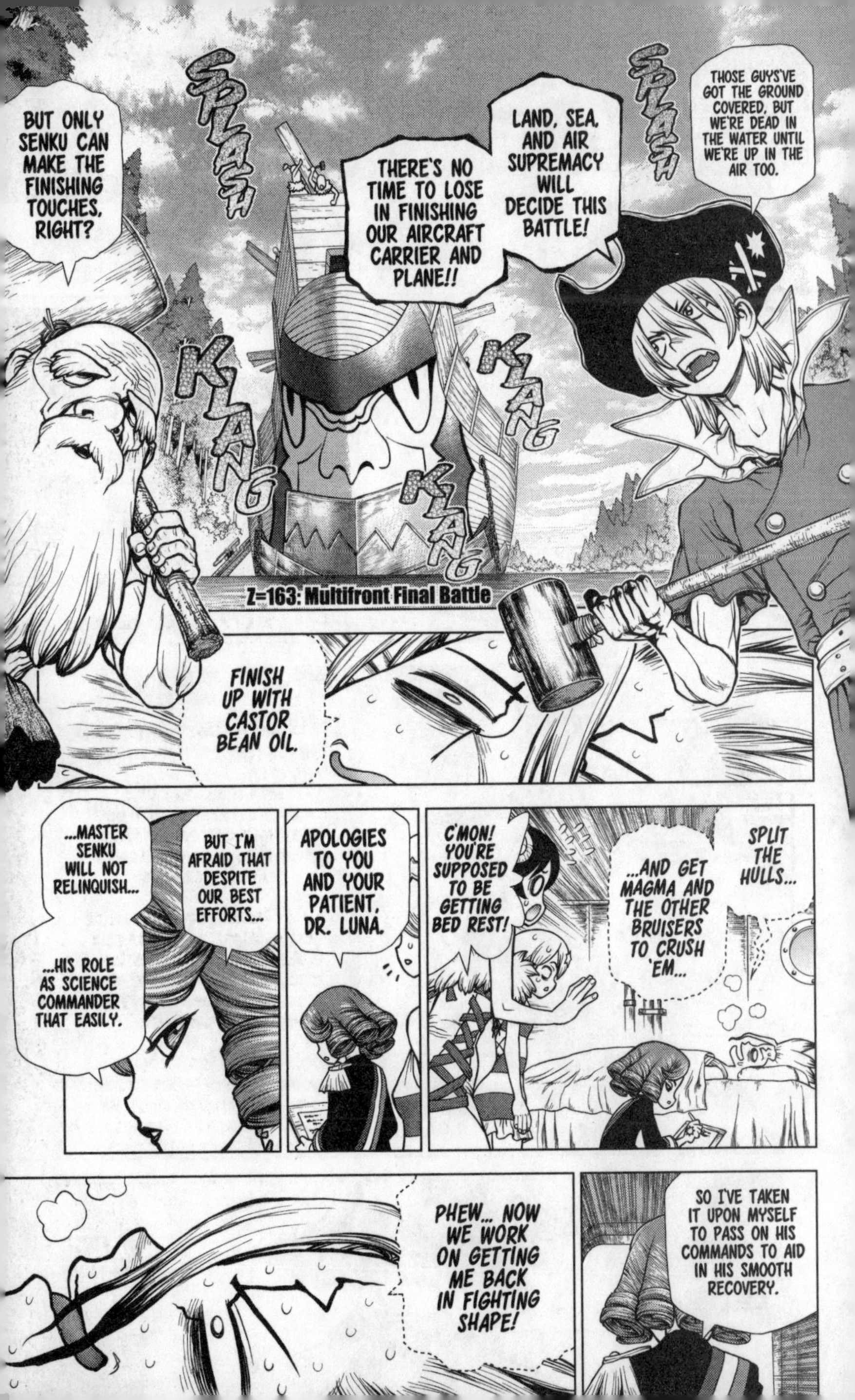
SPLASH
THOSE GUYS'VE GOT THE GROUND COVERED, BUT WE'RE DEAD IN THE WATER UNTIL WE'RE UP IN THE AIR TOO.
LAND, SEA, AND AIR SUPREMACY WILL DECIDE THIS BATTLE!
THERE'S NO TIME TO LOSE IN FINISHING OUR AIRCRAFT CARRIER AND PLANE!!
SPLASH
BUT ONLY SENKU CAN MAKE THE FINISHING TOUCHES, RIGHT?
KLANG
KLANG
KLANG
Z=163: Multifront Final Battle
FINISH UP WITH CASTOR BEAN OIL.
SPLIT THE HULLS...
...AND GET MAGMA AND THE OTHER BRUISERS TO CRUSH 'EM...
C'MON! YOU'RE SUPPOSED TO BE GETTING BED REST!
APOLOGIES TO YOU AND YOUR PATIENT, DR. LUNA.
BUT I'M AFRAID THAT DESPITE OUR BEST EFFORTS...
...MASTER SENKU WILL NOT RELINQUISH...
...HIS ROLE AS SCIENCE COMMANDER THAT EASILY.
SO I'VE TAKEN IT UPON MYSELF TO PASS ON HIS COMMANDS TO AID IN HIS SMOOTH RECOVERY.
PHEW... NOW WE WORK ON GETTING ME BACK IN FIGHTING SHAPE!

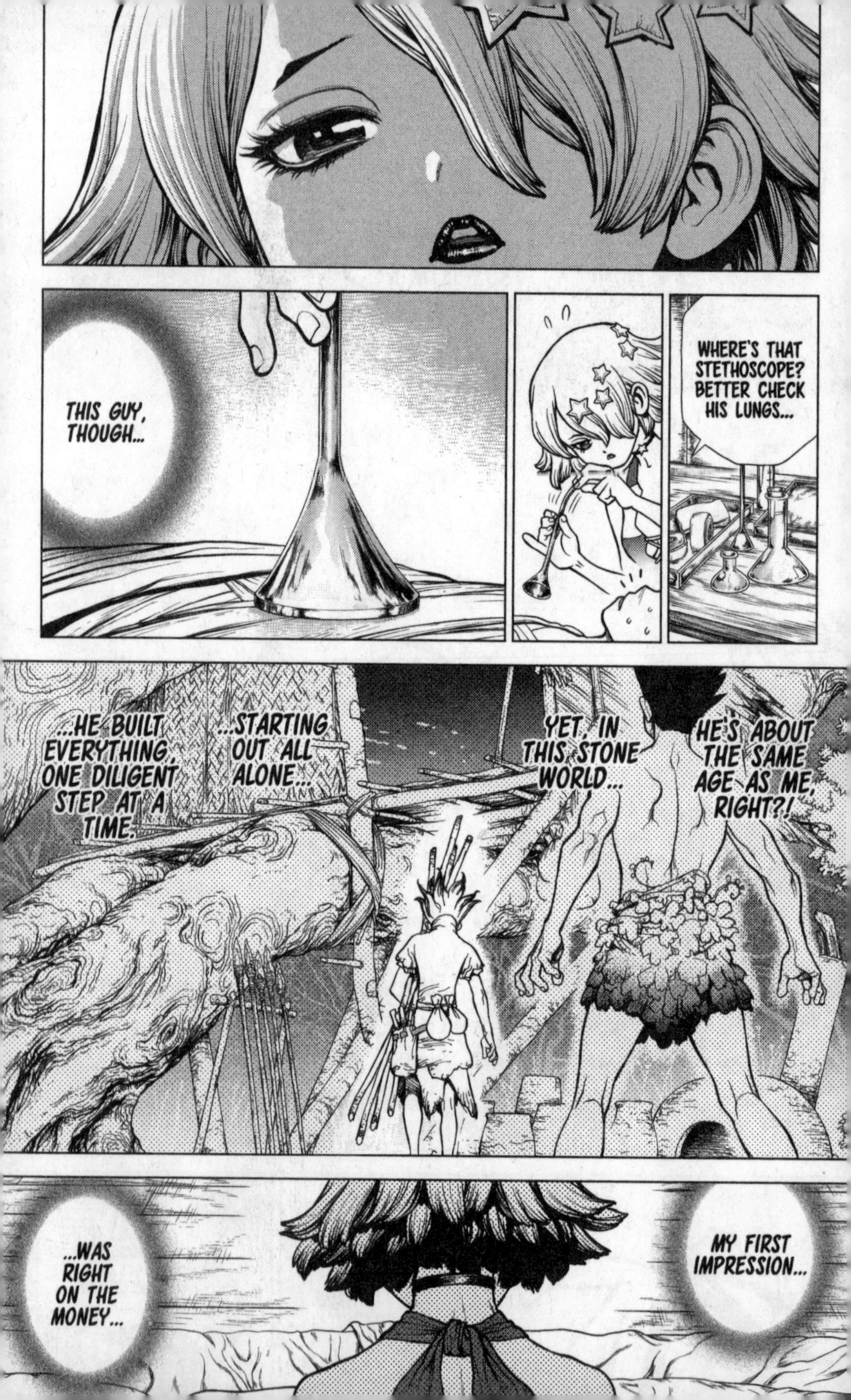
WHERE'S THAT STETHOSCOPE? BETTER CHECK HIS LUNGS...
THIS GUY, THOUGH...
HE'S ABOUT THE SAME AGE AS ME, RIGHT?!
YET, IN THIS STONE WORLD...
...STARTING OUT ALL ALONE...
...HE BUILT EVERYTHING, ONE DILIGENT STEP AT A TIME.
MY FIRST IMPRESSION...
...WAS RIGHT ON THE MONEY...

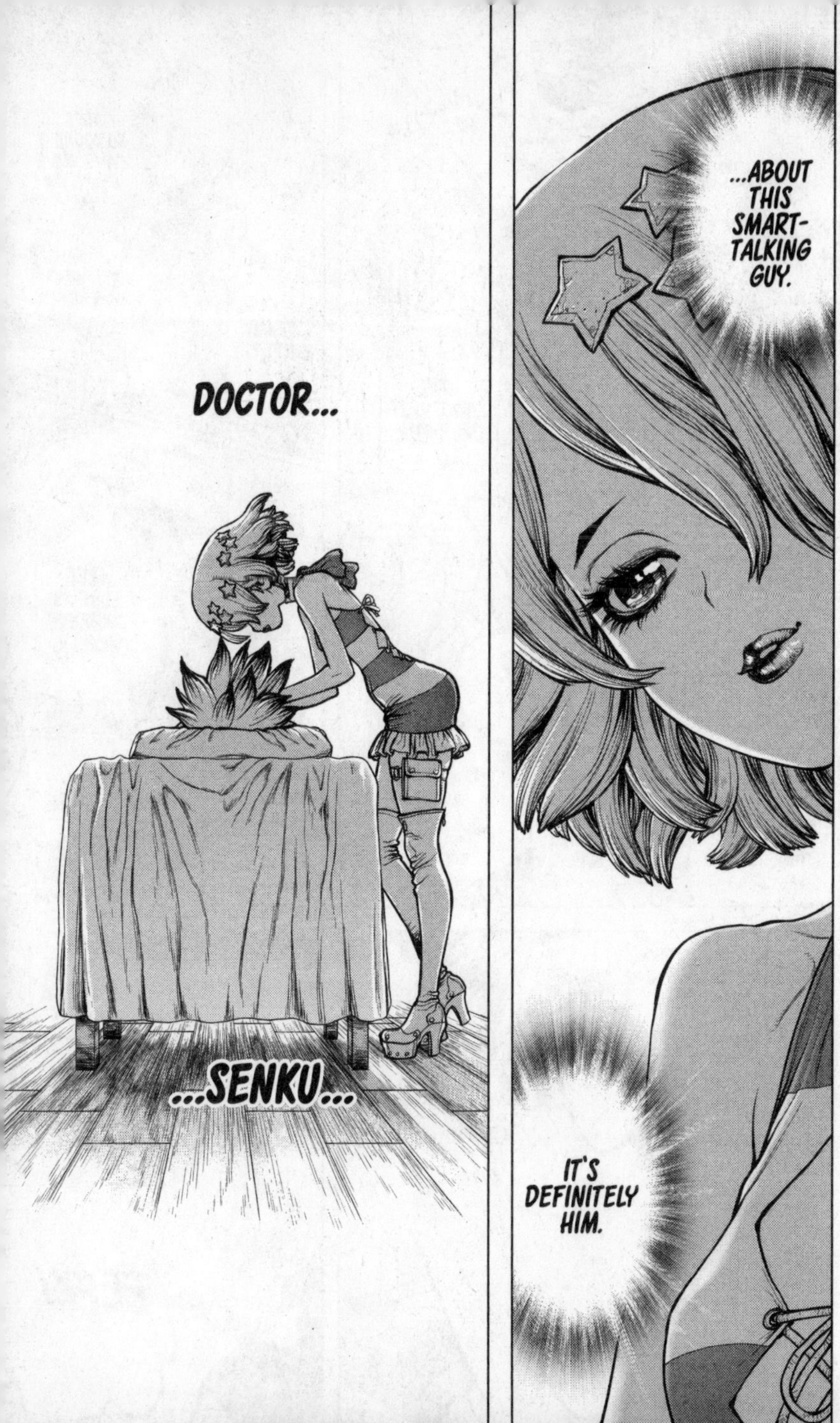
...ABOUT THIS SMART-TALKING GUY.
IT'S DEFINITELY HIM.
DOCTOR...
...SENKU...

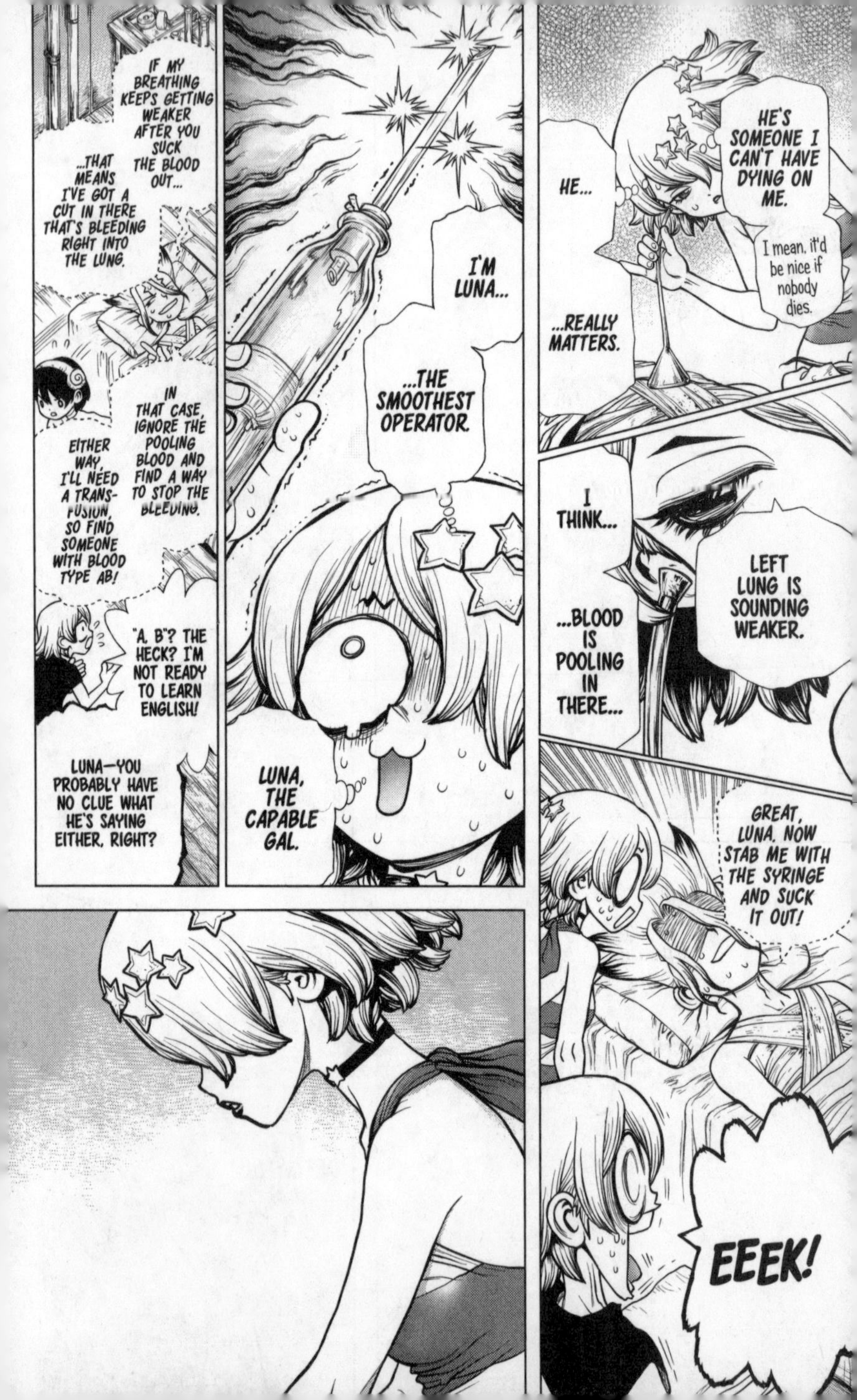

HE'S SOMEONE I CAN'T HAVE DYING ON ME.
I mean, it'd be nice if nobody dies.
HE...
...REALLY MATTERS.
LEFT LUNG IS SOUNDING WEAKER.
I THINK...
...BLOOD IS POOLING IN THERE...
GREAT, LUNA. NOW STAB ME WITH THE SYRINGE AND SUCK IT OUT!
EEEK!
I'M LUNA...
...THE SMOOTHEST OPERATOR.
LUNA, THE CAPABLE GAL.
IF MY BREATHING KEEPS GETTING WEAKER AFTER YOU SUCK THE BLOOD OUT...
...THAT MEANS I'VE GOT A CUT IN THERE THAT'S BLEEDING RIGHT INTO THE LUNG.
IN THAT CASE, IGNORE THE POOLING BLOOD AND FIND A WAY TO STOP THE BLEEDING.
EITHER WAY, I'LL NEED A TRANSFUSION, SO FIND SOMEONE WITH BLOOD TYPE AB!
"A, B"? THE HECK? I'M NOT READY TO LEARN ENGLISH!
LUNA—YOU PROBABLY HAVE NO CLUE WHAT HE'S SAYING EITHER, RIGHT?

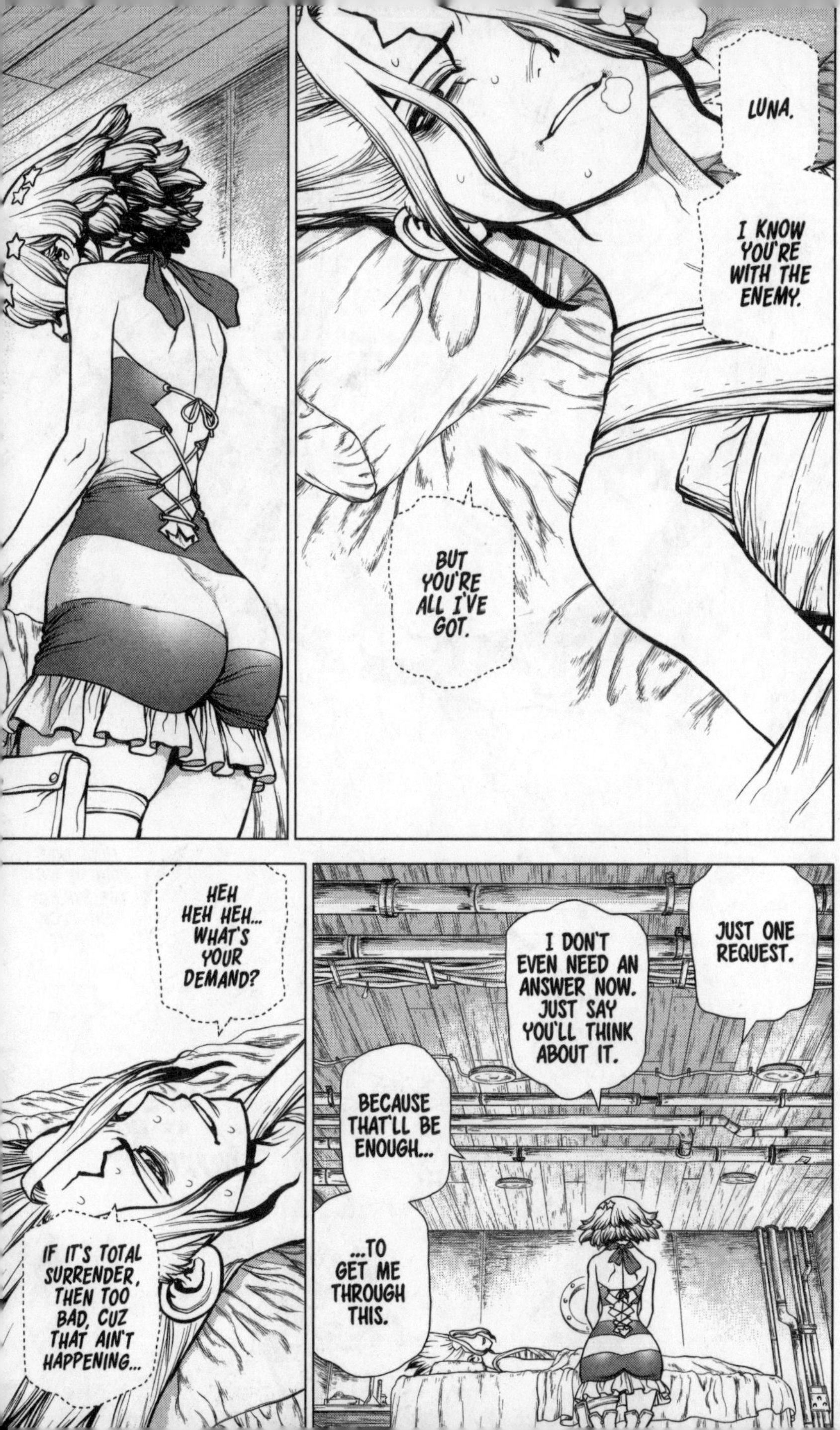
LUNA.
I KNOW YOU'RE WITH THE ENEMY.
BUT YOU'RE ALL I'VE GOT.
JUST ONE REQUEST.
I DON'T EVEN NEED AN ANSWER NOW. JUST SAY YOU'LL THINK ABOUT IT.
BECAUSE THAT'LL BE ENOUGH...
...TO GET ME THROUGH THIS.
HEH HEH HEH... WHAT'S YOUR DEMAND?
IF IT'S TOTAL SURRENDER, THEN TOO BAD, CUZ THAT AIN'T HAPPENING...

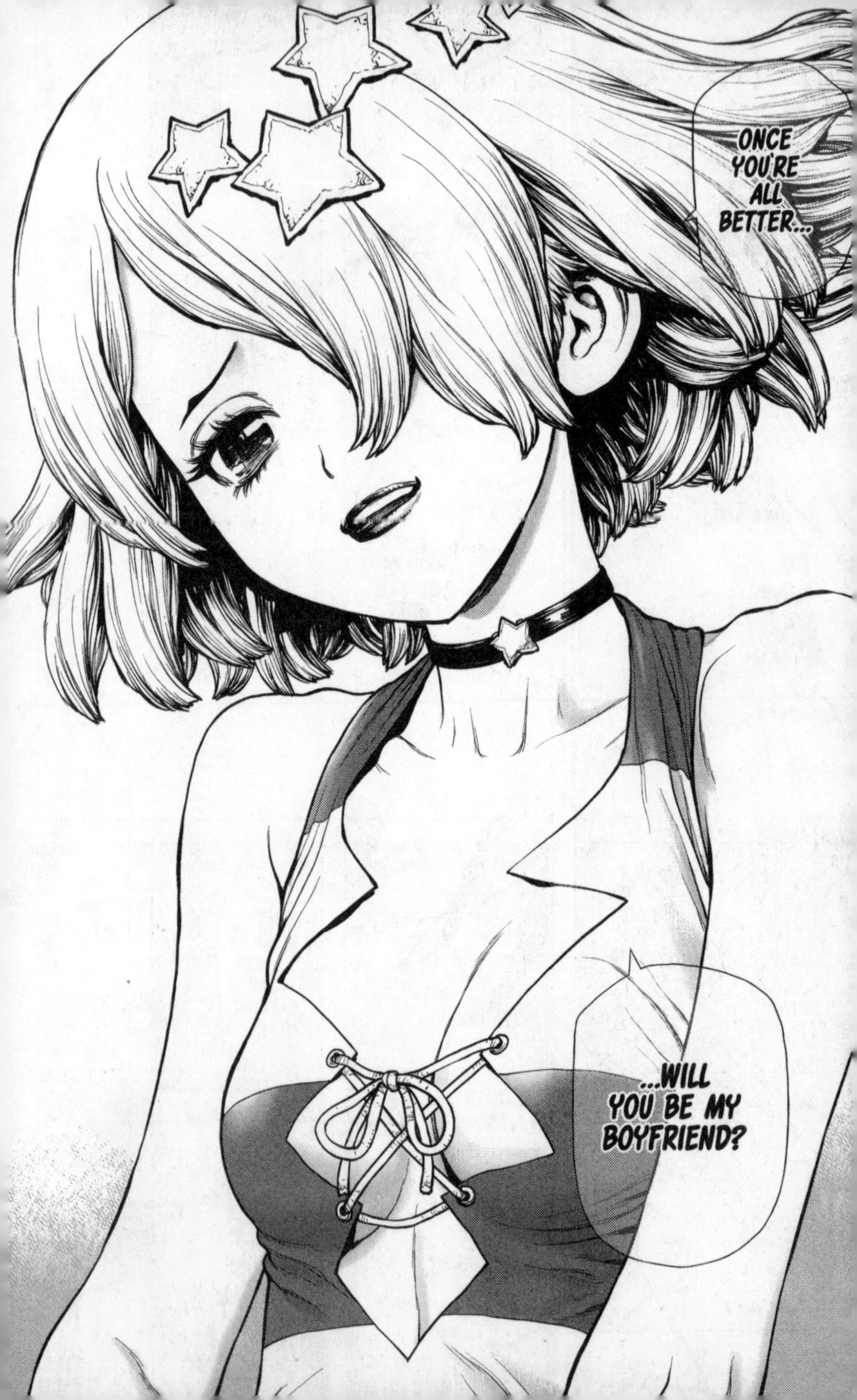
ONCE YOU'RE ALL BETTER...
...WILL YOU BE MY BOYFRIEND?

Z=163: Multifront Final Battle

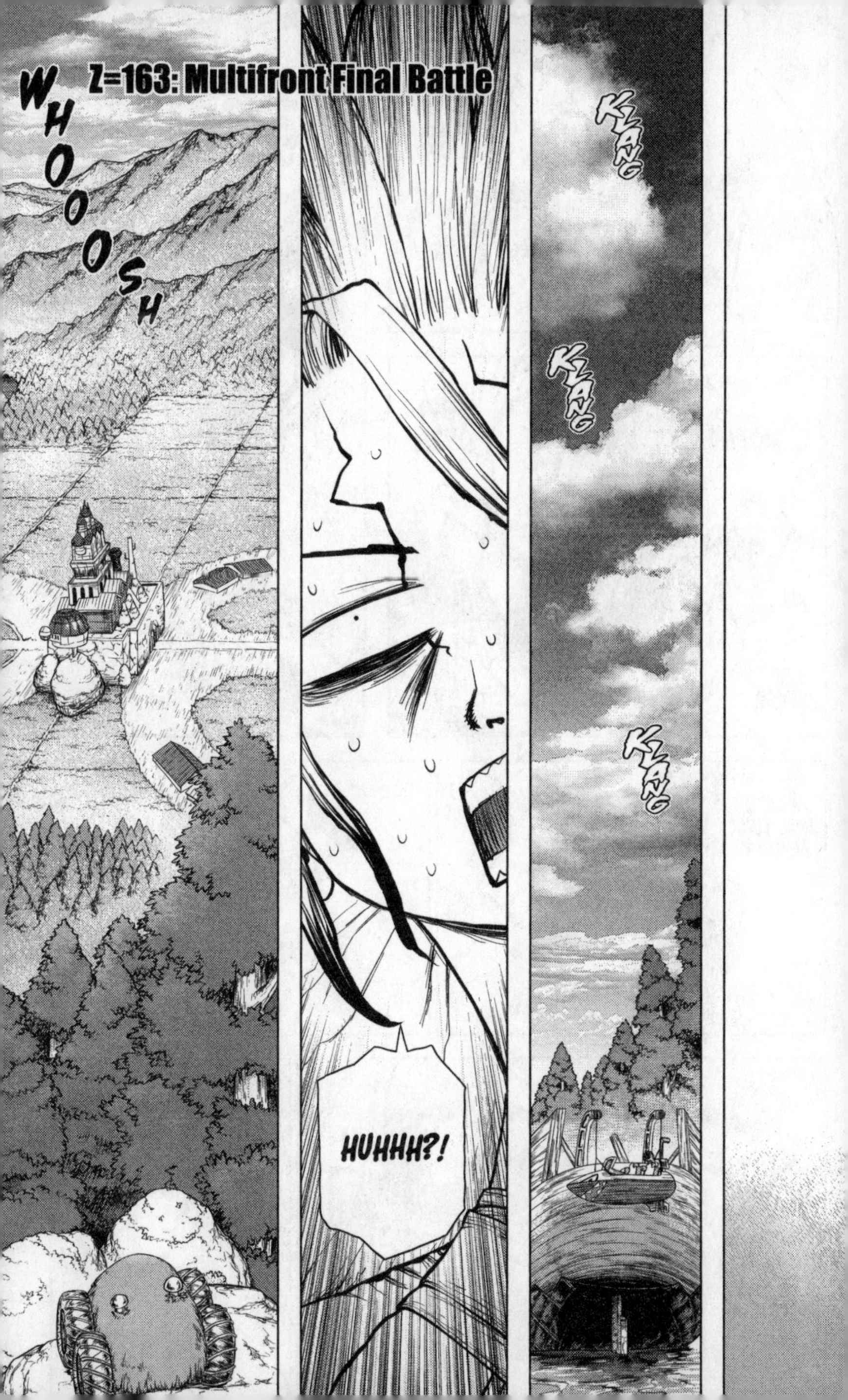
KLANG
KLANG
KLANG
HUHHH?!
WHOOOOSH

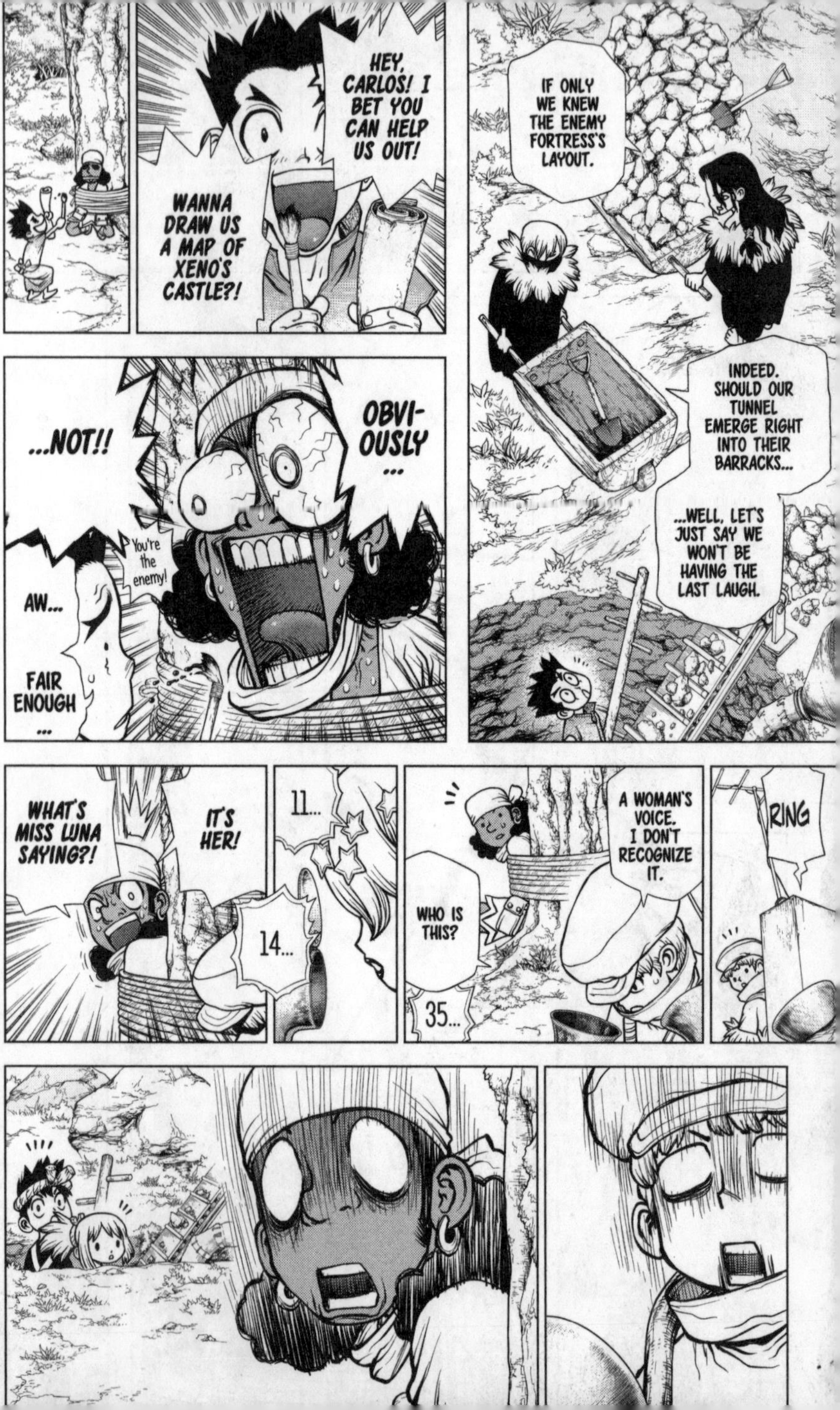
IF ONLY WE KNEW THE ENEMY FORTRESS'S LAYOUT.
INDEED. SHOULD OUR TUNNEL EMERGE RIGHT INTO THEIR BARRACKS...
...WELL, LET'S JUST SAY WE WON'T BE HAVING THE LAST LAUGH.
HEY, CARLOS! I BET YOU CAN HELP US OUT!
WANNA DRAW US A MAP OF XENO'S CASTLE?!
OBVI-OUSLY...
...NOT!!
You're the enemy!
AW...
FAIR ENOUGH...
RING
A WOMAN'S VOICE. I DON'T RECOGNIZE IT.
WHO IS THIS?
35...
11...
14...
IT'S HER!
WHAT'S MISS LUNA SAYING?!

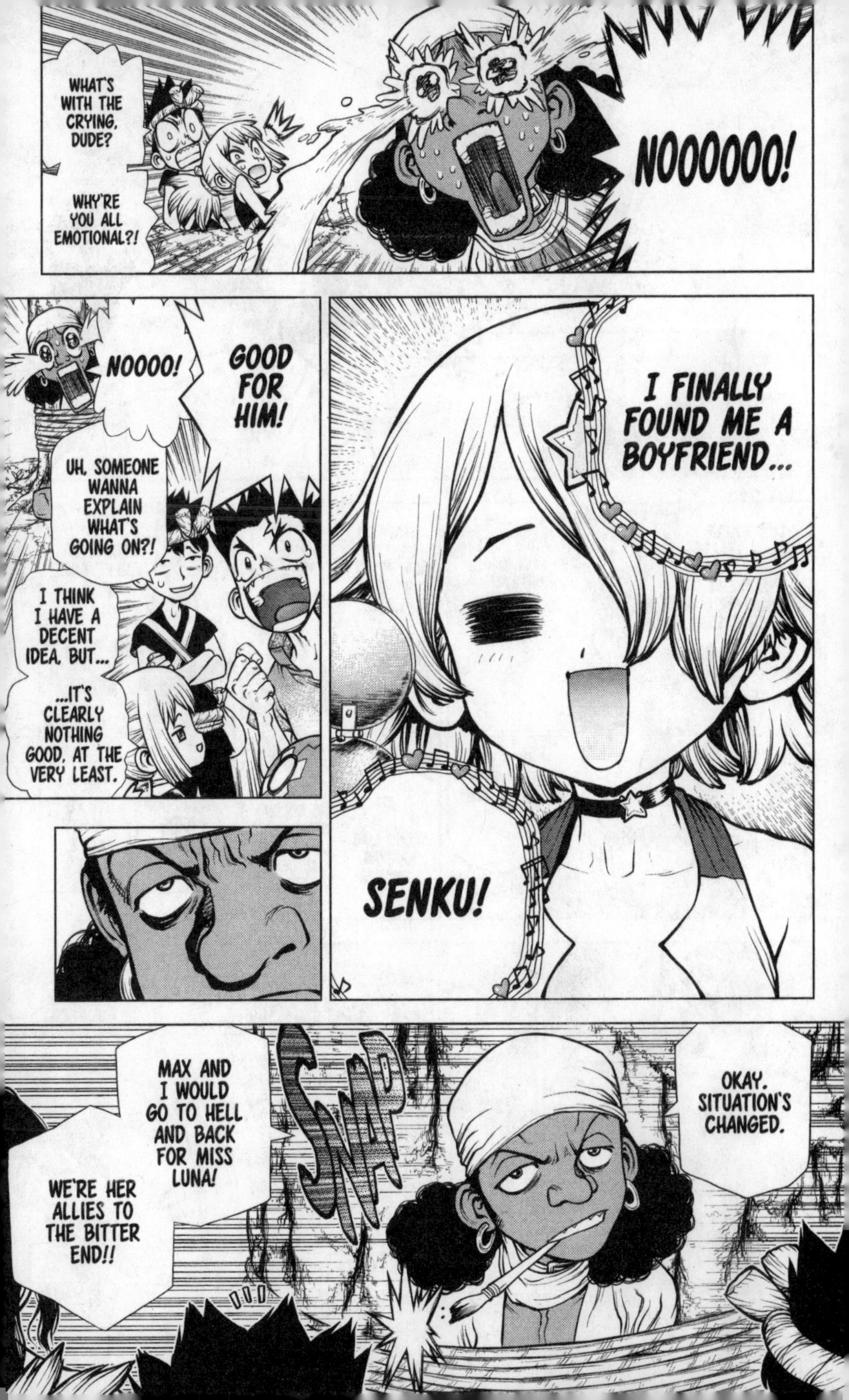
NOOOOOO!
WHAT'S WITH THE CRYING, DUDE?
WHY'RE YOU ALL EMOTIONAL?!
I FINALLY FOUND ME A BOYFRIEND...
SENKU!
GOOD FOR HIM!
NOOOO!
UH, SOMEONE WANNA EXPLAIN WHAT'S GOING ON?!
I THINK I HAVE A DECENT IDEA, BUT...
...IT'S CLEARLY NOTHING GOOD, AT THE VERY LEAST.
OKAY. SITUATION'S CHANGED.
SNAP
MAX AND I WOULD GO TO HELL AND BACK FOR MISS LUNA!
WE'RE HER ALLIES TO THE BITTER END!!

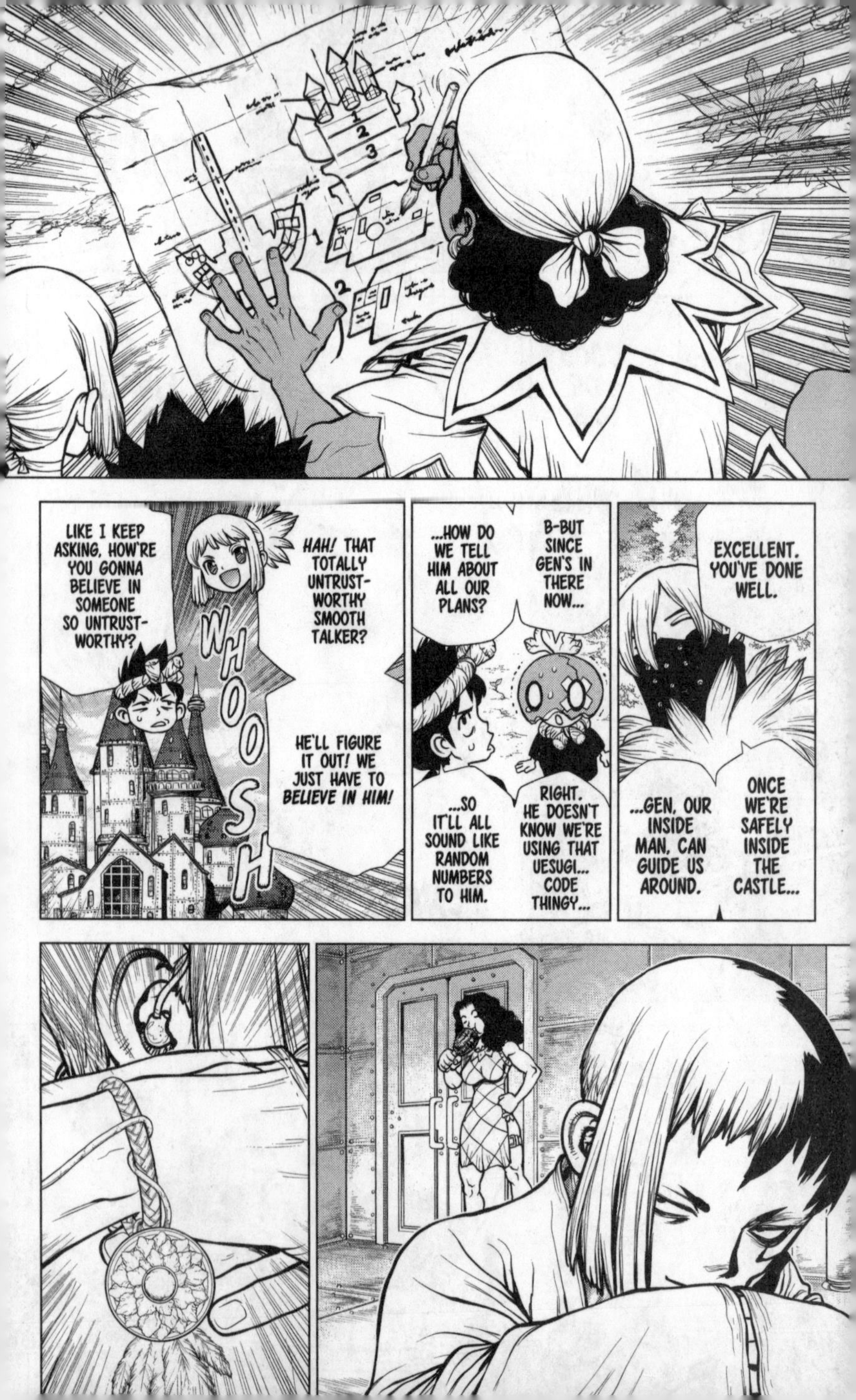
EXCELLENT. YOU'VE DONE WELL.
ONCE WE'RE SAFELY INSIDE THE CASTLE...
...GEN, OUR INSIDE MAN, CAN GUIDE US AROUND.
B-BUT SINCE GEN'S IN THERE NOW...
...HOW DO WE TELL HIM ABOUT ALL OUR PLANS?
RIGHT. HE DOESN'T KNOW WE'RE USING THAT UESUGI... CODE THINGY...
...SO IT'LL ALL SOUND LIKE RANDOM NUMBERS TO HIM.
HAH! THAT TOTALLY UNTRUST-WORTHY SMOOTH TALKER?
LIKE I KEEP ASKING, HOW'RE YOU GONNA BELIEVE IN SOMEONE SO UNTRUST-WORTHY?
WHOOSH
HE'LL FIGURE IT OUT! WE JUST HAVE TO *BELIEVE IN HIM!*

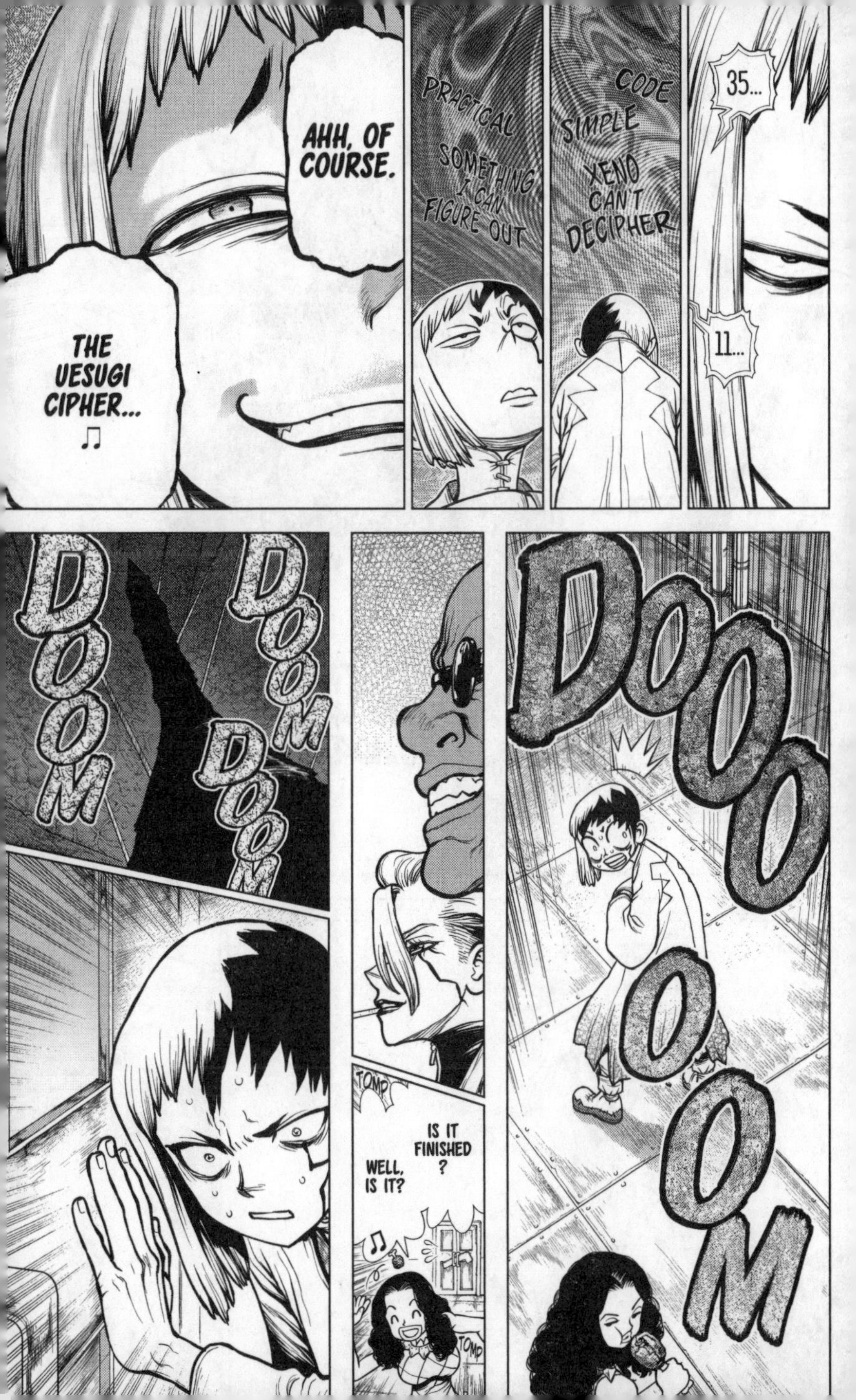

35...
11...
CODE
SIMPLE
XENO CAN'T DECIPHER
PRACTICAL
SOMETHING I CAN FIGURE OUT
AHH, OF COURSE.
THE UESUGI CIPHER... ♫
DOOOOOOOM
TOMP
IS IT FINISHED?
WELL, IS IT?
♫
TOMP
DOOOM
DOOOM
DOOOM

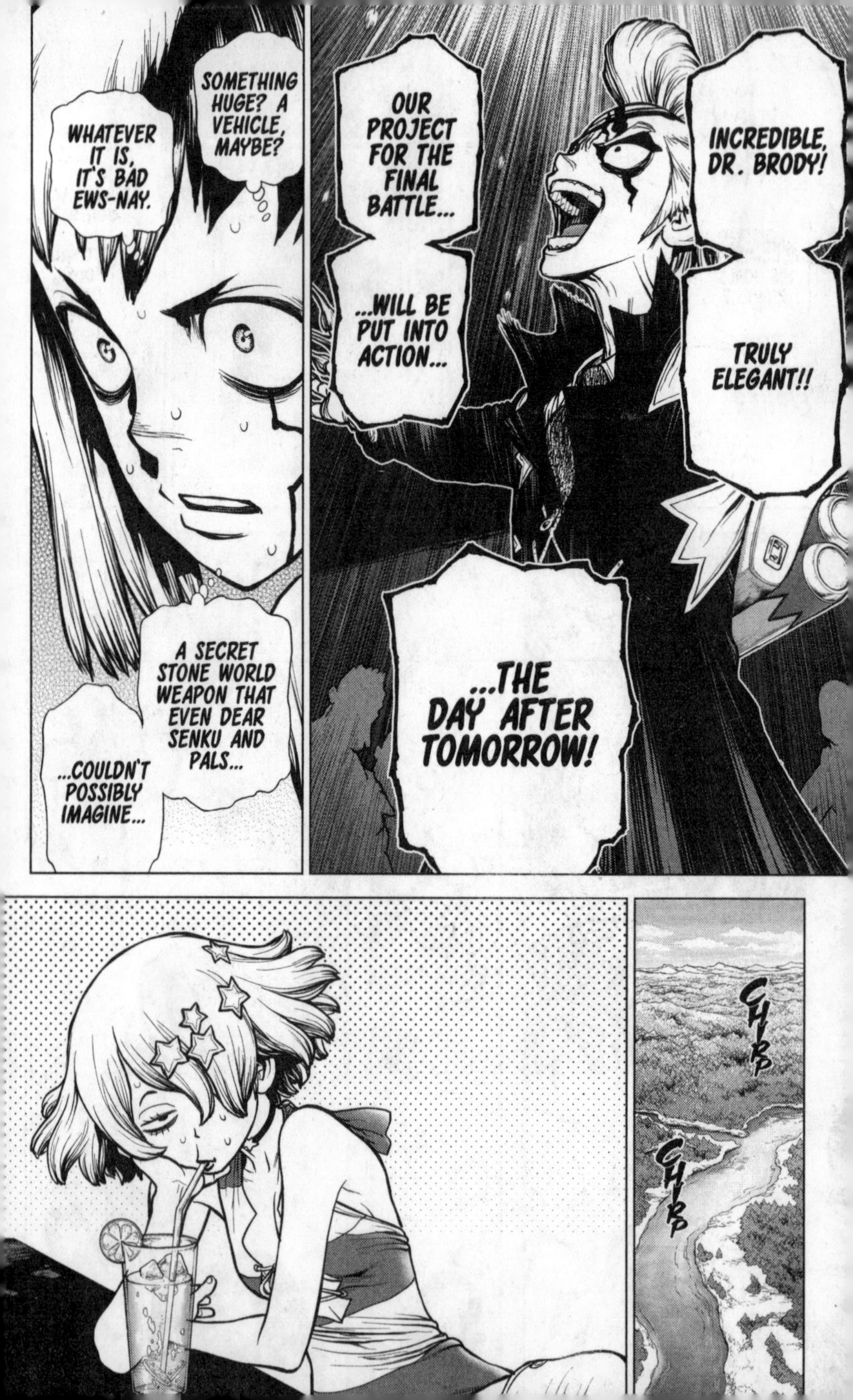
INCREDIBLE, DR. BRODY!
TRULY ELEGANT!!
OUR PROJECT FOR THE FINAL BATTLE...
...WILL BE PUT INTO ACTION...
...THE DAY AFTER TOMORROW!
SOMETHING HUGE? A VEHICLE, MAYBE?
WHATEVER IT IS, IT'S BAD EWS-NAY.
A SECRET STONE WORLD WEAPON THAT EVEN DEAR SENKU AND PALS...
...COULDN'T POSSIBLY IMAGINE...
CHIRP
CHIRP

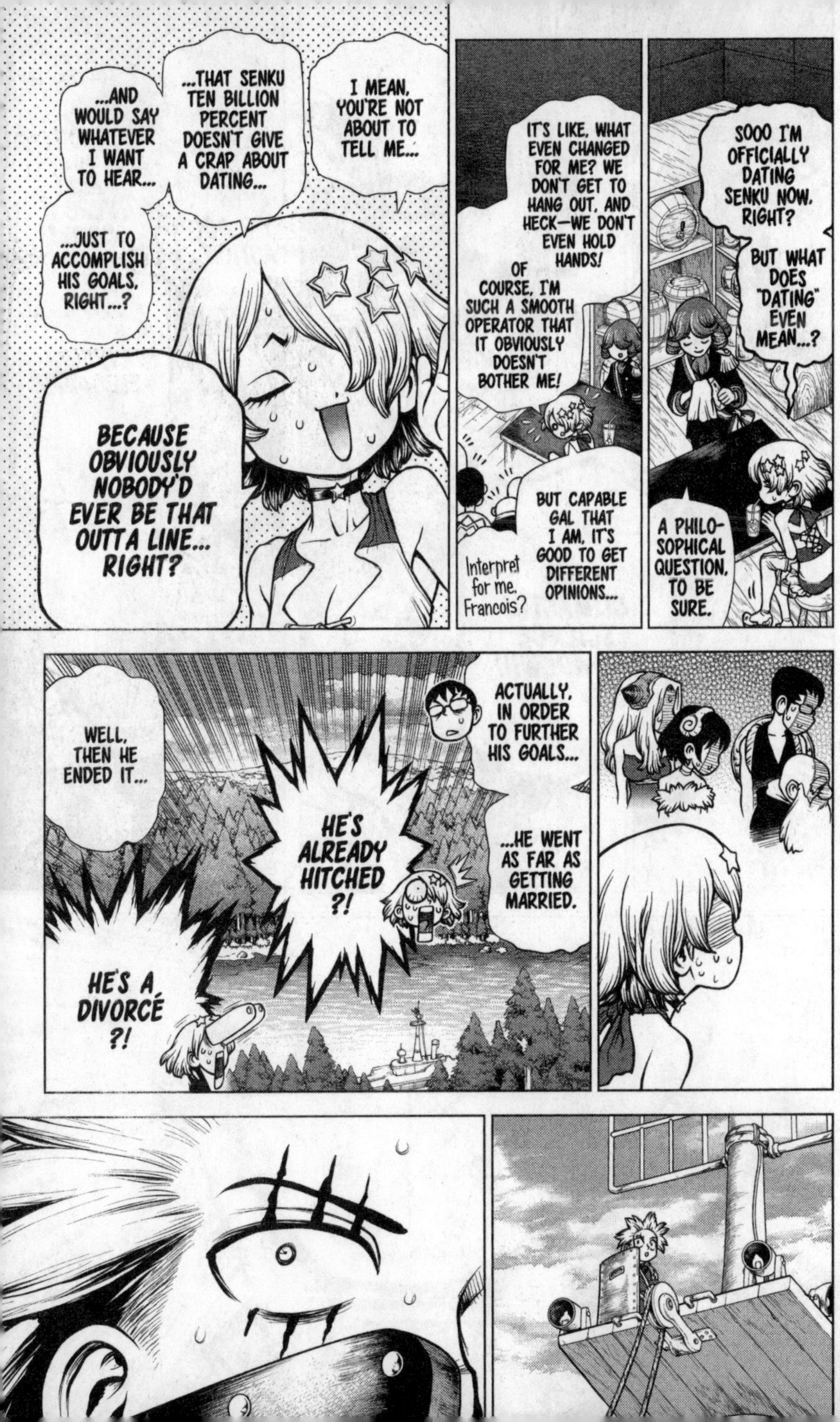
SOOO I'M OFFICIALLY DATING SENKU NOW, RIGHT?
BUT WHAT DOES "DATING" EVEN MEAN...?
A PHILOSOPHICAL QUESTION, TO BE SURE.
IT'S LIKE, WHAT EVEN CHANGED FOR ME? WE DON'T GET TO HANG OUT, AND HECK—WE DON'T EVEN HOLD HANDS!
OF COURSE, I'M SUCH A SMOOTH OPERATOR THAT IT OBVIOUSLY DOESN'T BOTHER ME!
BUT CAPABLE GAL THAT I AM, IT'S GOOD TO GET DIFFERENT OPINIONS...
Interpret for me, Francois?
I MEAN, YOU'RE NOT ABOUT TO TELL ME...
...THAT SENKU TEN BILLION PERCENT DOESN'T GIVE A CRAP ABOUT DATING...
...AND WOULD SAY WHATEVER I WANT TO HEAR...
...JUST TO ACCOMPLISH HIS GOALS, RIGHT...?
BECAUSE OBVIOUSLY NOBODY'D EVER BE THAT OUTTA LINE... RIGHT?
ACTUALLY, IN ORDER TO FURTHER HIS GOALS...
...HE WENT AS FAR AS GETTING MARRIED.
HE'S ALREADY HITCHED?!
WELL, THEN HE ENDED IT...
HE'S A DIVORCÉ?!

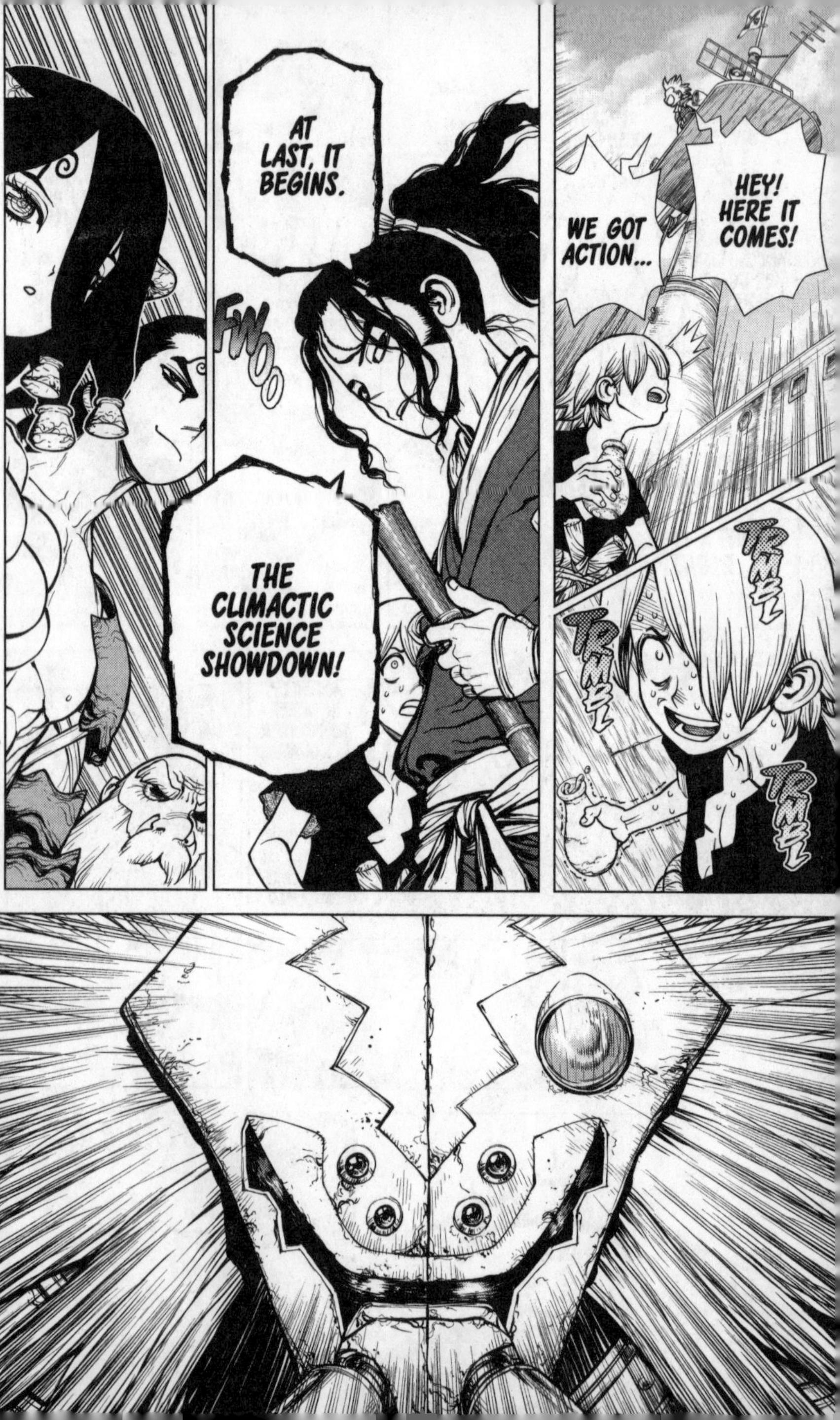
HEY! HERE IT COMES!
WE GOT ACTION...
TRMBL
TRMBL
TRMBL
AT LAST, IT BEGINS.
FWOOO
THE CLIMACTIC SCIENCE SHOWDOWN!

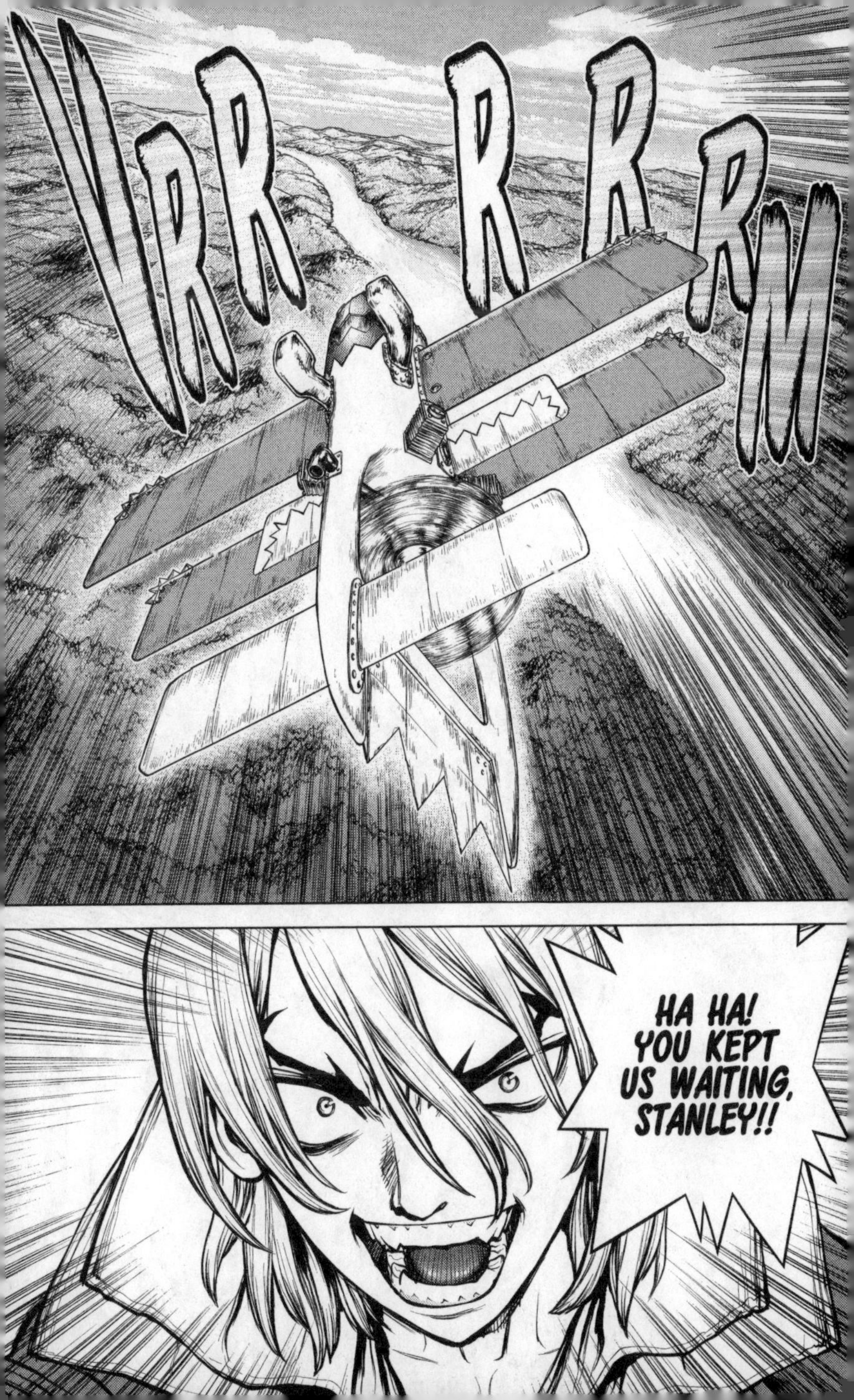
VRRRRRM
HA HA! YOU KEPT US WAITING, STANLEY!!

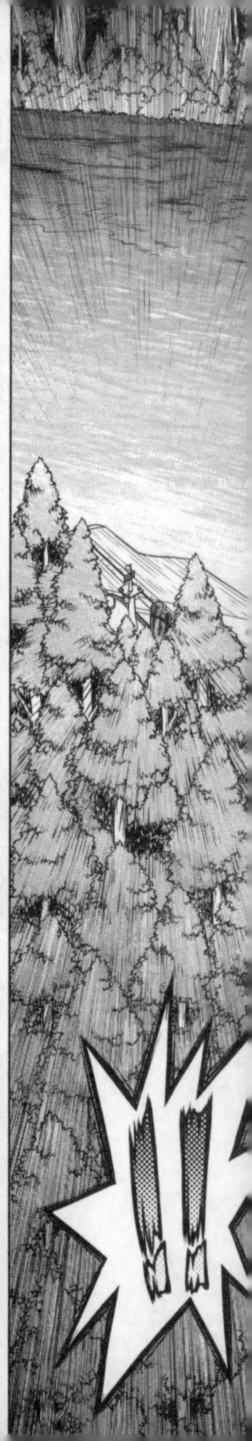
!!

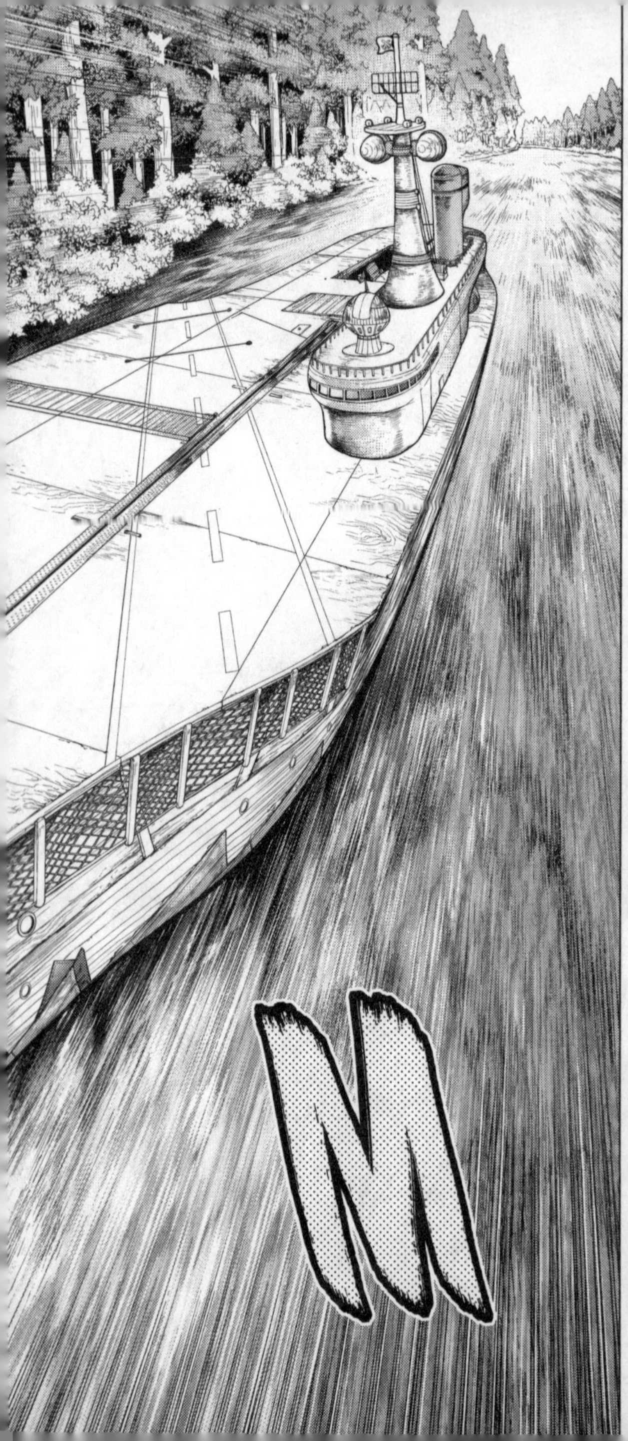
M

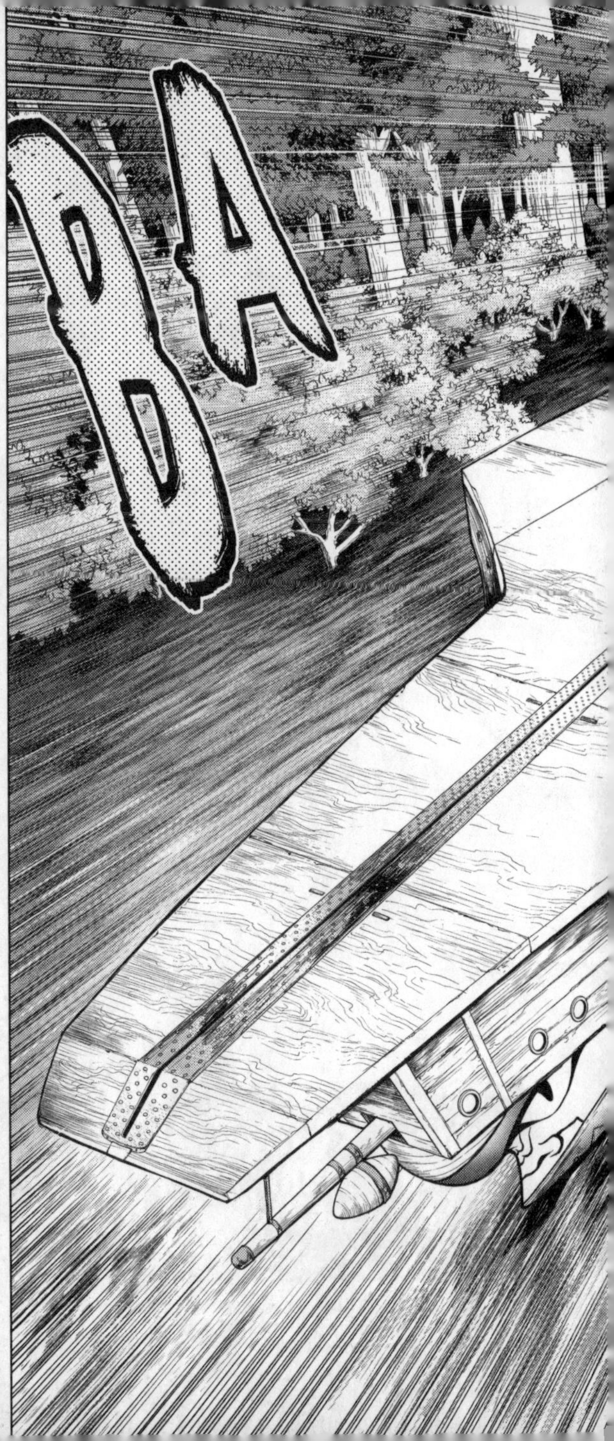
BA
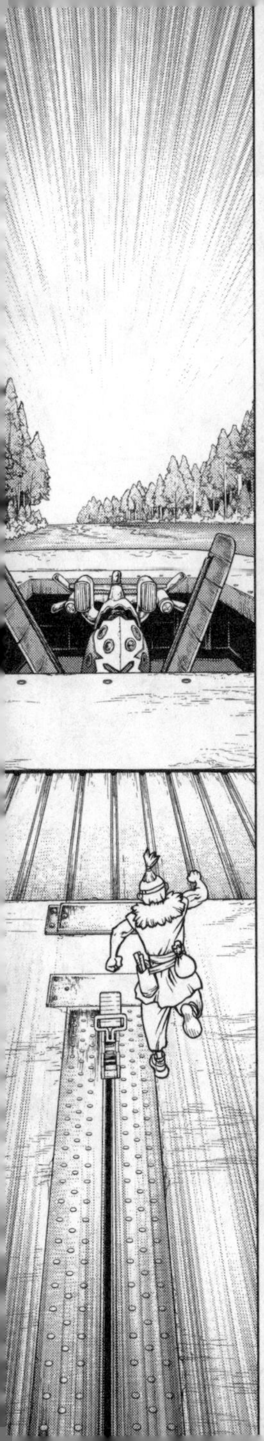

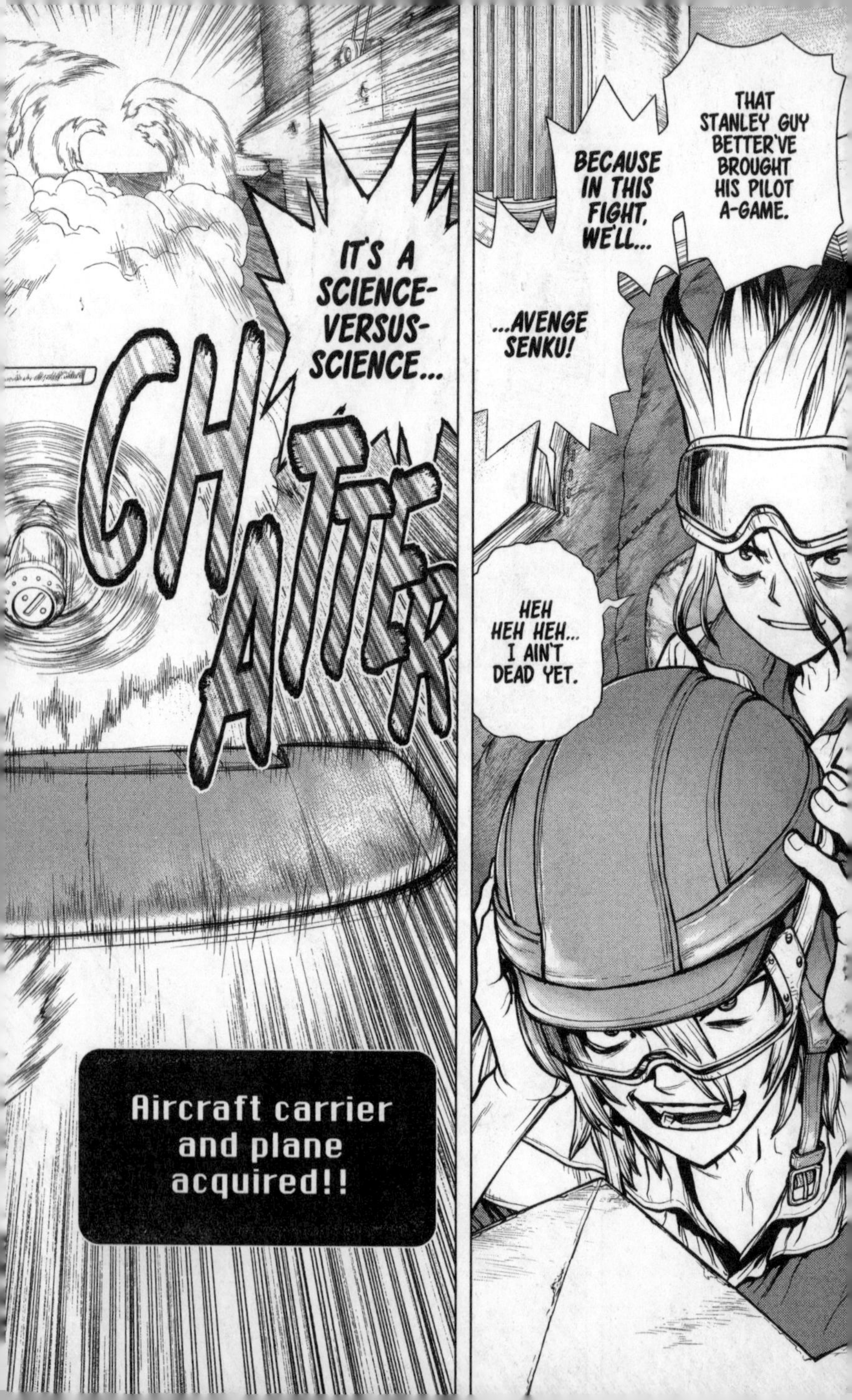
THAT STANLEY GUY BETTER'VE BROUGHT HIS PILOT A-GAME.
BECAUSE IN THIS FIGHT, WE'LL...
...AVENGE SENKU!
HEH HEH HEH... I AIN'T DEAD YET.
IT'S A SCIENCE-VERSUS-SCIENCE...
CHATTER
Aircraft carrier and plane acquired!!

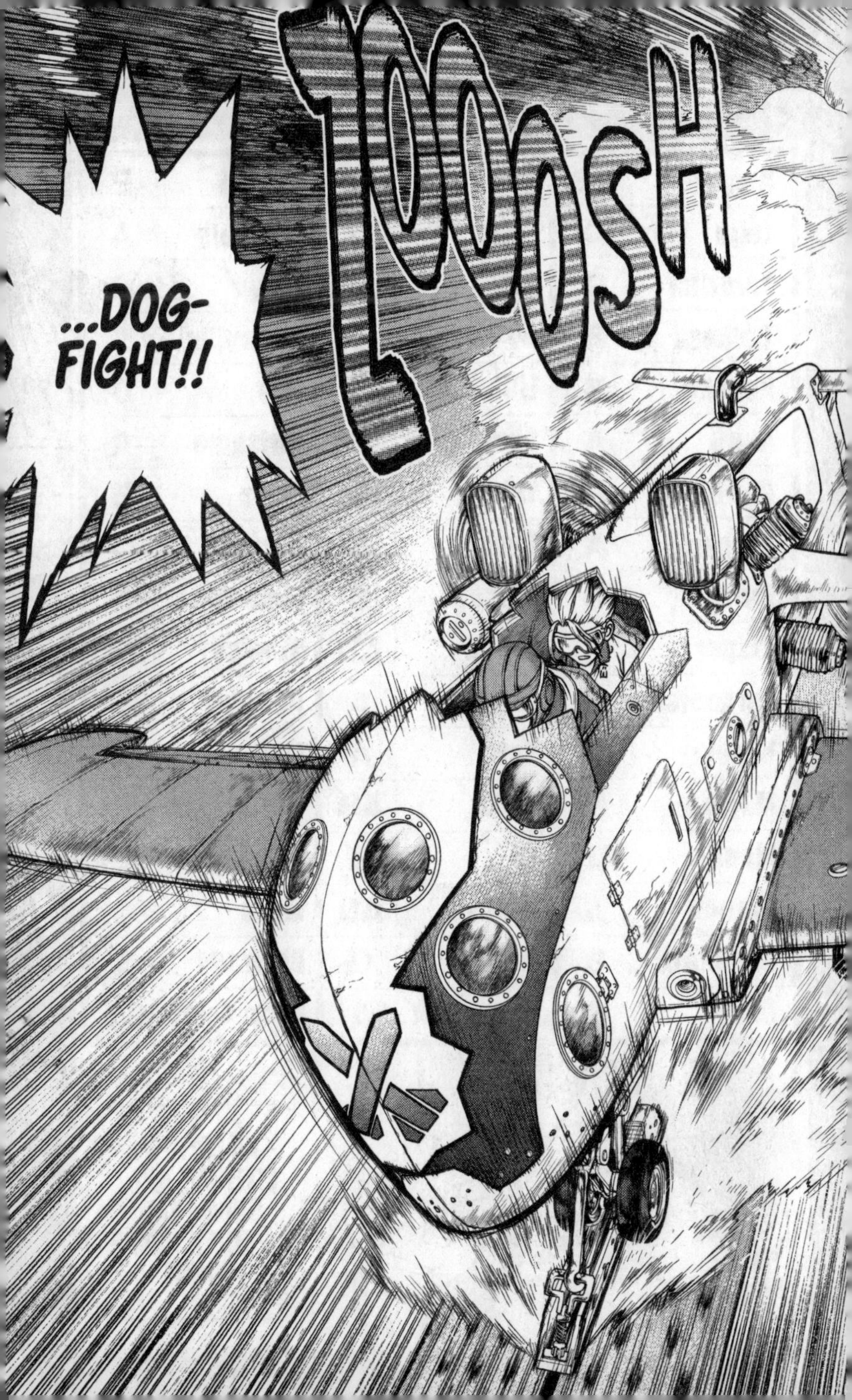
ZOOOOSH
...DOG-
FIGHT!!

BLOOD TYPE OVERVIEW

Senku	AB	Kokyo	B	Ryusui	B
Taiju	A	Suika	O	Francois	A
Yuzuriha	O	Gen	B	Soyuz	O
Tsukasa	B	Byakuya	O	Amaryllis	A
Kohaku	B	Lillian	A	Moz	B
Kinro	A	Shamil	B	Kirisame	A
Ginro	B	Yakov	O	Ibara	B
Chrome	A	Connie	A	Oarashi	O
Ruri	O	Darya	B	Matsukaze	A
Jasper	A	Hyoga	AB	Stanley	B
Turquoise	B	Homura	A	Dr. Xeno	A
Kaseki	AB	Ukyo	A	Luna	A
Magma	B	Nikki	AB	Carlos	B
Mantle	AB	Yo	B	Max	AB
Garnet	A	Minami	AB	Maya	O
Sapphire	B	Mirai	O	Dr. Brody	A
Ruby	O	Manga Artist	A	Mecha Senku	OIL

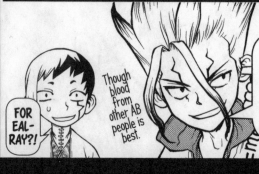

AB TYPES LIKE ME ARE UNIVERSAL RECIPIENTS, Y'KNOW.
Though blood from other AB people is best.
FOR EAL-RAY?!

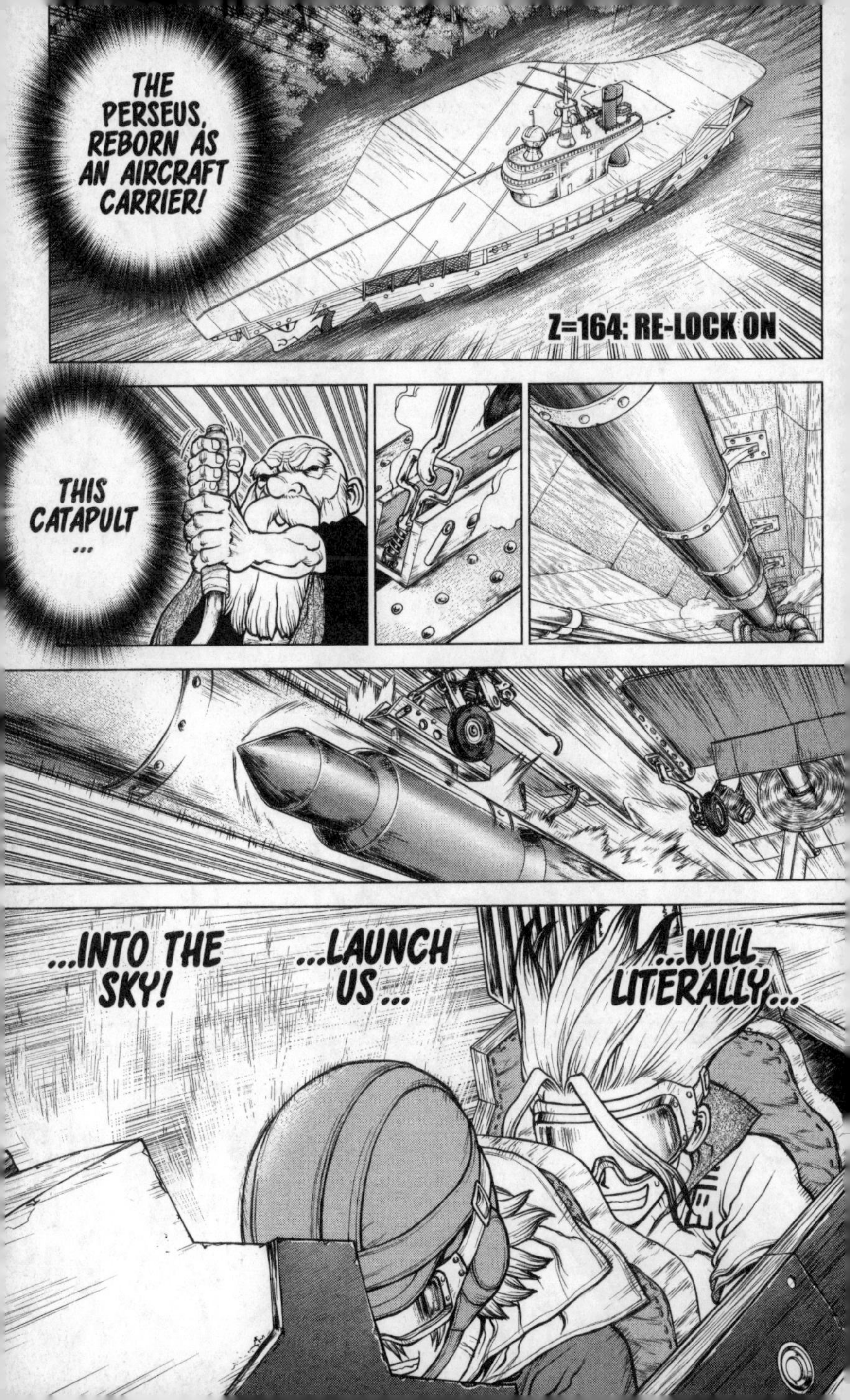
THE PERSEUS, REBORN AS AN AIRCRAFT CARRIER!
Z=164: RE-LOCK ON
THIS CATAPULT ...
...WILL LITERALLY...
...LAUNCH US ...
...INTO THE SKY!

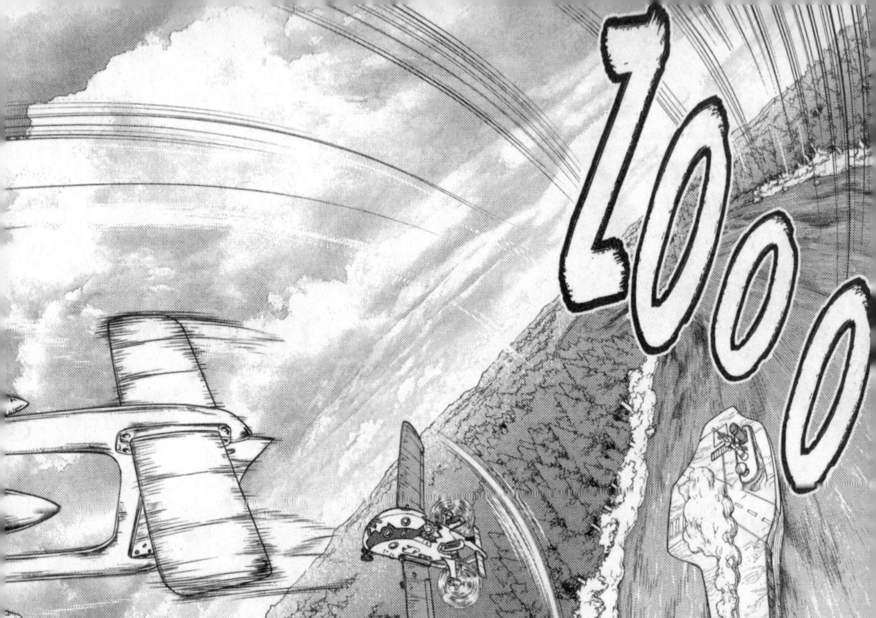
ZOOOOOSH
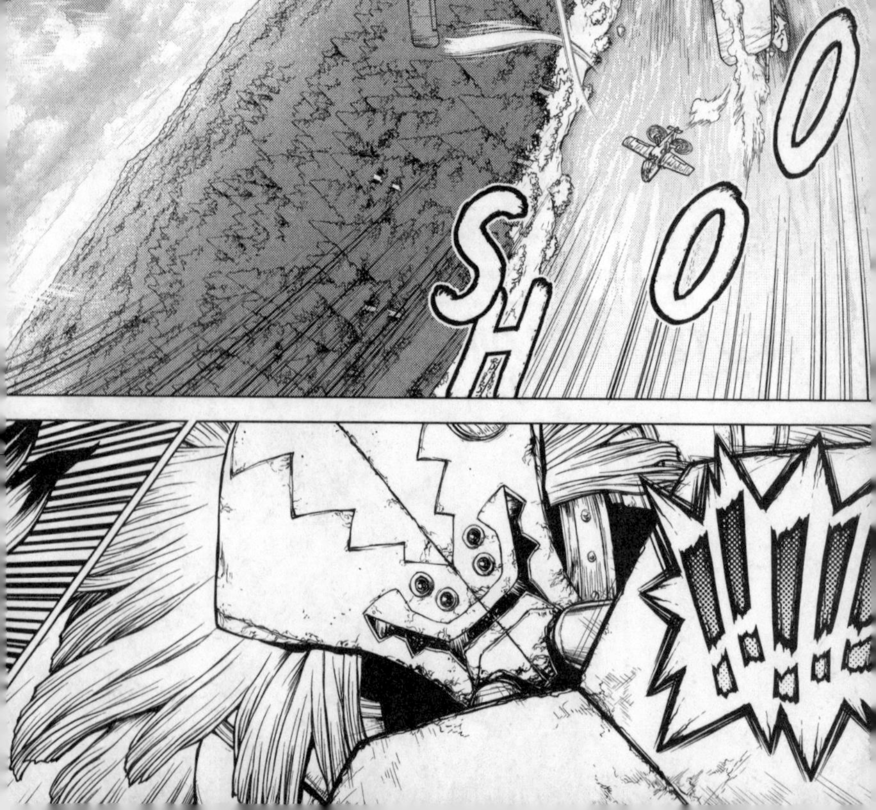
!!!!!

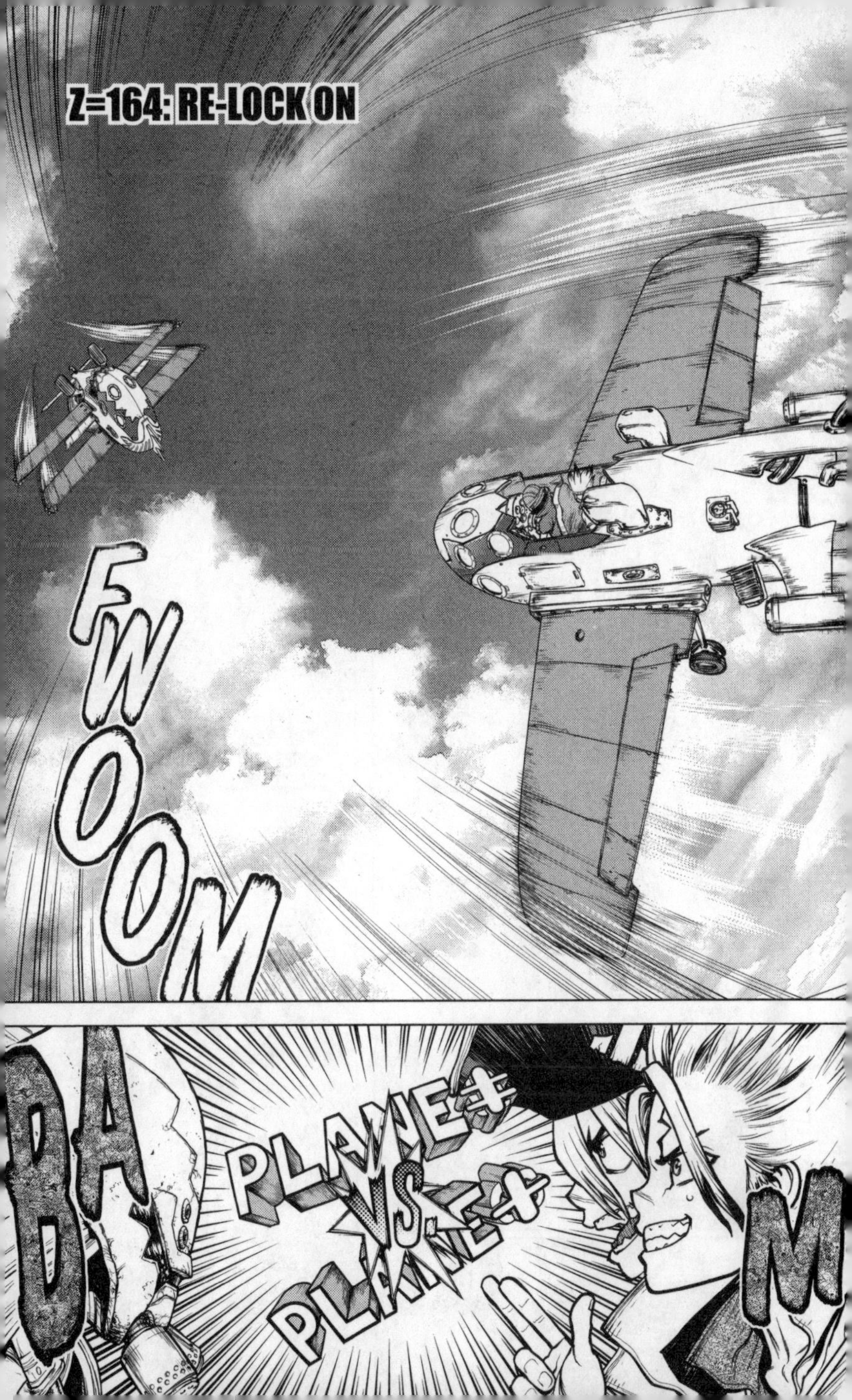
Z=164: RE-LOCK ON
FWOOOM
BAM
PLANE
VS.
PLANE

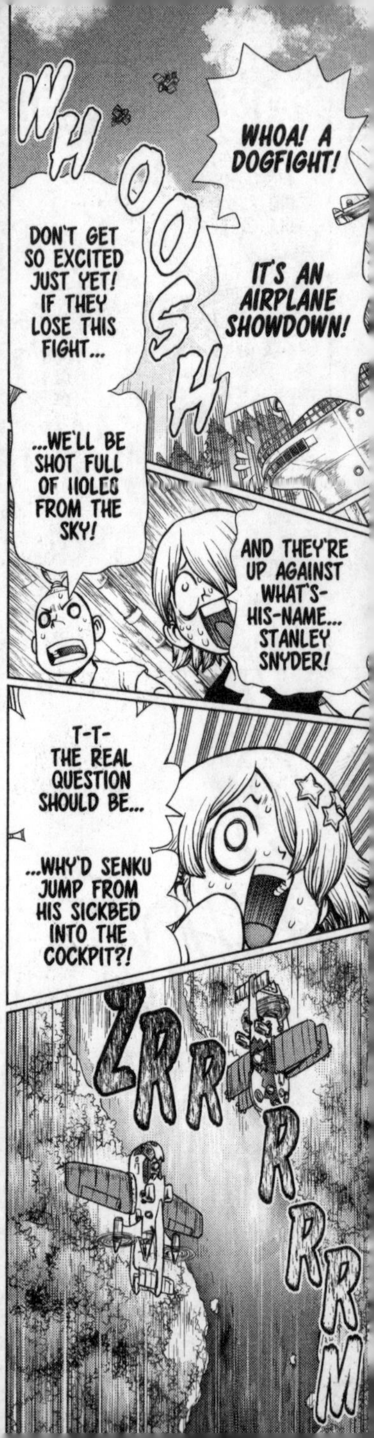
WHOA! A DOGFIGHT!
IT'S AN AIRPLANE SHOWDOWN!
WHOOOSH
DON'T GET SO EXCITED JUST YET! IF THEY LOSE THIS FIGHT...
...WE'LL BE SHOT FULL OF HOLES FROM THE SKY!
AND THEY'RE UP AGAINST WHAT'S-HIS-NAME... STANLEY SNYDER!
T-T-THE REAL QUESTION SHOULD BE...
...WHY'D SENKU JUMP FROM HIS SICKBED INTO THE COCKPIT?!
ZRRRRRRM

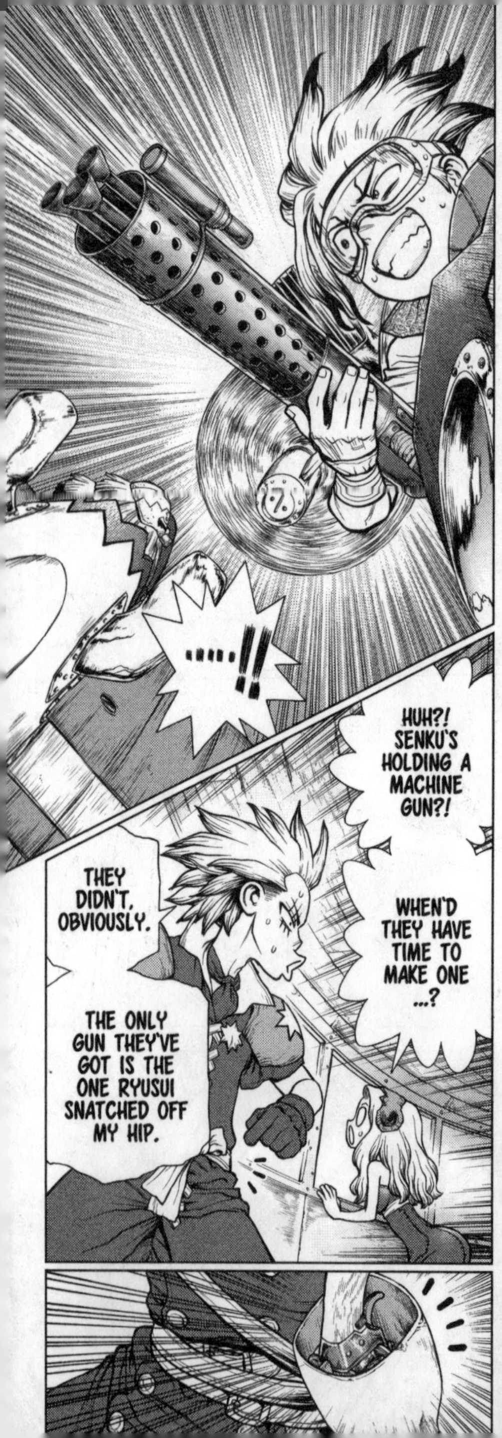
.....!!
HUH?! SENKU'S HOLDING A MACHINE GUN?!
WHEN'D THEY HAVE TIME TO MAKE ONE ...?
THEY DIDN'T, OBVIOUSLY.
THE ONLY GUN THEY'VE GOT IS THE ONE RYUSUI SNATCHED OFF MY HIP.

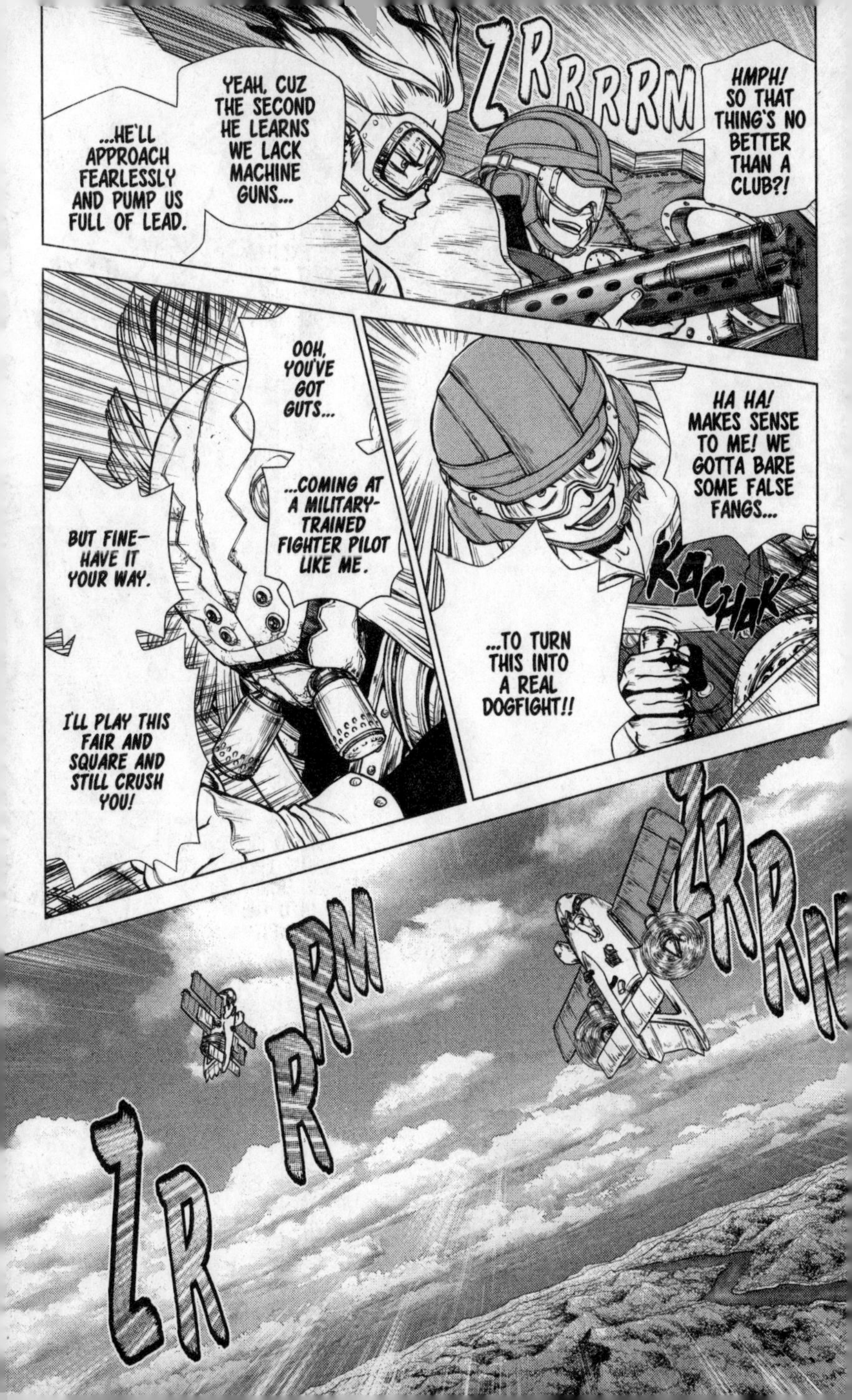
ZRRRRM
HMPH! SO THAT THING'S NO BETTER THAN A CLUB?!
YEAH, CUZ THE SECOND HE LEARNS WE LACK MACHINE GUNS...
...HE'LL APPROACH FEARLESSLY AND PUMP US FULL OF LEAD.
HA HA! MAKES SENSE TO ME! WE GOTTA BARE SOME FALSE FANGS...
KACHAK
...TO TURN THIS INTO A REAL DOGFIGHT!!
OOH, YOU'VE GOT GUTS...
...COMING AT A MILITARY-TRAINED FIGHTER PILOT LIKE ME.
BUT FINE—HAVE IT YOUR WAY.
I'LL PLAY THIS FAIR AND SQUARE AND STILL CRUSH YOU!
ZRRRM

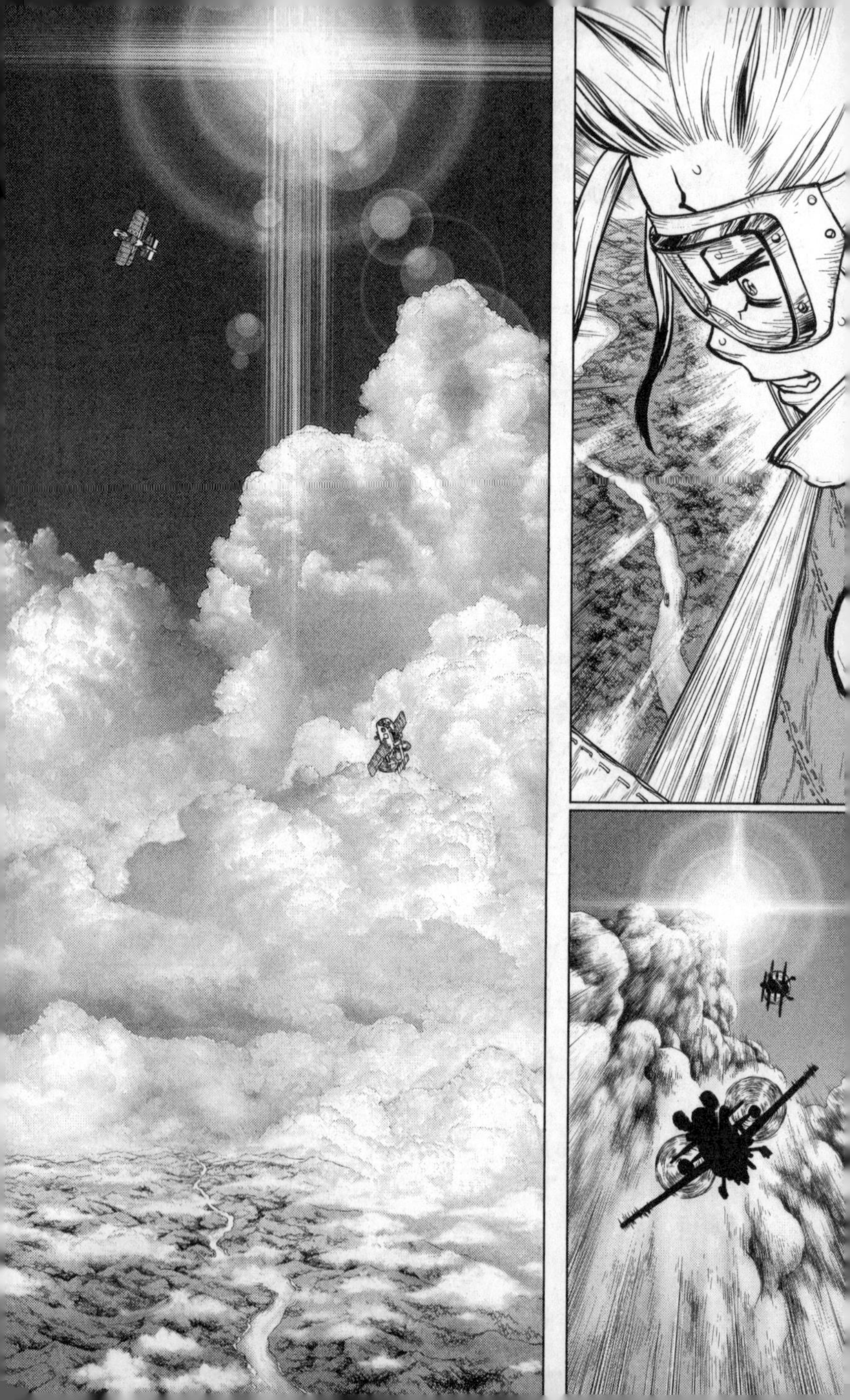

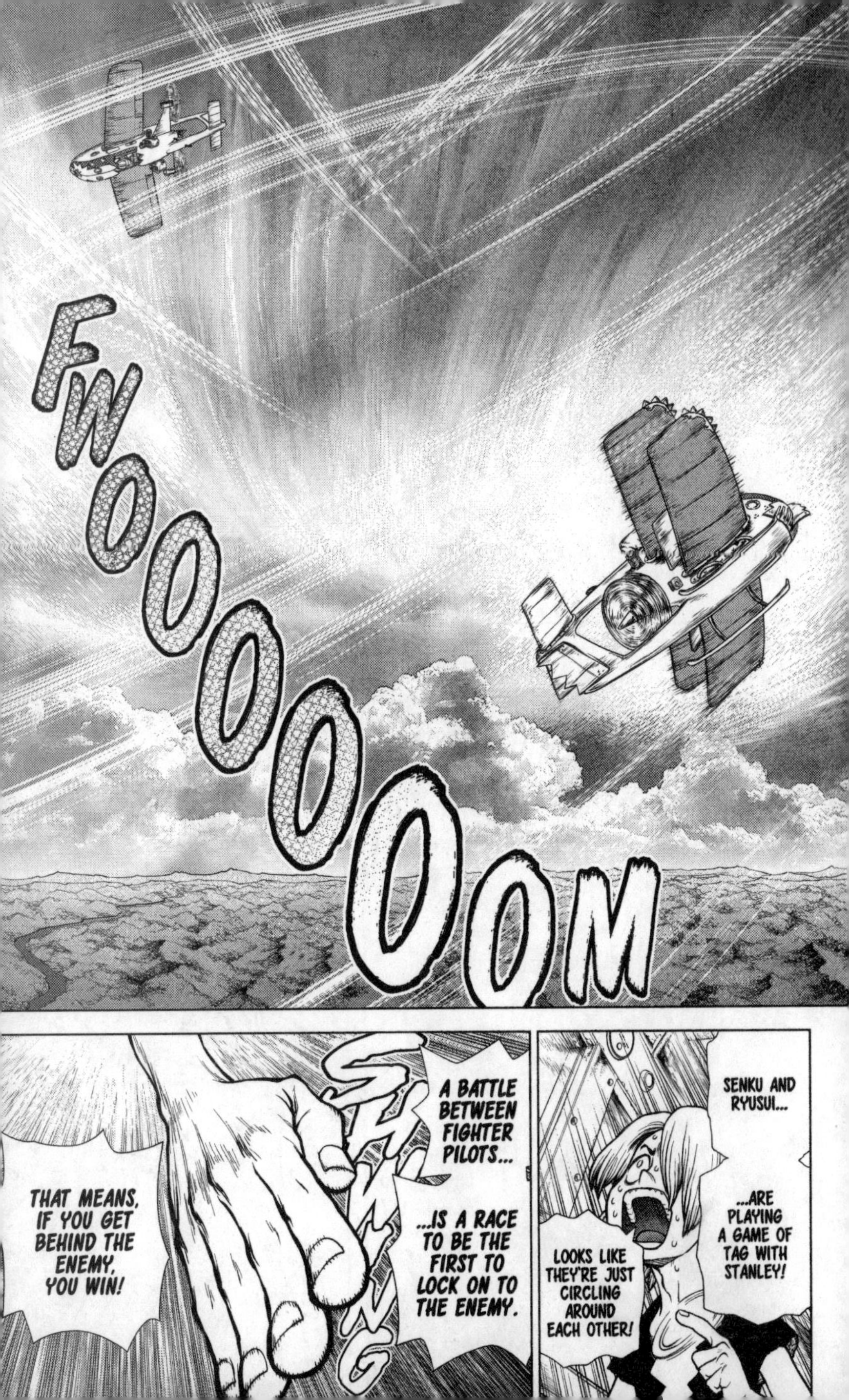
FWOOOOOOOOM
SENKU AND RYUSUI...
...ARE PLAYING A GAME OF TAG WITH STANLEY!
LOOKS LIKE THEY'RE JUST CIRCLING AROUND EACH OTHER!
A BATTLE BETWEEN FIGHTER PILOTS...
...IS A RACE TO BE THE FIRST TO LOCK ON TO THE ENEMY.
THAT MEANS, IF YOU GET BEHIND THE ENEMY, YOU WIN!

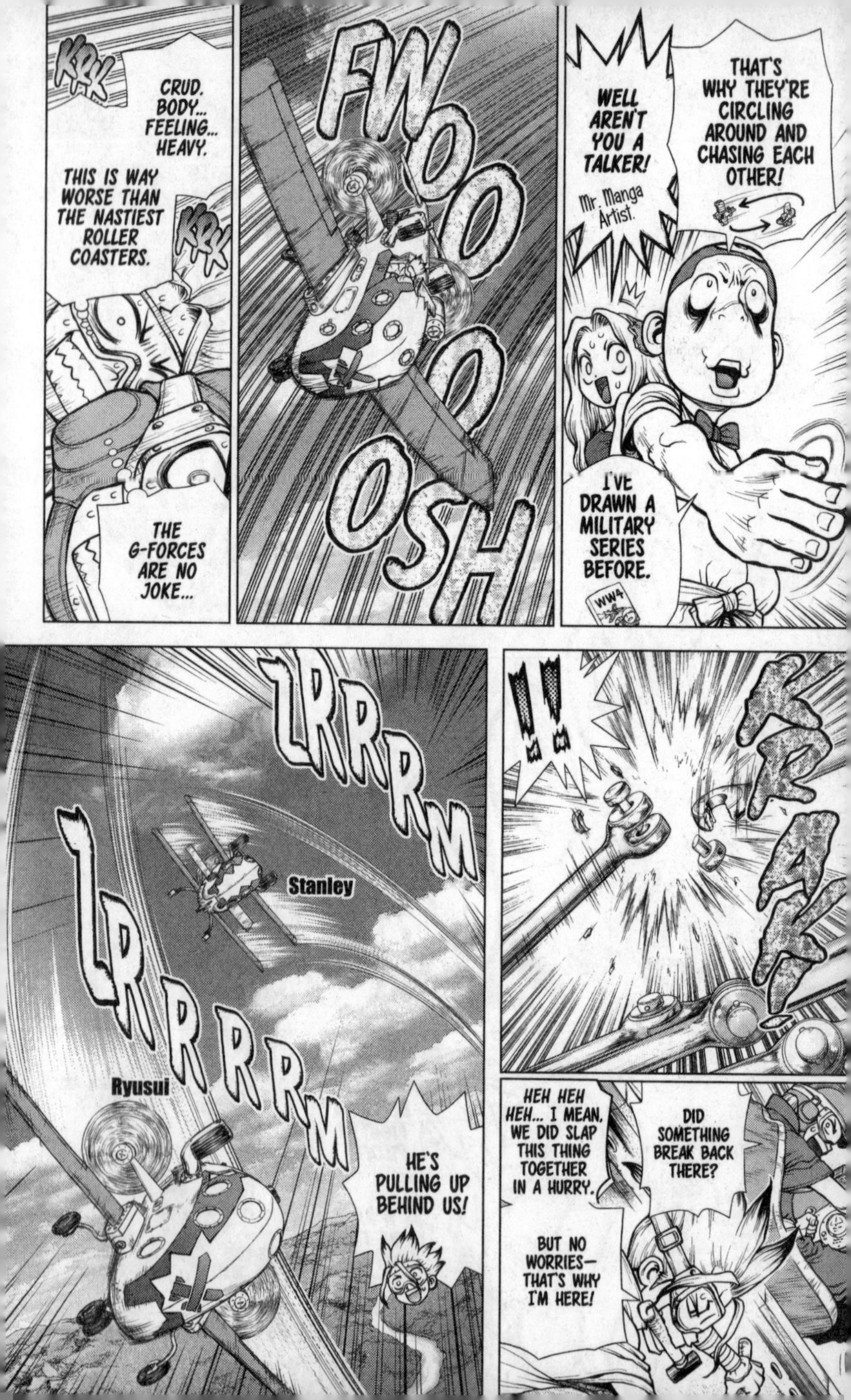
THAT'S WHY THEY'RE CIRCLING AROUND AND CHASING EACH OTHER!
WELL AREN'T YOU A TALKER!
Mr. Manga Artist.
I'VE DRAWN A MILITARY SERIES BEFORE.
WW4
FWOOOOOSH
KRK
CRUD. BODY... FEELING... HEAVY.
THIS IS WAY WORSE THAN THE NASTIEST ROLLER COASTERS.
KRK
THE G-FORCES ARE NO JOKE...
!!
KRAK
DID SOMETHING BREAK BACK THERE?
HEH HEH HEH... I MEAN, WE DID SLAP THIS THING TOGETHER IN A HURRY.
BUT NO WORRIES—THAT'S WHY I'M HERE!
ZRRRM
Stanley
ZRRRRRM
Ryusui
HE'S PULLING UP BEHIND US!

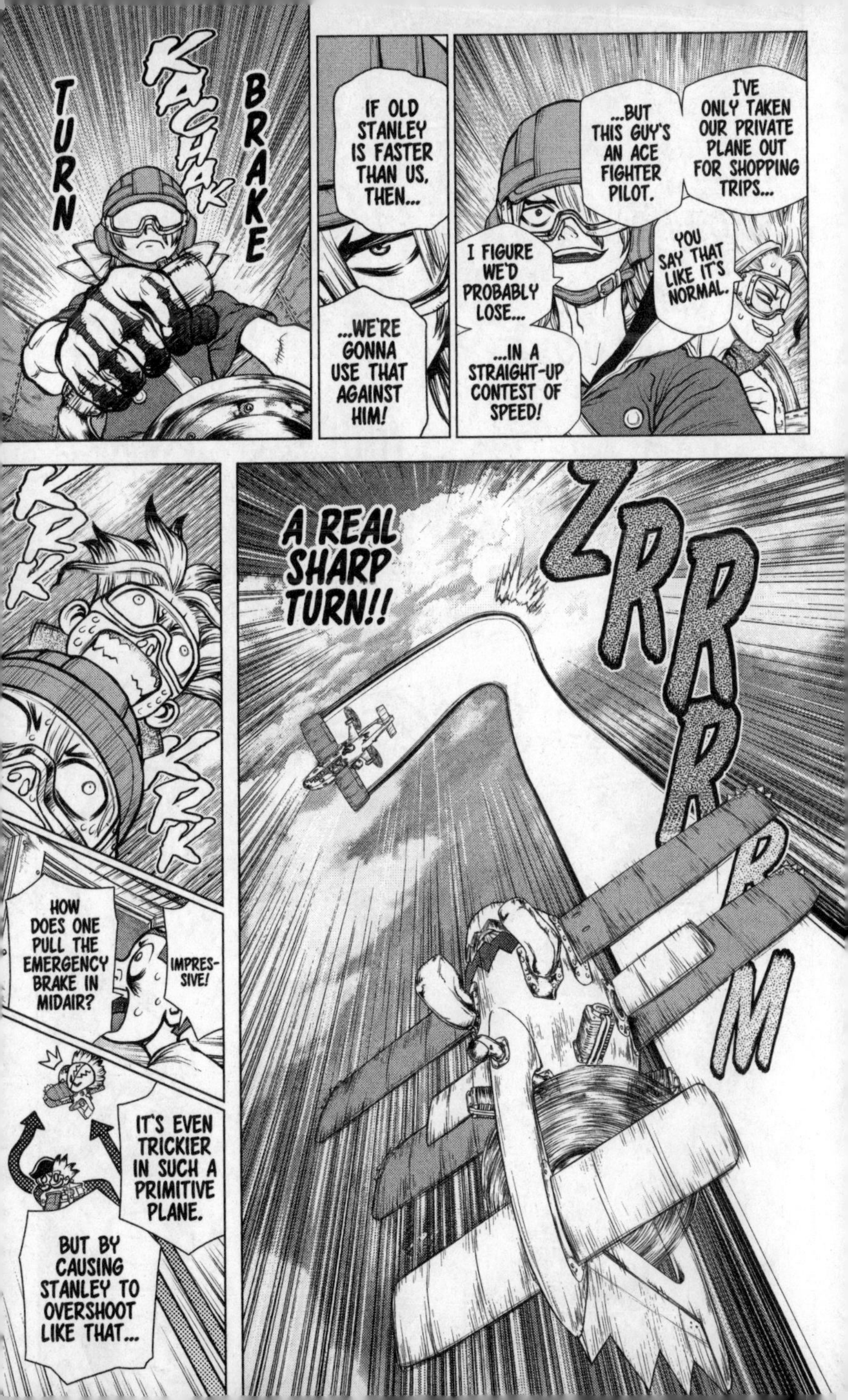
I'VE ONLY TAKEN OUR PRIVATE PLANE OUT FOR SHOPPING TRIPS...
...BUT THIS GUY'S AN ACE FIGHTER PILOT.
YOU SAY THAT LIKE IT'S NORMAL.
I FIGURE WE'D PROBABLY LOSE...
...IN A STRAIGHT-UP CONTEST OF SPEED!
IF OLD STANLEY IS FASTER THAN US, THEN...
...WE'RE GONNA USE THAT AGAINST HIM!
BRAKE
KACHAK
TURN
ZRRRRM
A REAL SHARP TURN!!
KRK
KRK
IMPRES-SIVE!
HOW DOES ONE PULL THE EMERGENCY BRAKE IN MIDAIR?
IT'S EVEN TRICKIER IN SUCH A PRIMITIVE PLANE.
BUT BY CAUSING STANLEY TO OVERSHOOT LIKE THAT...

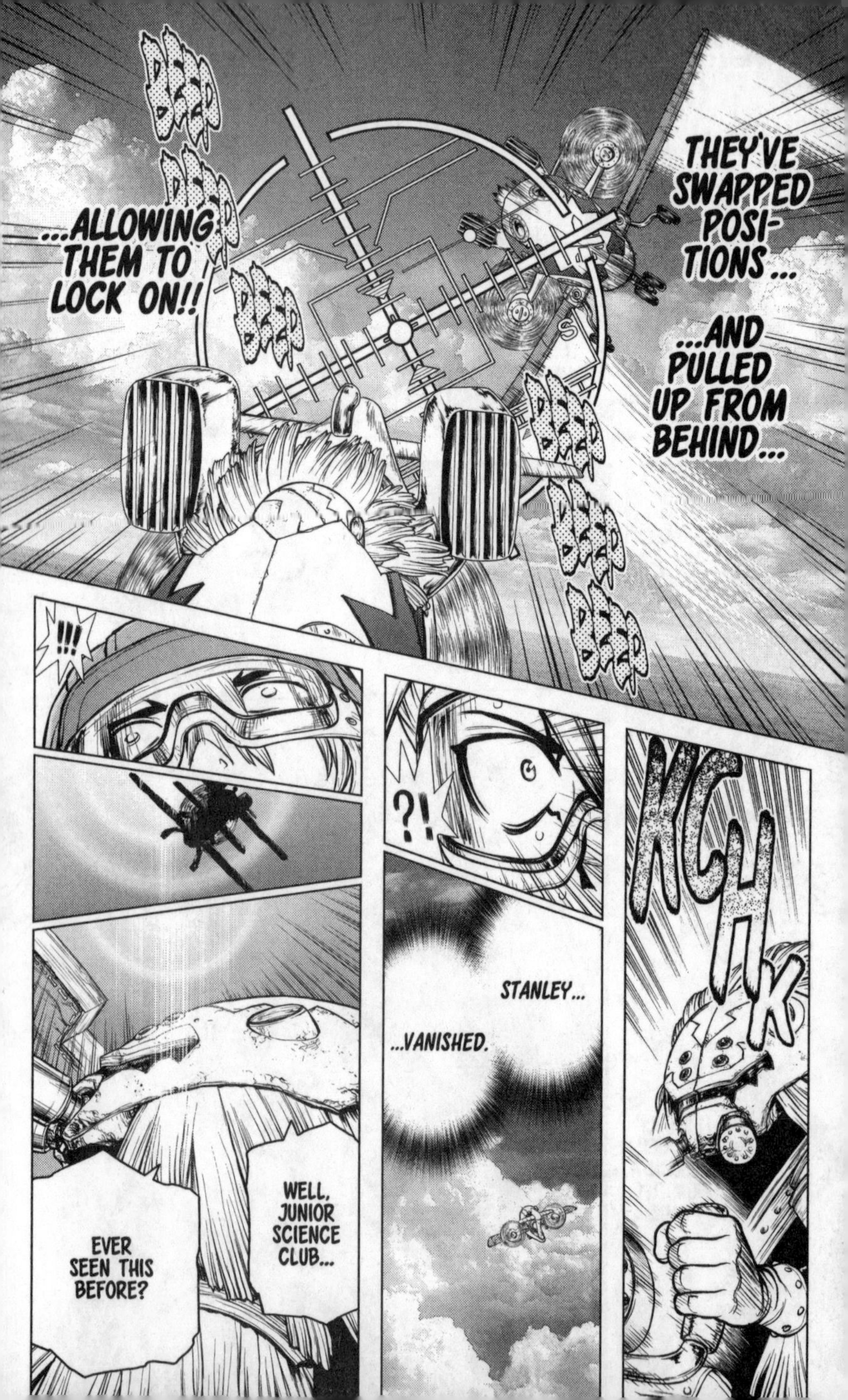
THEY'VE SWAPPED POSI-TIONS...
...AND PULLED UP FROM BEHIND...
...ALLOWING THEM TO LOCK ON!!
BEEP BEEP
BEEP BEEP
BEEP BEEP
BEEP
KCHK
?!
STANLEY...
...VANISHED.
!!!
WELL, JUNIOR SCIENCE CLUB...
EVER SEEN THIS BEFORE?

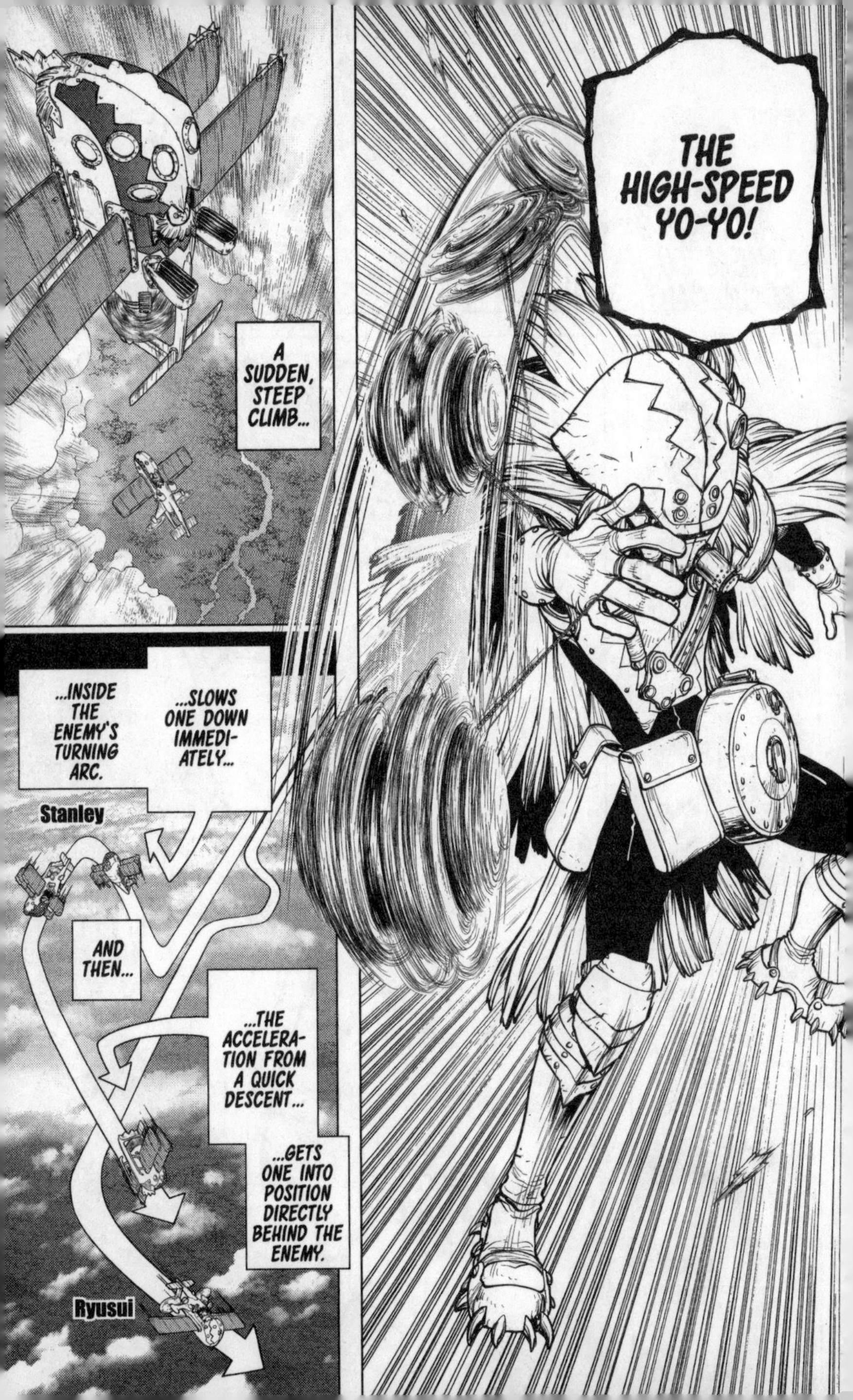
THE HIGH-SPEED YO-YO!
A SUDDEN, STEEP CLIMB...
...SLOWS ONE DOWN IMMEDIATELY...
...INSIDE THE ENEMY'S TURNING ARC.
Stanley
AND THEN...
...THE ACCELERATION FROM A QUICK DESCENT...
...GETS ONE INTO POSITION DIRECTLY BEHIND THE ENEMY.
Ryusui

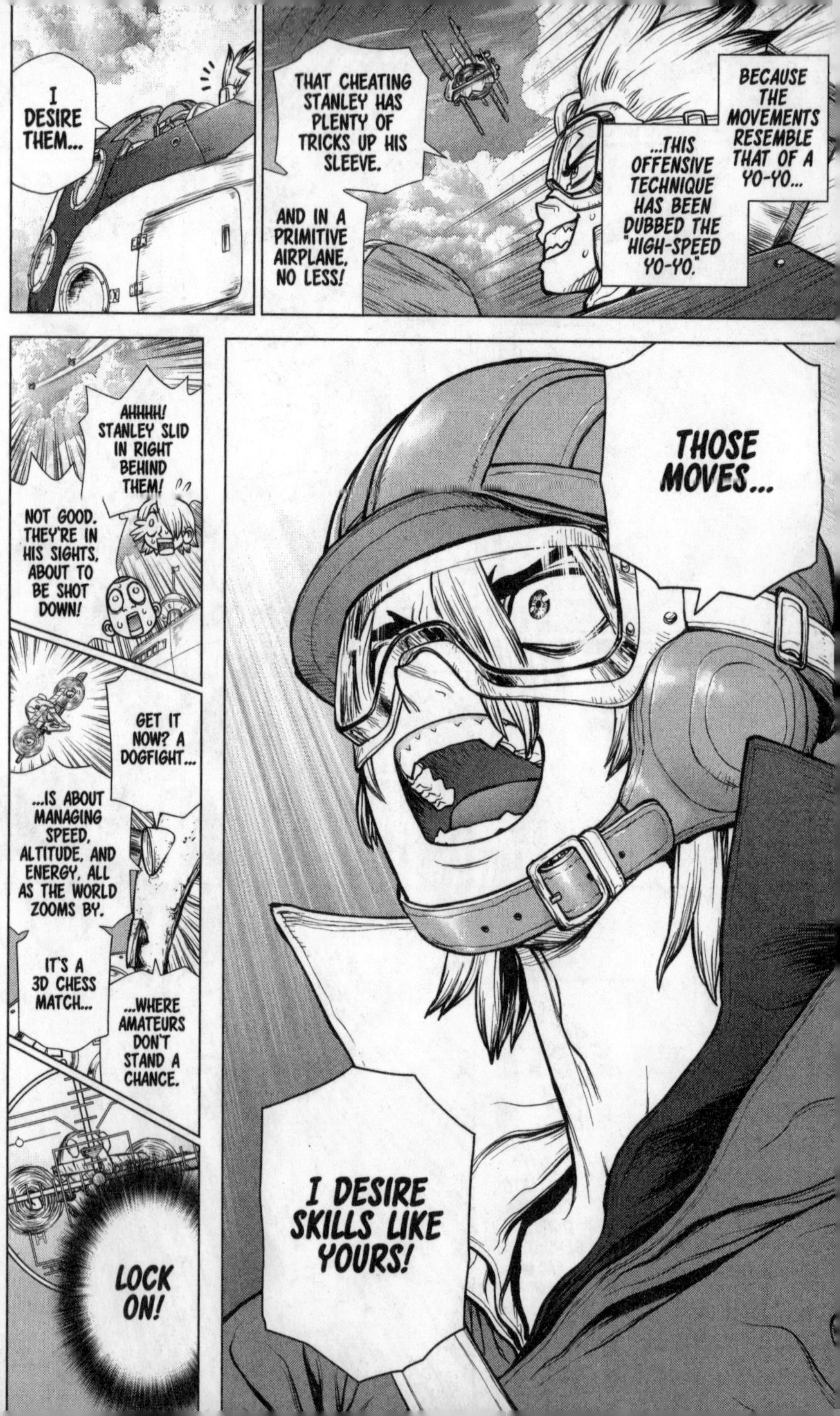
BECAUSE THE MOVEMENTS RESEMBLE THAT OF A YO-YO...
...THIS OFFENSIVE TECHNIQUE HAS BEEN DUBBED THE "HIGH-SPEED YO-YO."
THAT CHEATING STANLEY HAS PLENTY OF TRICKS UP HIS SLEEVE.
AND IN A PRIMITIVE AIRPLANE, NO LESS!
I DESIRE THEM...
THOSE MOVES...
I DESIRE SKILLS LIKE YOURS!
AHHHH! STANLEY SLID IN RIGHT BEHIND THEM!
NOT GOOD. THEY'RE IN HIS SIGHTS, ABOUT TO BE SHOT DOWN!
GET IT NOW? A DOGFIGHT...
...IS ABOUT MANAGING SPEED, ALTITUDE, AND ENERGY, ALL AS THE WORLD ZOOMS BY.
IT'S A 3D CHESS MATCH...
...WHERE AMATEURS DON'T STAND A CHANCE.
LOCK ON!

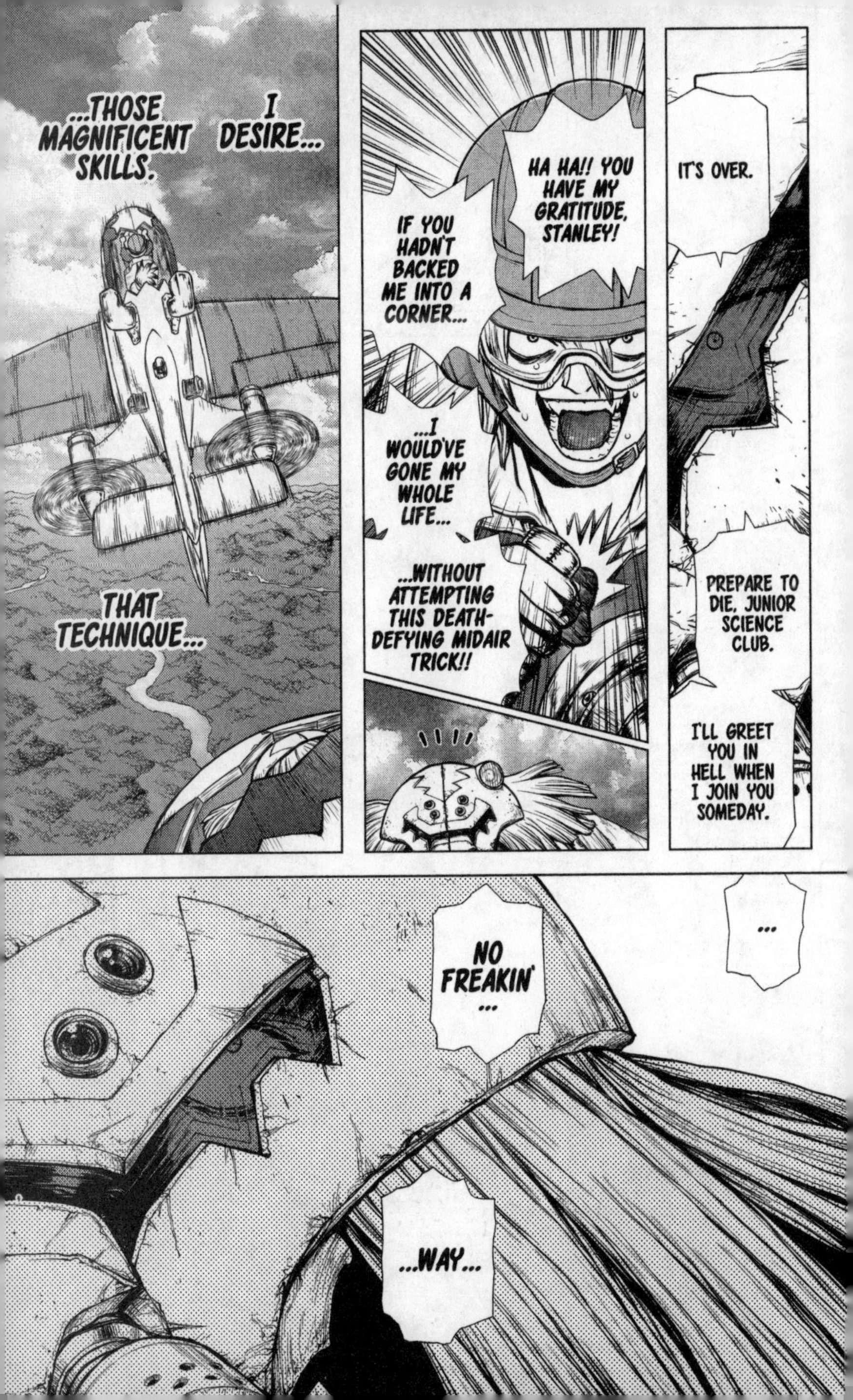
IT'S OVER.
PREPARE TO DIE, JUNIOR SCIENCE CLUB.
I'LL GREET YOU IN HELL WHEN I JOIN YOU SOMEDAY.
HA HA!! YOU HAVE MY GRATITUDE, STANLEY!
IF YOU HADN'T BACKED ME INTO A CORNER...
...I WOULD'VE GONE MY WHOLE LIFE...
...WITHOUT ATTEMPTING THIS DEATH-DEFYING MIDAIR TRICK!!
I DESIRE...
...THOSE MAGNIFICENT SKILLS.
THAT TECHNIQUE...
...
NO FREAKIN' ...
...WAY...

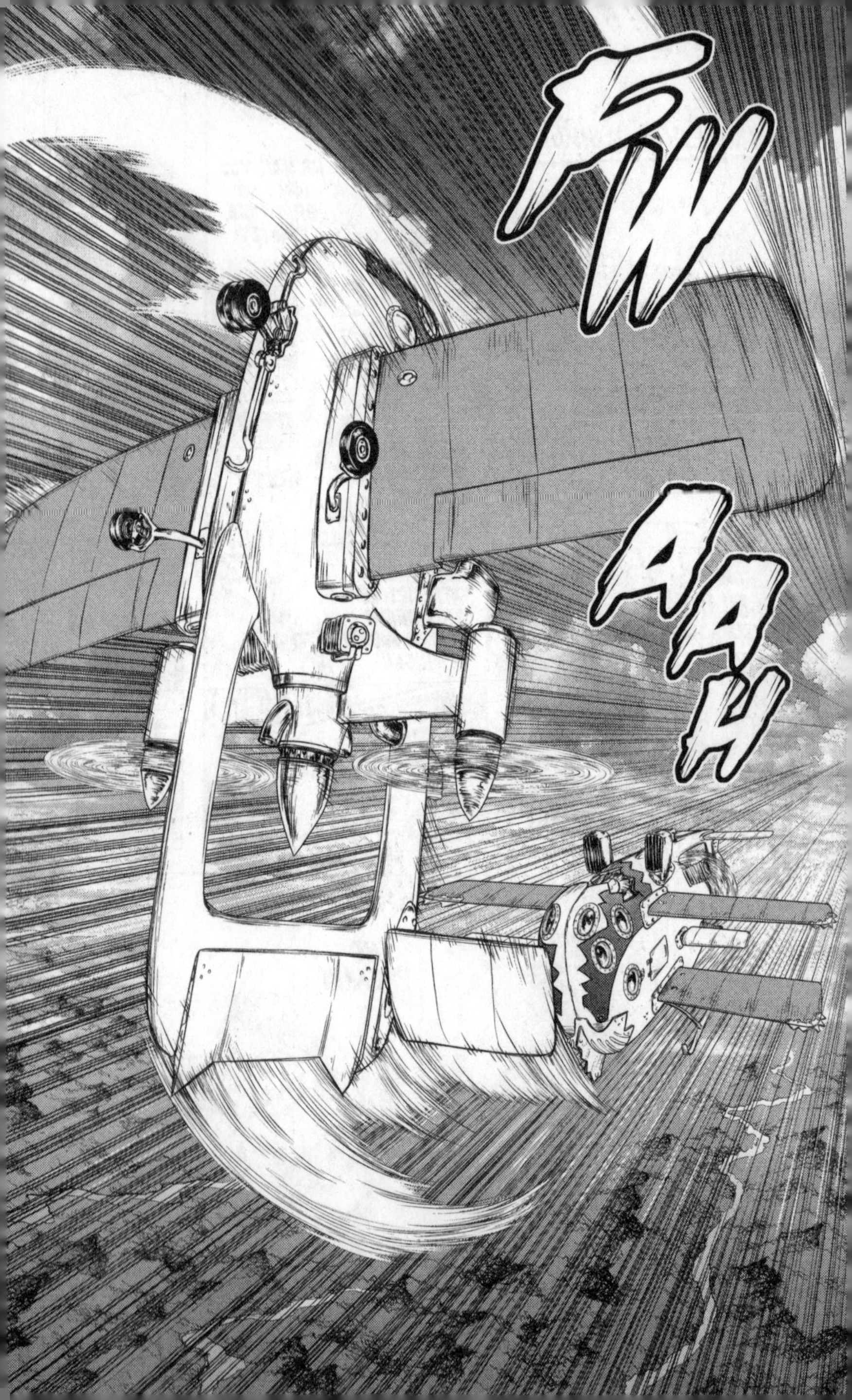
FWAAH

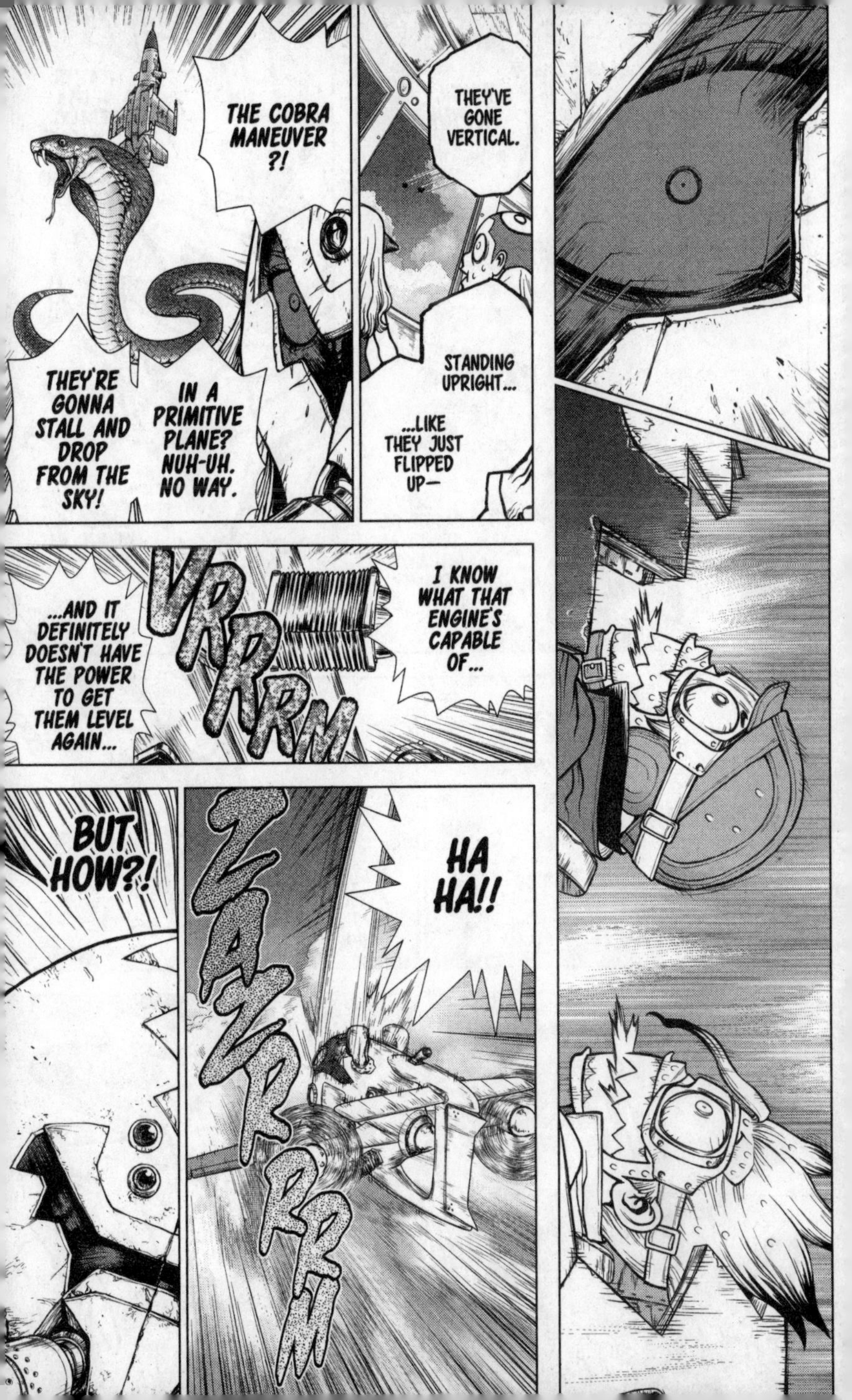
THEY'VE GONE VERTICAL.
STANDING UPRIGHT...
...LIKE THEY JUST FLIPPED UP—
THE COBRA MANEUVER ?!
IN A PRIMITIVE PLANE? NUH-UH. NO WAY.
THEY'RE GONNA STALL AND DROP FROM THE SKY!
I KNOW WHAT THAT ENGINE'S CAPABLE OF...
VRRRM
...AND IT DEFINITELY DOESN'T HAVE THE POWER TO GET THEM LEVEL AGAIN...
HA HA!!
ZARRRRM
BUT HOW?!

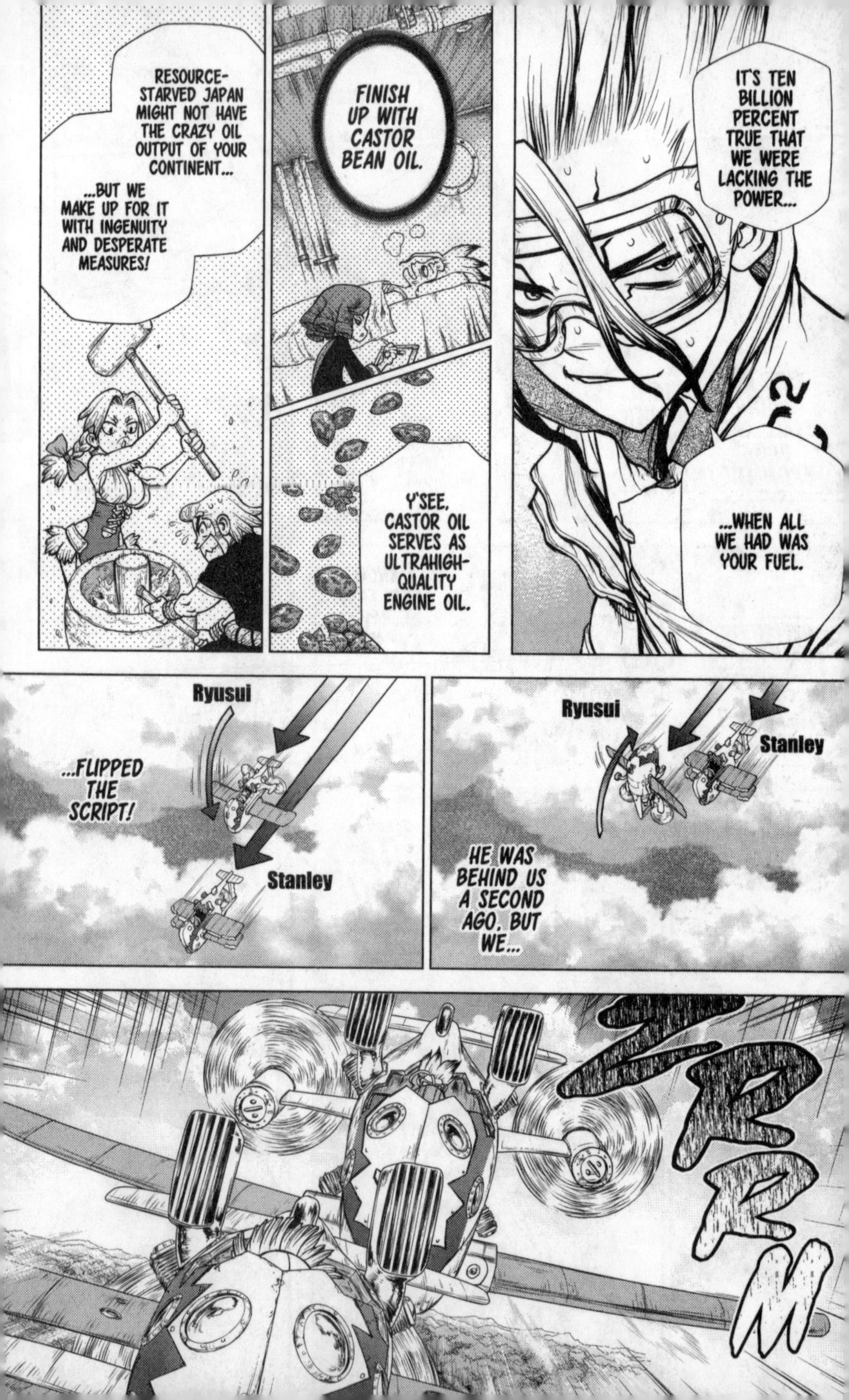
IT'S TEN BILLION PERCENT TRUE THAT WE WERE LACKING THE POWER...
...WHEN ALL WE HAD WAS YOUR FUEL.
FINISH UP WITH CASTOR BEAN OIL.
Y'SEE, CASTOR OIL SERVES AS ULTRAHIGH-QUALITY ENGINE OIL.
RESOURCE-STARVED JAPAN MIGHT NOT HAVE THE CRAZY OIL OUTPUT OF YOUR CONTINENT...
...BUT WE MAKE UP FOR IT WITH INGENUITY AND DESPERATE MEASURES!
Ryusui
Stanley
HE WAS BEHIND US A SECOND AGO, BUT WE...
Ryusui
...FLIPPED THE SCRIPT!
Stanley
VRRM

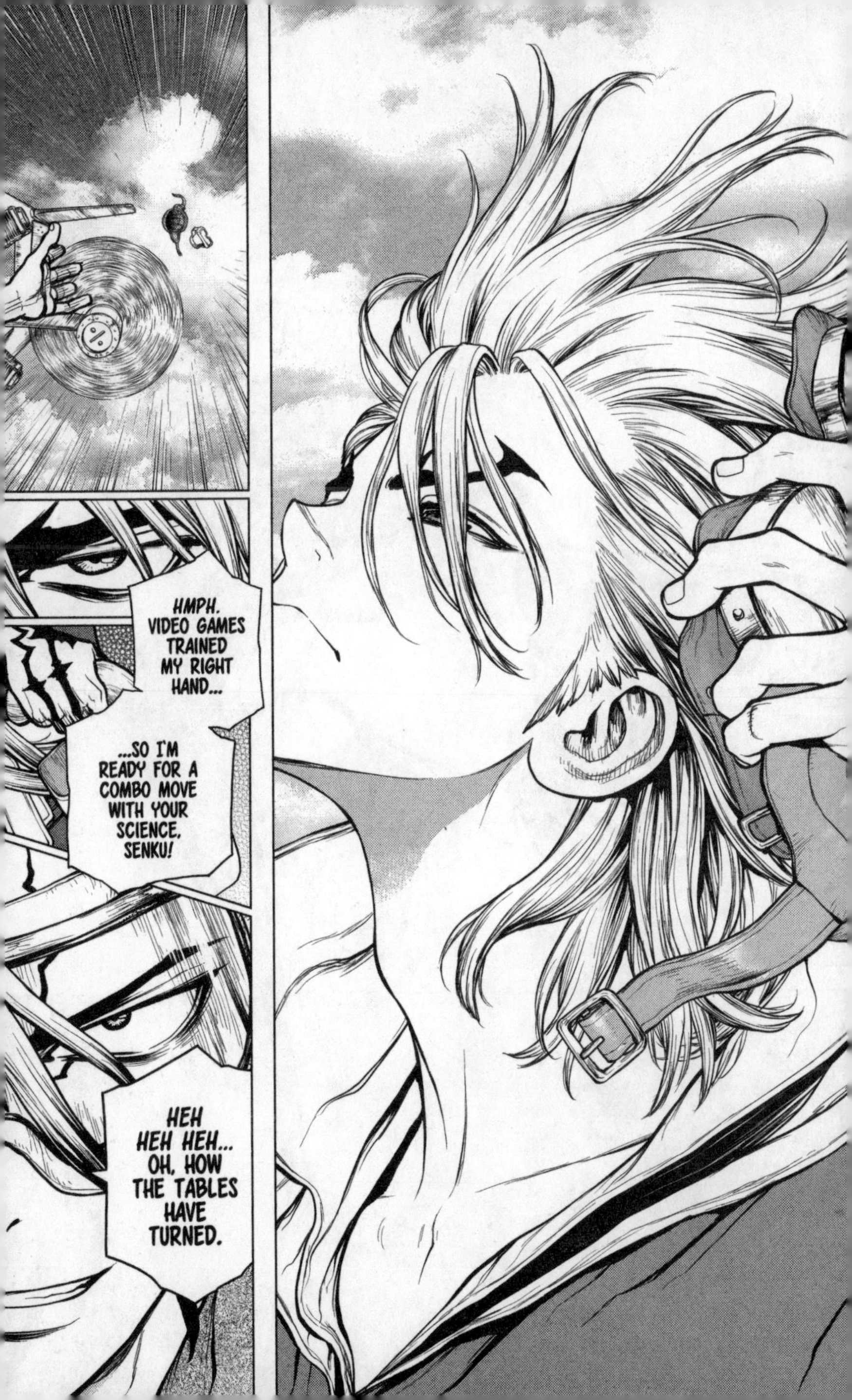
HMPH. VIDEO GAMES TRAINED MY RIGHT HAND...
...SO I'M READY FOR A COMBO MOVE WITH YOUR SCIENCE, SENKU!
HEH HEH HEH... OH, HOW THE TABLES HAVE TURNED.

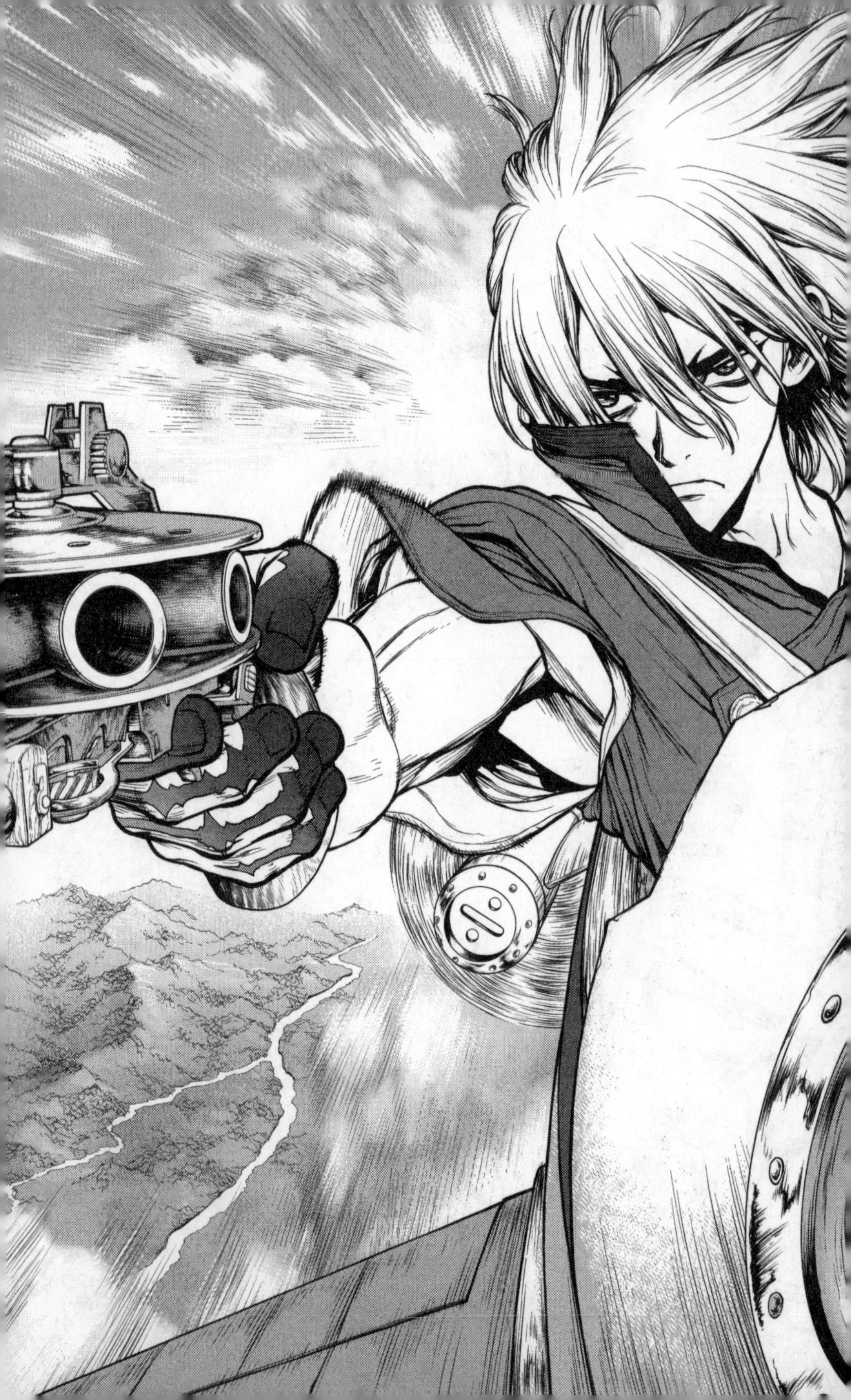

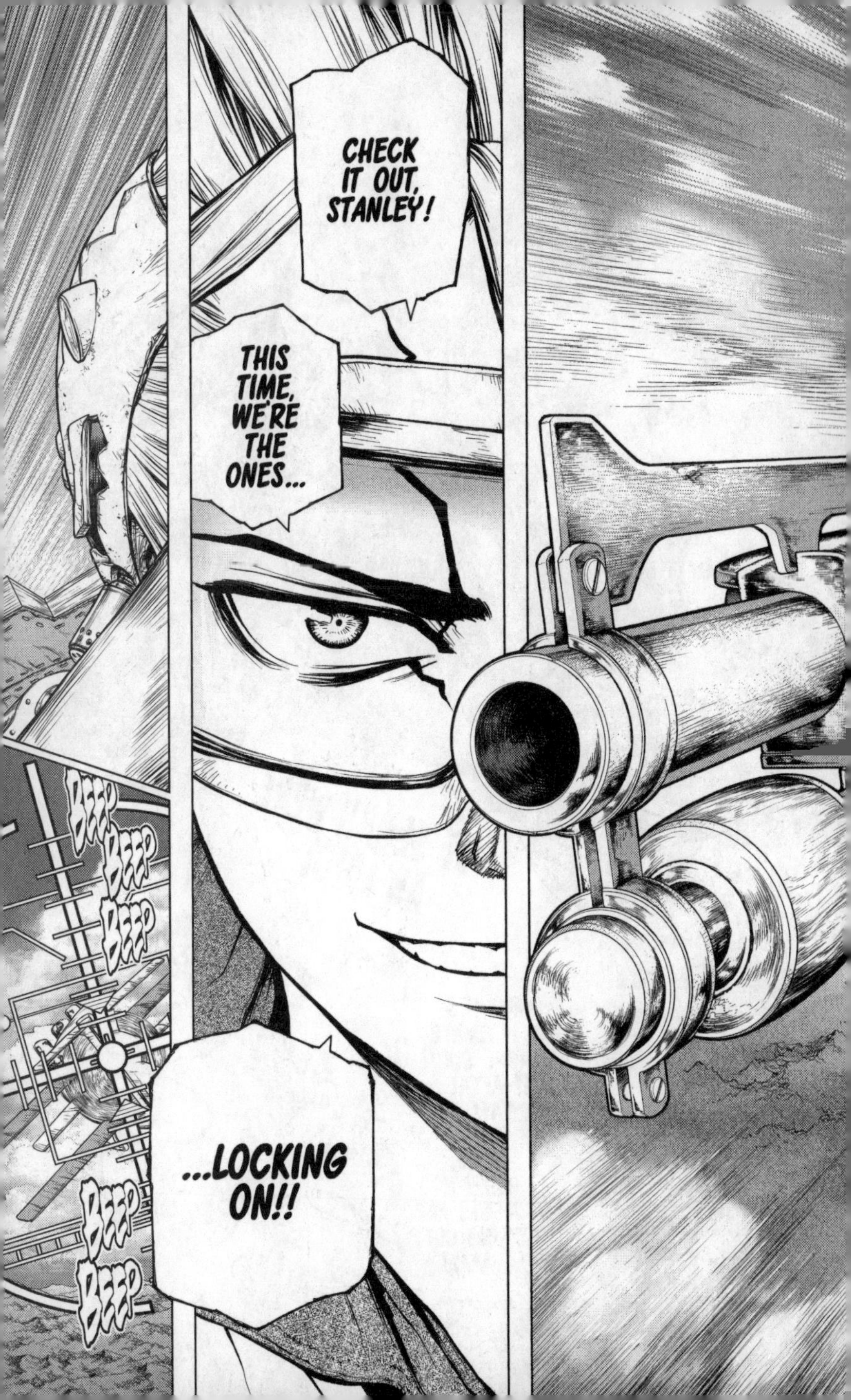
CHECK IT OUT, STANLEY!
THIS TIME, WE'RE THE ONES...
...LOCKING ON!!
BEEP BEEP BEEP
BEEP BEEP

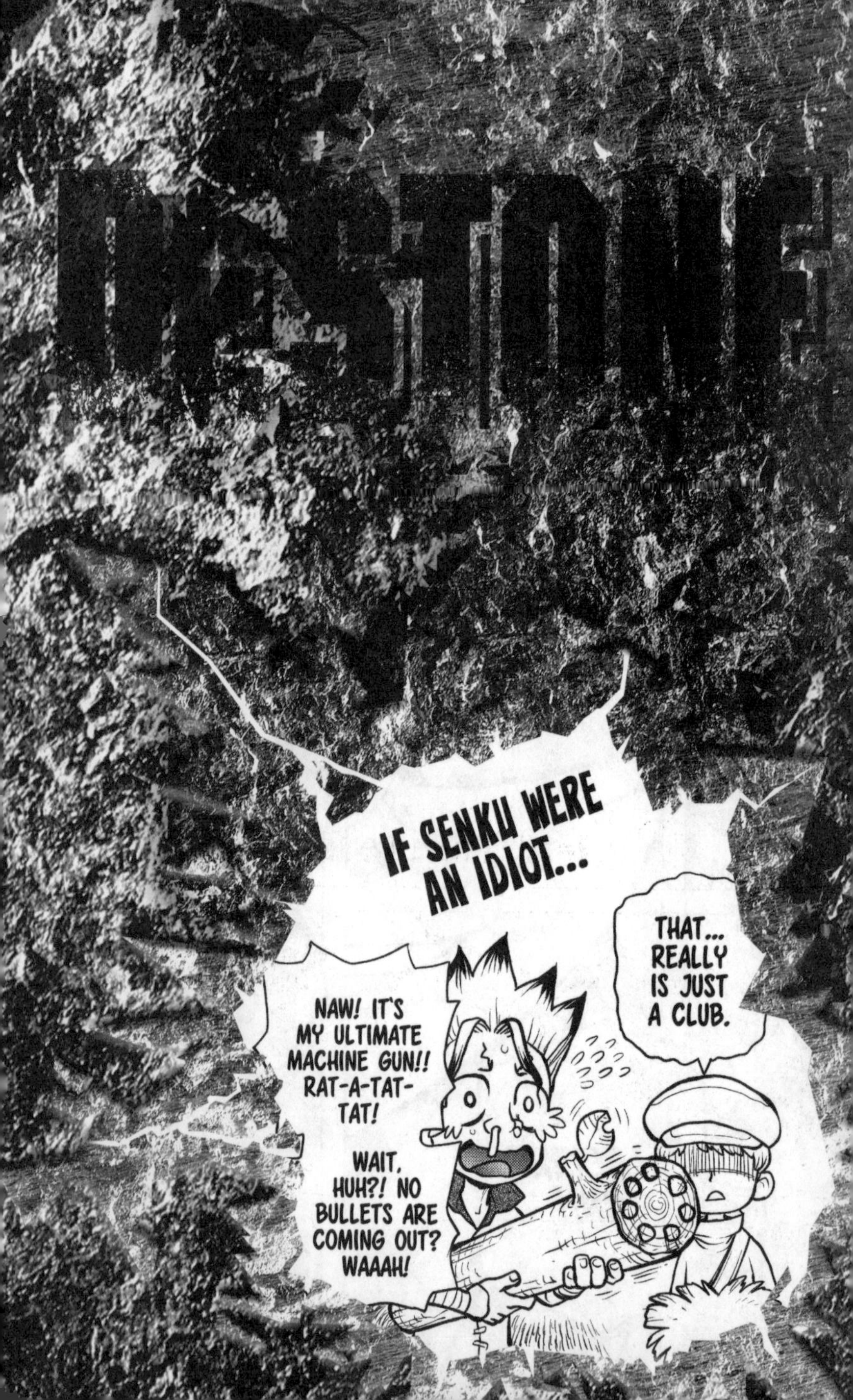
Dr.STONE
IF SENKU WERE AN IDIOT...
THAT... REALLY IS JUST A CLUB.
NAW! IT'S MY ULTIMATE MACHINE GUN!! RAT-A-TAT-TAT!
WAIT, HUH?! NO BULLETS ARE COMING OUT? WAAAH!

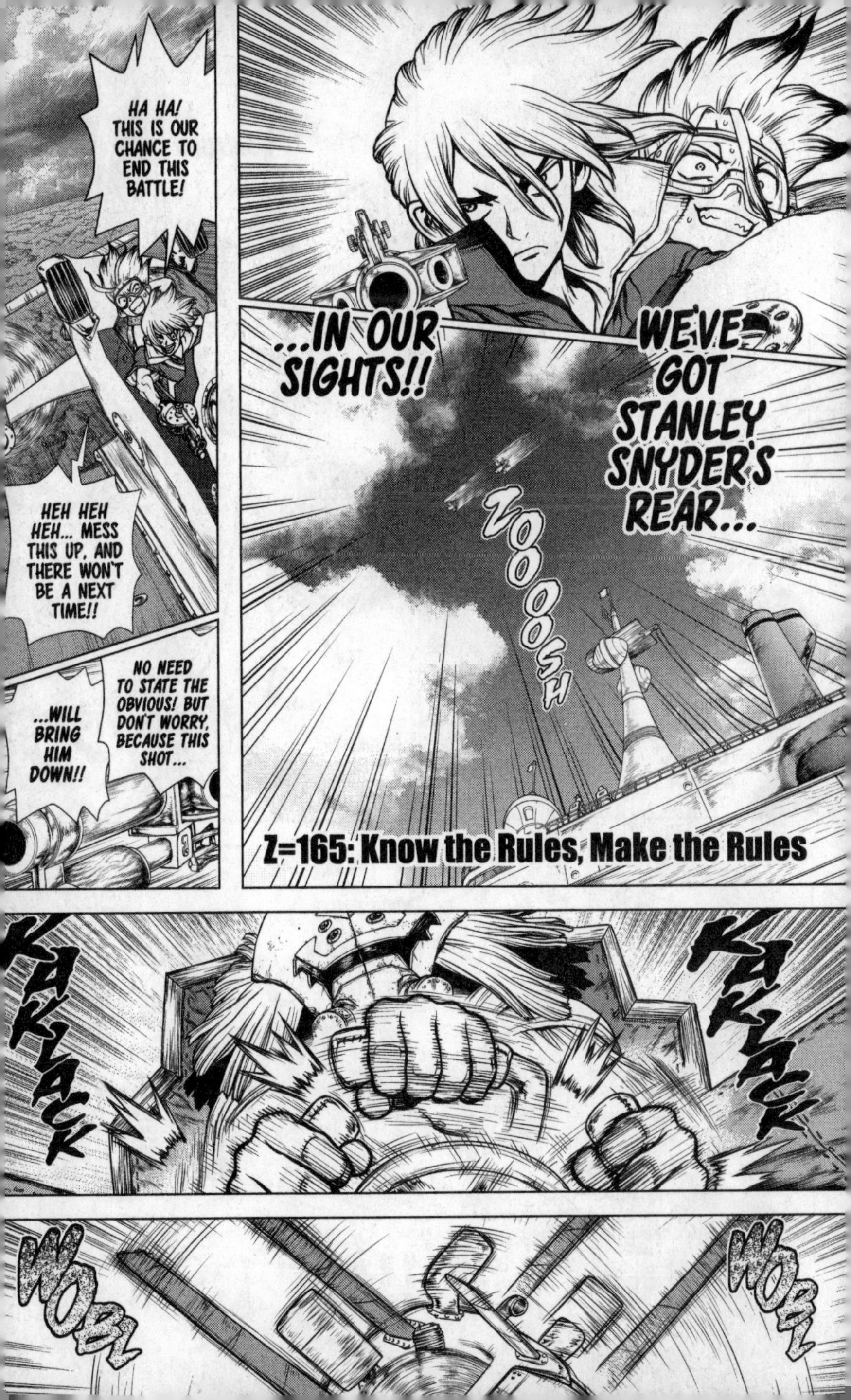
WE'VE GOT STANLEY SNYDER'S REAR...
...IN OUR SIGHTS!!
ZOOOOSH
Z=165: Know the Rules, Make the Rules
HA HA! THIS IS OUR CHANCE TO END THIS BATTLE!
HEH HEH HEH... MESS THIS UP, AND THERE WON'T BE A NEXT TIME!!
NO NEED TO STATE THE OBVIOUS! BUT DON'T WORRY, BECAUSE THIS SHOT...
...WILL BRING HIM DOWN!!
KAKLACK
KAKLACK
WOBBL
WOBBL

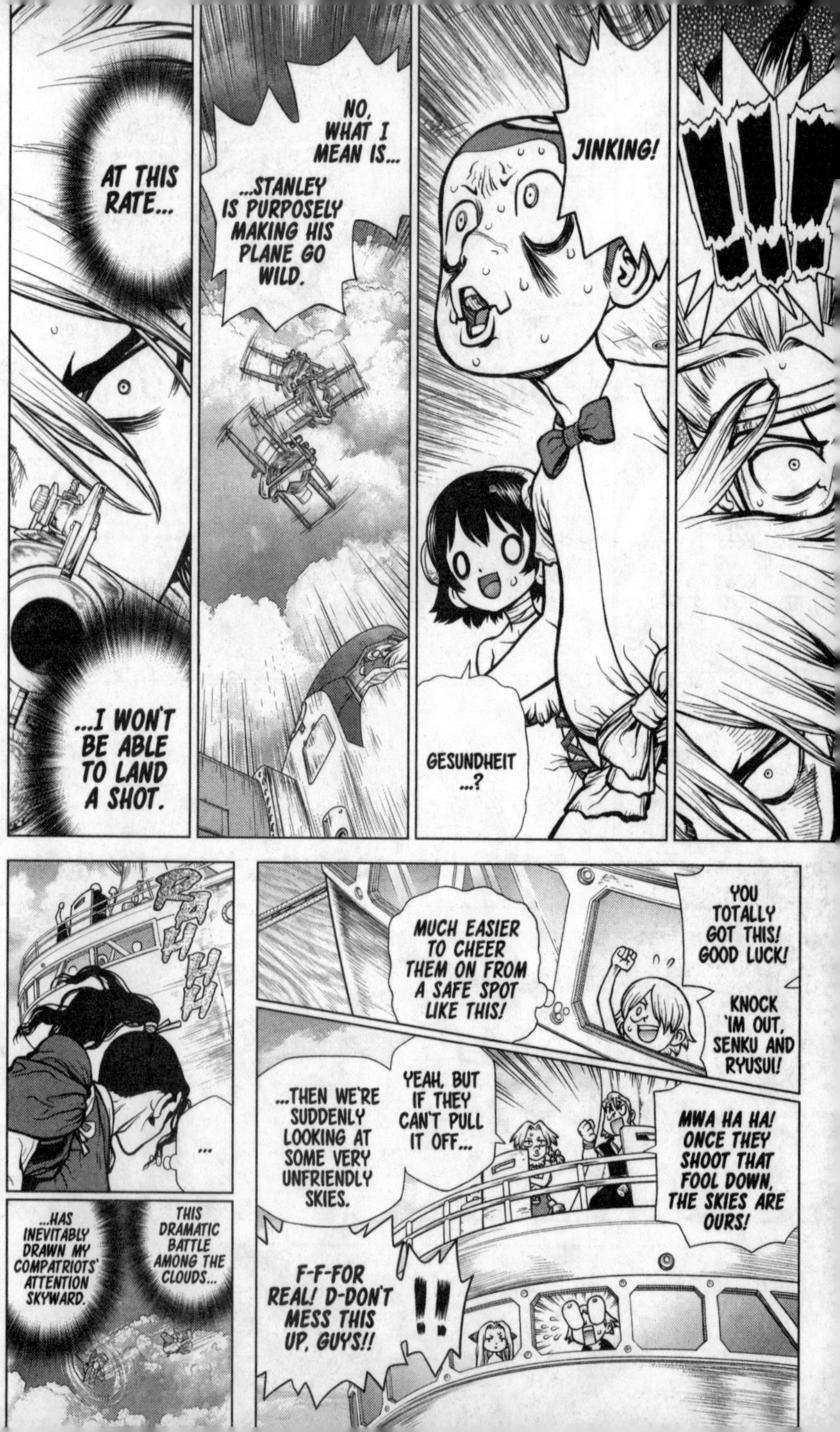
!!!
JINKING!
GESUNDHEIT ...?
NO, WHAT I MEAN IS...
...STANLEY IS PURPOSELY MAKING HIS PLANE GO WILD.
AT THIS RATE...
...I WON'T BE ABLE TO LAND A SHOT.
YOU TOTALLY GOT THIS! GOOD LUCK!
KNOCK 'IM OUT, SENKU AND RYUSUI!
MUCH EASIER TO CHEER THEM ON FROM A SAFE SPOT LIKE THIS!
MWA HA HA! ONCE THEY SHOOT THAT FOOL DOWN, THE SKIES ARE OURS!
YEAH, BUT IF THEY CAN'T PULL IT OFF...
...THEN WE'RE SUDDENLY LOOKING AT SOME VERY UNFRIENDLY SKIES.
!!
F-F-FOR REAL! D-DON'T MESS THIS UP, GUYS!!
...
THIS DRAMATIC BATTLE AMONG THE CLOUDS...
...HAS INEVITABLY DRAWN MY COMPATRIOTS' ATTENTION SKYWARD.

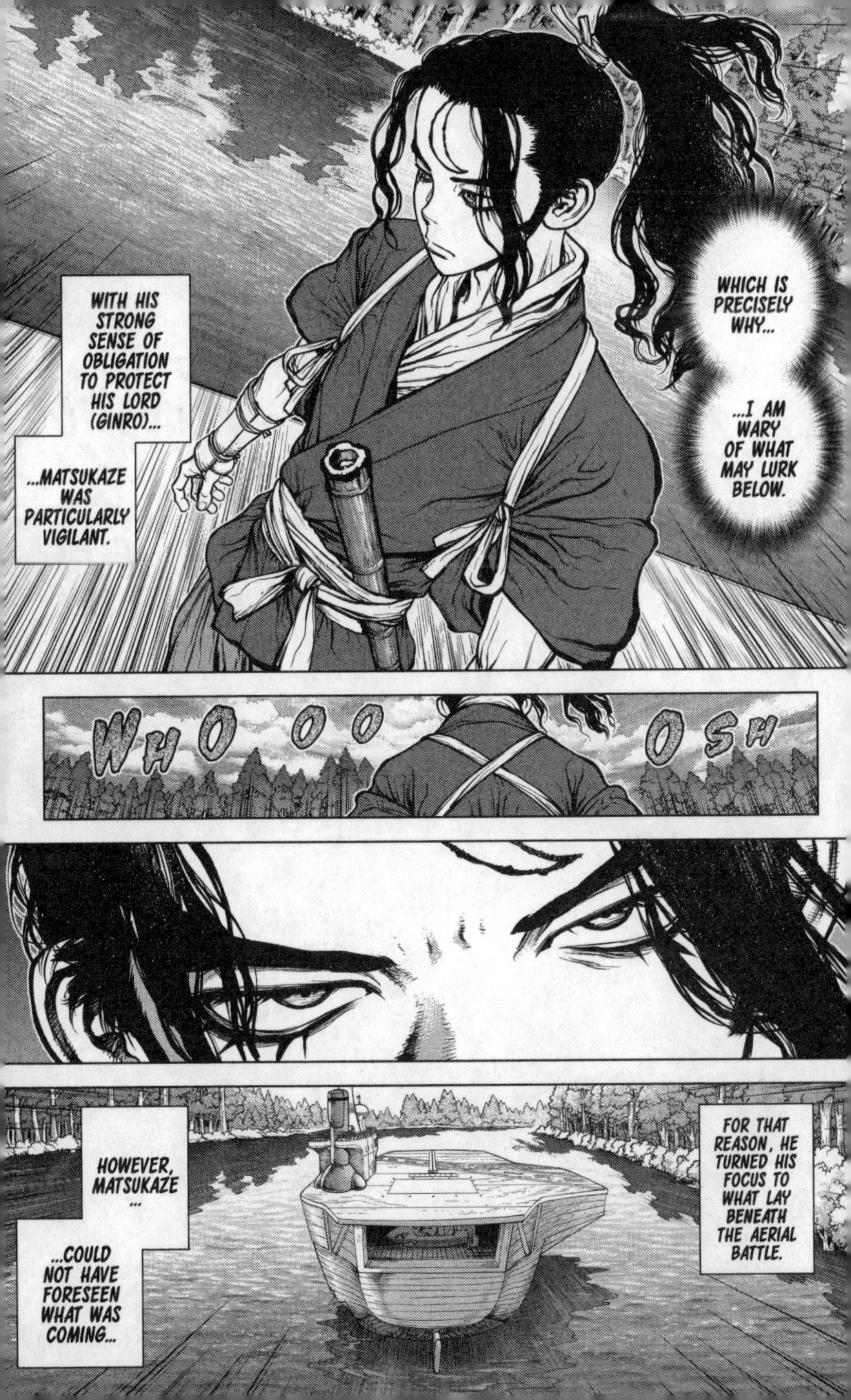
WHICH IS PRECISELY WHY...
...I AM WARY OF WHAT MAY LURK BELOW.
WITH HIS STRONG SENSE OF OBLIGATION TO PROTECT HIS LORD (GINRO)...
...MATSUKAZE WAS PARTICULARLY VIGILANT.
WHOOOOSH
FOR THAT REASON, HE TURNED HIS FOCUS TO WHAT LAY BENEATH THE AERIAL BATTLE.
HOWEVER, MATSUKAZE...
...COULD NOT HAVE FORESEEN WHAT WAS COMING...

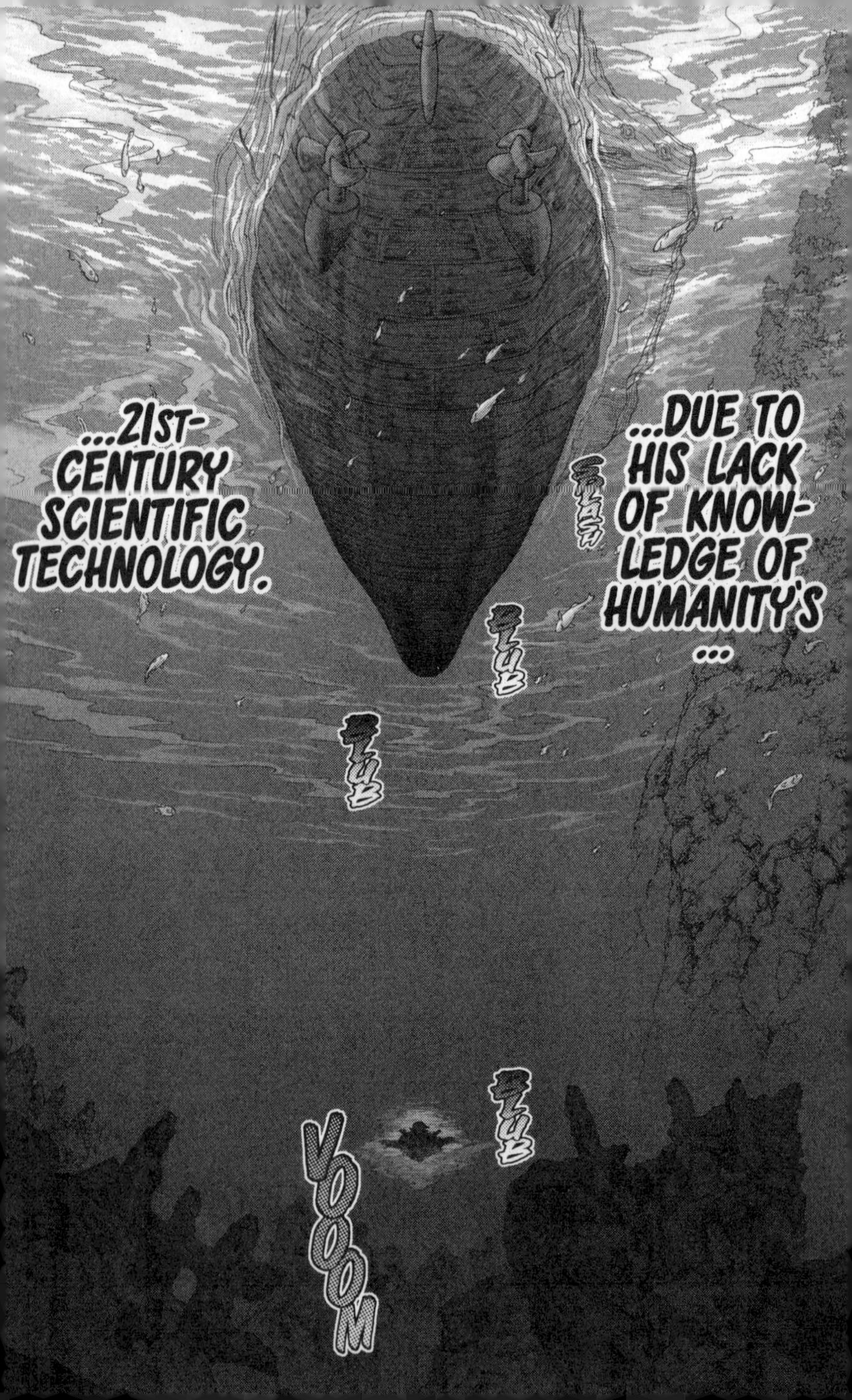

...DUE TO HIS LACK OF KNOW-LEDGE OF HUMANITY'S ...
SPLASH
...21ST-CENTURY SCIENTIFIC TECHNOLOGY.
BLUB
BLUB
BLUB
VOOOOM

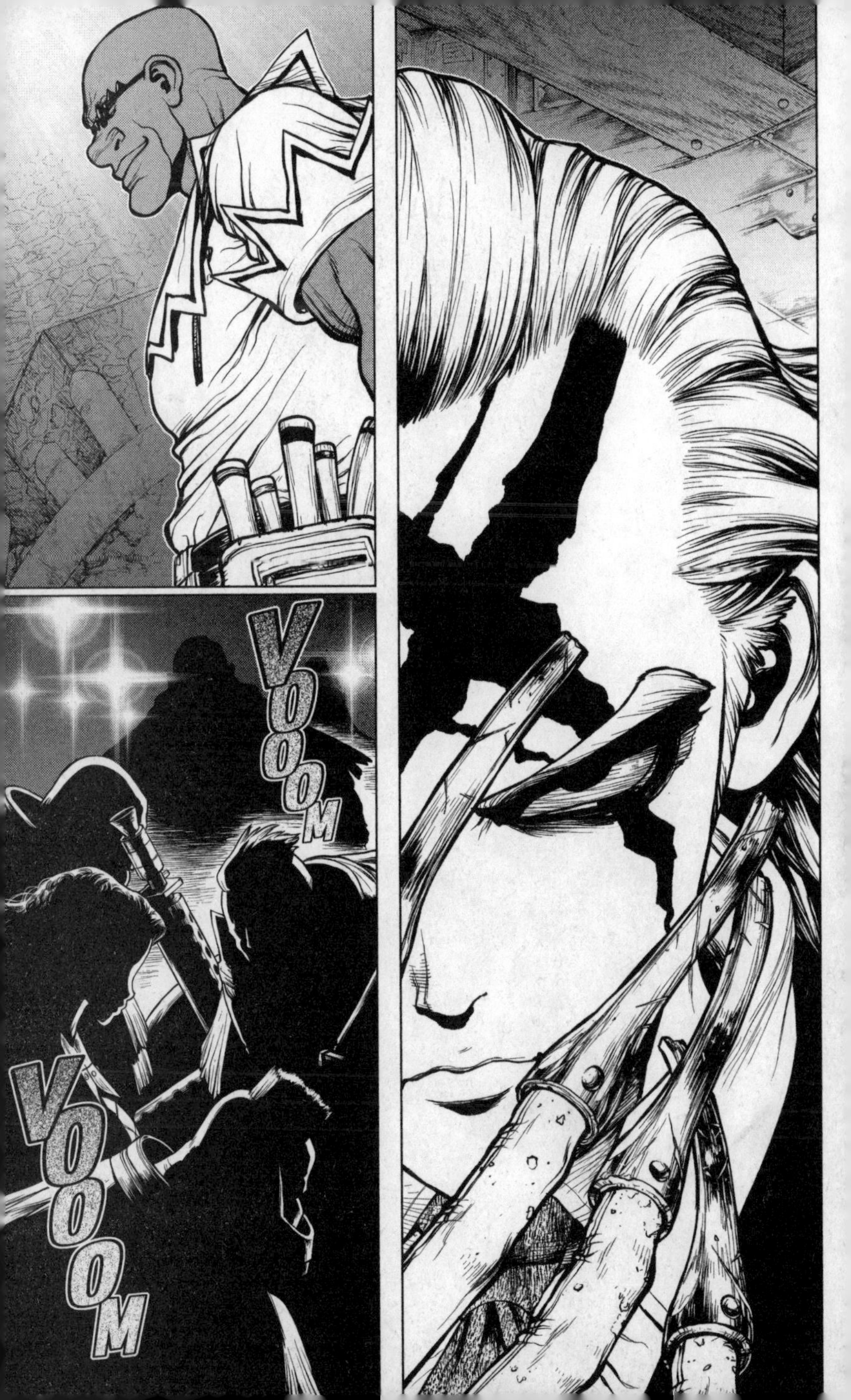
VOOOM
VOOOM

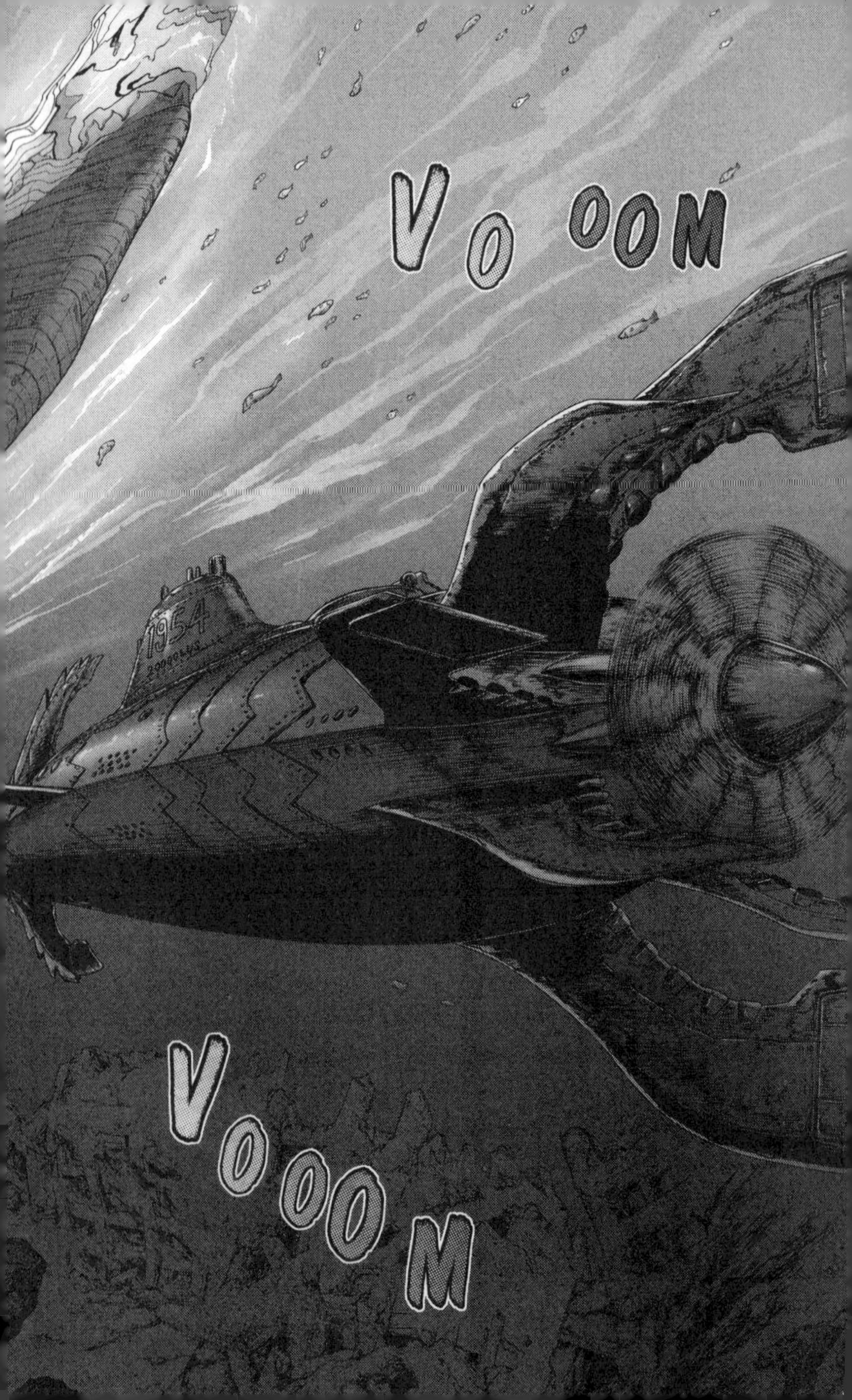
VO OOM
VOOOOM

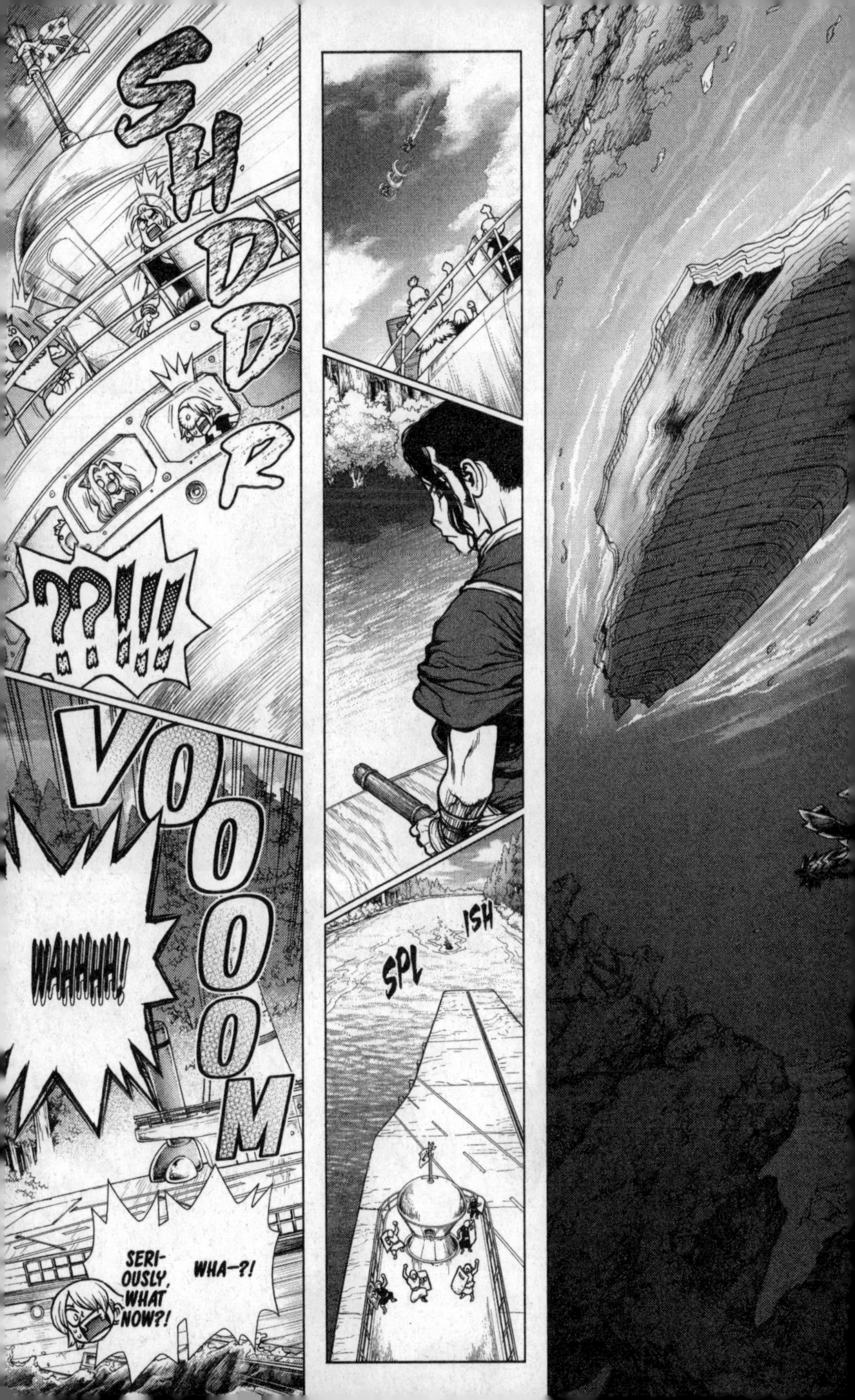
SPL
ISH
SHDDR
??!!!
VOOOOOM
WAHHHH!
WHA-?!
SERI-OUSLY, WHAT NOW?!

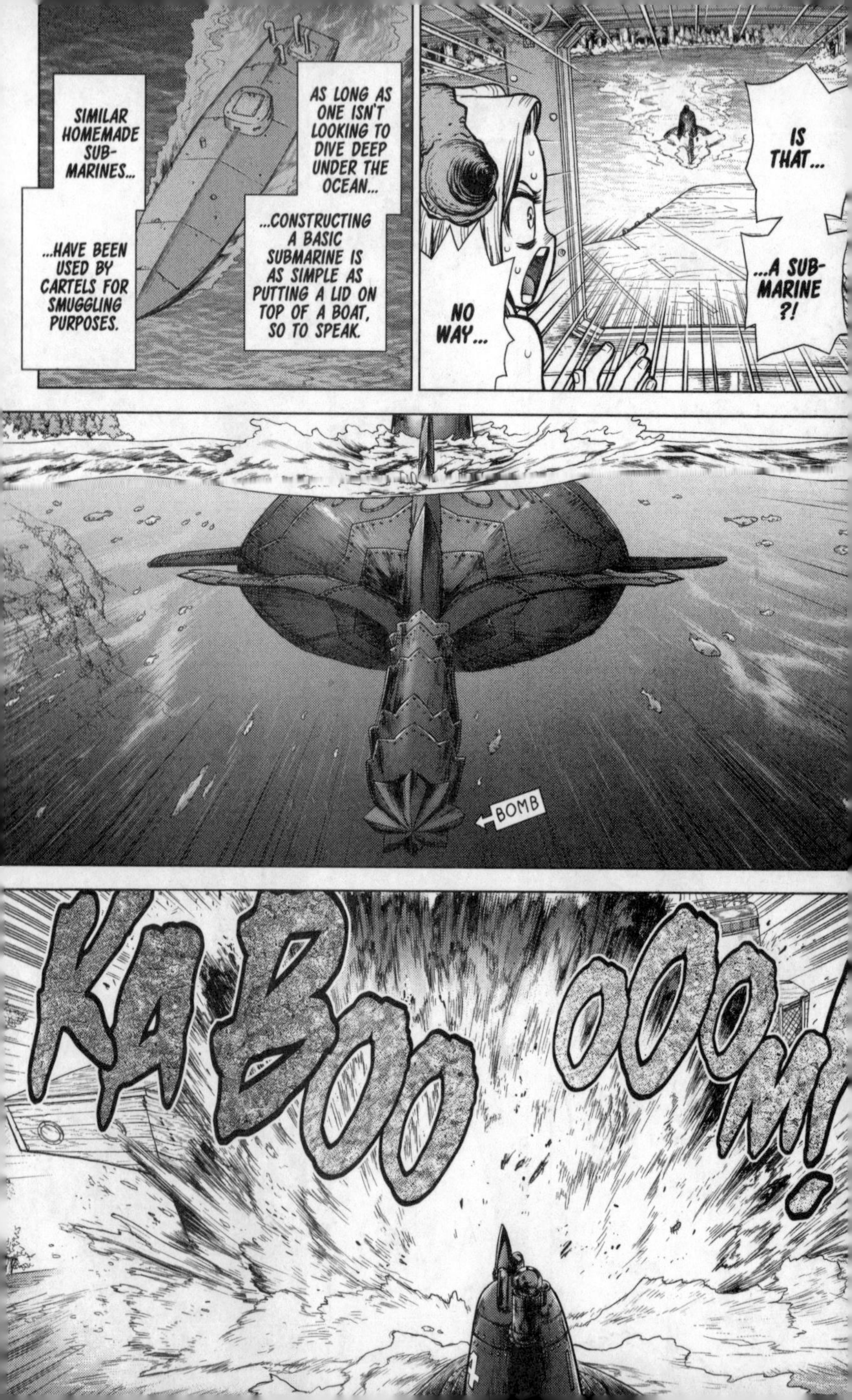
IS THAT...
...A SUB-MARINE?!
NO WAY...
AS LONG AS ONE ISN'T LOOKING TO DIVE DEEP UNDER THE OCEAN...
...CONSTRUCTING A BASIC SUBMARINE IS AS SIMPLE AS PUTTING A LID ON TOP OF A BOAT, SO TO SPEAK.
SIMILAR HOMEMADE SUB-MARINES...
...HAVE BEEN USED BY CARTELS FOR SMUGGLING PURPOSES.
BOMB
KABOOOOOOM!

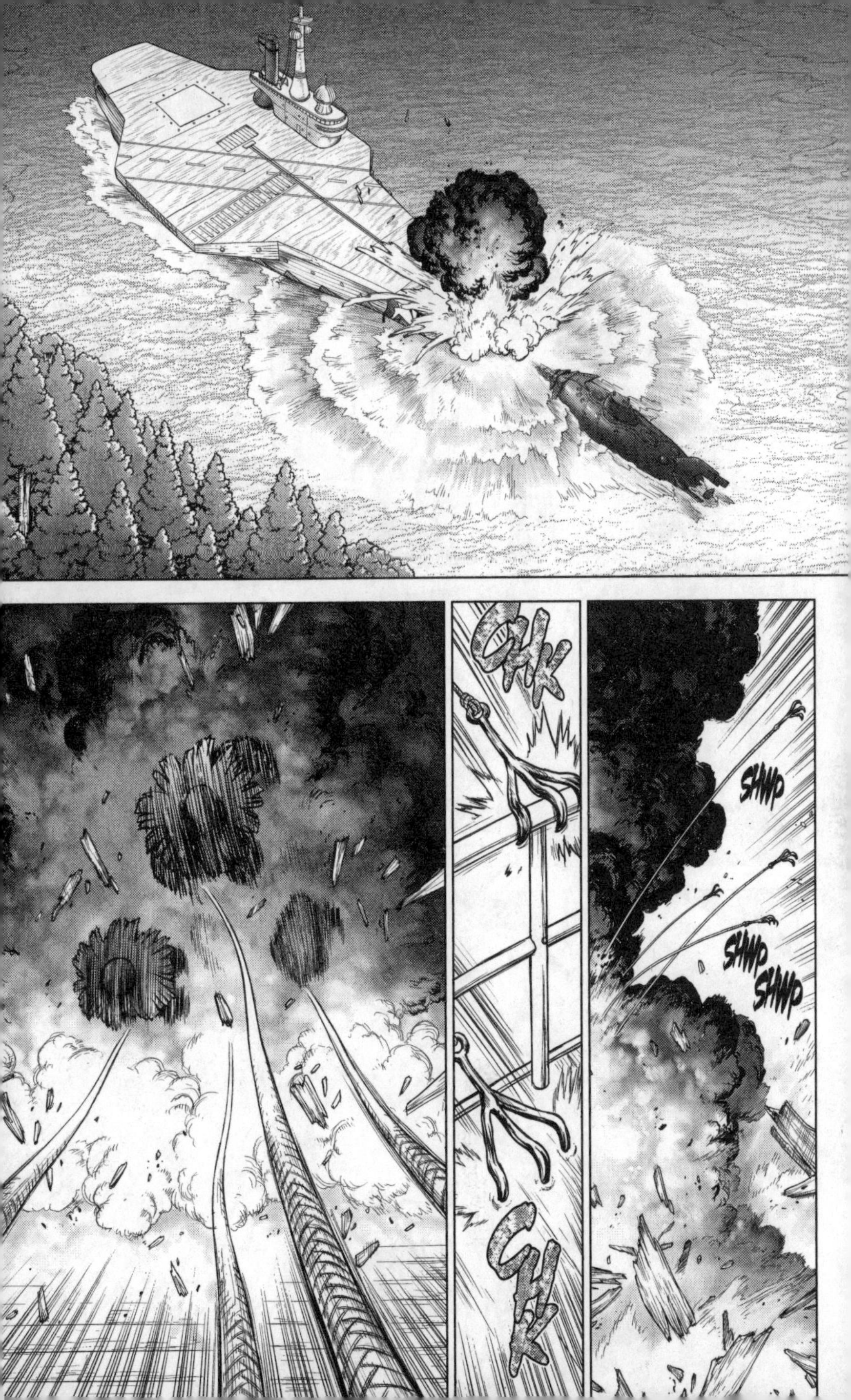
SHWP
SHWP
SHWP
CHK
CHK

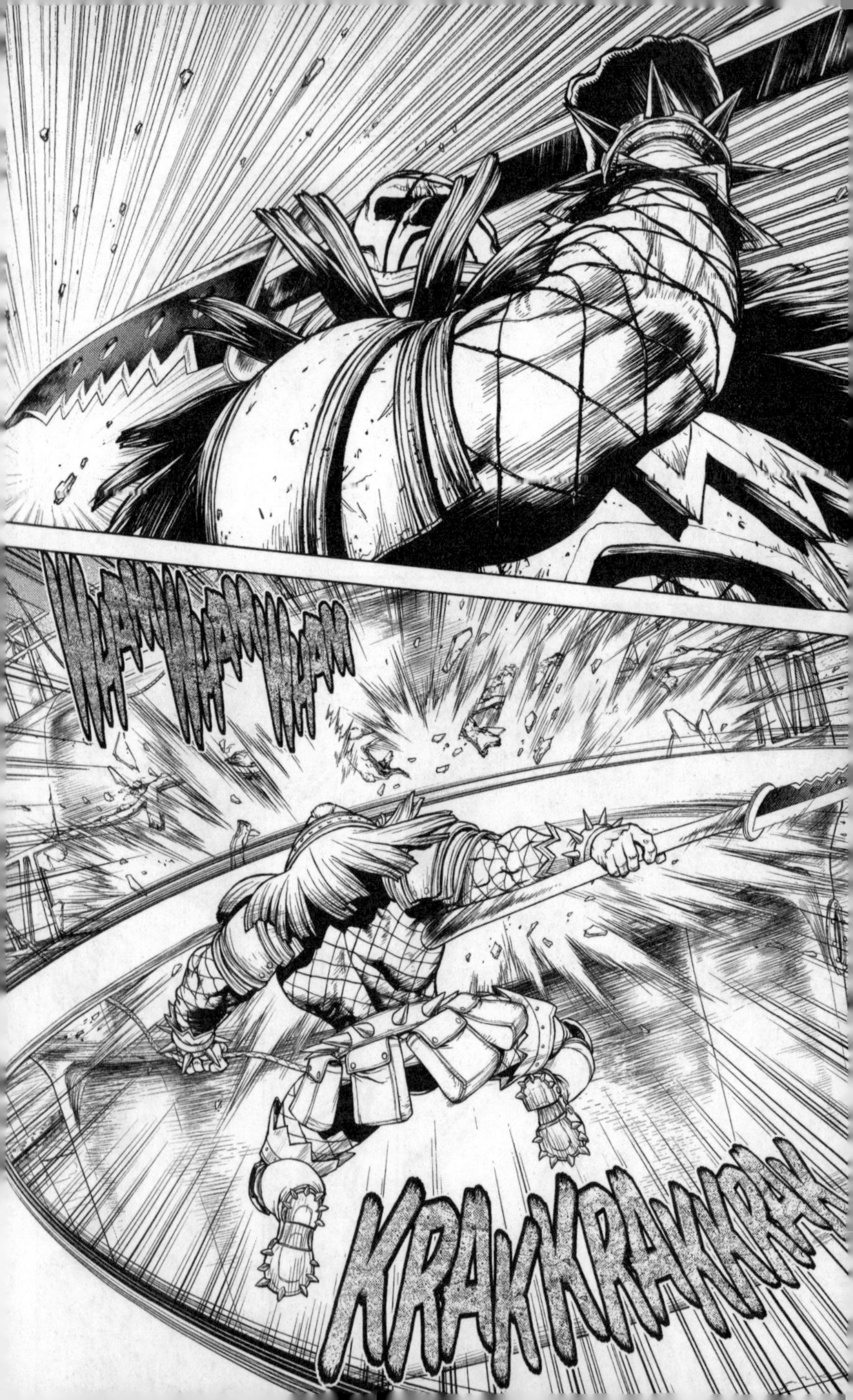
WHAM WHAM WHAM
KRAK KRAK KRAK

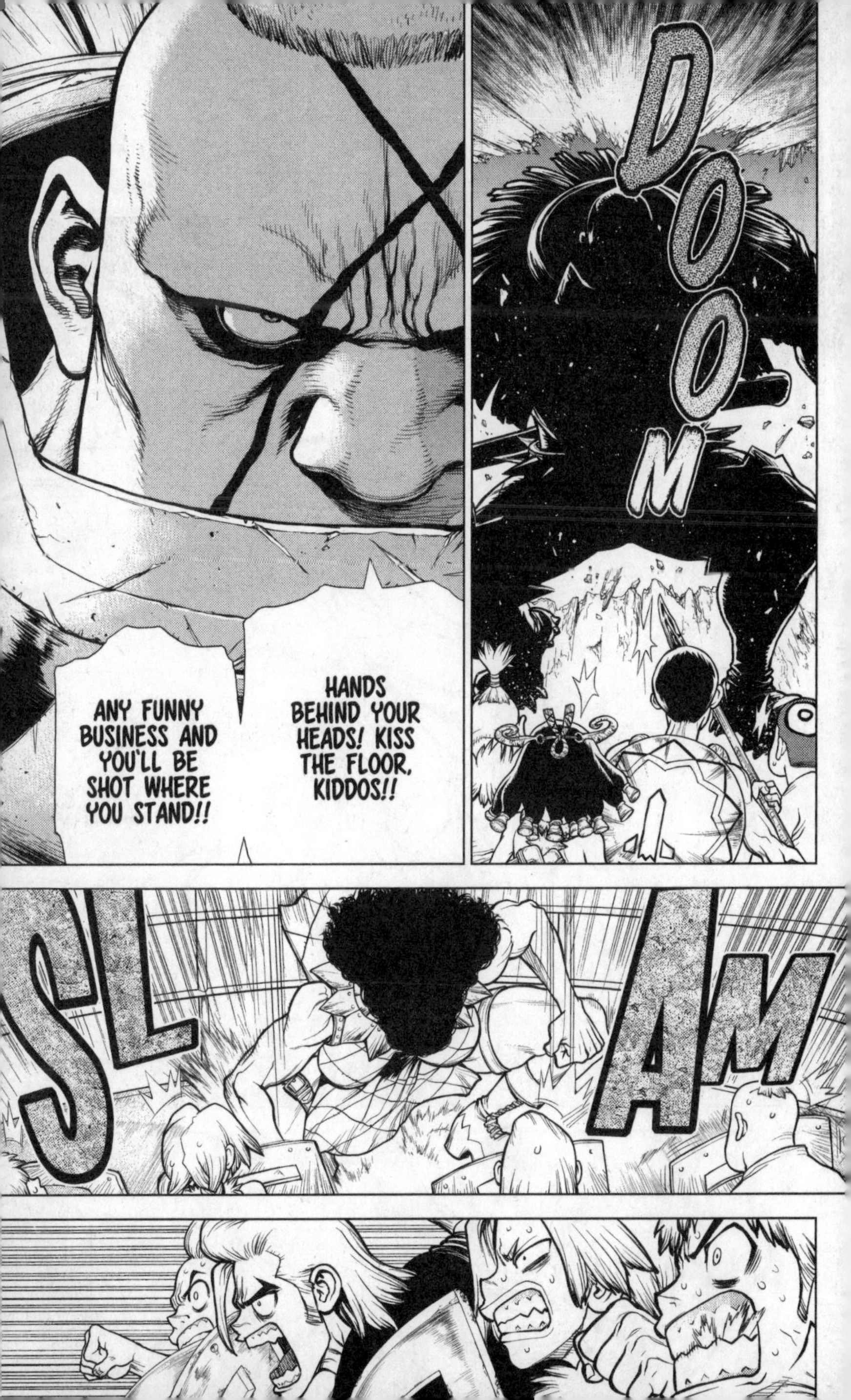
DOOOM
HANDS BEHIND YOUR HEADS! KISS THE FLOOR, KIDDOS!!
ANY FUNNY BUSINESS AND YOU'LL BE SHOT WHERE YOU STAND!!
SLAM

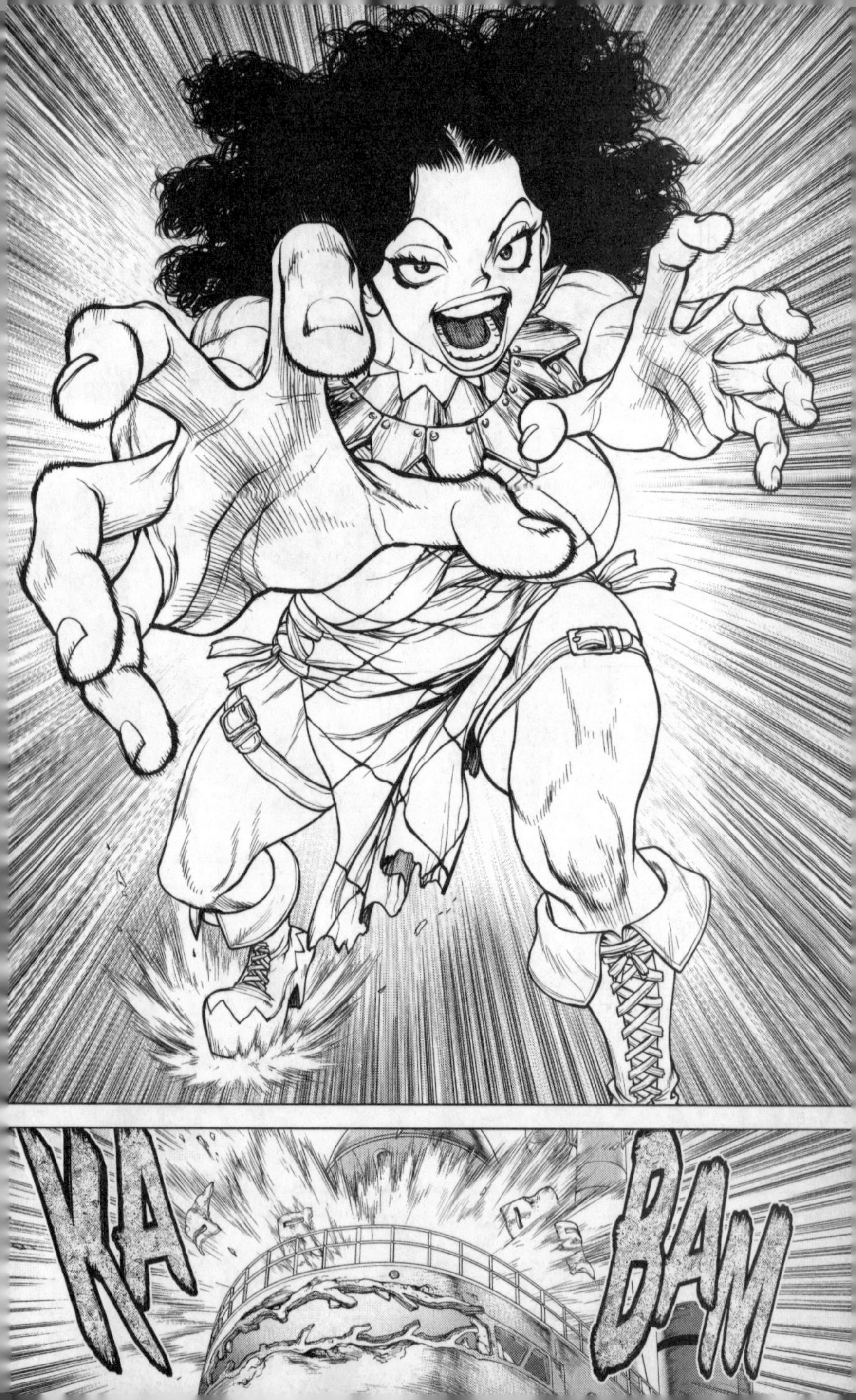
KA-BAM

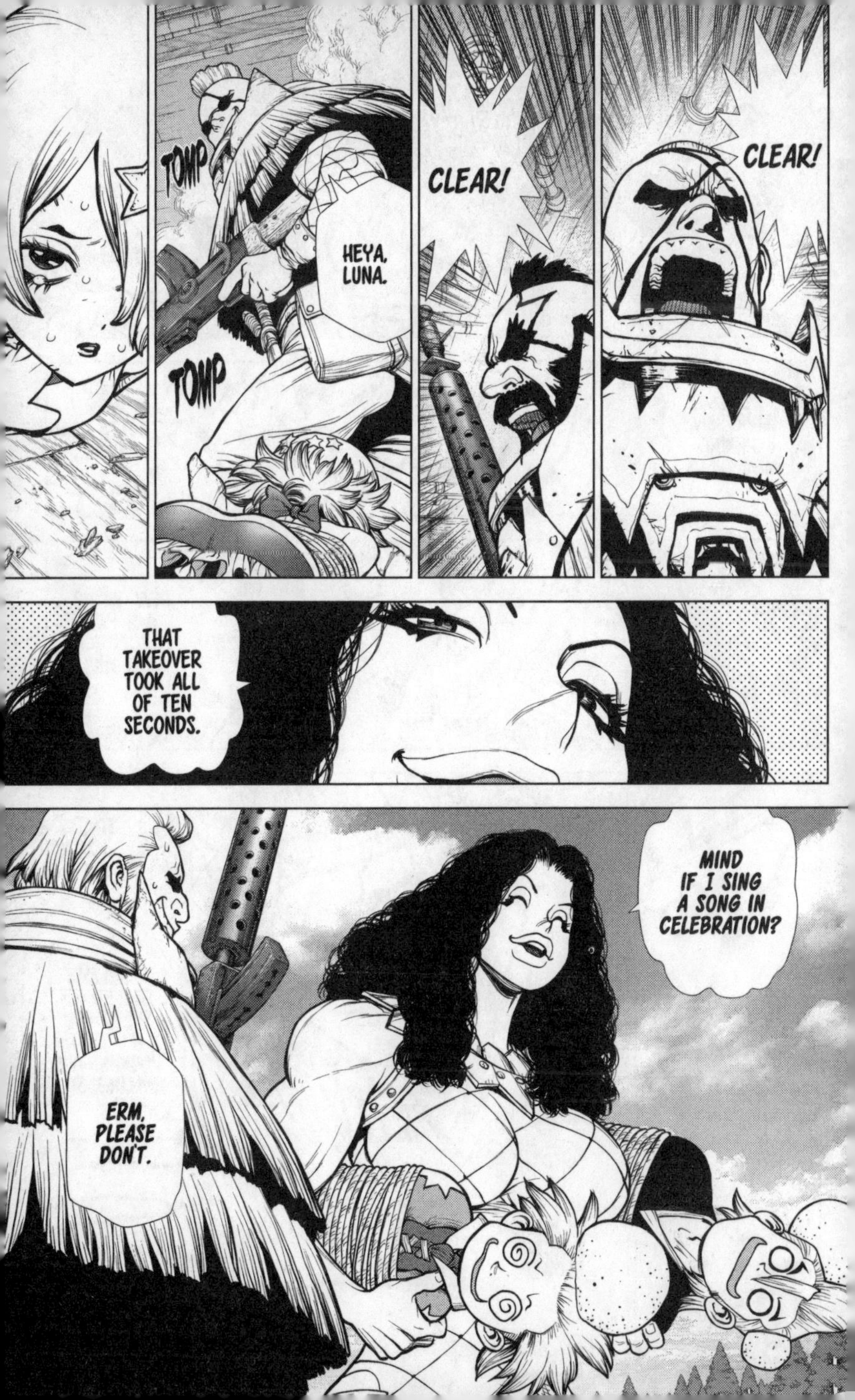
CLEAR!
CLEAR!
HEYA, LUNA.
TOMP
TOMP
THAT TAKEOVER TOOK ALL OF TEN SECONDS.
MIND IF I SING A SONG IN CELEBRATION?
ERM, PLEASE DON'T.

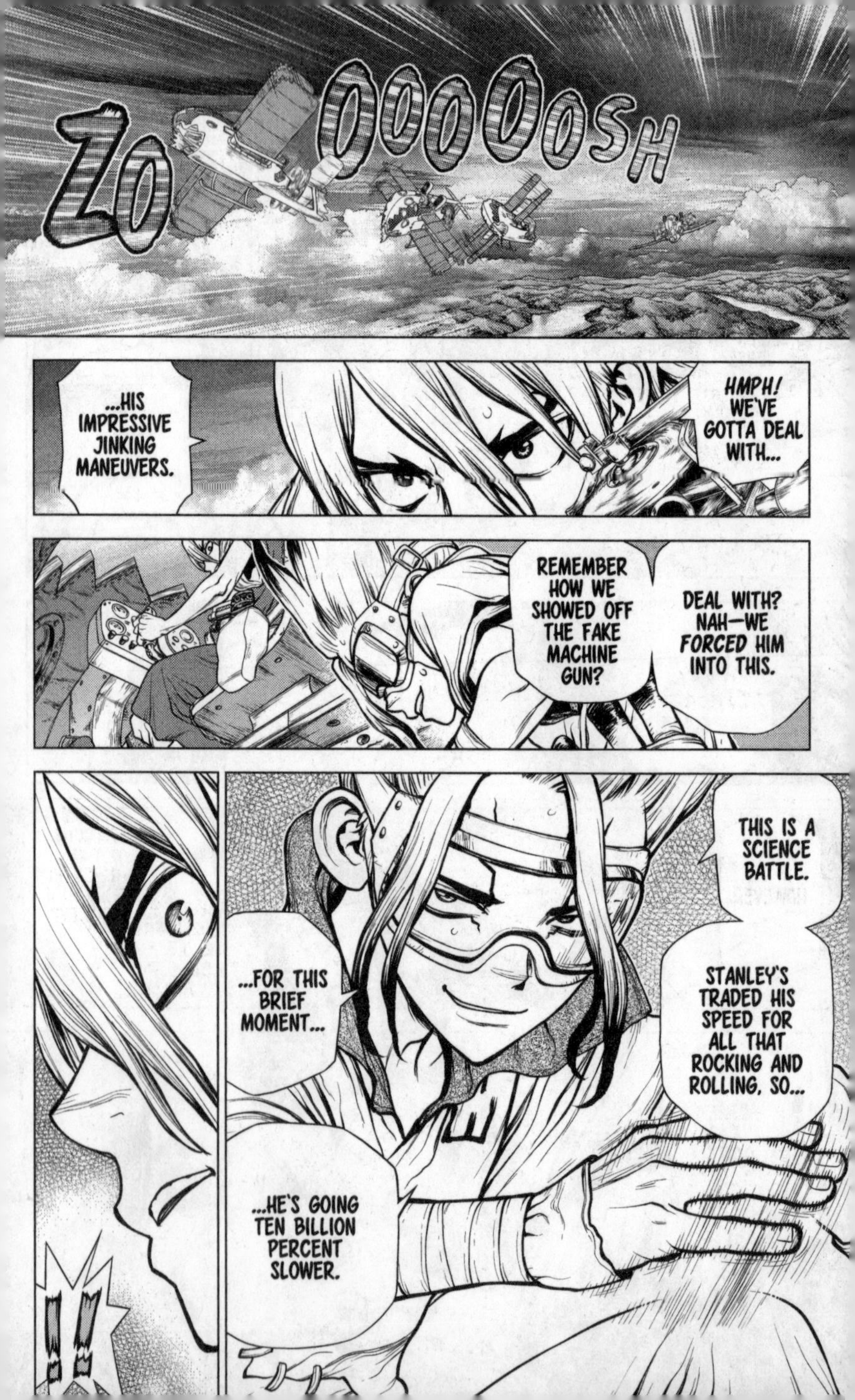
ZOOOOOOOSH
HMPH! WE'VE GOTTA DEAL WITH...
...HIS IMPRESSIVE JINKING MANEUVERS.
DEAL WITH? NAH—WE *FORCED* HIM INTO THIS.
REMEMBER HOW WE SHOWED OFF THE FAKE MACHINE GUN?
THIS IS A SCIENCE BATTLE.
STANLEY'S TRADED HIS SPEED FOR ALL THAT ROCKING AND ROLLING, SO...
...FOR THIS BRIEF MOMENT...
...HE'S GOING TEN BILLION PERCENT SLOWER.
!!

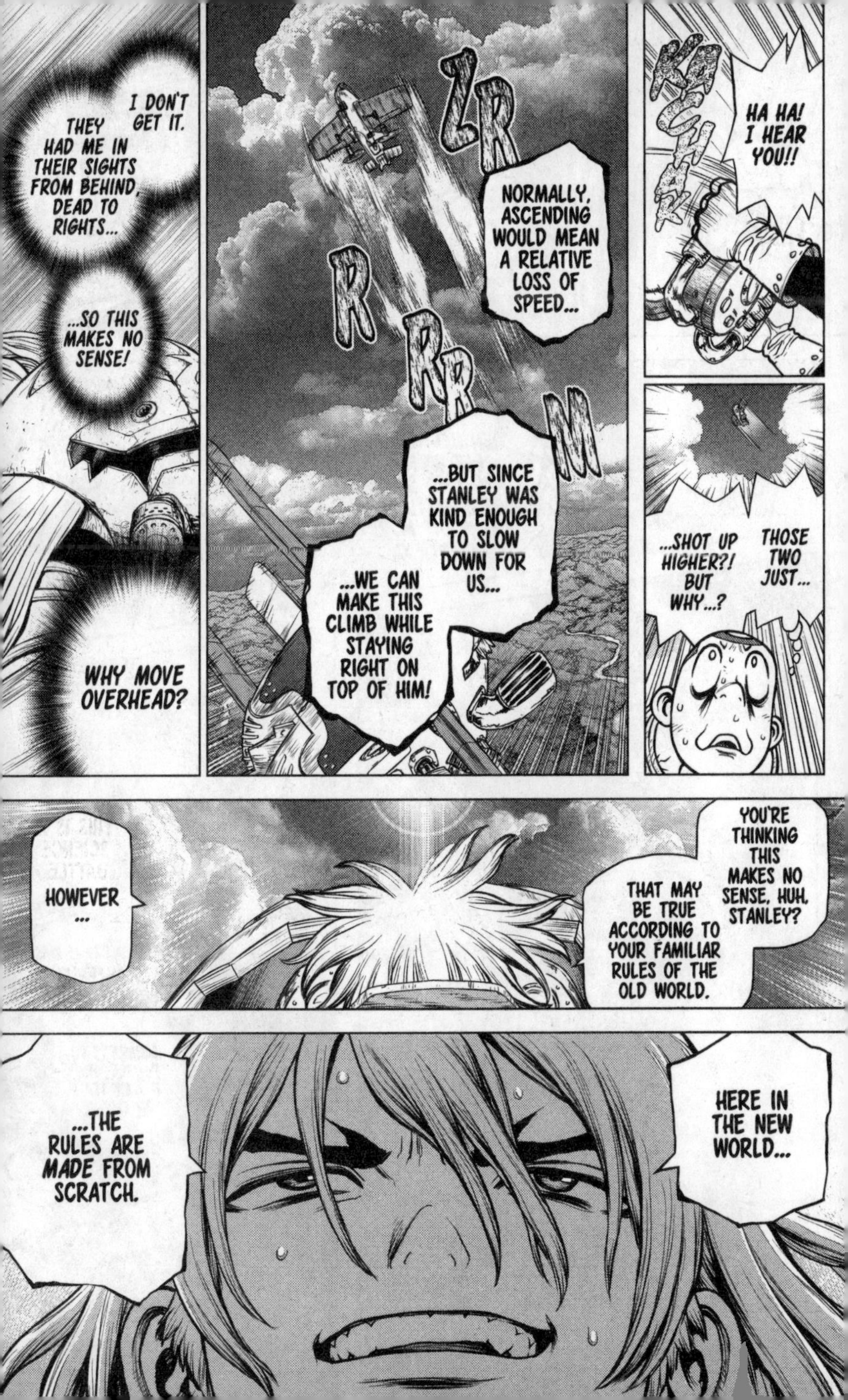
HA HA! I HEAR YOU!!
THOSE TWO JUST...
...SHOT UP HIGHER?! BUT WHY...?
ZRRRRM
NORMALLY, ASCENDING WOULD MEAN A RELATIVE LOSS OF SPEED...
...BUT SINCE STANLEY WAS KIND ENOUGH TO SLOW DOWN FOR US...
...WE CAN MAKE THIS CLIMB WHILE STAYING RIGHT ON TOP OF HIM!
I DON'T GET IT.
THEY HAD ME IN THEIR SIGHTS FROM BEHIND, DEAD TO RIGHTS...
...SO THIS MAKES NO SENSE!
WHY MOVE OVERHEAD?
YOU'RE THINKING THIS MAKES NO SENSE, HUH, STANLEY?
THAT MAY BE TRUE ACCORDING TO YOUR FAMILIAR RULES OF THE OLD WORLD.
HOWEVER...
HERE IN THE NEW WORLD...
...THE RULES ARE MADE FROM SCRATCH.

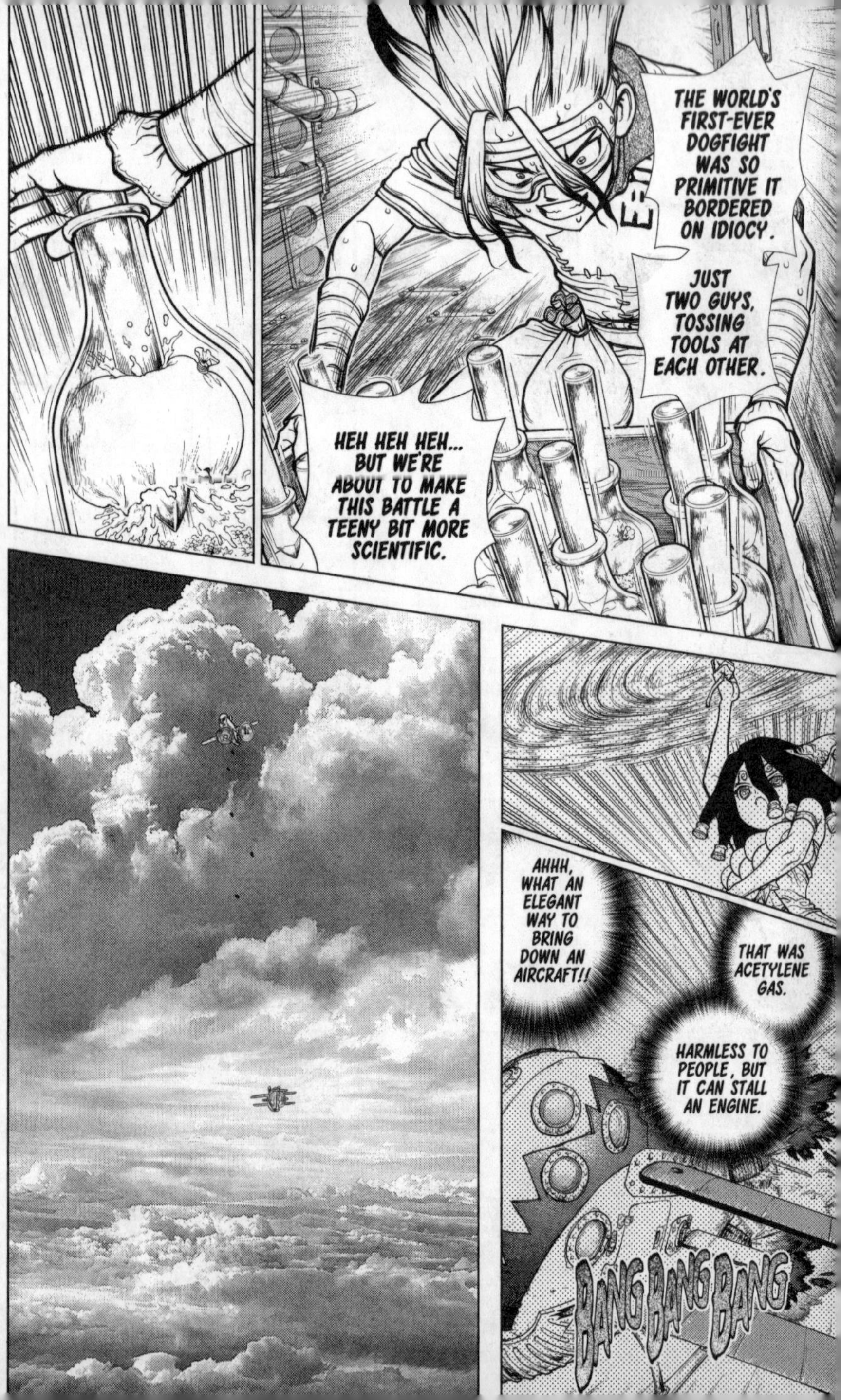
THE WORLD'S FIRST-EVER DOGFIGHT WAS SO PRIMITIVE IT BORDERED ON IDIOCY.
JUST TWO GUYS, TOSSING TOOLS AT EACH OTHER.
HEH HEH HEH... BUT WE'RE ABOUT TO MAKE THIS BATTLE A TEENY BIT MORE SCIENTIFIC.
AHHH, WHAT AN ELEGANT WAY TO BRING DOWN AN AIRCRAFT!!
THAT WAS ACETYLENE GAS.
HARMLESS TO PEOPLE, BUT IT CAN STALL AN ENGINE.
BANG BANG BANG

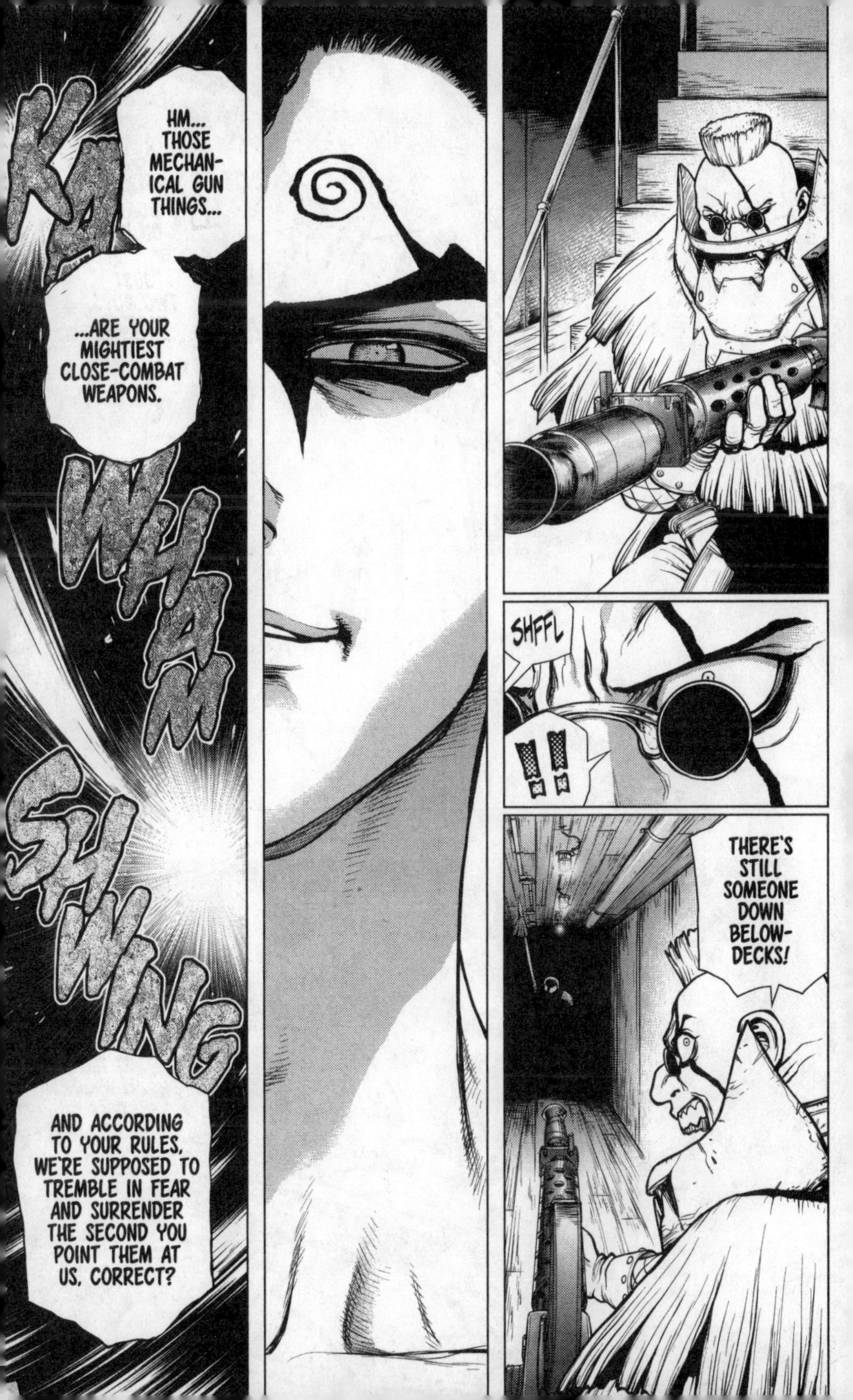
SHFFL
!!
THERE'S STILL SOMEONE DOWN BELOW-DECKS!
KA
HM... THOSE MECHANICAL GUN THINGS...
...ARE YOUR MIGHTIEST CLOSE-COMBAT WEAPONS.
WHAM
SHWING
AND ACCORDING TO YOUR RULES, WE'RE SUPPOSED TO TREMBLE IN FEAR AND SURRENDER THE SECOND YOU POINT THEM AT US, CORRECT?

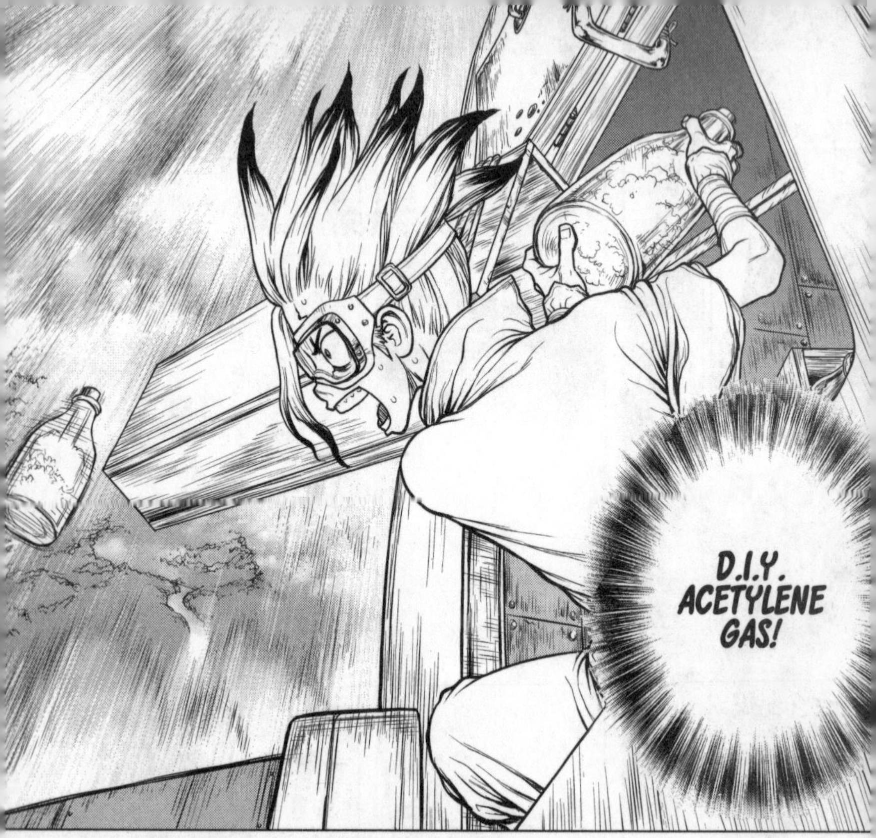
D.I.Y. ACETYLENE GAS!
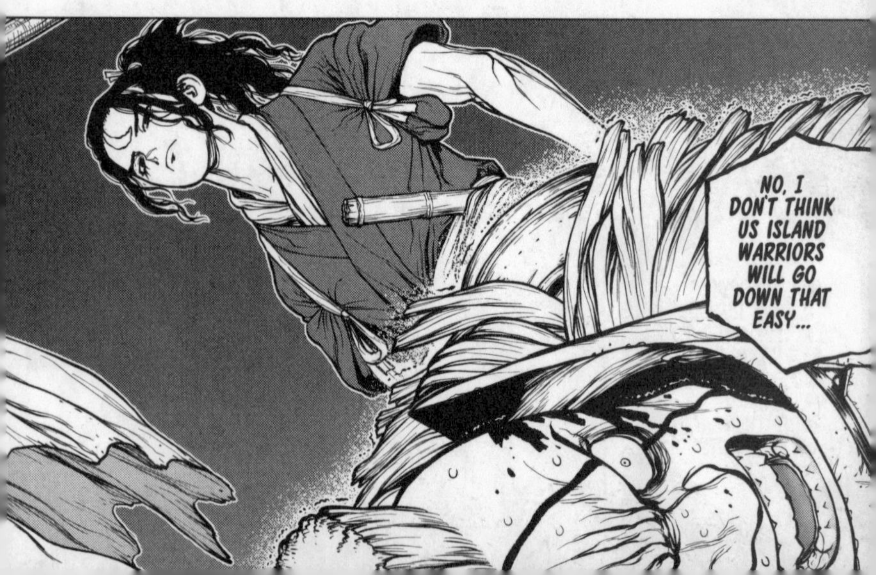
NO, I DON'T THINK US ISLAND WARRIORS WILL GO DOWN THAT EASY...

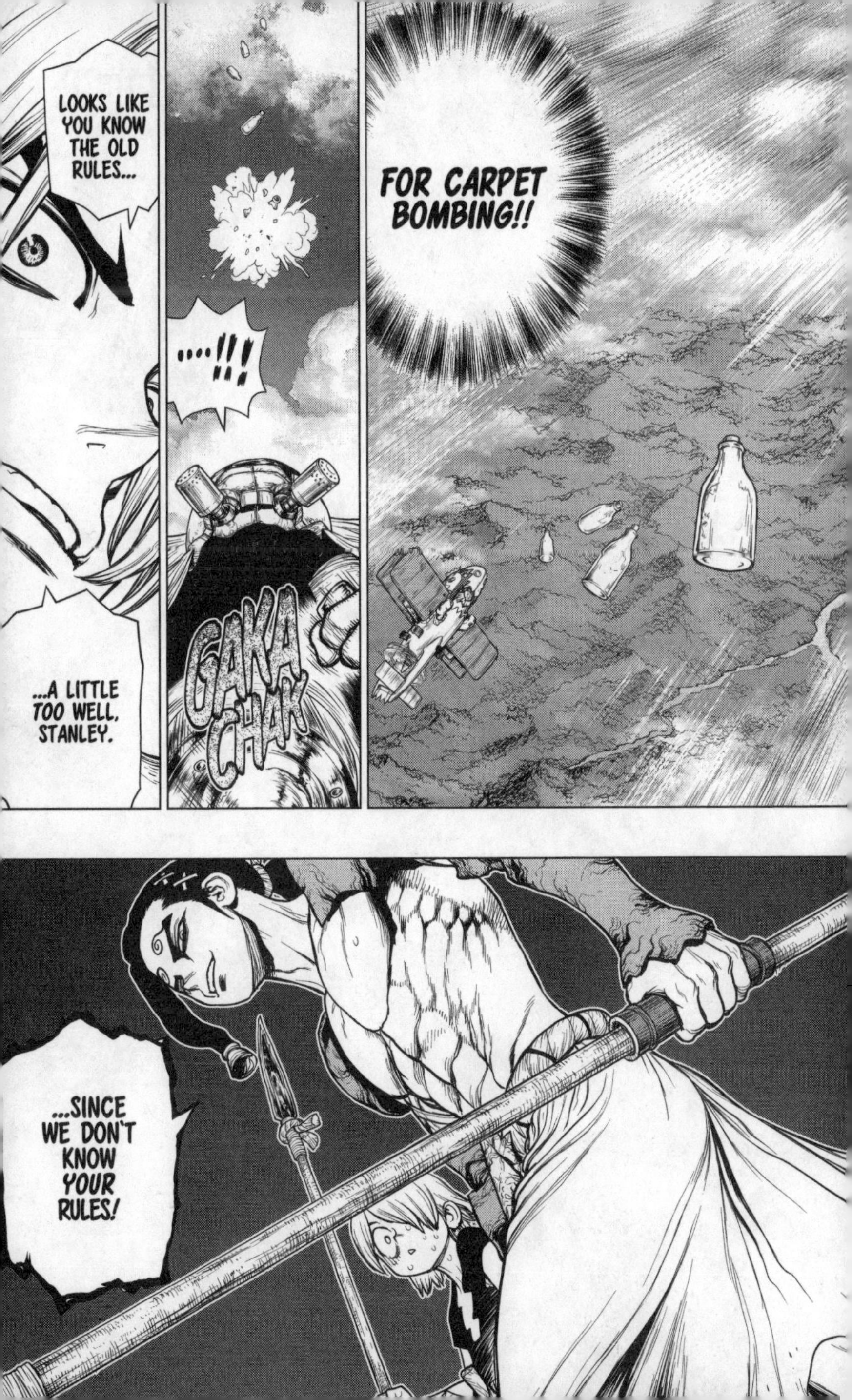
FOR CARPET BOMBING!!
....!!!
GAKA CHAK
LOOKS LIKE YOU KNOW THE OLD RULES...
...A LITTLE TOO WELL, STANLEY.
...SINCE WE DON'T KNOW YOUR RULES!

Z=166: Ultimate Knight

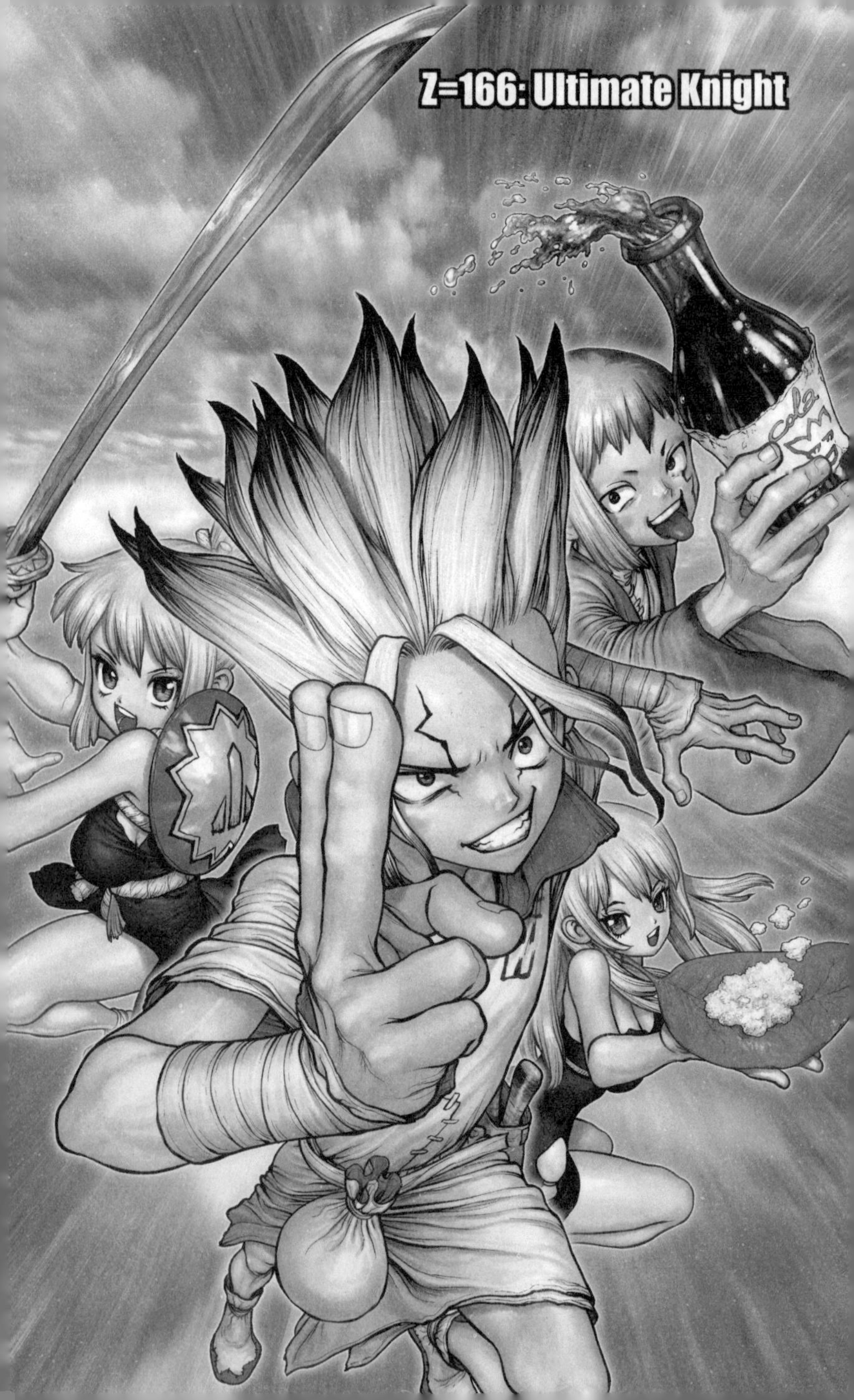

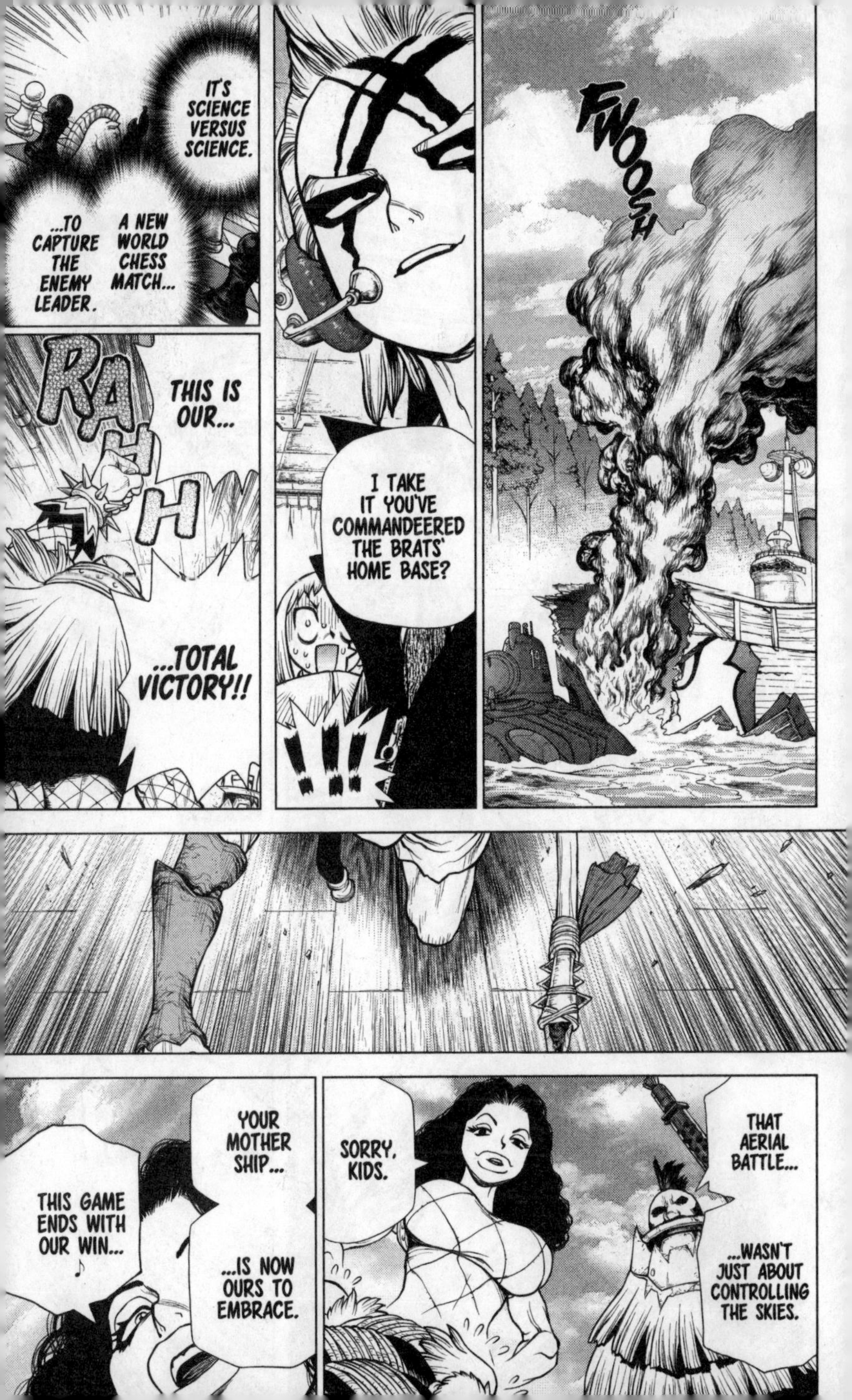
FWOOOSH
I TAKE IT YOU'VE COMMANDEERED THE BRATS' HOME BASE?
!!!
IT'S SCIENCE VERSUS SCIENCE.
A NEW WORLD CHESS MATCH...
...TO CAPTURE THE ENEMY LEADER.
RAHH
THIS IS OUR...
...TOTAL VICTORY!!
THAT AERIAL BATTLE...
SORRY, KIDS.
...WASN'T JUST ABOUT CONTROLLING THE SKIES.
YOUR MOTHER SHIP...
...IS NOW OURS TO EMBRACE.
THIS GAME ENDS WITH OUR WIN... ♪

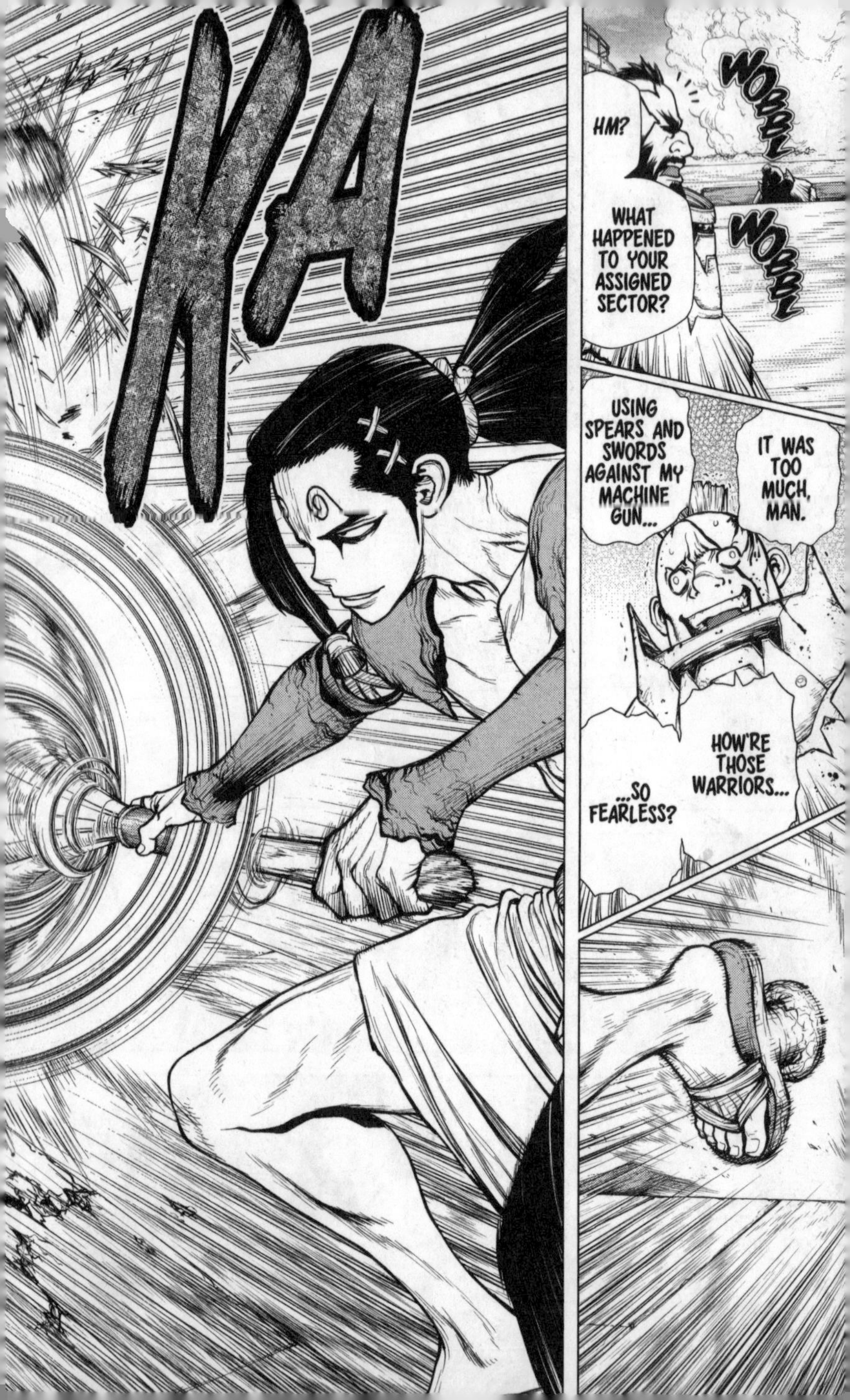
WOBBL
WOBBL
HM?
WHAT HAPPENED TO YOUR ASSIGNED SECTOR?
IT WAS TOO MUCH, MAN.
USING SPEARS AND SWORDS AGAINST MY MACHINE GUN...
HOW'RE THOSE WARRIORS...
...SO FEARLESS?
KA

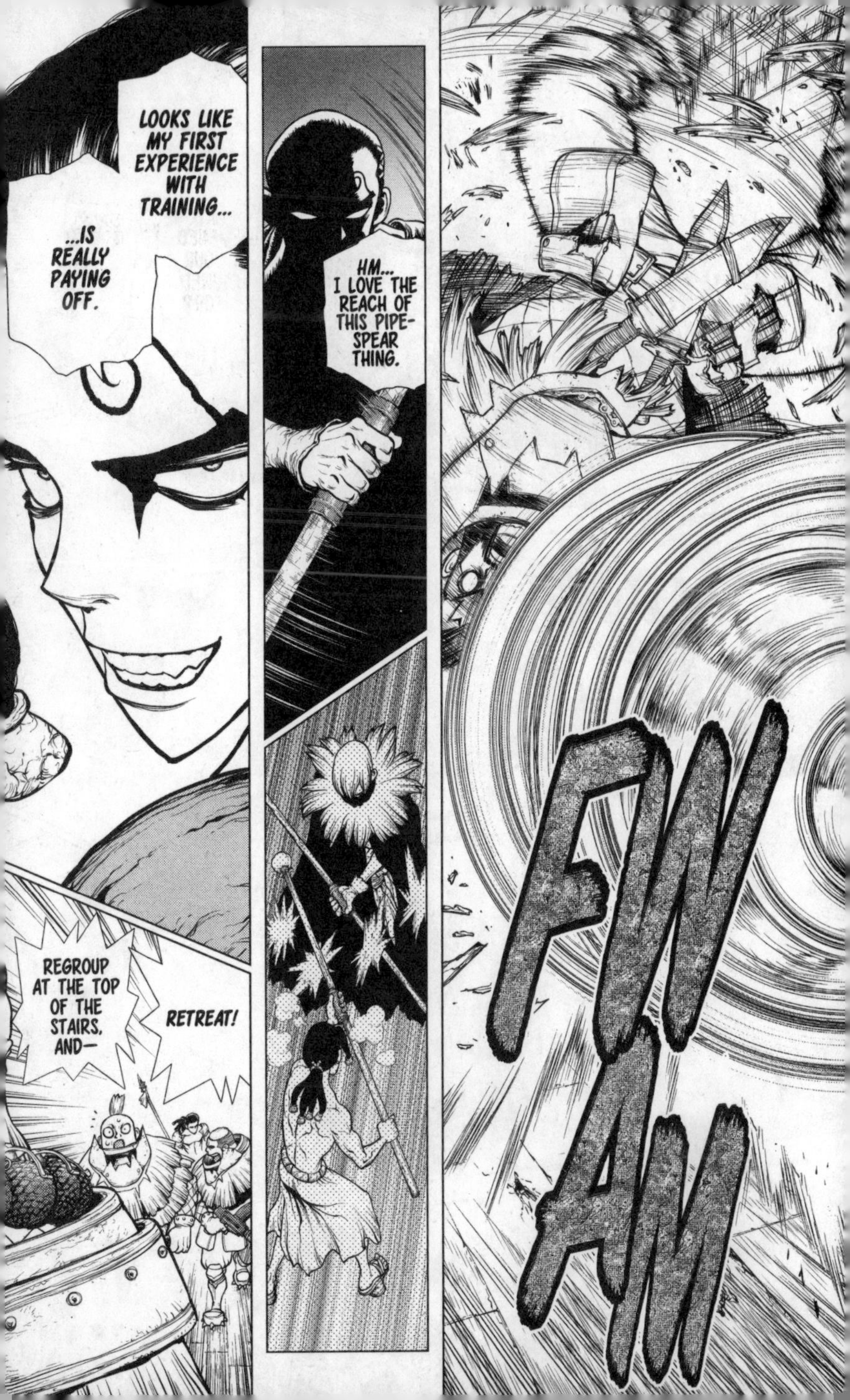

FWAM
HM... I LOVE THE REACH OF THIS PIPE-SPEAR THING.
LOOKS LIKE MY FIRST EXPERIENCE WITH TRAINING...
...IS REALLY PAYING OFF.
REGROUP AT THE TOP OF THE STAIRS, AND—
RETREAT!

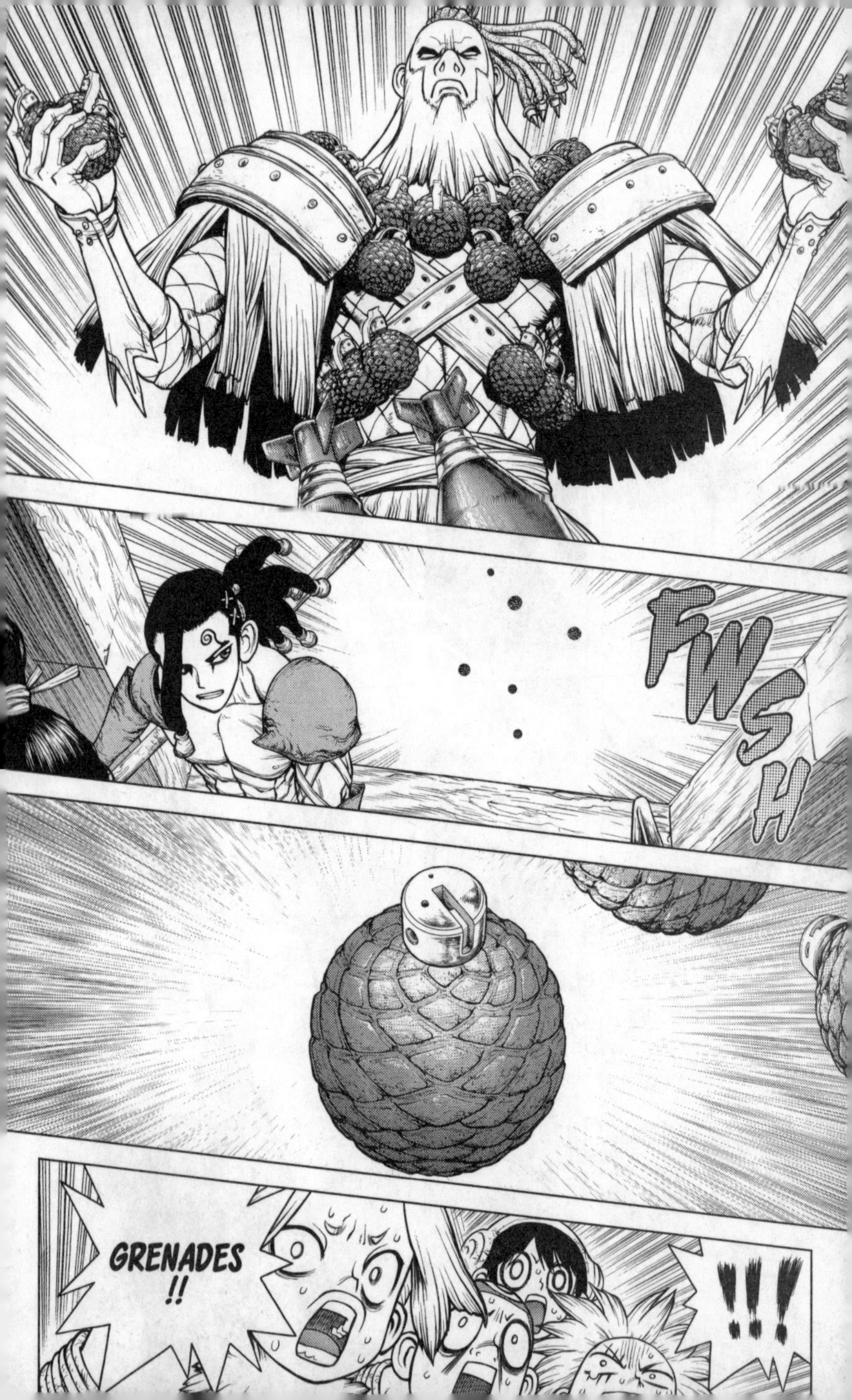
FWSH
GRENADES !!
!!!

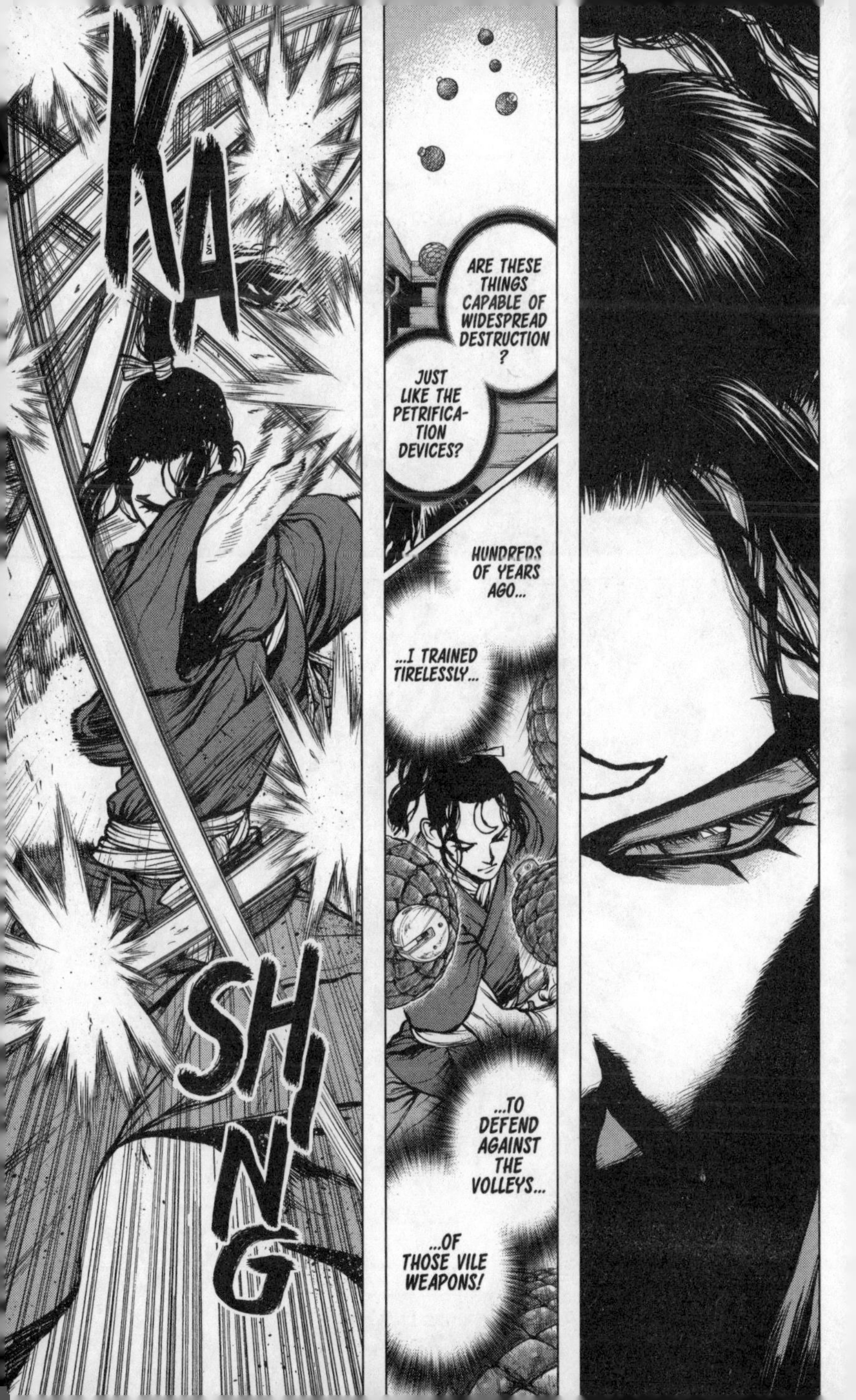
ARE THESE THINGS CAPABLE OF WIDESPREAD DESTRUCTION?
JUST LIKE THE PETRIFICATION DEVICES?
HUNDREDS OF YEARS AGO...
...I TRAINED TIRELESSLY...
...TO DEFEND AGAINST THE VOLLEYS...
...OF THOSE VILE WEAPONS!
KA
SHING

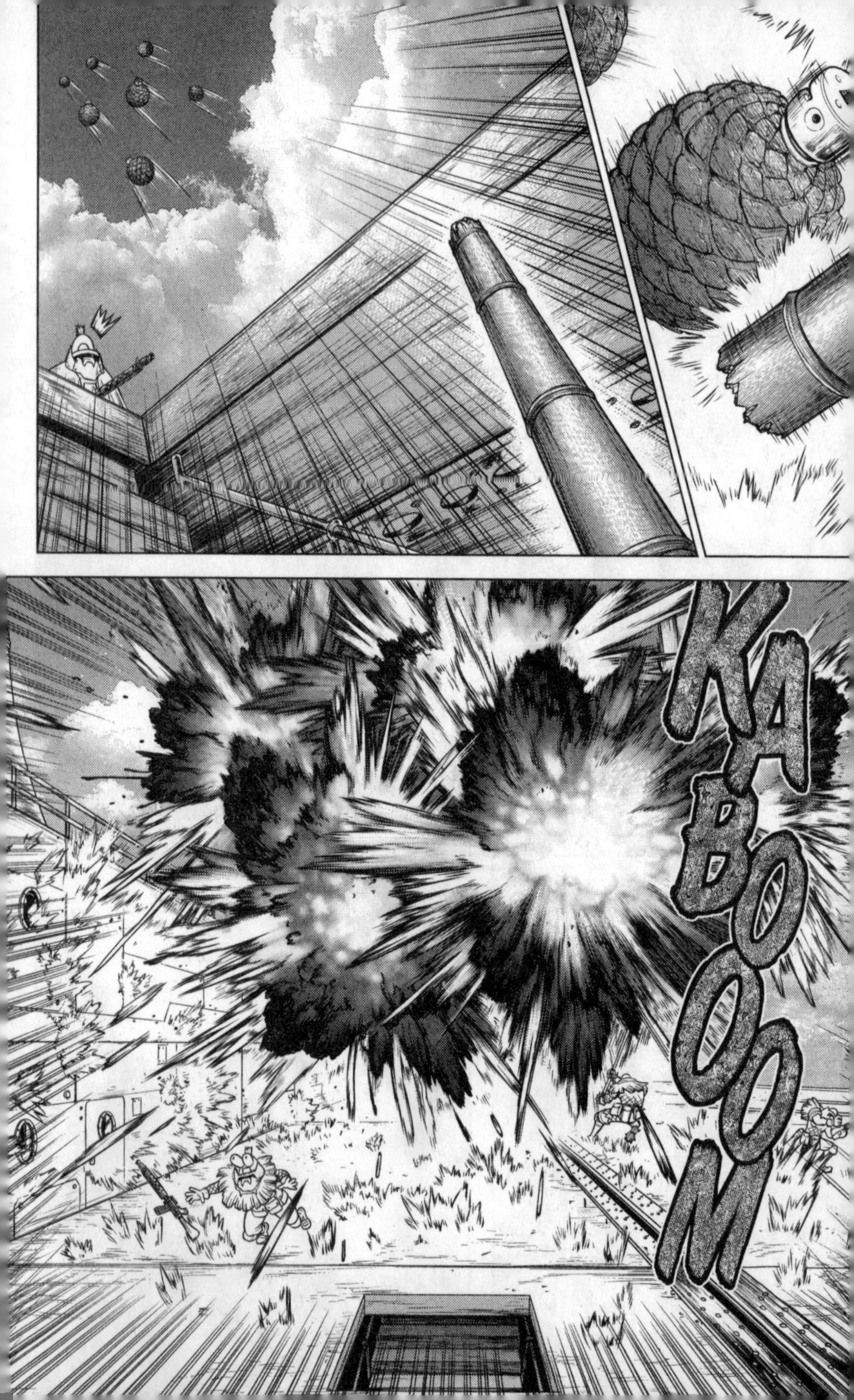
KABOOOM

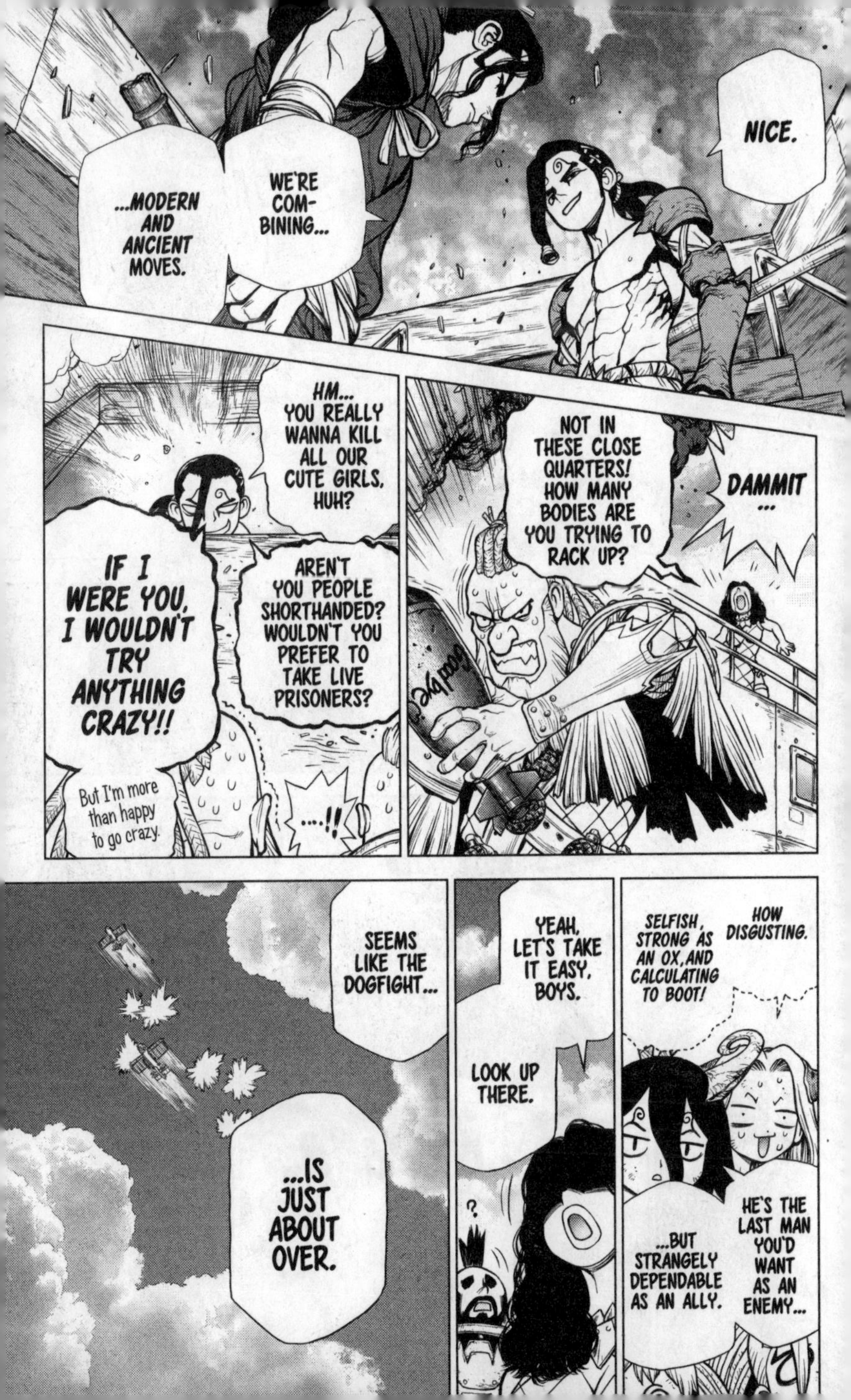
NICE.
WE'RE COM-BINING...
...MODERN AND ANCIENT MOVES.
DAMMIT...
NOT IN THESE CLOSE QUARTERS! HOW MANY BODIES ARE YOU TRYING TO RACK UP?
HM... YOU REALLY WANNA KILL ALL OUR CUTE GIRLS, HUH?
AREN'T YOU PEOPLE SHORTHANDED? WOULDN'T YOU PREFER TO TAKE LIVE PRISONERS?
IF I WERE YOU, I WOULDN'T TRY ANYTHING CRAZY!!
But I'm more than happy to go crazy.
....!!
HOW DISGUSTING.
SELFISH, STRONG AS AN OX, AND CALCULATING TO BOOT!
HE'S THE LAST MAN YOU'D WANT AS AN ENEMY...
...BUT STRANGELY DEPENDABLE AS AN ALLY.
YEAH, LET'S TAKE IT EASY, BOYS.
LOOK UP THERE.
?
SEEMS LIKE THE DOGFIGHT...
...IS JUST ABOUT OVER.

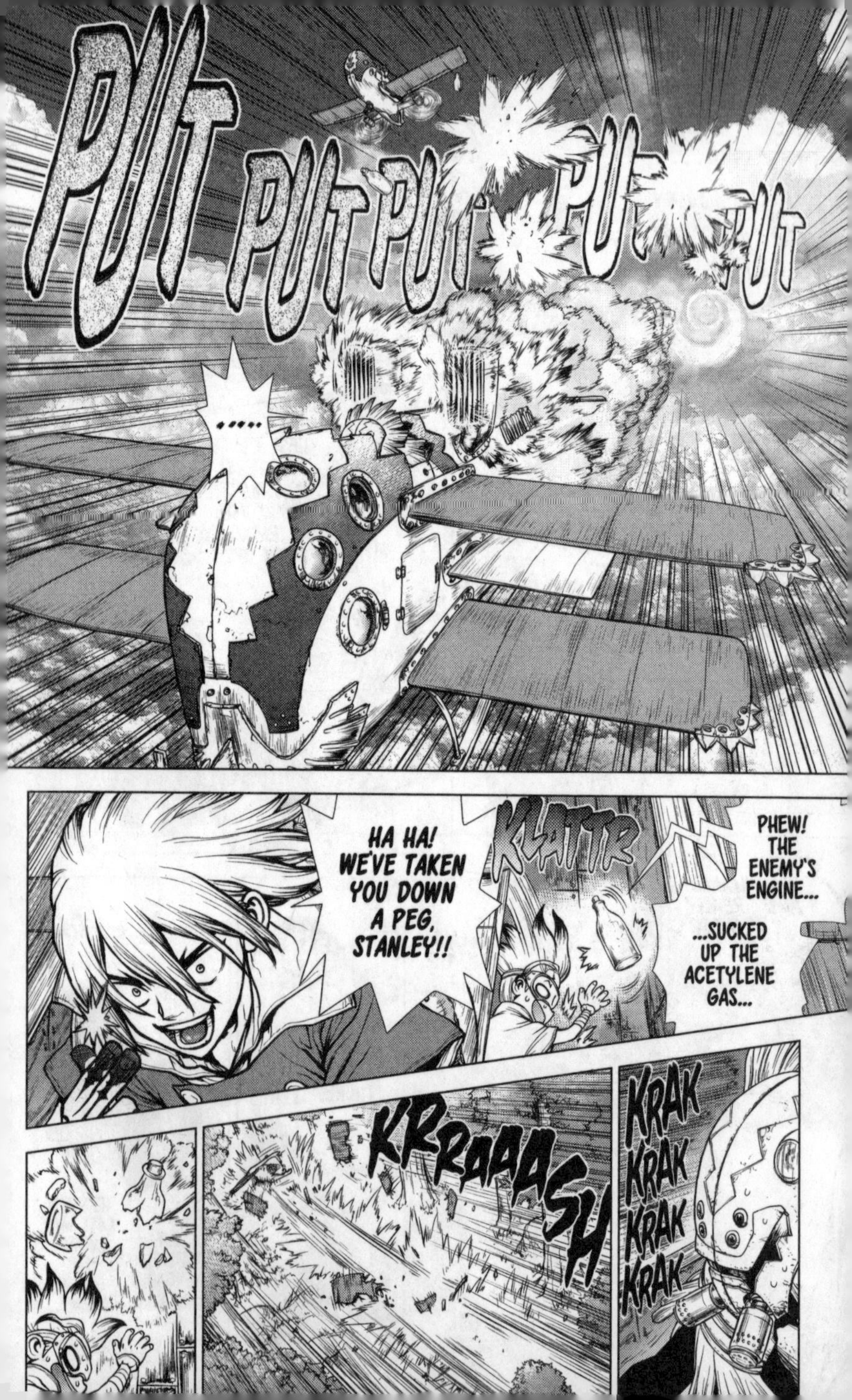
PUT PUT PUT PUT PUT PUT
....
PHEW! THE ENEMY'S ENGINE...
...SUCKED UP THE ACETYLENE GAS...
KLATTR
HA HA! WE'VE TAKEN YOU DOWN A PEG, STANLEY!!
KRAK KRAK KRAK KRAK
KRRAAASH

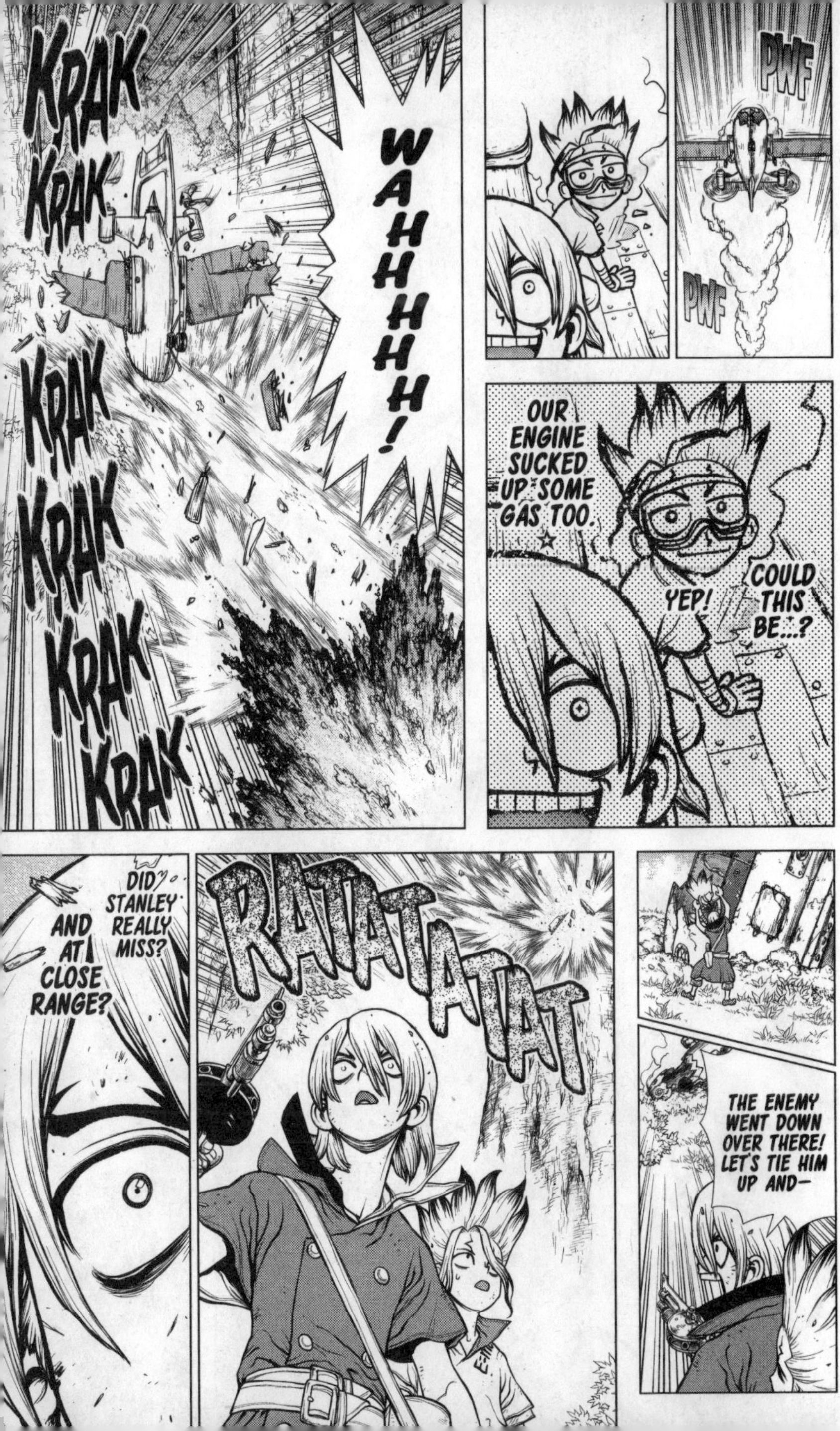
PWF
PWF
OUR ENGINE SUCKED UP SOME GAS TOO.
COULD THIS BE...?
YEP!
WAHHHHHHH!
KRAK KRAK
KRAK KRAK KRAK KRAK
THE ENEMY WENT DOWN OVER THERE! LET'S TIE HIM UP AND—
RATATATATAT
DID STANLEY REALLY MISS?
AND AT CLOSE RANGE?

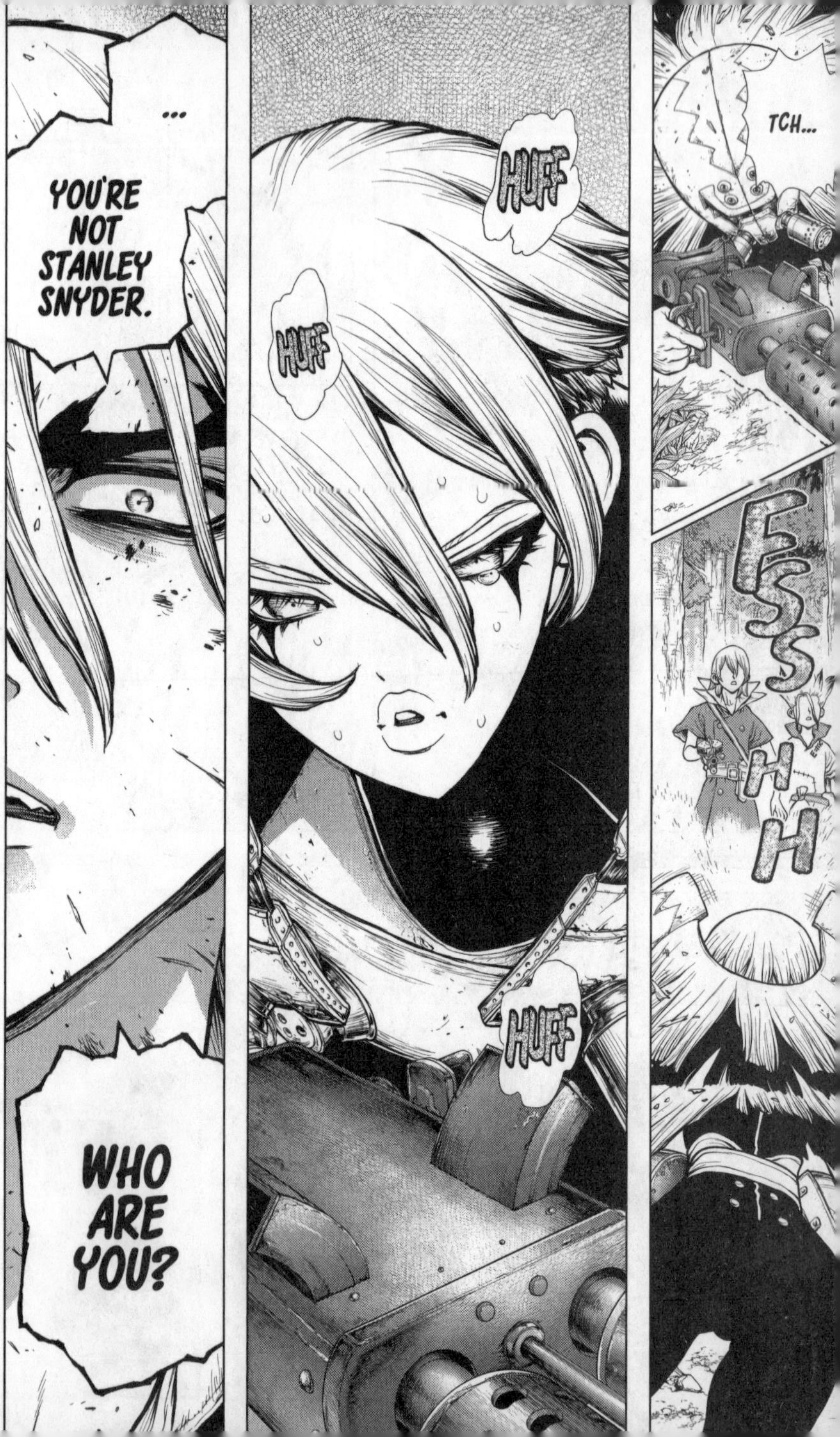
TCH...
FSSHH
HUFF
HUFF
HUFF
...
YOU'RE NOT STANLEY SNYDER.
WHO ARE YOU?

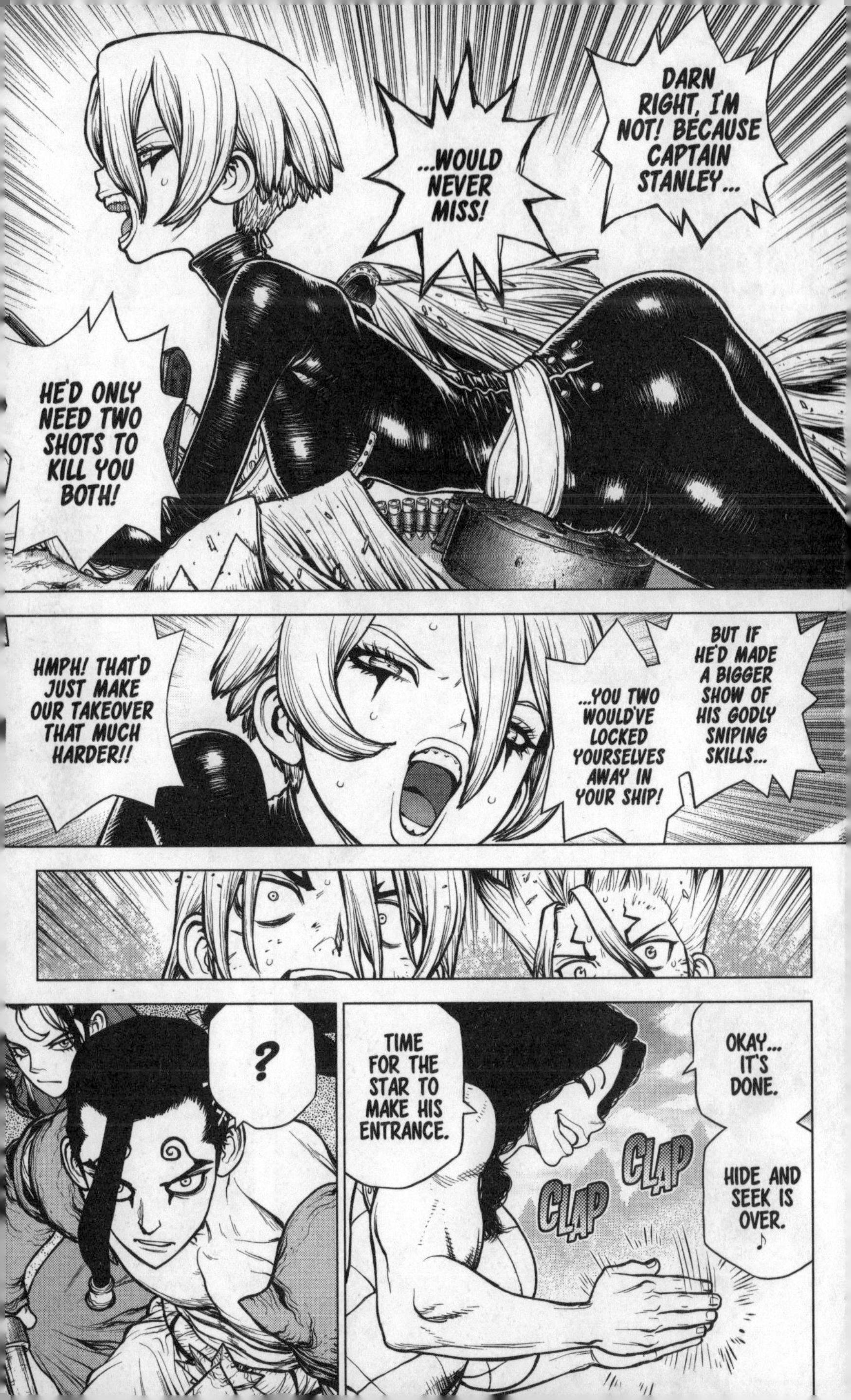
DARN RIGHT, I'M NOT! BECAUSE CAPTAIN STANLEY...
...WOULD NEVER MISS!
HE'D ONLY NEED TWO SHOTS TO KILL YOU BOTH!
BUT IF HE'D MADE A BIGGER SHOW OF HIS GODLY SNIPING SKILLS...
...YOU TWO WOULD'VE LOCKED YOURSELVES AWAY IN YOUR SHIP!
HMPH! THAT'D JUST MAKE OUR TAKEOVER THAT MUCH HARDER!!
OKAY... IT'S DONE.
HIDE AND SEEK IS OVER. ♪
CLAP
CLAP
TIME FOR THE STAR TO MAKE HIS ENTRANCE.
?

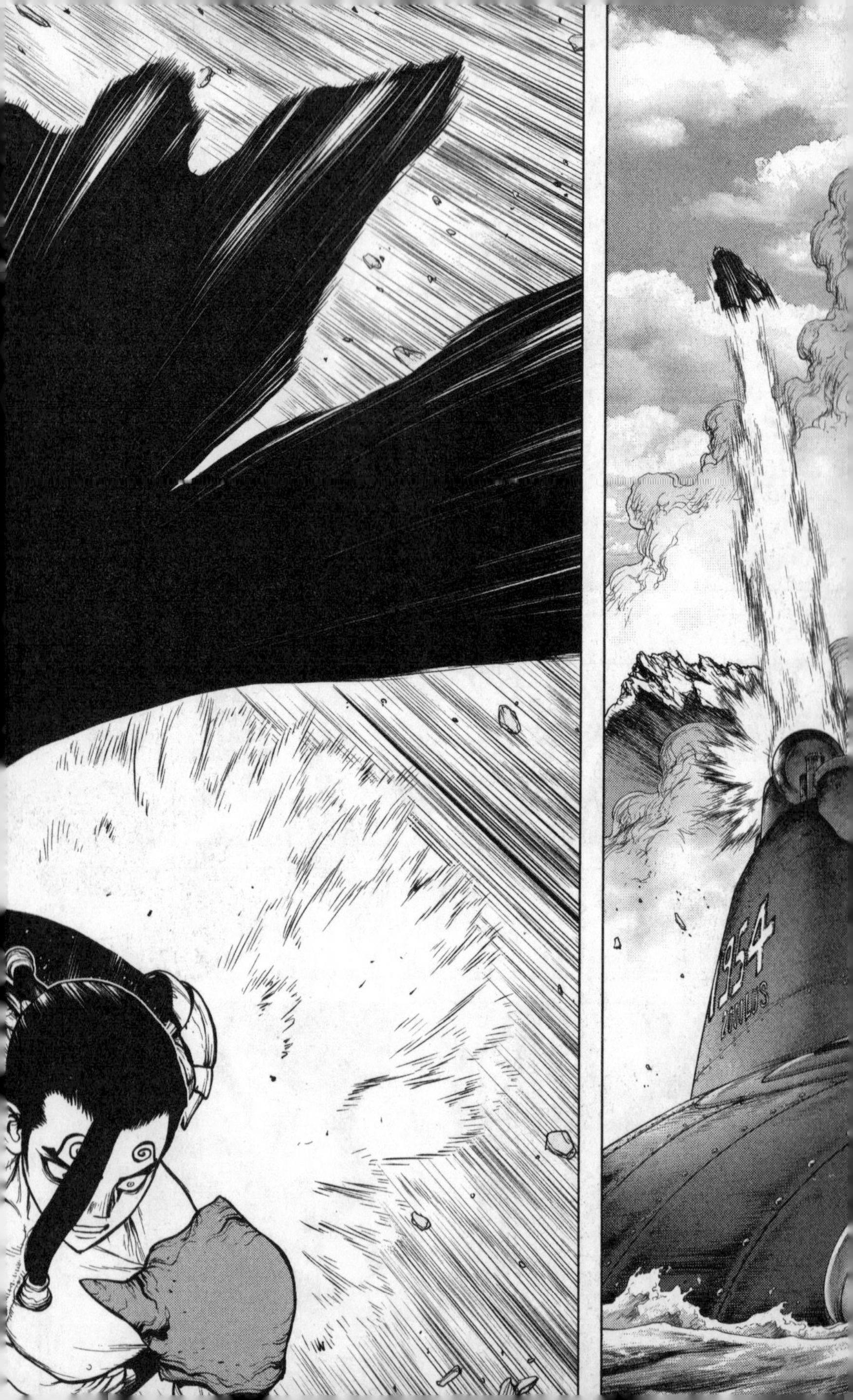
1954

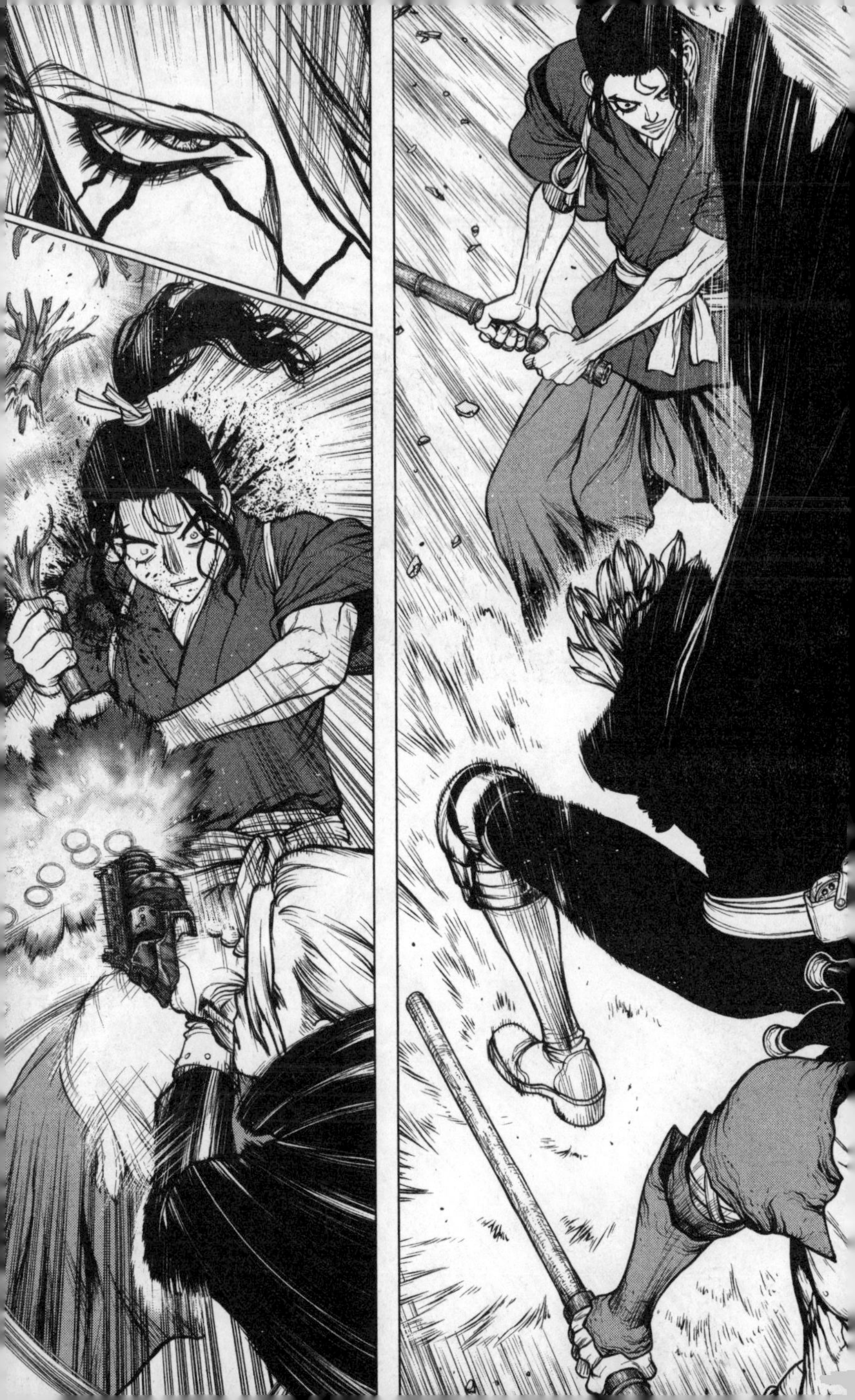

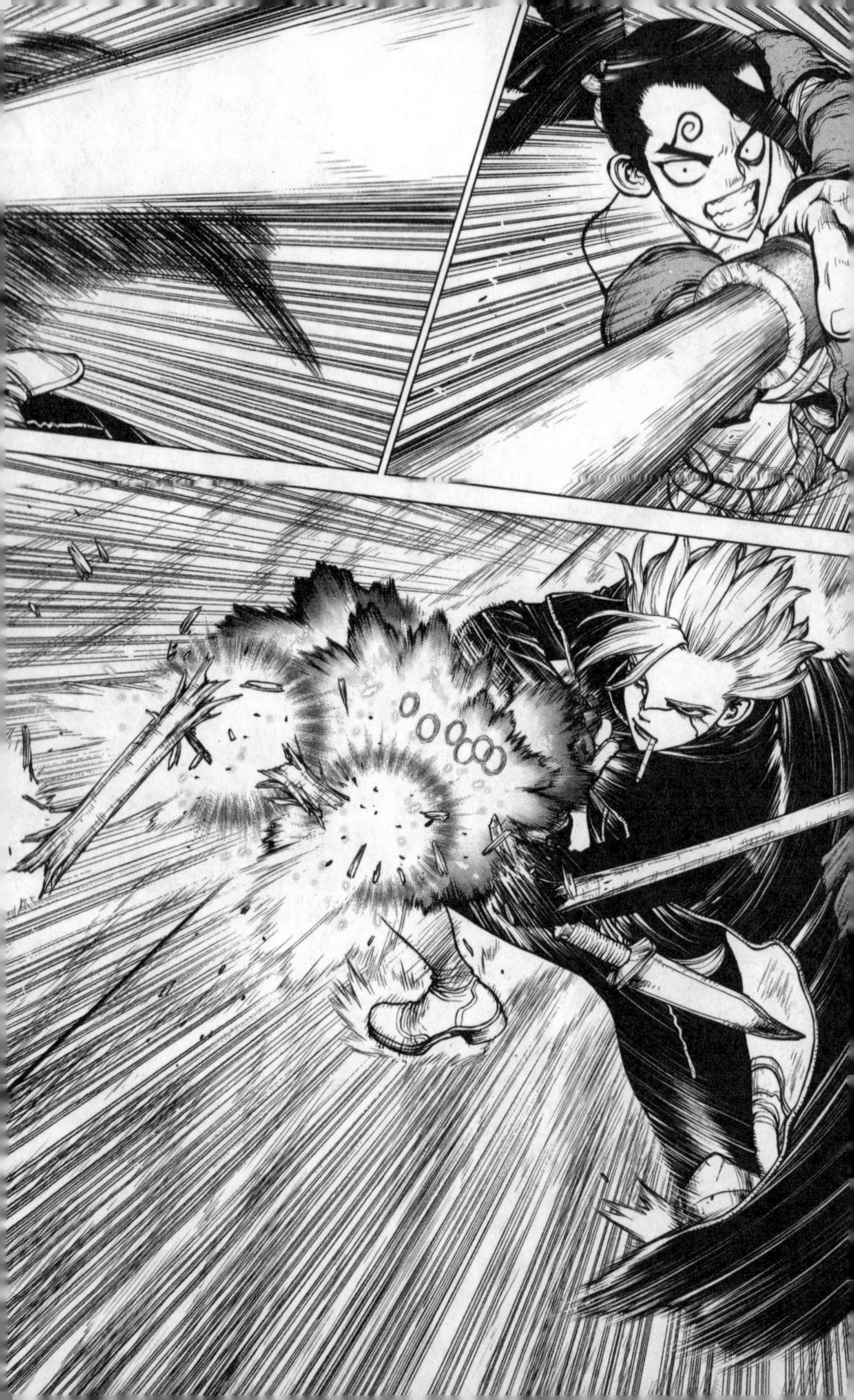

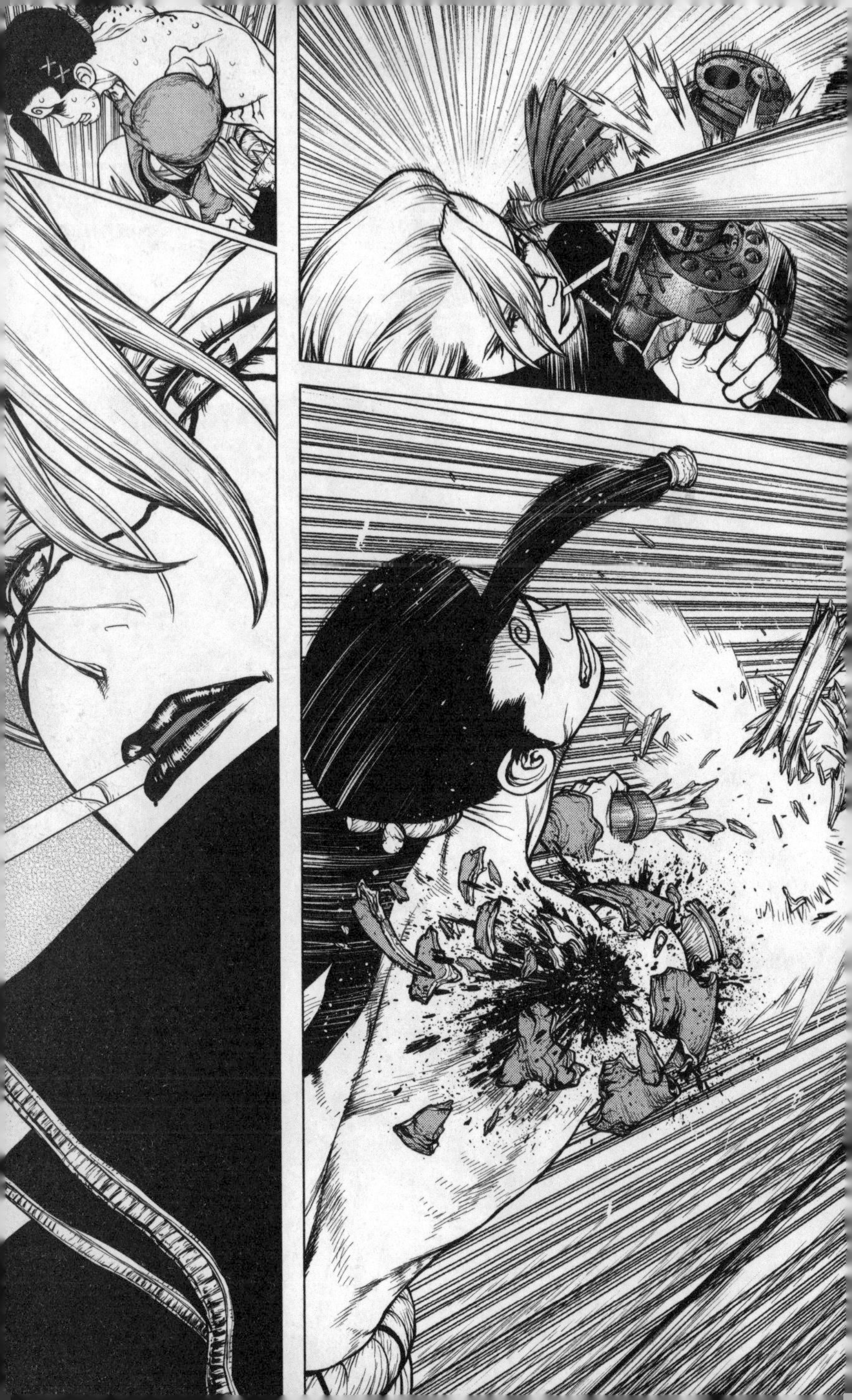

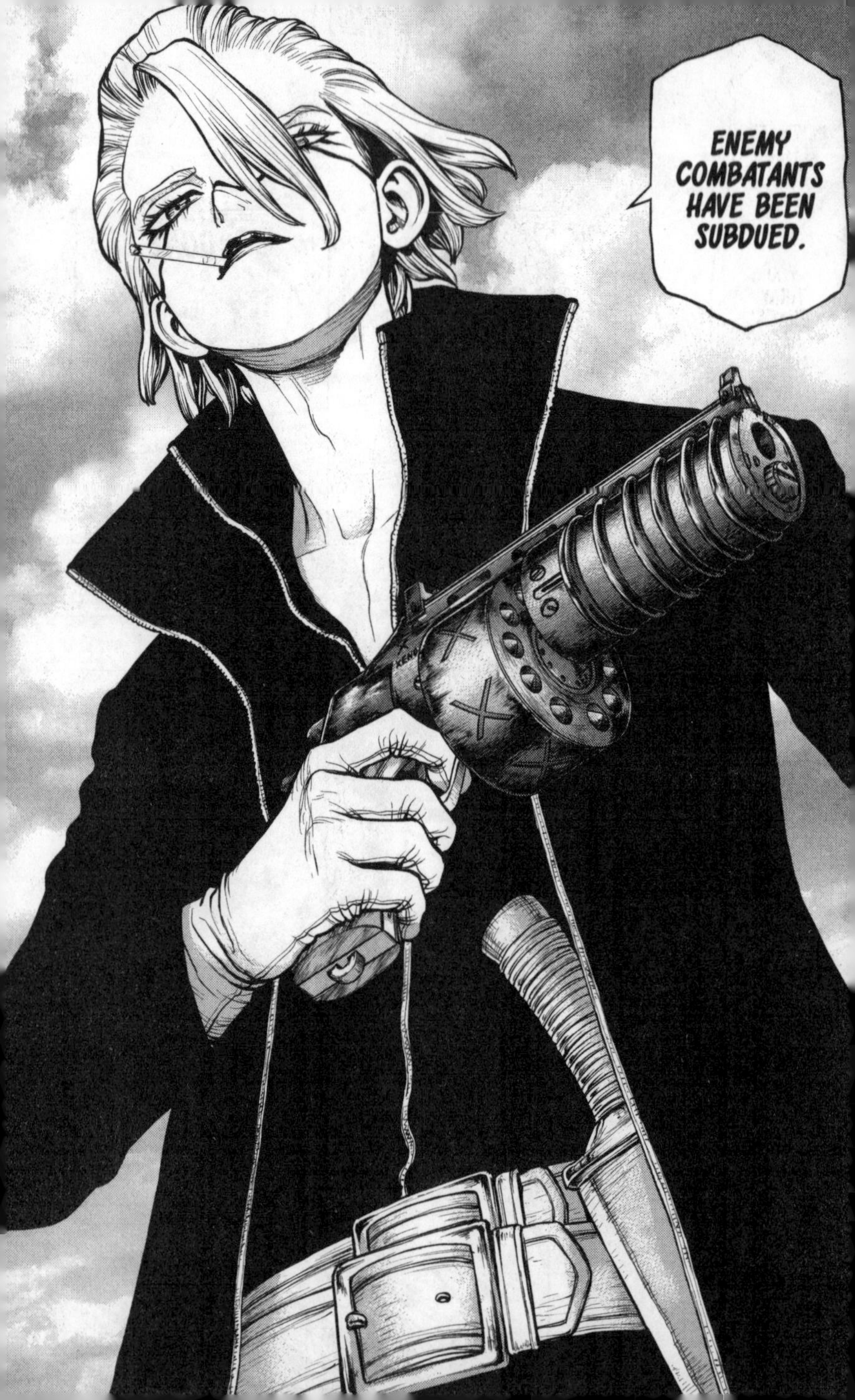
ENEMY COMBATANTS HAVE BEEN SUBDUED.

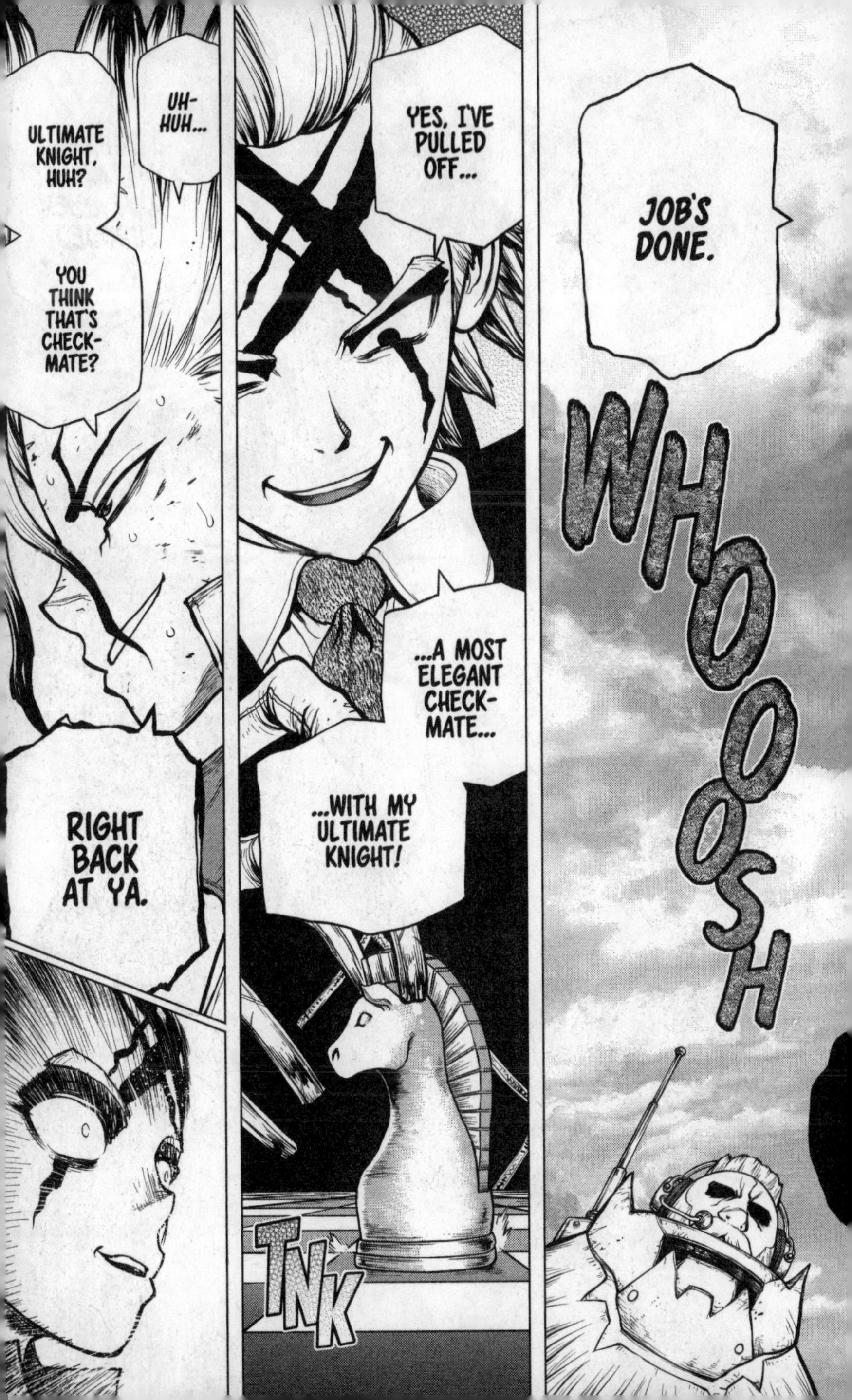

JOB'S DONE.
WHOOOOSH
YES, I'VE PULLED OFF...
...A MOST ELEGANT CHECKMATE...
...WITH MY ULTIMATE KNIGHT!
TNK
UH-HUH...
ULTIMATE KNIGHT, HUH?
YOU THINK THAT'S CHECKMATE?
RIGHT BACK AT YA.

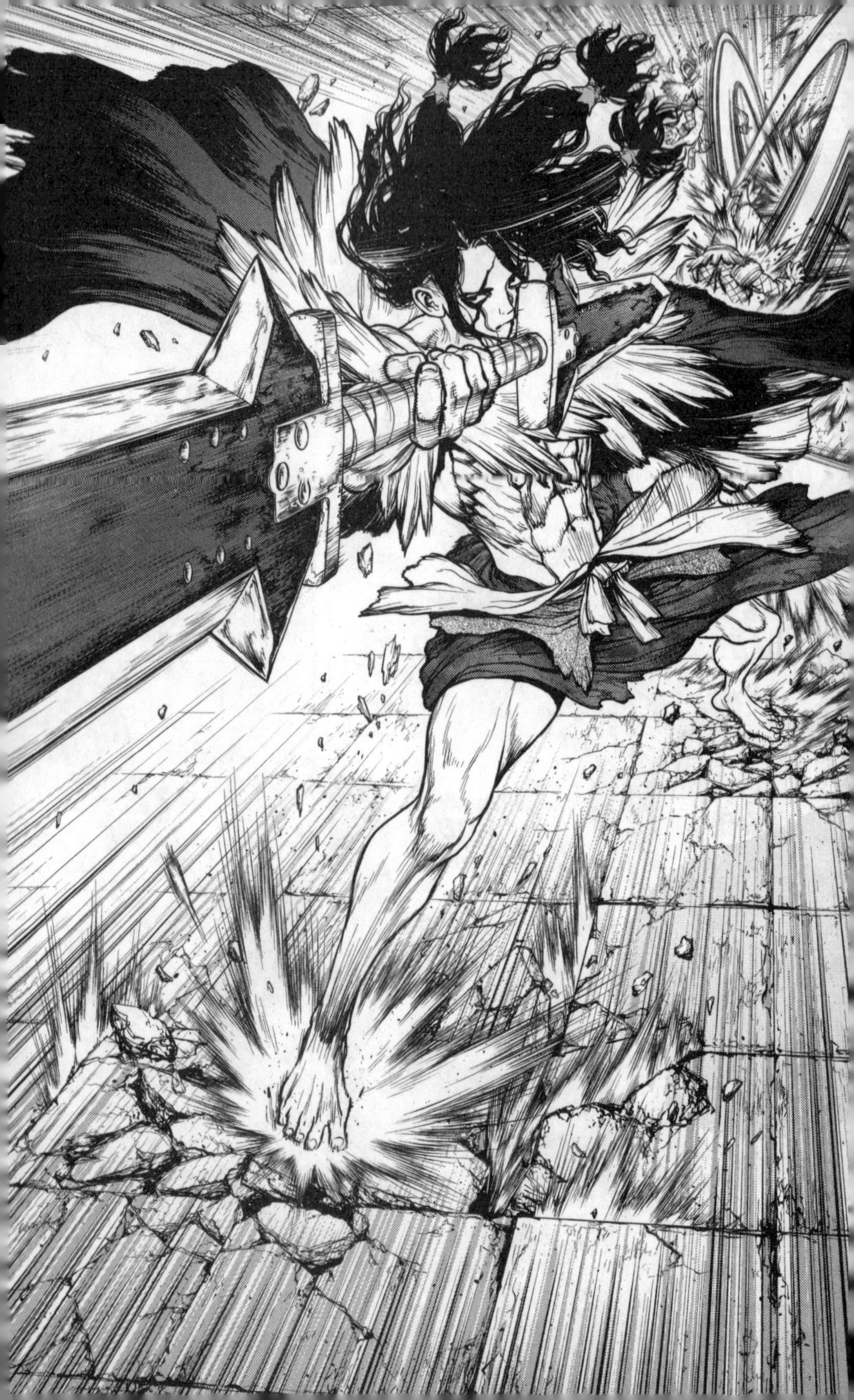

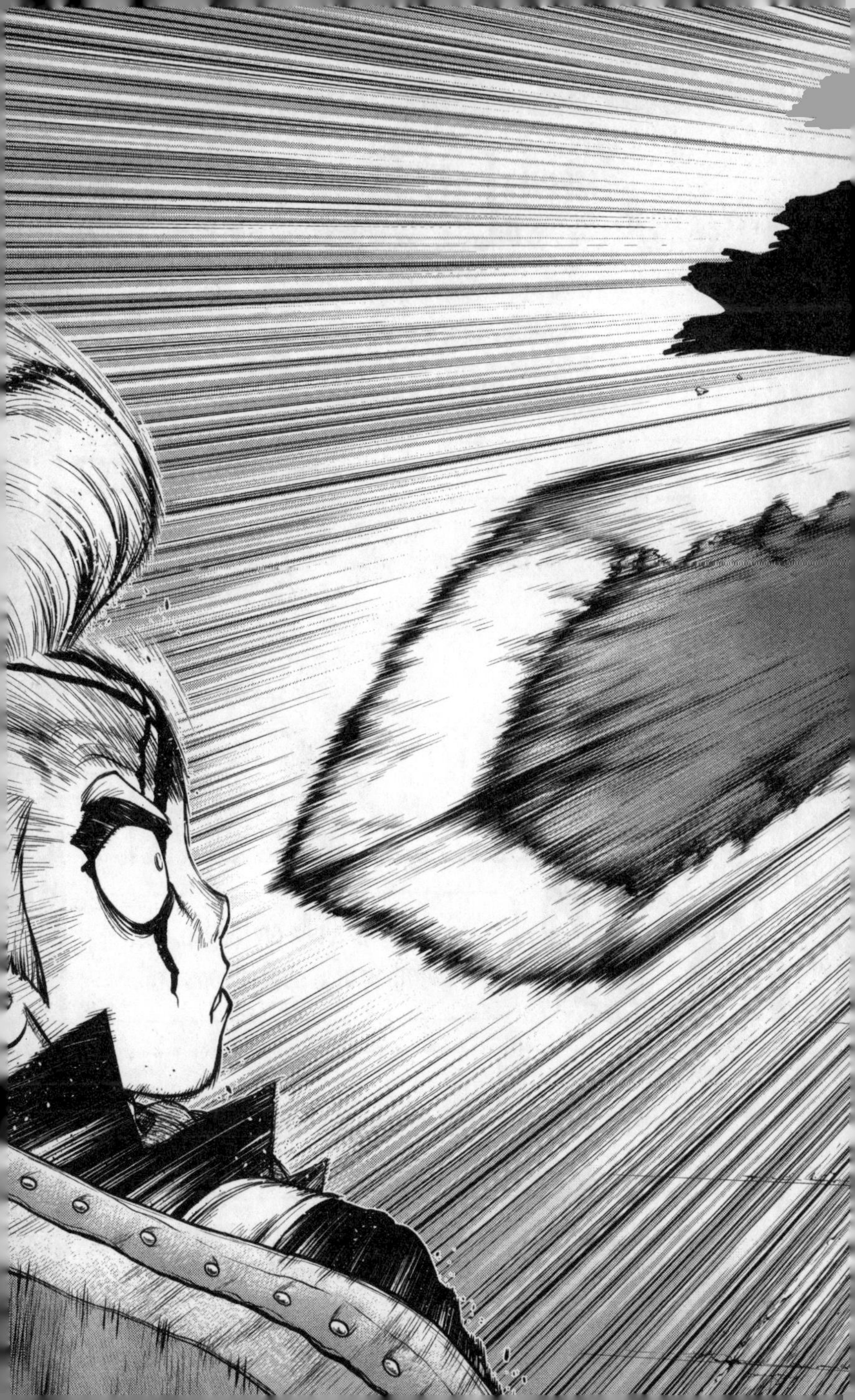

MECHA SENKU Q&A

SEARCH

Question Corner

Stanley shot Senku, but has he
ever killed anyone before the earth
turned into the Stone World?

K.M. from Hokkaido SEARCH

Sure have. While on the job, as
a member of a special-ops unit.

And so on and so forth! Any questions at all!!

This Q&A section is currently being held in
Japan for use in Japanese graphic novels.

Z=167: Different Strokes

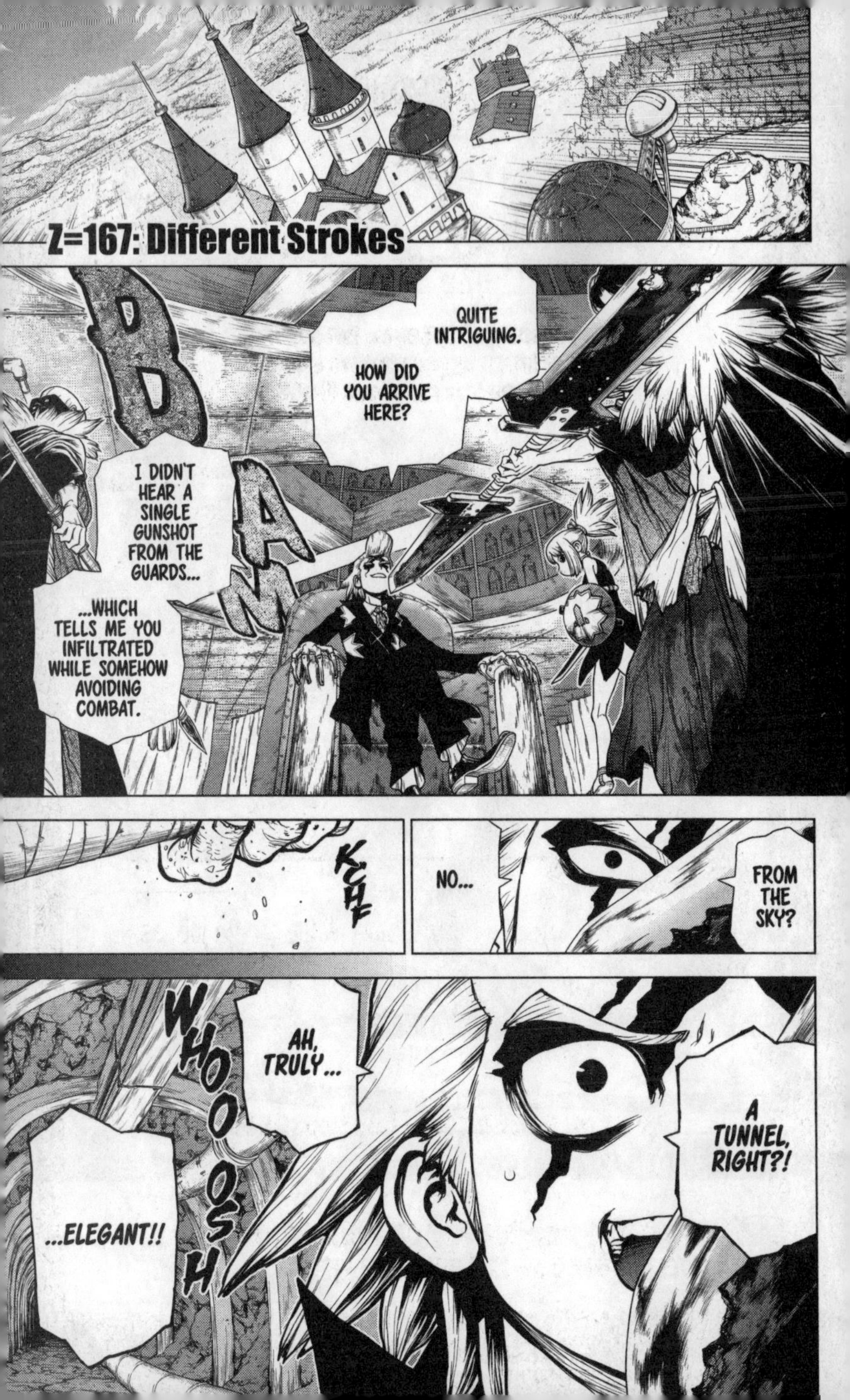
QUITE INTRIGUING.
HOW DID YOU ARRIVE HERE?
BAM
I DIDN'T HEAR A SINGLE GUNSHOT FROM THE GUARDS...
...WHICH TELLS ME YOU INFILTRATED WHILE SOMEHOW AVOIDING COMBAT.
FROM THE SKY?
NO...
K'CHF
A TUNNEL, RIGHT?!
AH, TRULY...
WHOOOOSH
...ELEGANT!!

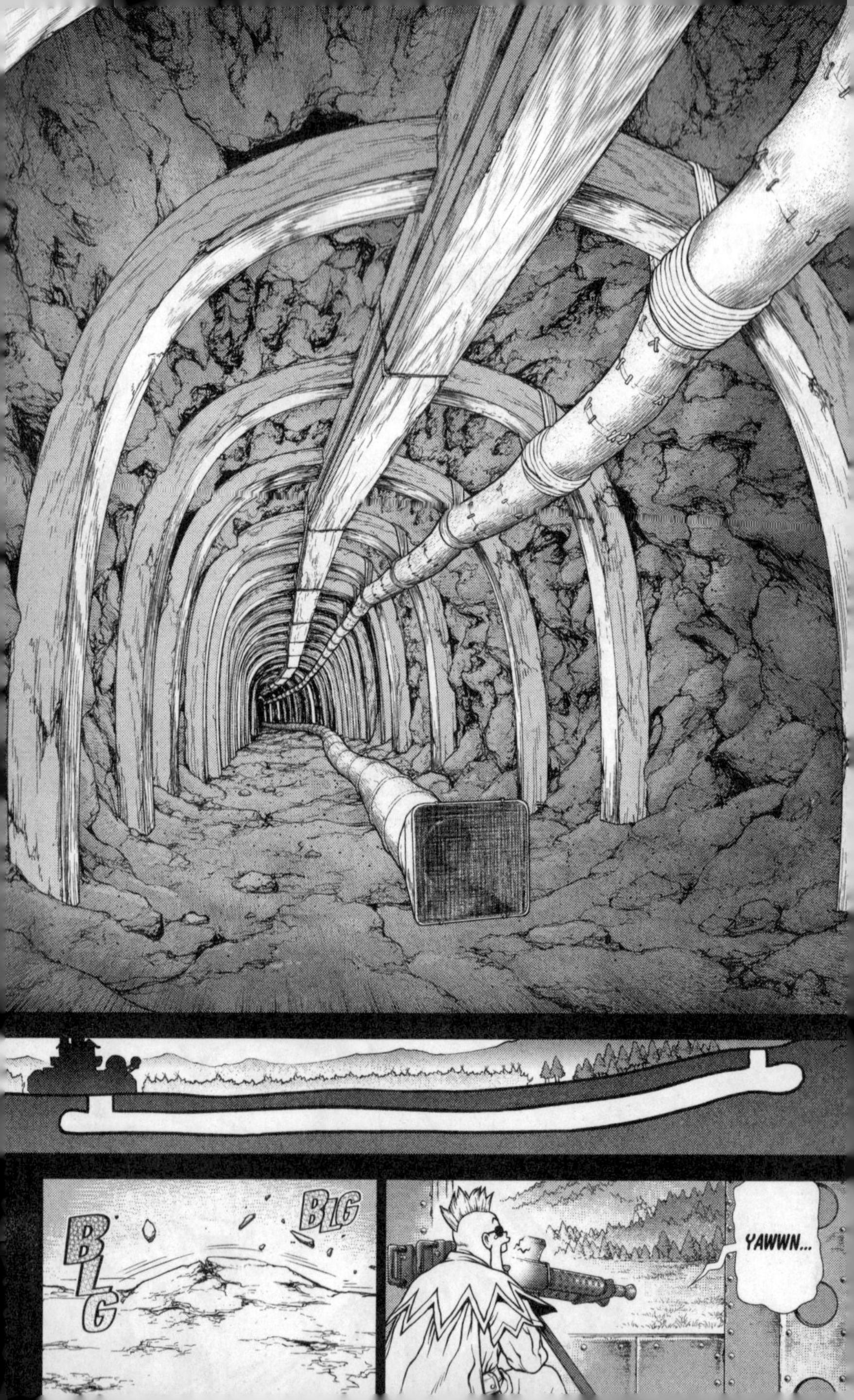
YAWWN...
BLG
BLG

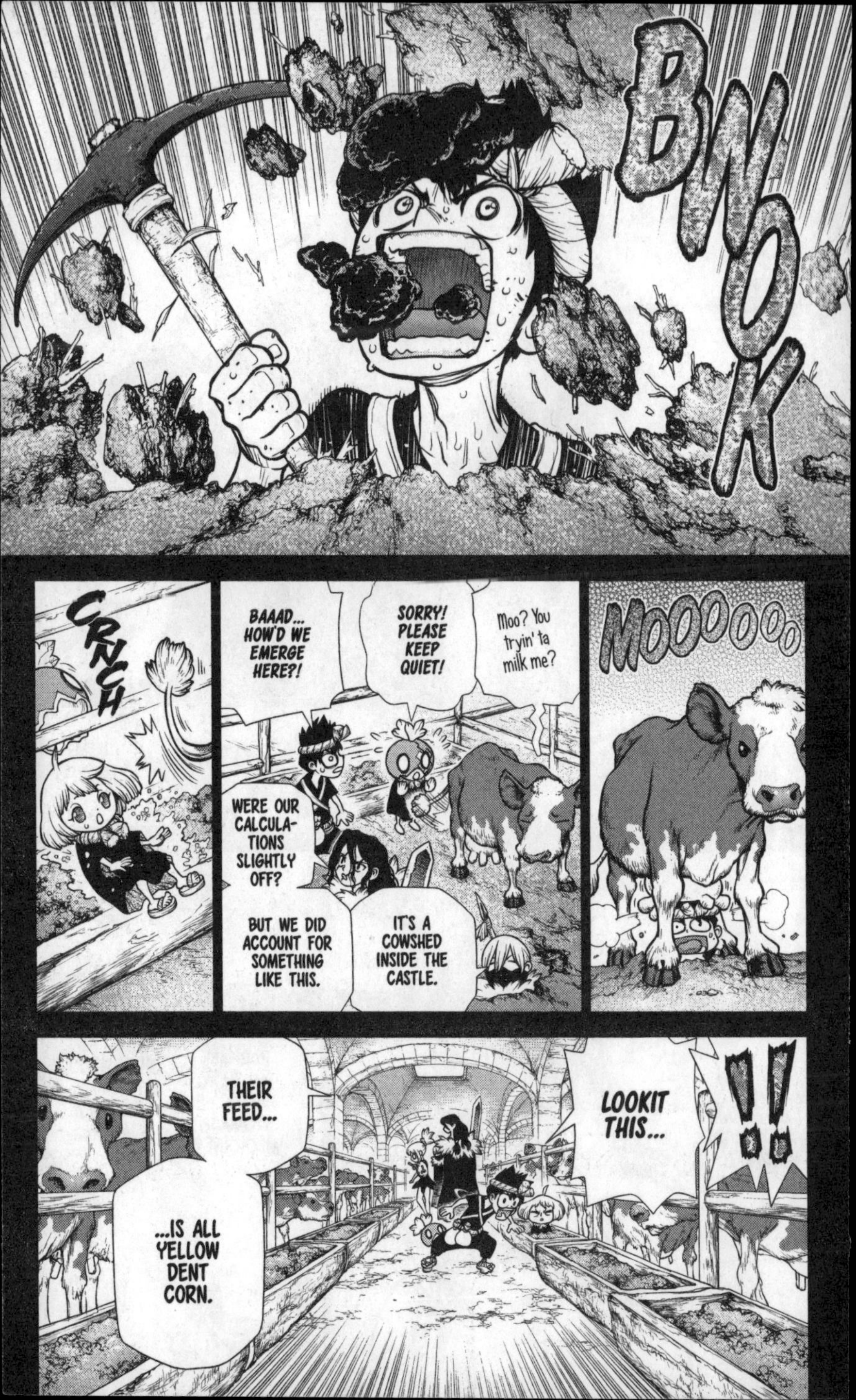
BWOOK
MOOOOOOO
Moo? You tryin' ta milk me?
SORRY! PLEASE KEEP QUIET!
BAAAD... HOW'D WE EMERGE HERE?!
WERE OUR CALCULATIONS SLIGHTLY OFF?
BUT WE DID ACCOUNT FOR SOMETHING LIKE THIS.
IT'S A COWSHED INSIDE THE CASTLE.
CRNCH
!!
LOOKIT THIS...
THEIR FEED...
...IS ALL YELLOW DENT CORN.

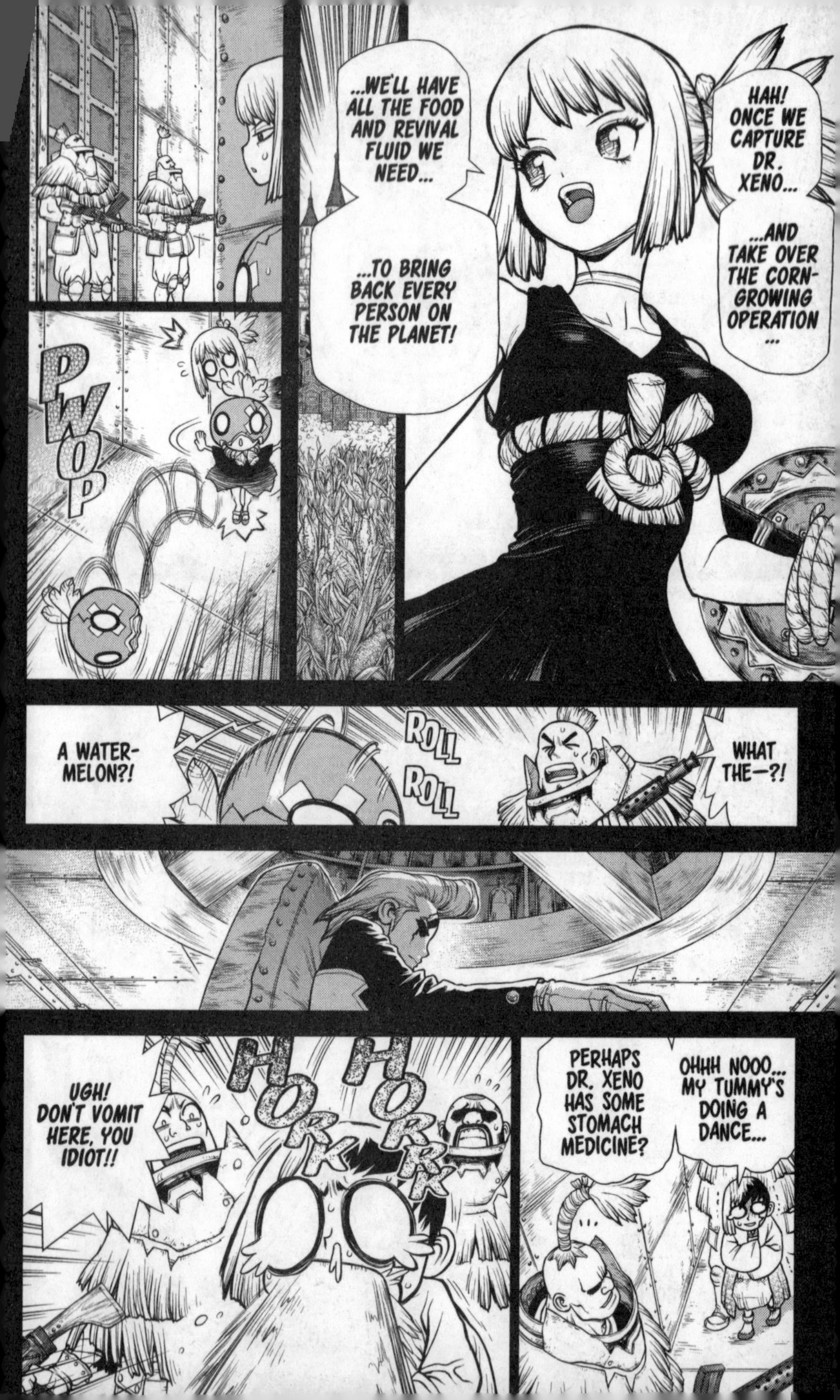
HAH! ONCE WE CAPTURE DR. XENO...
...AND TAKE OVER THE CORN-GROWING OPERATION...
...WE'LL HAVE ALL THE FOOD AND REVIVAL FLUID WE NEED...
...TO BRING BACK EVERY PERSON ON THE PLANET!
PWOP
WHAT THE—?!
ROLL ROLL
A WATER-MELON?!
OHHH NOOO... MY TUMMY'S DOING A DANCE...
PERHAPS DR. XENO HAS SOME STOMACH MEDICINE?
HORK HORK
UGH! DON'T VOMIT HERE, YOU IDIOT!!

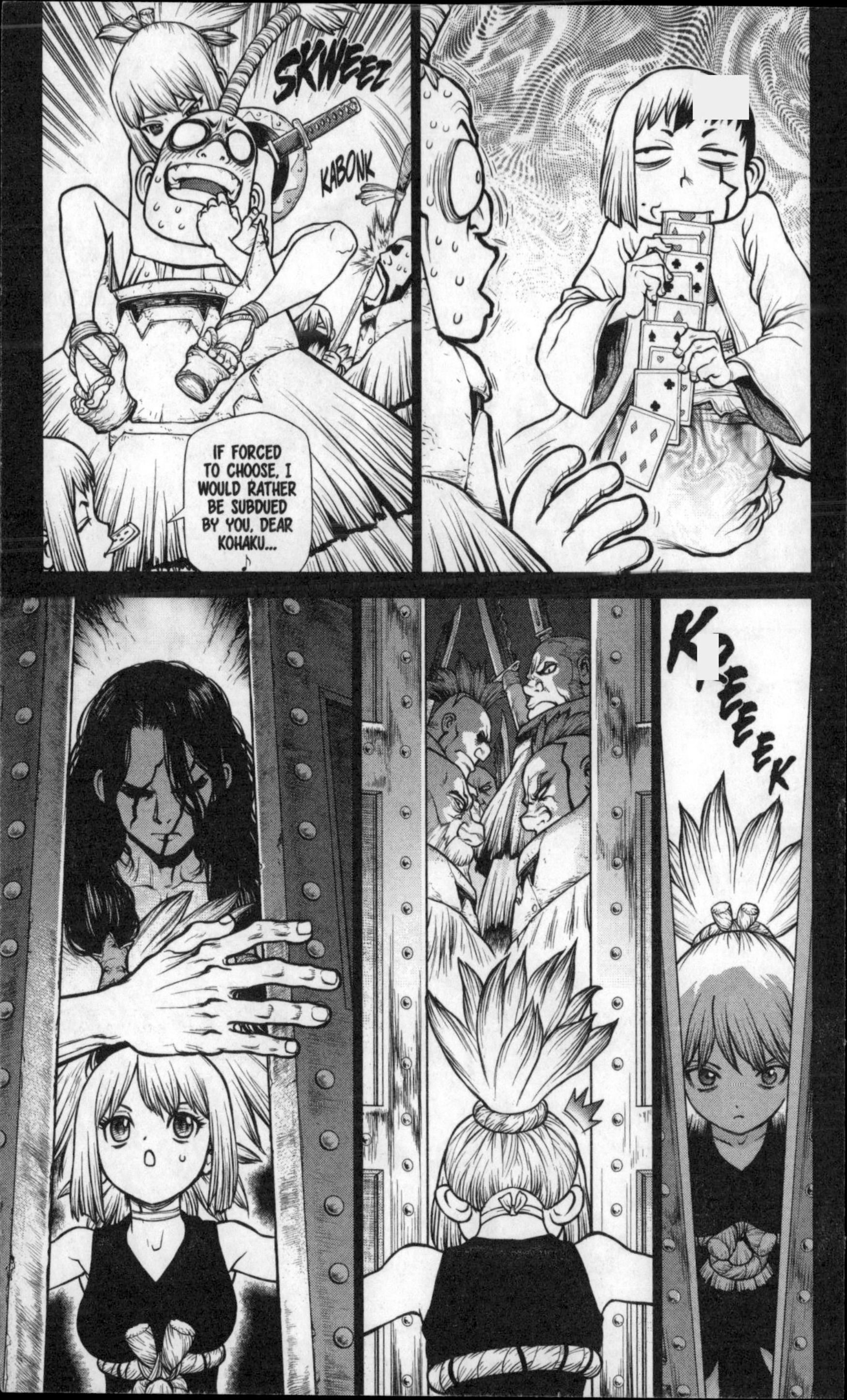

SKWEEZ
KABONK
IF FORCED TO CHOOSE, I WOULD RATHER BE SUBDUED BY YOU, DEAR KOHAKU... ♪
K EEEEK

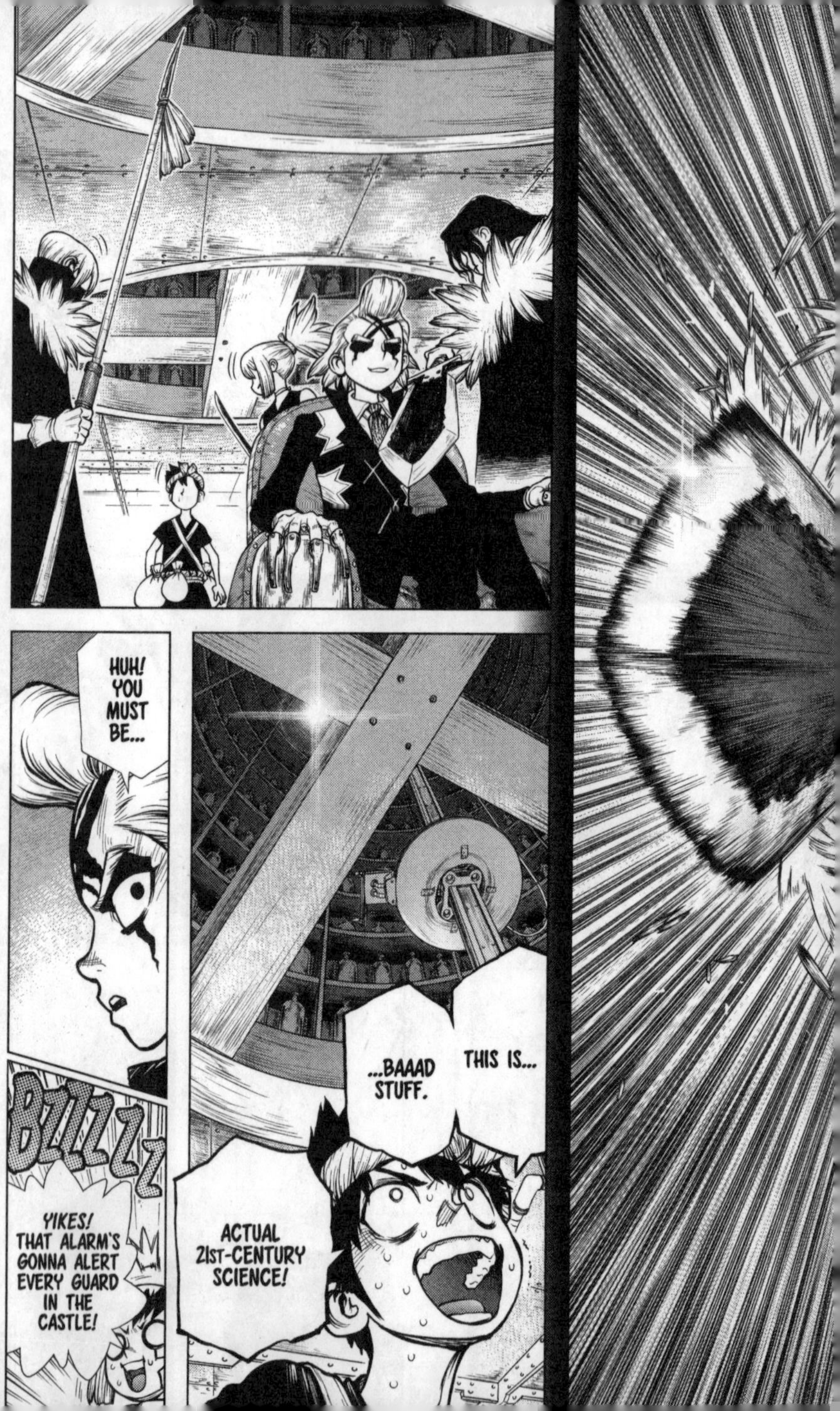
THIS IS...
...BAAAD STUFF.
ACTUAL 21ST-CENTURY SCIENCE!
HUH! YOU MUST BE...
BZZZZZ
YIKES! THAT ALARM'S GONNA ALERT EVERY GUARD IN THE CASTLE!

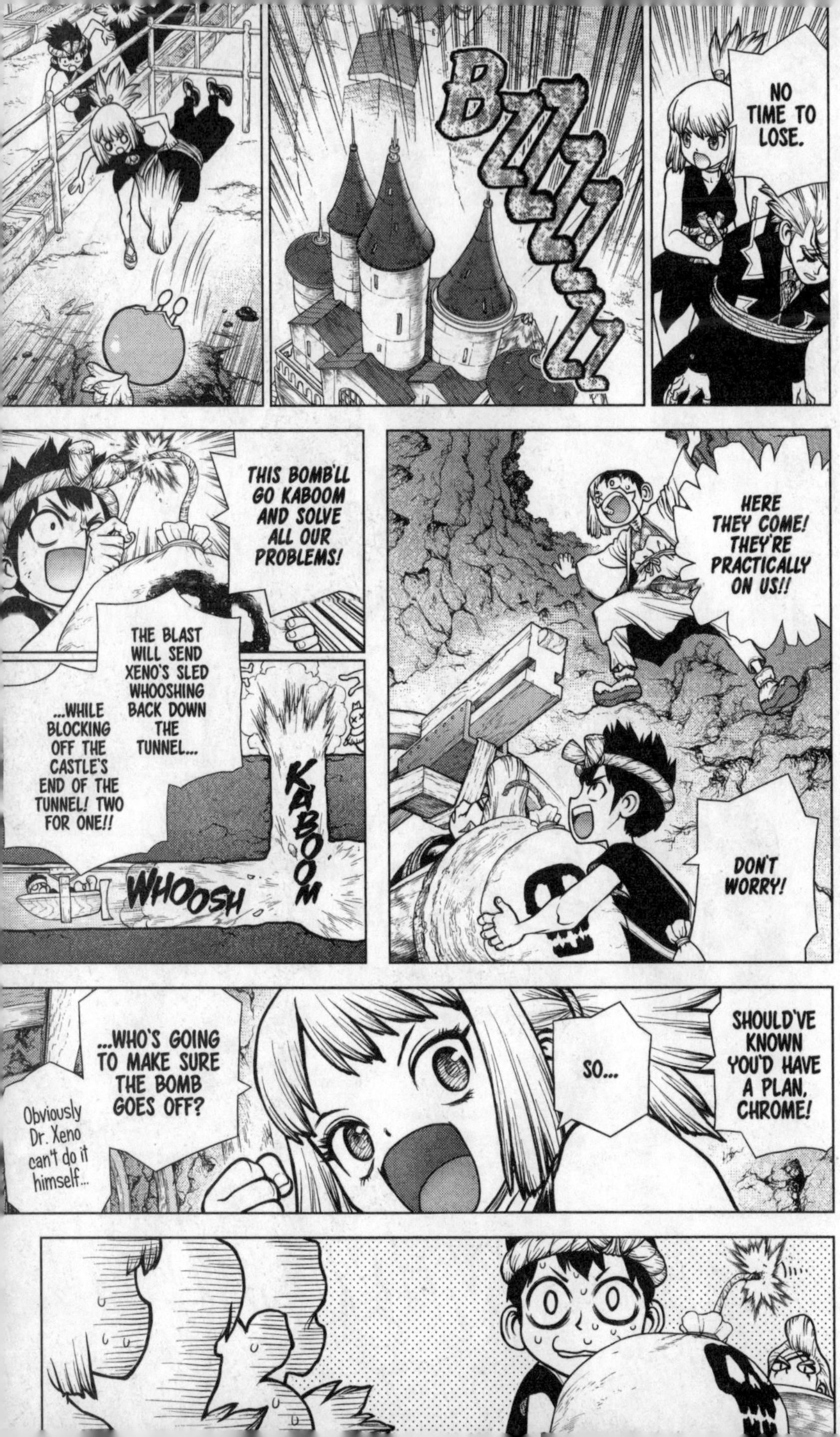
NO TIME TO LOSE.
BZZZZZZZ
HERE THEY COME! THEY'RE PRACTICALLY ON US!!
DON'T WORRY!
THIS BOMB'LL GO KABOOM AND SOLVE ALL OUR PROBLEMS!
THE BLAST WILL SEND XENO'S SLED WHOOSHING BACK DOWN THE TUNNEL...
...WHILE BLOCKING OFF THE CASTLE'S END OF THE TUNNEL! TWO FOR ONE!!
KABOOM
WHOOSH
SHOULD'VE KNOWN YOU'D HAVE A PLAN, CHROME!
SO...
...WHO'S GOING TO MAKE SURE THE BOMB GOES OFF?
Obviously Dr. Xeno can't do it himself...

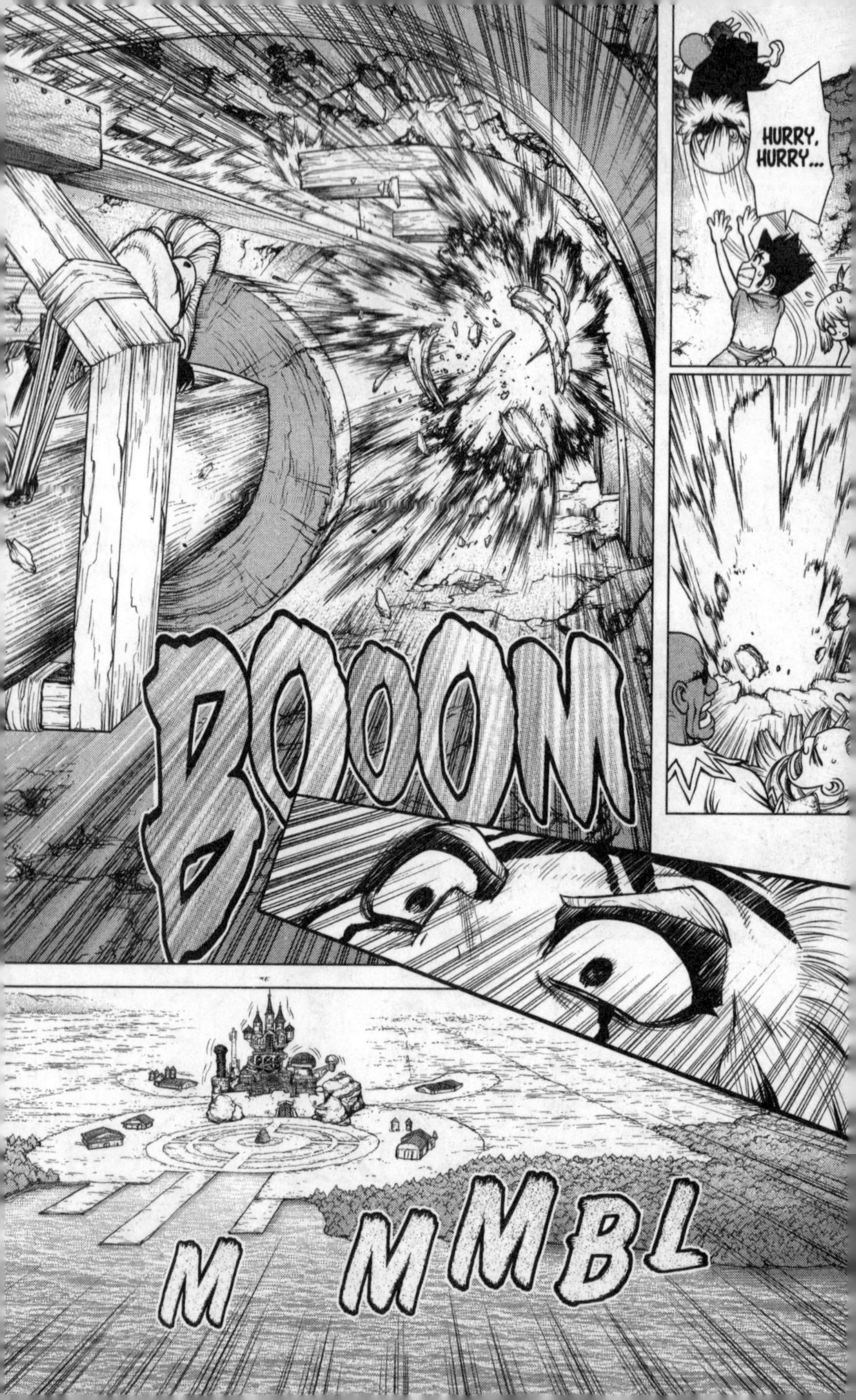
HURRY, HURRY...
BOOOM
M MMBL

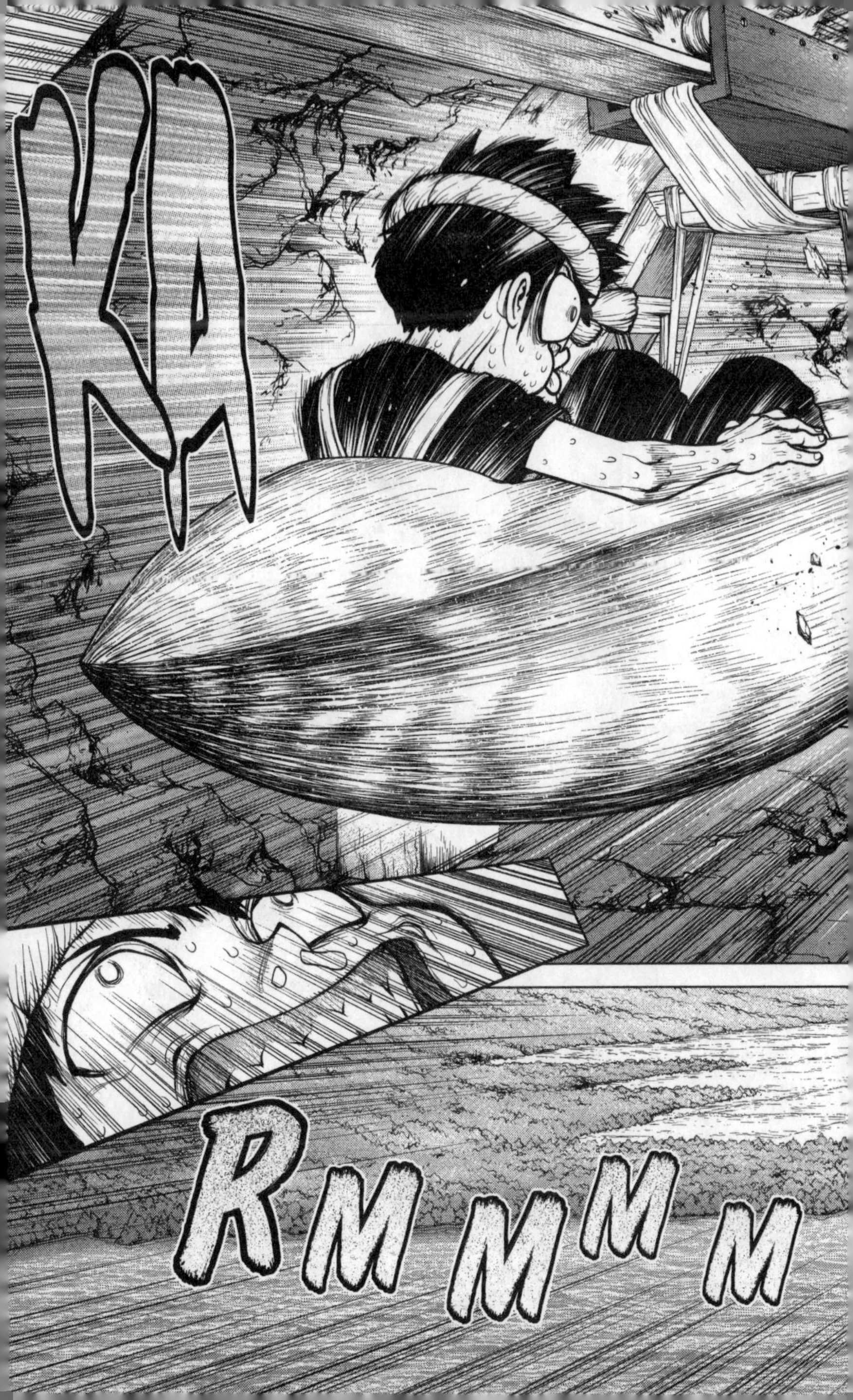
RMMMM

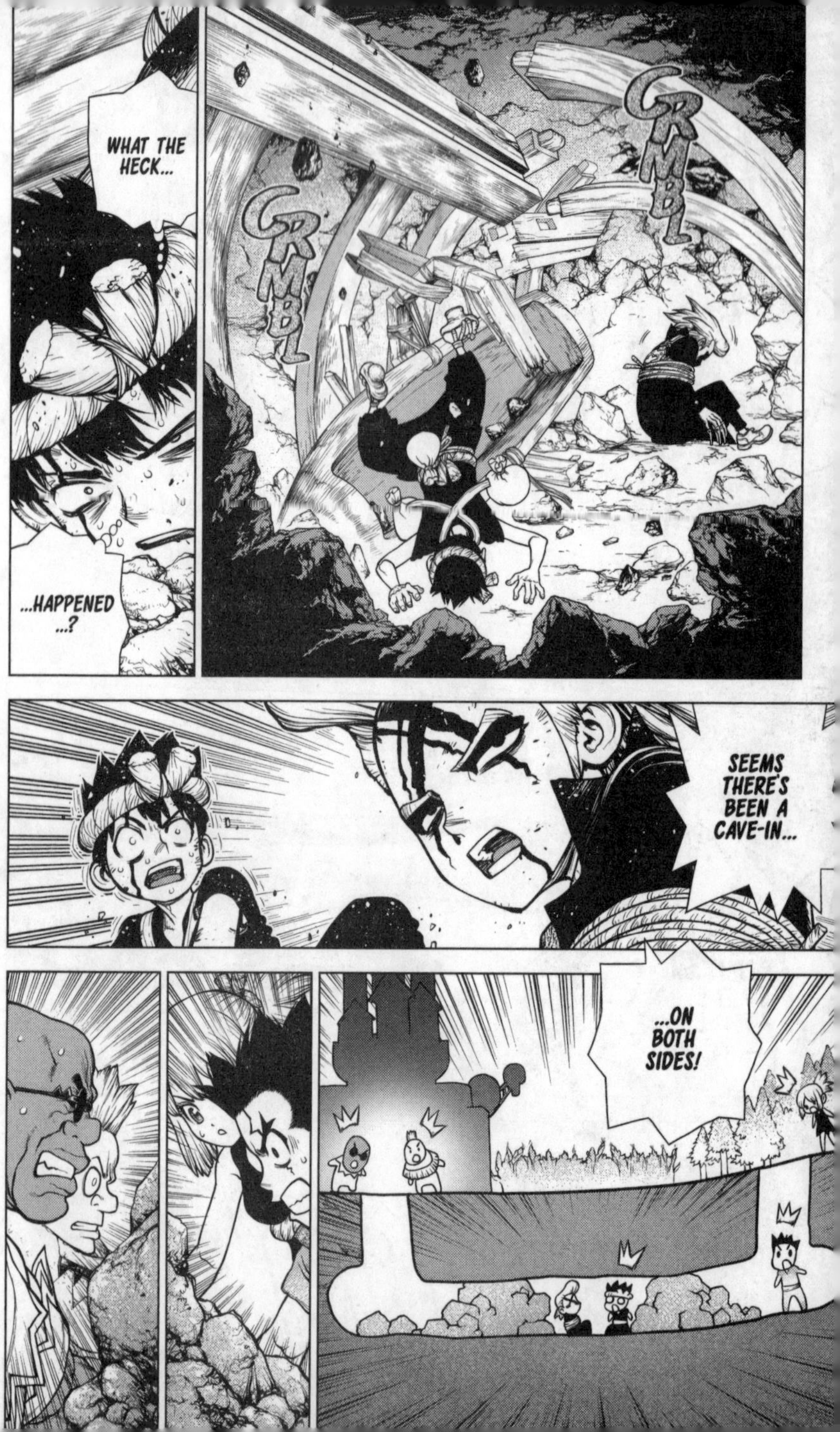
GRMBL
GRMBL
WHAT THE HECK...
...HAPPENED ...?
SEEMS THERE'S BEEN A CAVE-IN...
...ON BOTH SIDES!

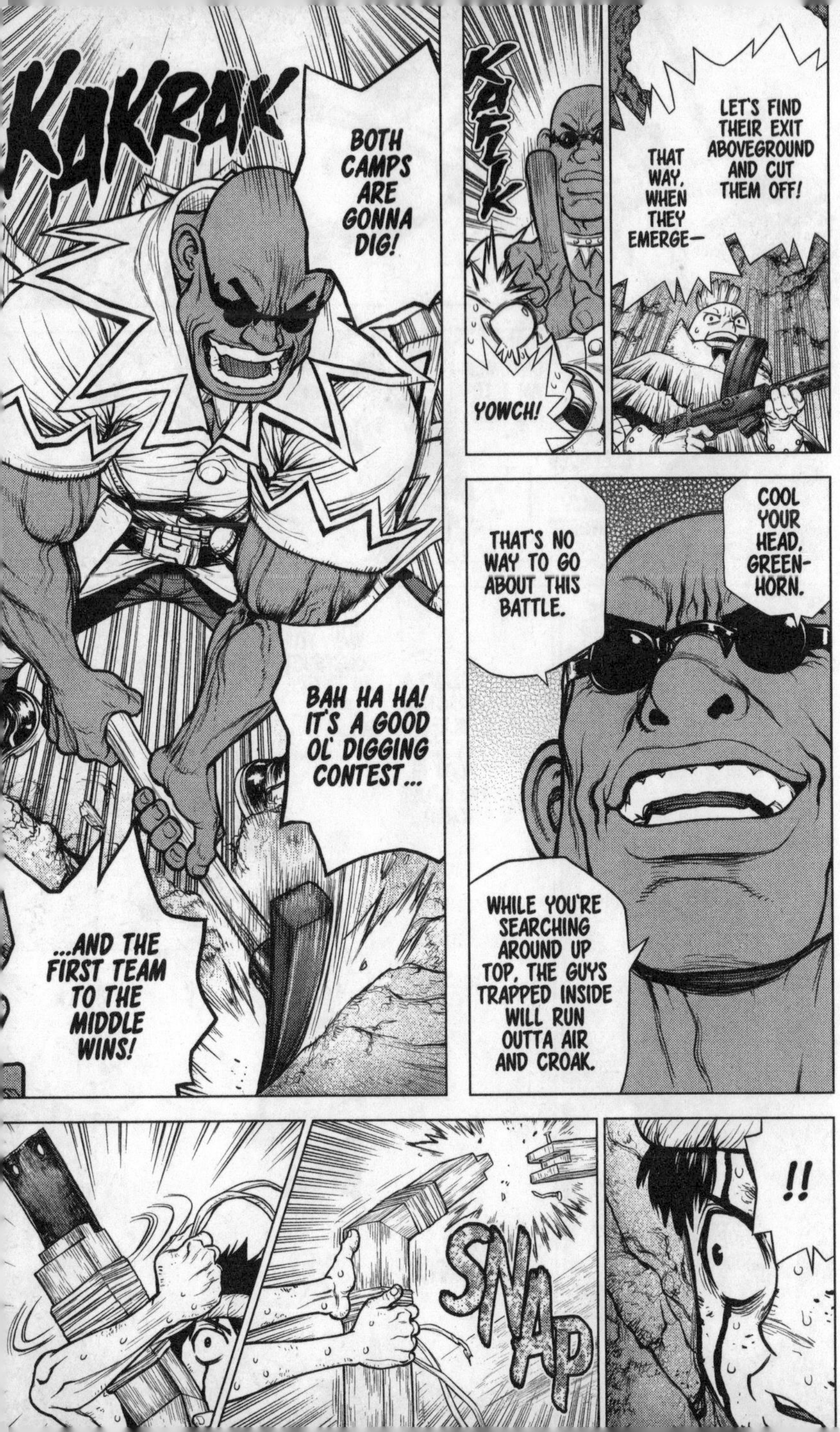
LET'S FIND THEIR EXIT ABOVEGROUND AND CUT THEM OFF!
THAT WAY, WHEN THEY EMERGE—
KAFLIK
YOWCH!
COOL YOUR HEAD, GREEN-HORN.
THAT'S NO WAY TO GO ABOUT THIS BATTLE.
WHILE YOU'RE SEARCHING AROUND UP TOP, THE GUYS TRAPPED INSIDE WILL RUN OUTTA AIR AND CROAK.
KAKRAK
BOTH CAMPS ARE GONNA DIG!
BAH HA HA! IT'S A GOOD OL' DIGGING CONTEST...
...AND THE FIRST TEAM TO THE MIDDLE WINS!
!!
SNAP

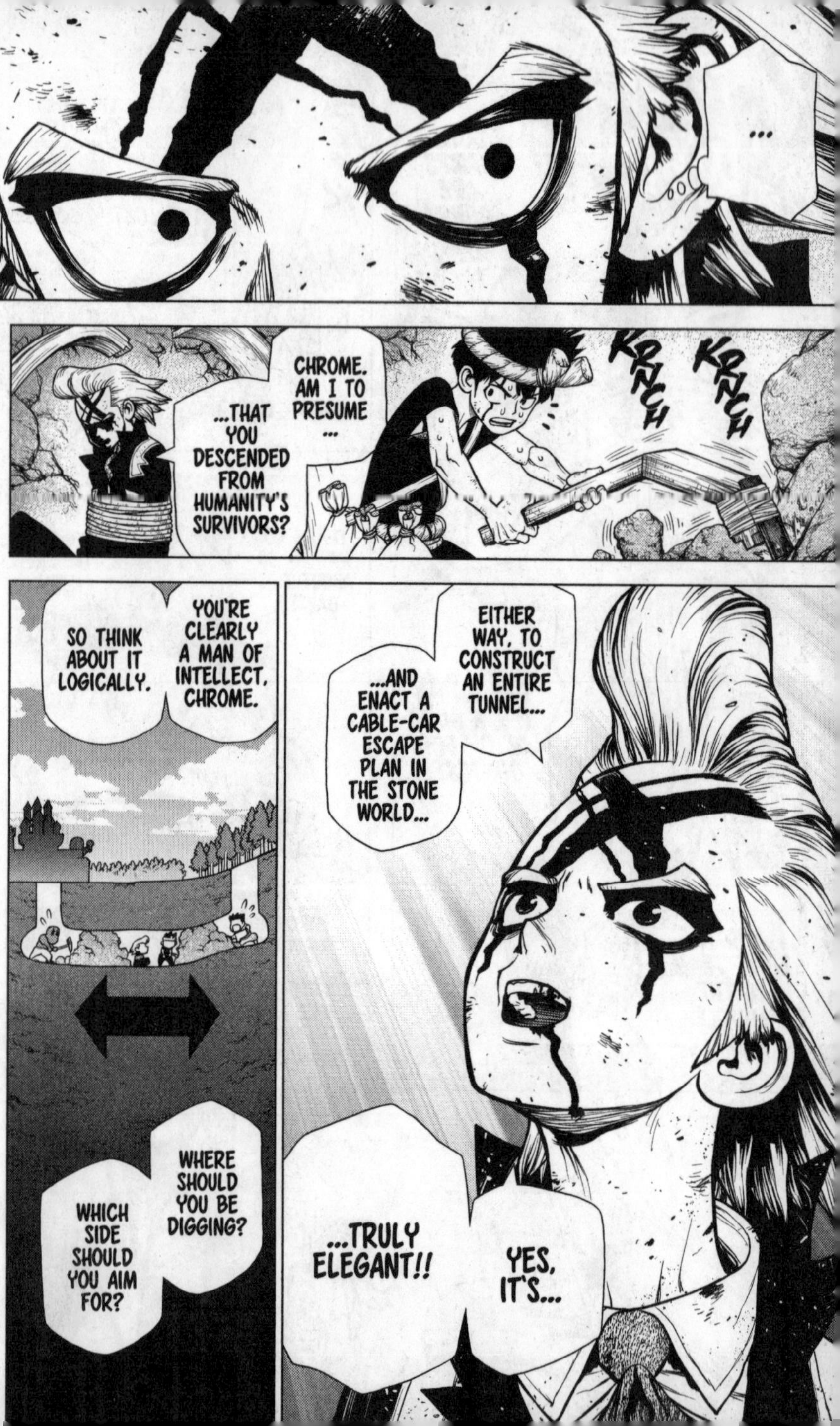
...
KRNCH
KRNCH
CHROME. AM I TO PRESUME...
...THAT YOU DESCENDED FROM HUMANITY'S SURVIVORS?
EITHER WAY, TO CONSTRUCT AN ENTIRE TUNNEL...
...AND ENACT A CABLE-CAR ESCAPE PLAN IN THE STONE WORLD...
YES, IT'S...
...TRULY ELEGANT!!
YOU'RE CLEARLY A MAN OF INTELLECT, CHROME.
SO THINK ABOUT IT LOGICALLY.
WHERE SHOULD YOU BE DIGGING?
WHICH SIDE SHOULD YOU AIM FOR?

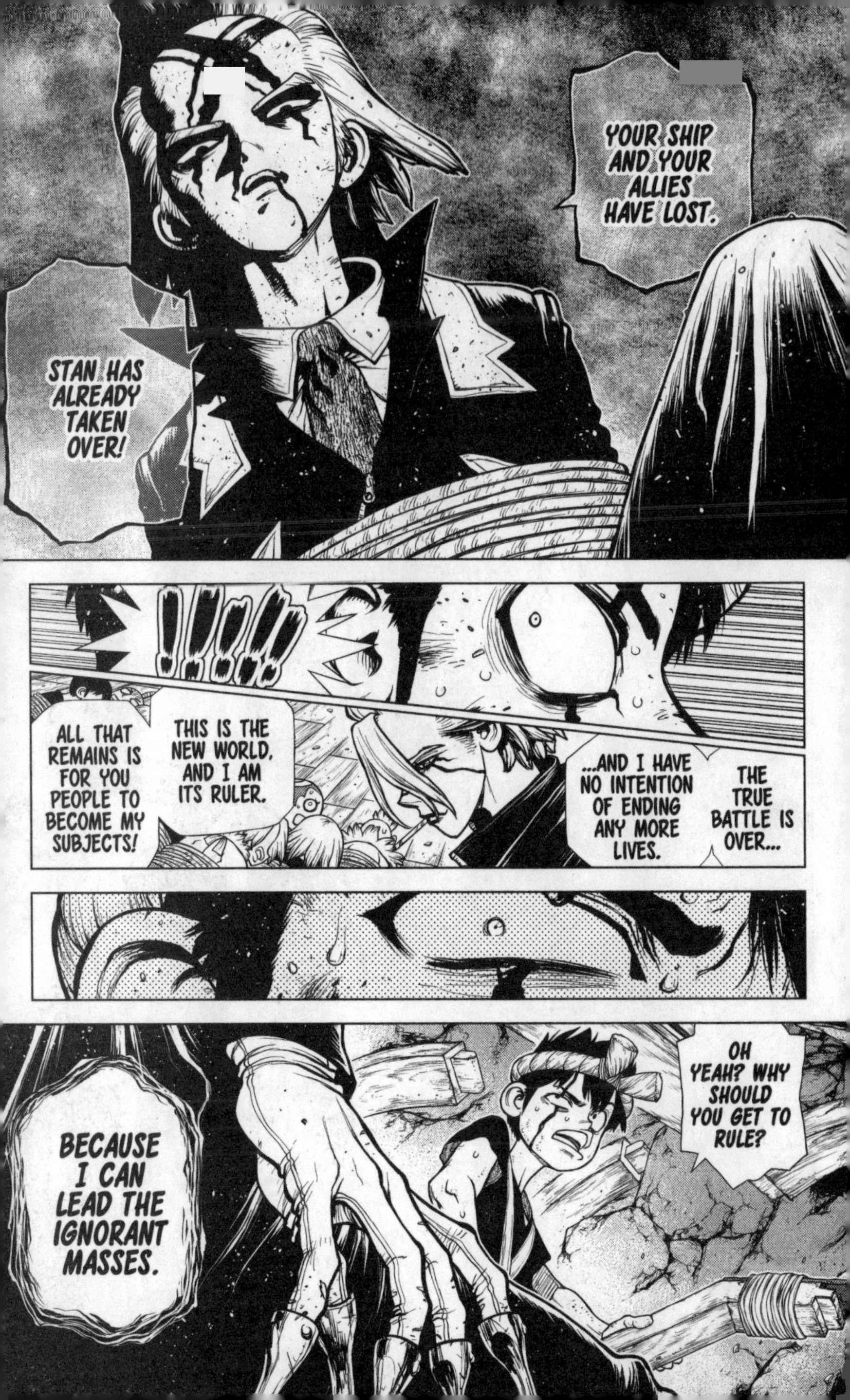
YOUR SHIP AND YOUR ALLIES HAVE LOST.
STAN HAS ALREADY TAKEN OVER!
!!!!!
THE TRUE BATTLE IS OVER...
...AND I HAVE NO INTENTION OF ENDING ANY MORE LIVES.
THIS IS THE NEW WORLD, AND I AM ITS RULER.
ALL THAT REMAINS IS FOR YOU PEOPLE TO BECOME MY SUBJECTS!
OH YEAH? WHY SHOULD YOU GET TO RULE?
BECAUSE I CAN LEAD THE IGNORANT MASSES.

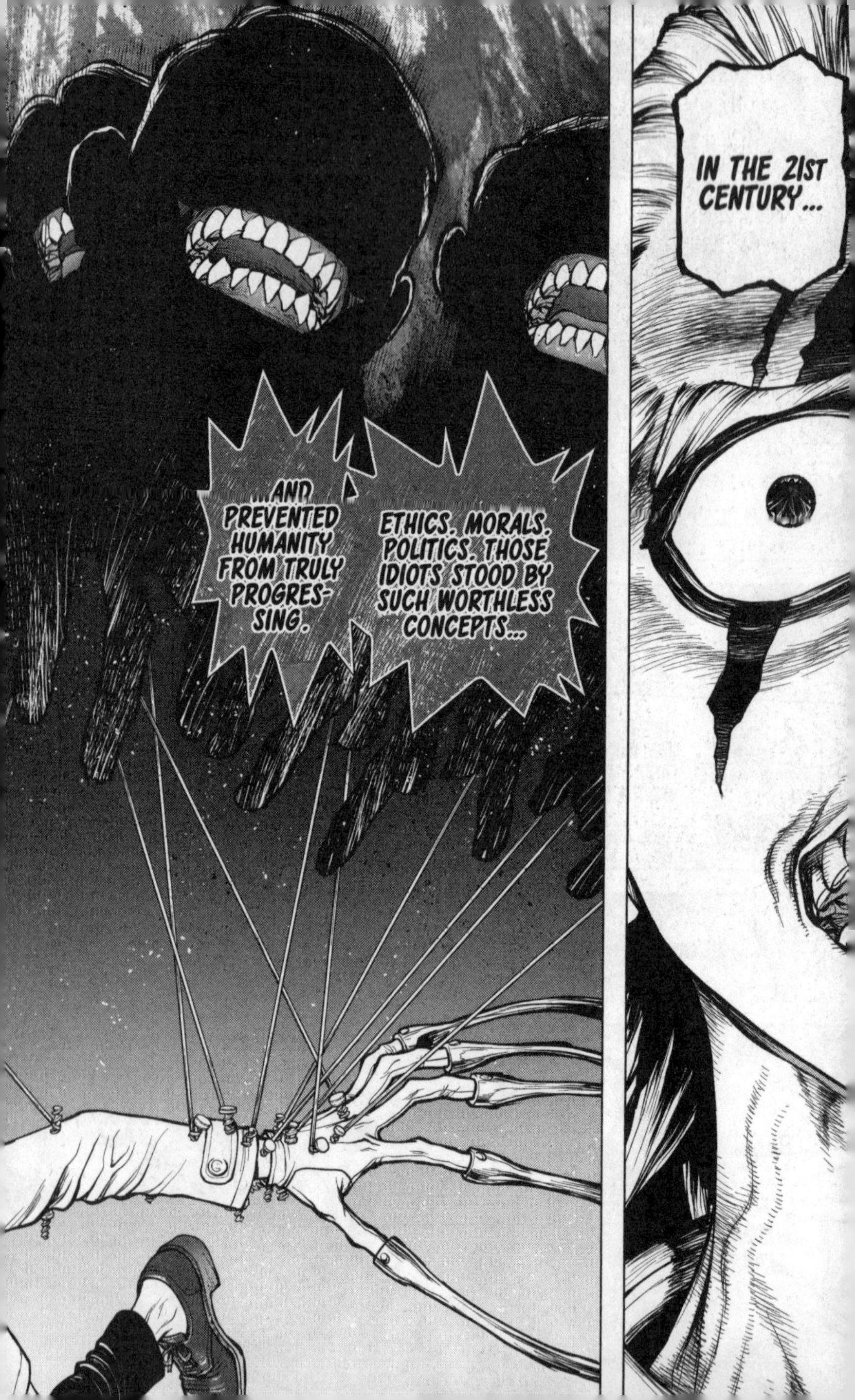
IN THE 21ST CENTURY...
ETHICS. MORALS. POLITICS. THOSE IDIOTS STOOD BY SUCH WORTHLESS CONCEPTS...
AND PREVENTED HUMANITY FROM TRULY PROGRES-SING.

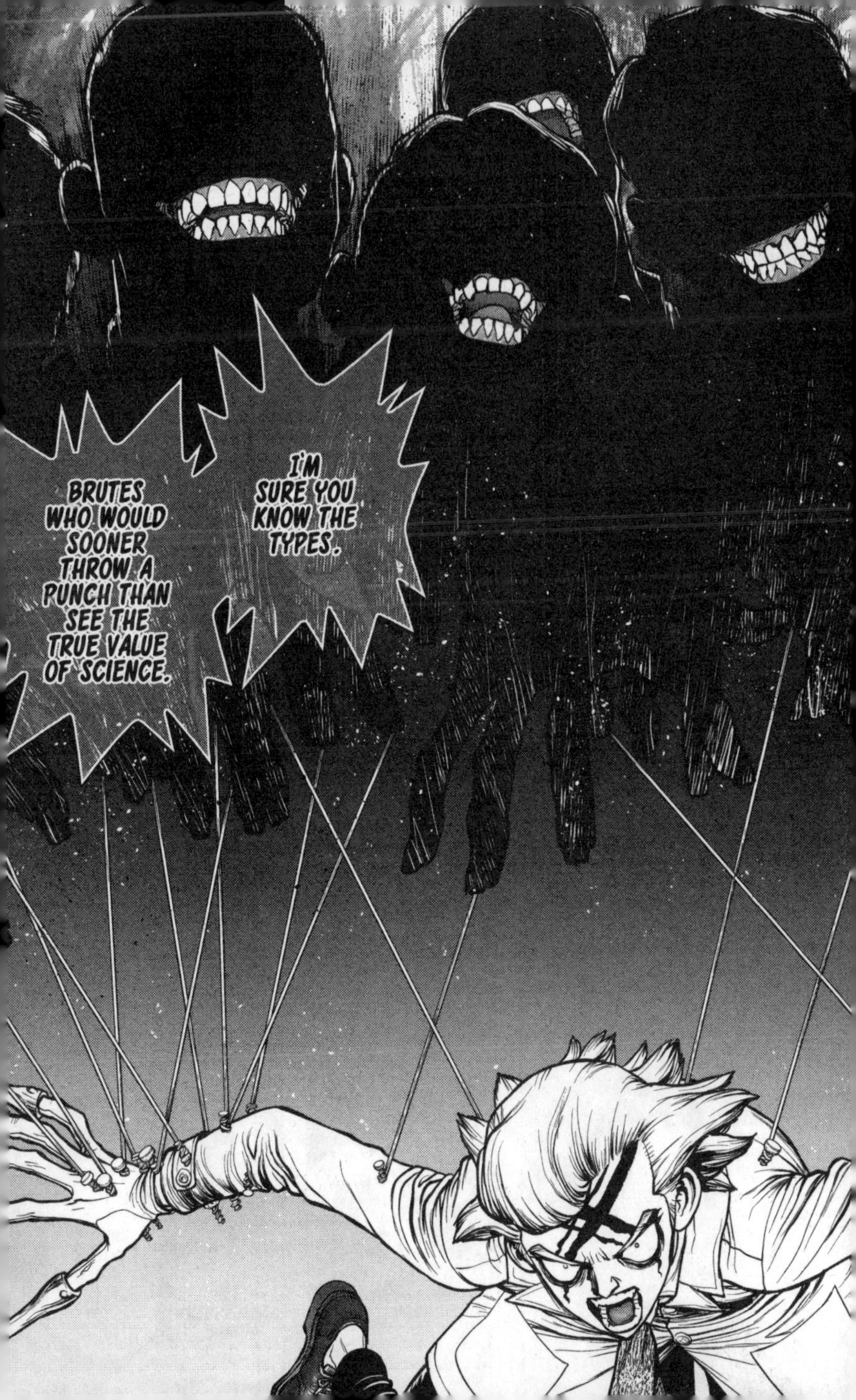
I'M SURE YOU KNOW THE TYPES.
BRUTES WHO WOULD SOONER THROW A PUNCH THAN SEE THE TRUE VALUE OF SCIENCE.

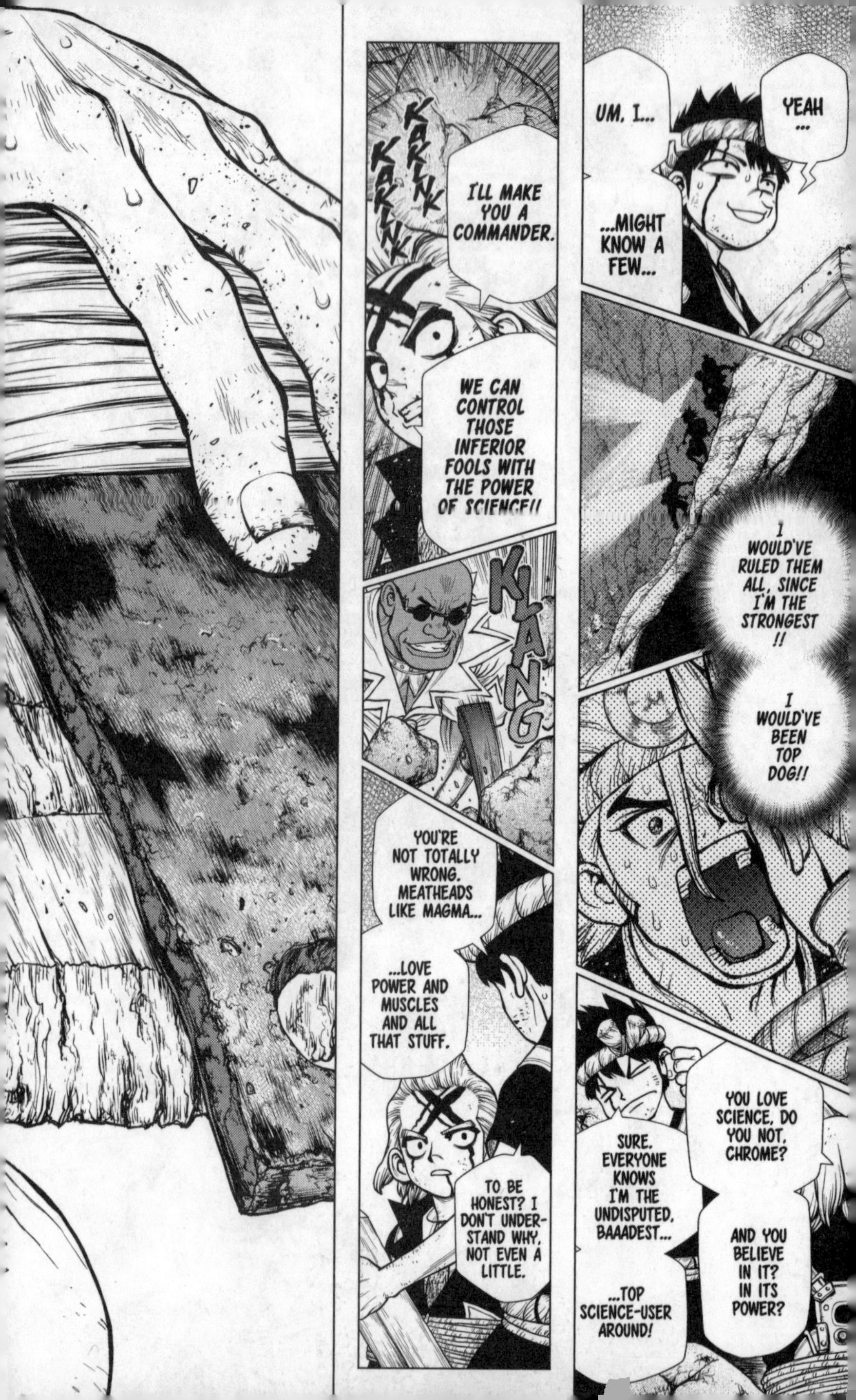
YEAH ...
UM, I...
...MIGHT KNOW A FEW...
I WOULD'VE RULED THEM ALL, SINCE I'M THE STRONGEST !!
I WOULD'VE BEEN TOP DOG!!
YOU LOVE SCIENCE, DO YOU NOT, CHROME?
SURE. EVERYONE KNOWS I'M THE UNDISPUTED, BAAADEST...
...TOP SCIENCE-USER AROUND!
AND YOU BELIEVE IN IT? IN ITS POWER?
KAKINK KAKINK
I'LL MAKE YOU A COMMANDER.
WE CAN CONTROL THOSE INFERIOR FOOLS WITH THE POWER OF SCIENCE!!
KLANG
YOU'RE NOT TOTALLY WRONG. MEATHEADS LIKE MAGMA...
...LOVE POWER AND MUSCLES AND ALL THAT STUFF.
TO BE HONEST? I DON'T UNDERSTAND WHY, NOT EVEN A LITTLE.

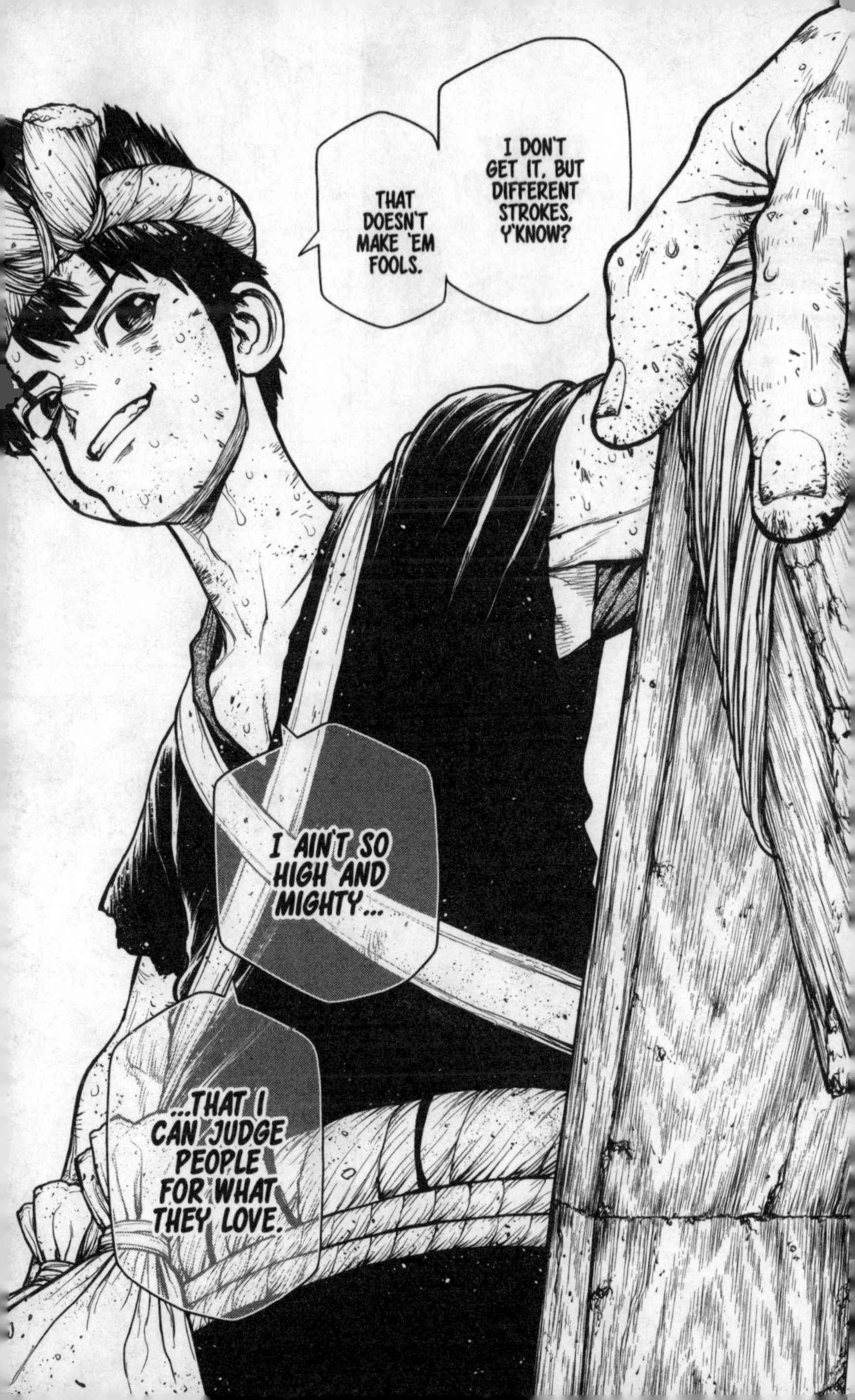
I DON'T GET IT, BUT DIFFERENT STROKES, Y'KNOW?
THAT DOESN'T MAKE 'EM FOOLS.
I AIN'T SO HIGH AND MIGHTY...
...THAT I CAN JUDGE PEOPLE FOR WHAT THEY LOVE.

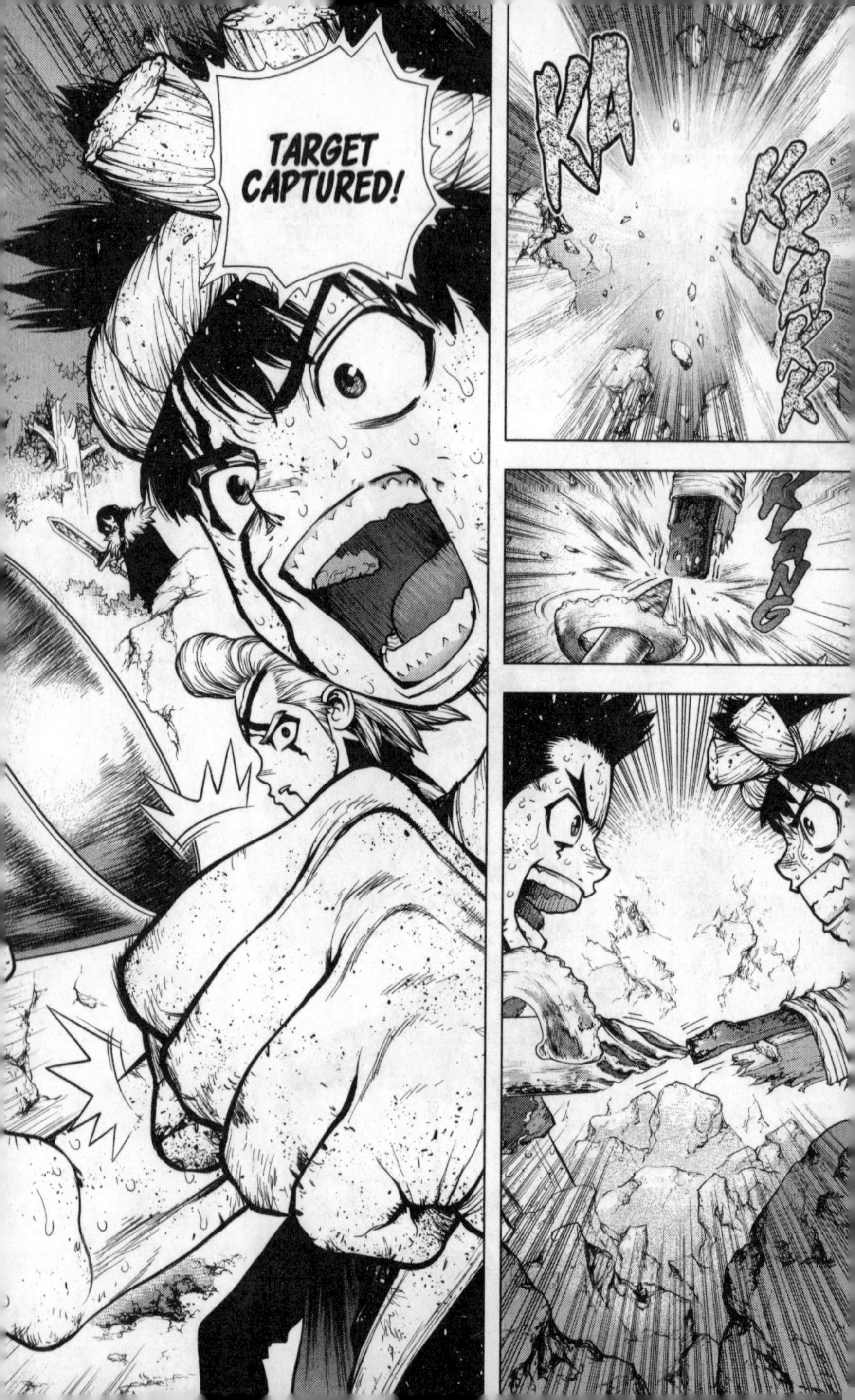
KA
KRAKK
KLANG
TARGET CAPTURED!

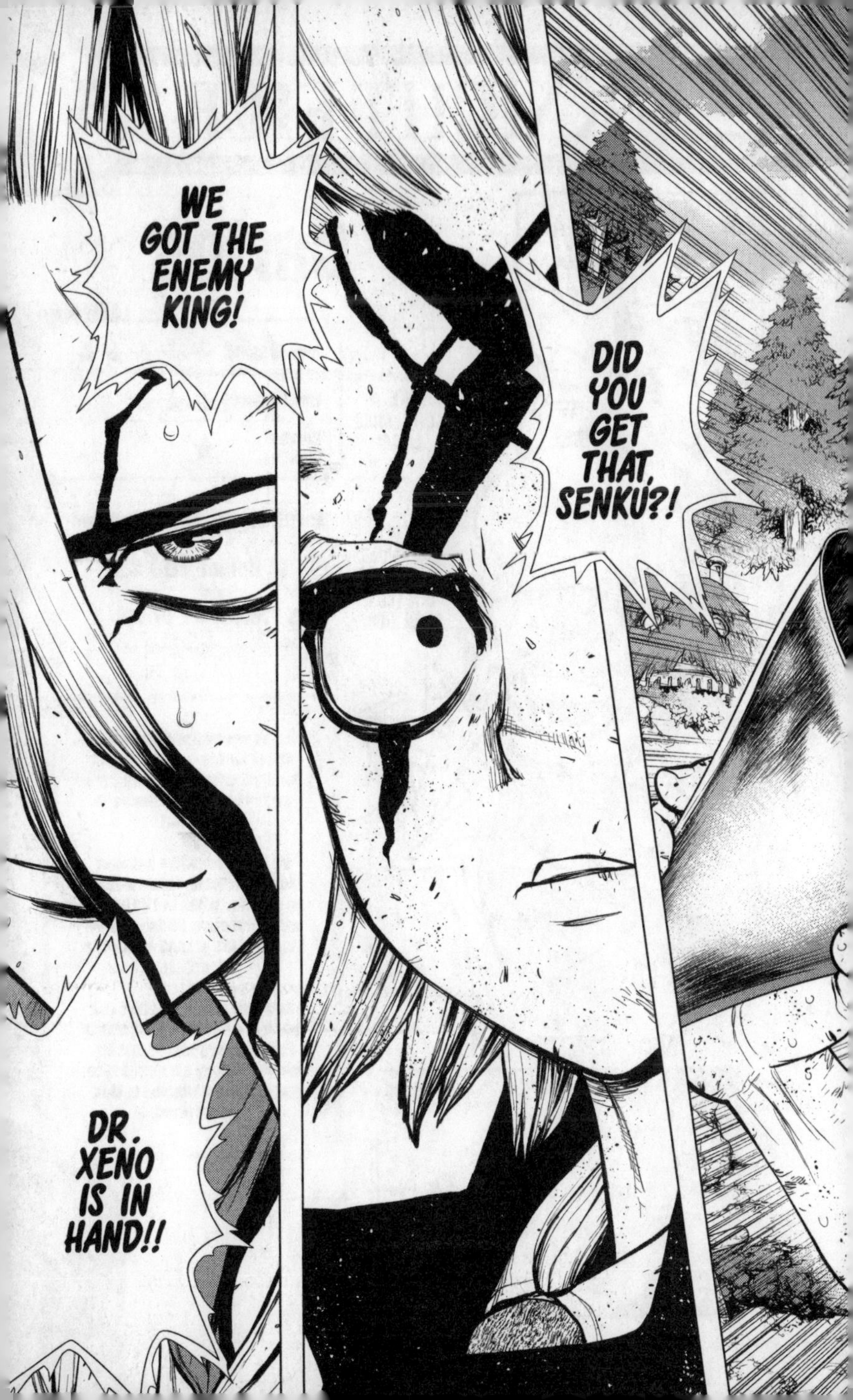
DID YOU GET THAT, SENKU?!
WE GOT THE ENEMY KING!
DR. XENO IS IN HAND!!

Xeno's Science Kingdom

KNIGHT FILE 5

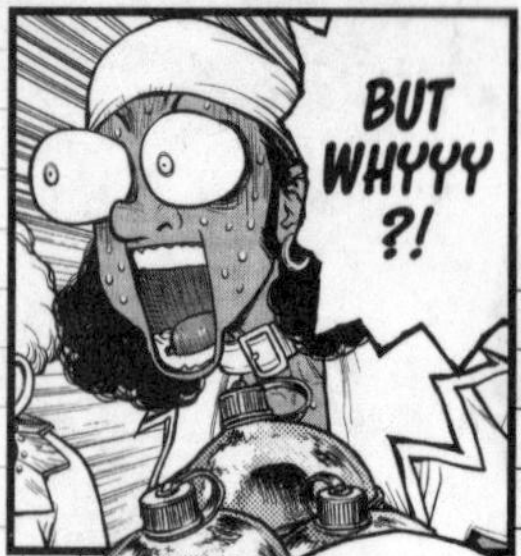
BUT WHYYY?!

Carlos

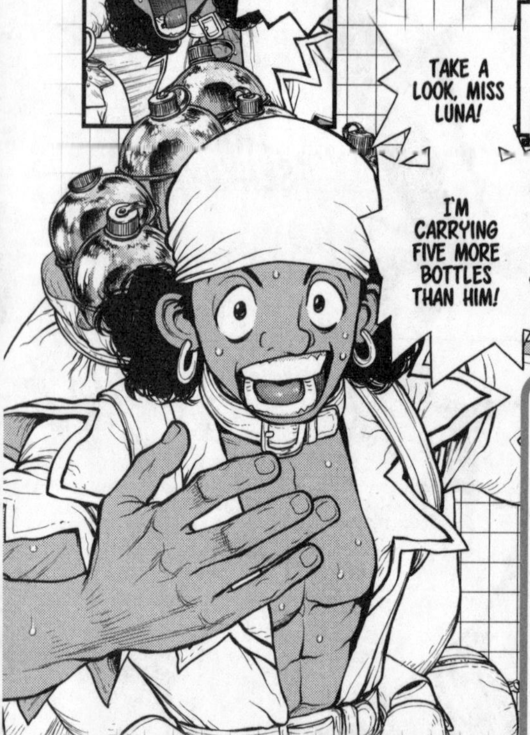
TAKE A LOOK, MISS LUNA!
I'M CARRYING FIVE MORE BOTTLES THAN HIM!

Driving Skills	★★★★★
Flirting Moves	★★★
Combat Abilities	★

- **Full Name:** Carlos Barrios
- **Height:** 185 cm
- **Profession:** Driver

As the longstanding personal driver for the wealthy Wright family, Carlos has known Luna for ten years, ever since she was a girl.

He treats Luna like a proper lady (just like he treats women he's flirting with), but he has no ulterior motive. Rather, Carlos almost looks at Luna as his own daughter.

He's fully aware that he's not much in a physical fight, which is why he suggested that Mr. Wright employ a bodyguard to protect Luna. That led to Max being hired.

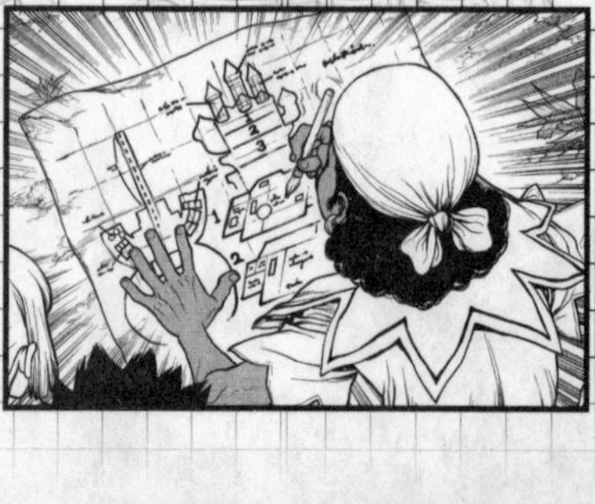

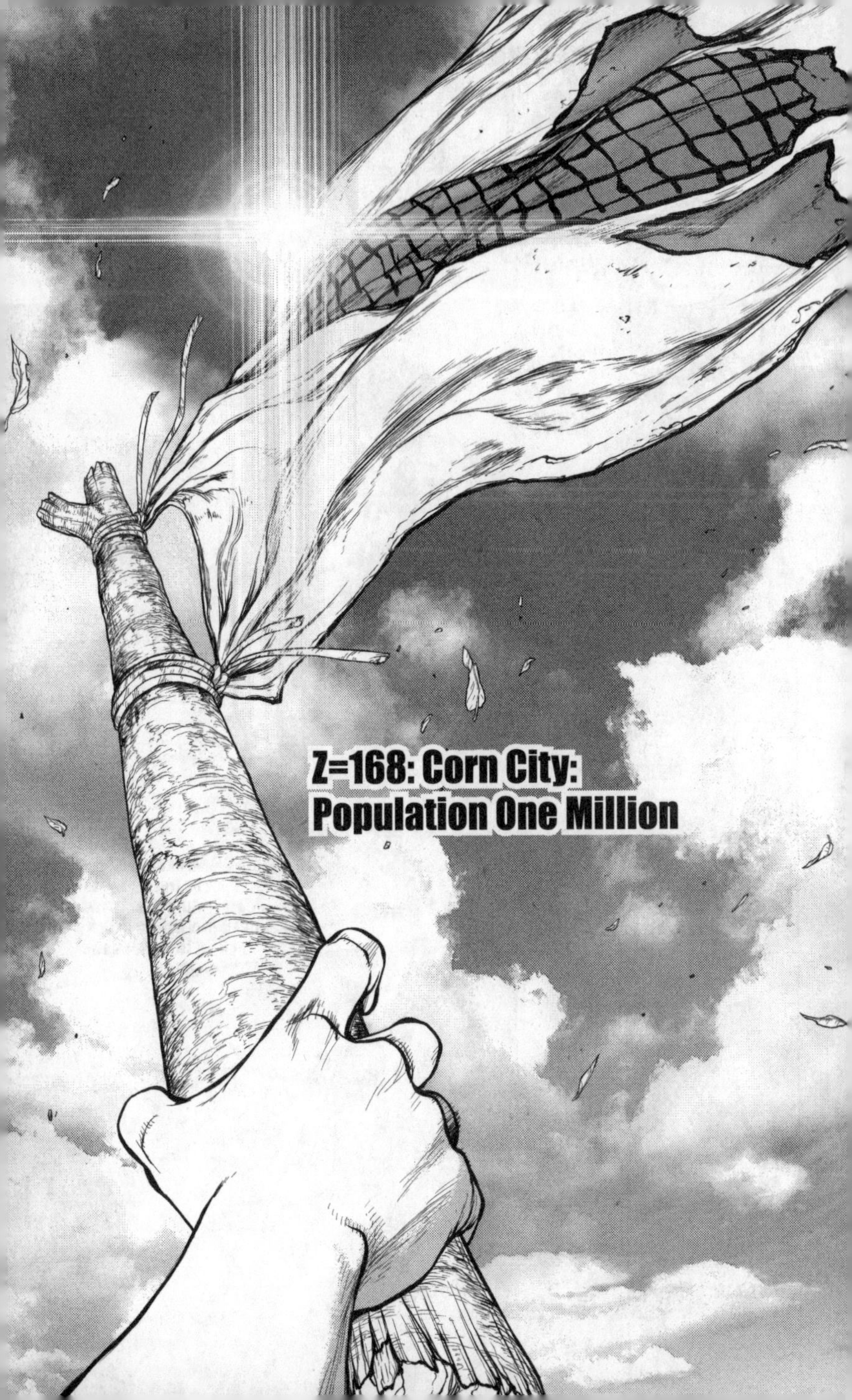
Z=168: Corn City:
Population One Million

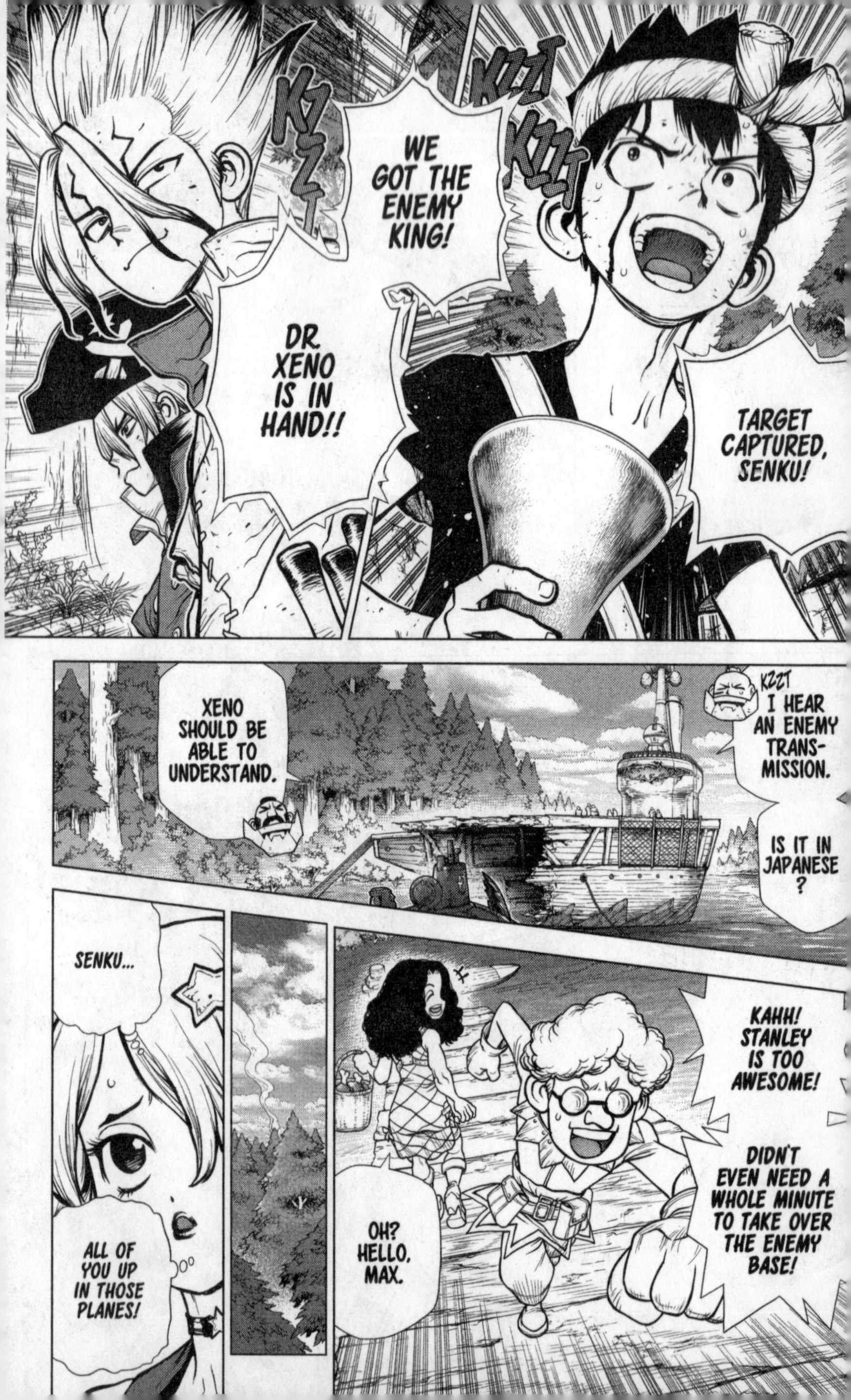
KZZT KZZT
WE GOT THE ENEMY KING!
TARGET CAPTURED, SENKU!
KZZT
DR. XENO IS IN HAND!!
KZZT
I HEAR AN ENEMY TRANS-MISSION.
IS IT IN JAPANESE?
XENO SHOULD BE ABLE TO UNDERSTAND.
KAHH! STANLEY IS TOO AWESOME!
DIDN'T EVEN NEED A WHOLE MINUTE TO TAKE OVER THE ENEMY BASE!
OH? HELLO, MAX.
SENKU...
ALL OF YOU UP IN THOSE PLANES!

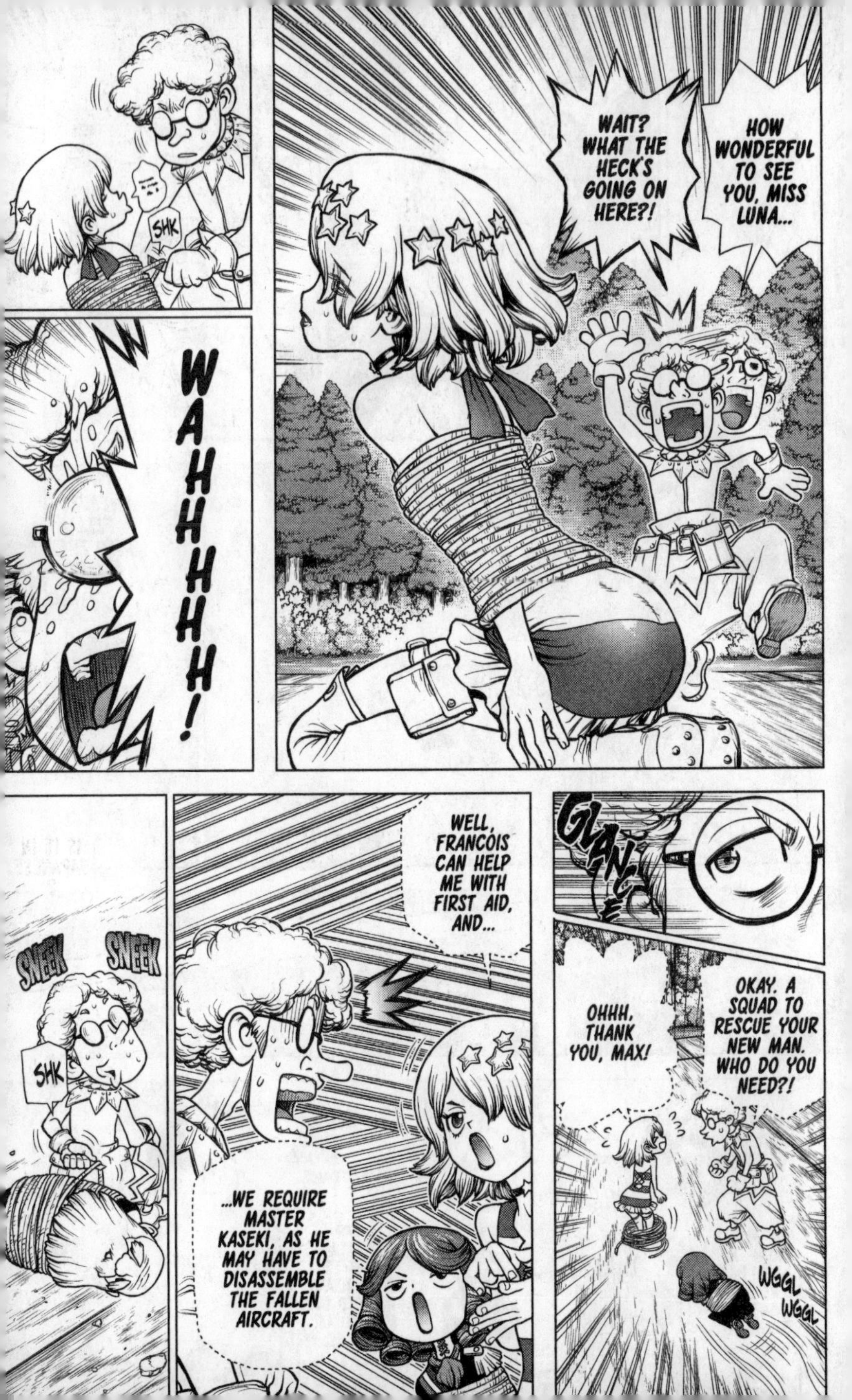
HOW WONDERFUL TO SEE YOU, MISS LUNA...
WAIT? WHAT THE HECK'S GOING ON HERE?!
SHK
WAHHHHHH!
GLANCE
OKAY. A SQUAD TO RESCUE YOUR NEW MAN. WHO DO YOU NEED?!
OHHH, THANK YOU, MAX!
WGGL WGGL
WELL, FRANCOIS CAN HELP ME WITH FIRST AID, AND...
...WE REQUIRE MASTER KASEKI, AS HE MAY HAVE TO DISASSEMBLE THE FALLEN AIRCRAFT.
SNEEK SNEEK
SHK

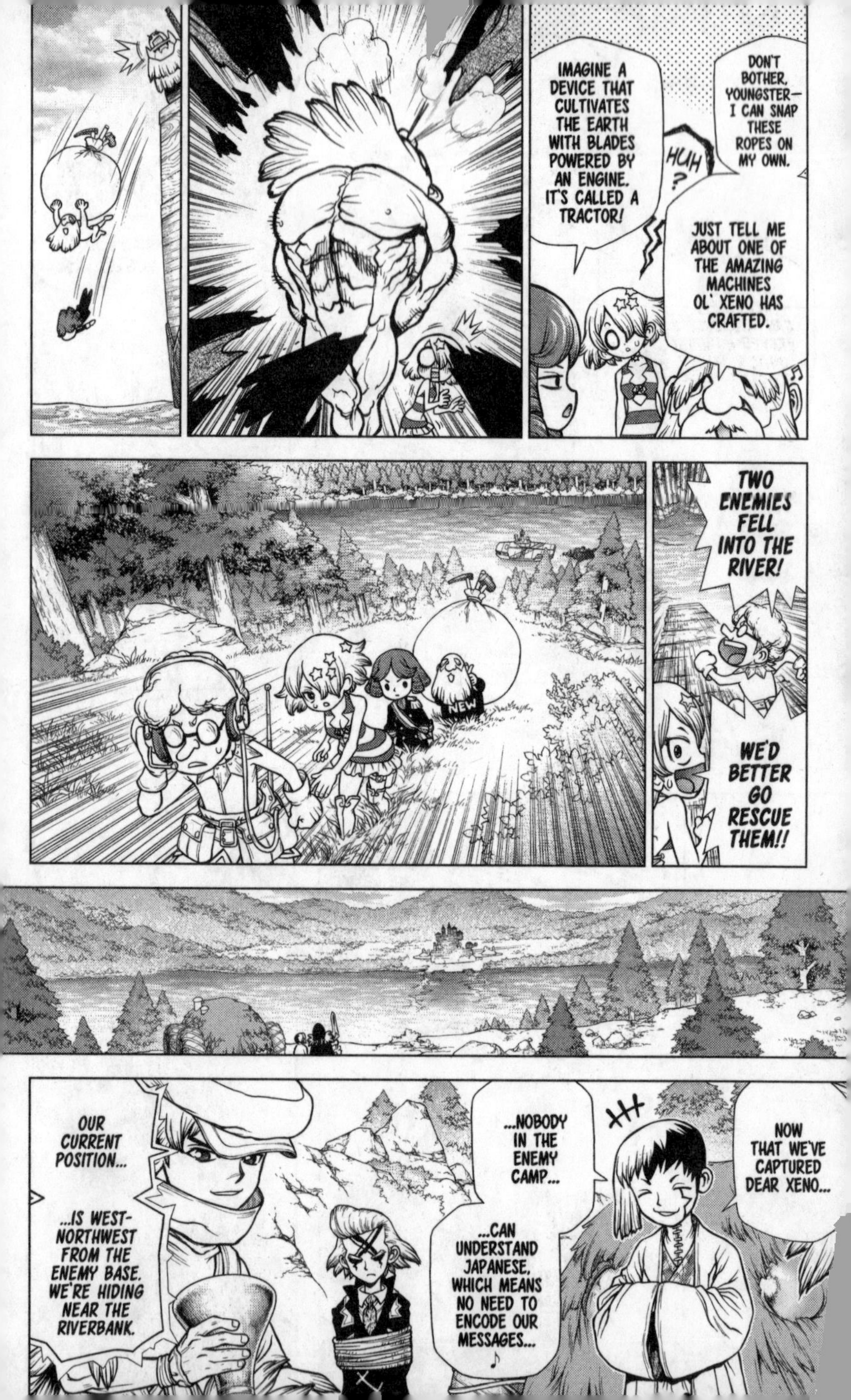
DON'T BOTHER, YOUNGSTER— I CAN SNAP THESE ROPES ON MY OWN.
HUH?
JUST TELL ME ABOUT ONE OF THE AMAZING MACHINES OL' XENO HAS CRAFTED.
IMAGINE A DEVICE THAT CULTIVATES THE EARTH WITH BLADES POWERED BY AN ENGINE. IT'S CALLED A TRACTOR!
TWO ENEMIES FELL INTO THE RIVER!
WE'D BETTER GO RESCUE THEM!!
NEW
NOW THAT WE'VE CAPTURED DEAR XENO...
...NOBODY IN THE ENEMY CAMP...
...CAN UNDERSTAND JAPANESE, WHICH MEANS NO NEED TO ENCODE OUR MESSAGES... ♪
OUR CURRENT POSITION...
...IS WEST-NORTHWEST FROM THE ENEMY BASE. WE'RE HIDING NEAR THE RIVERBANK.

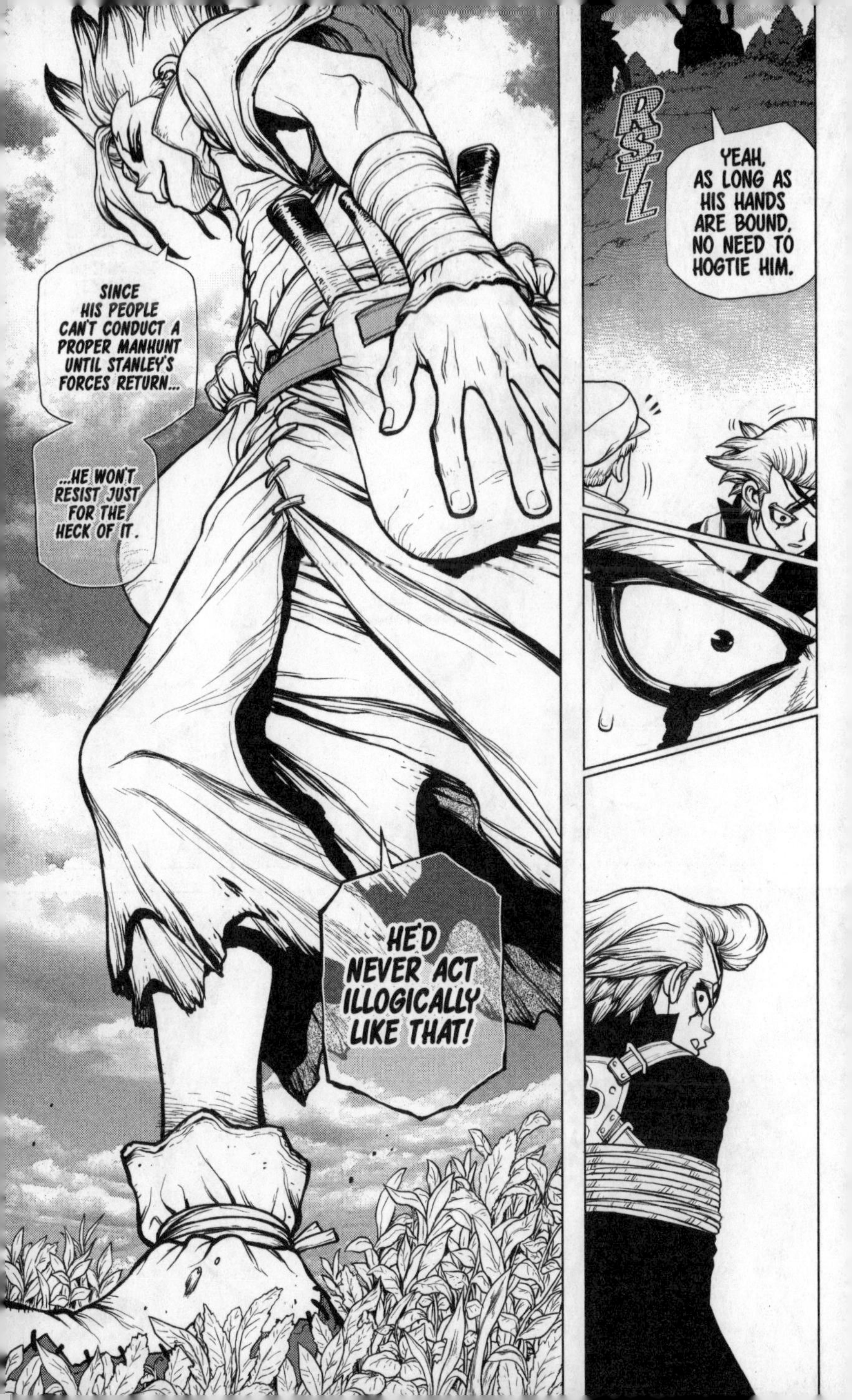
RSTL
YEAH, AS LONG AS HIS HANDS ARE BOUND, NO NEED TO HOGTIE HIM.
SINCE HIS PEOPLE CAN'T CONDUCT A PROPER MANHUNT UNTIL STANLEY'S FORCES RETURN...
...HE WON'T RESIST JUST FOR THE HECK OF IT.
HE'D NEVER ACT ILLOGICALLY LIKE THAT!

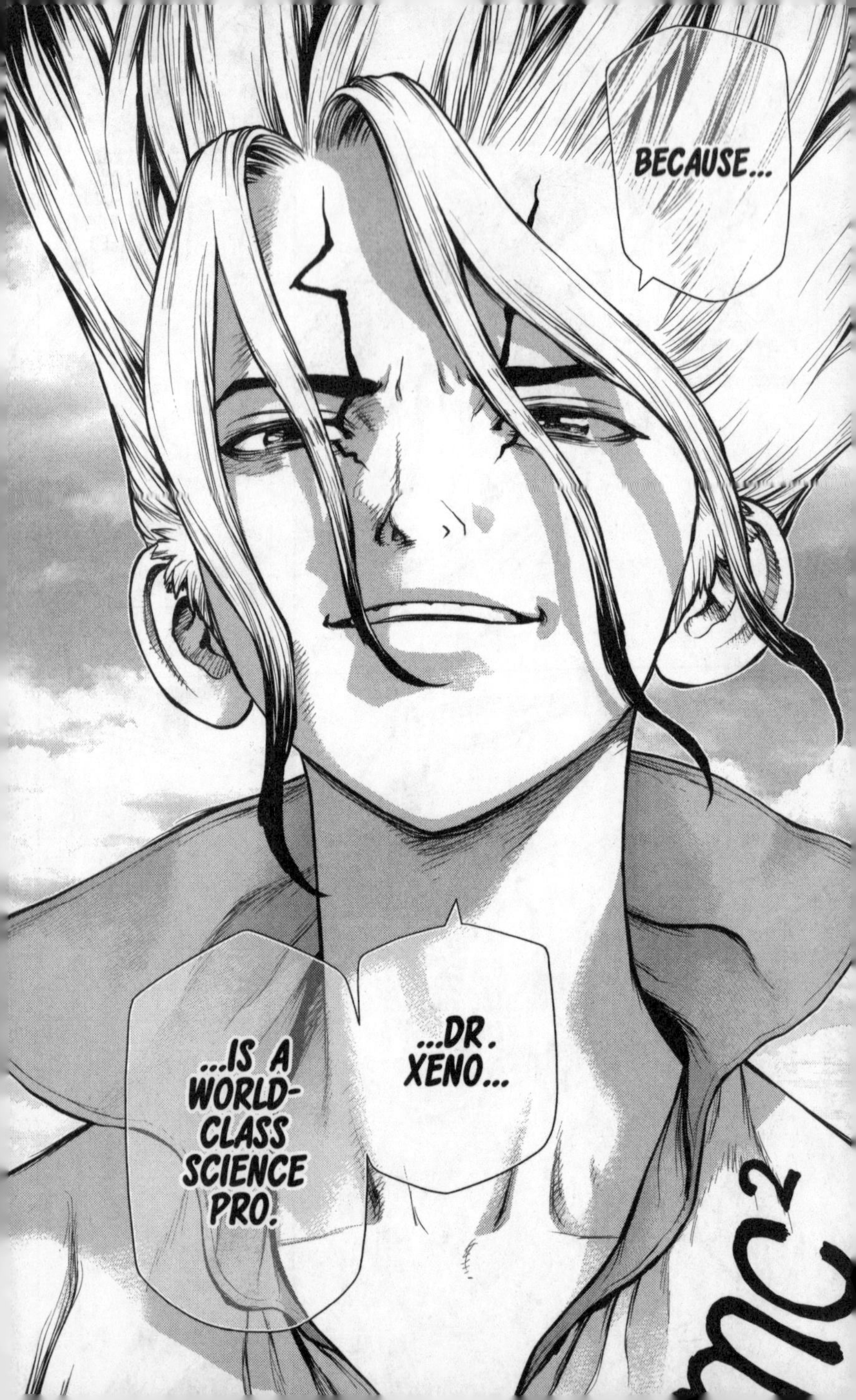
BECAUSE...
...DR. XENO...
...IS A WORLD-CLASS SCIENCE PRO.

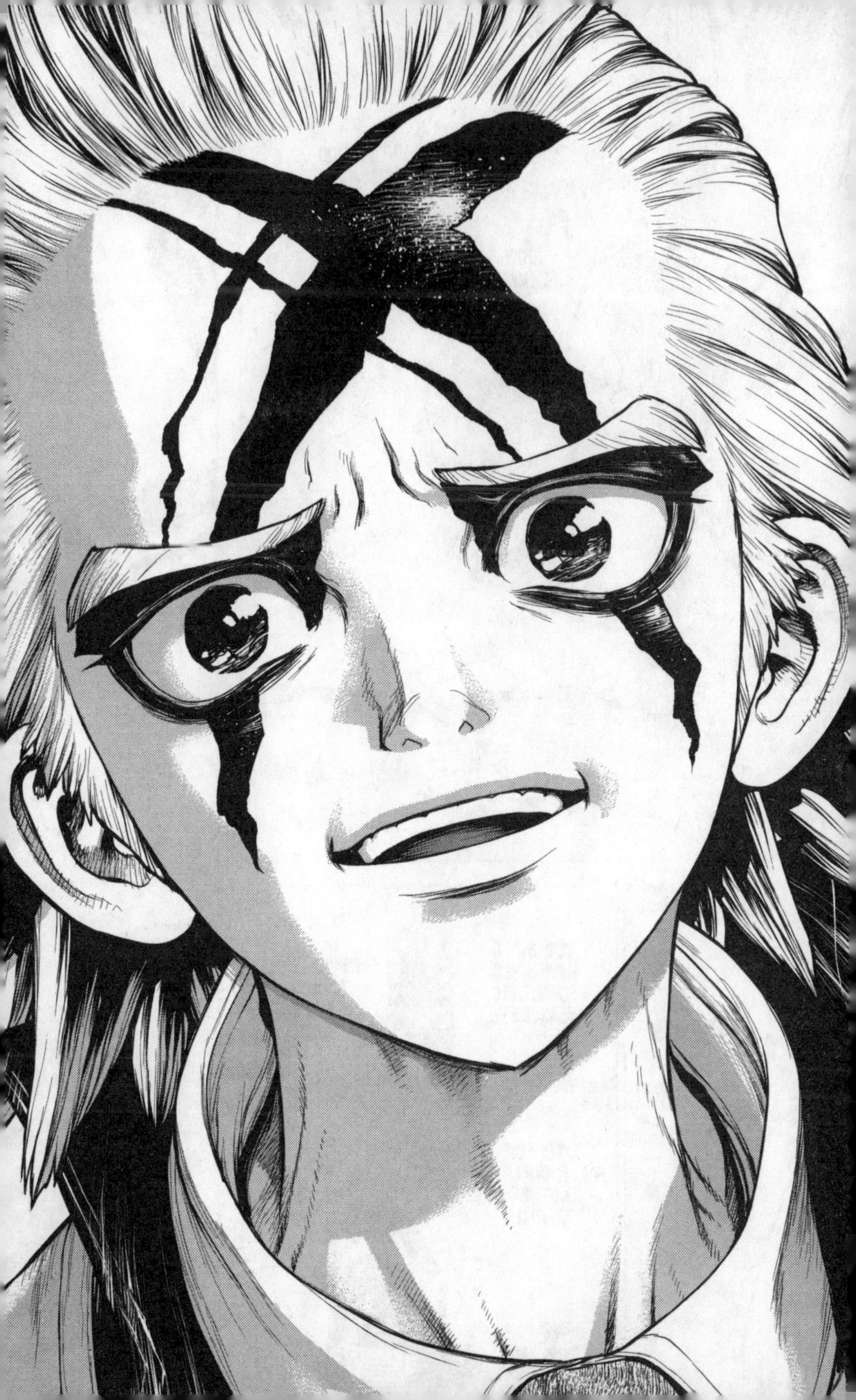

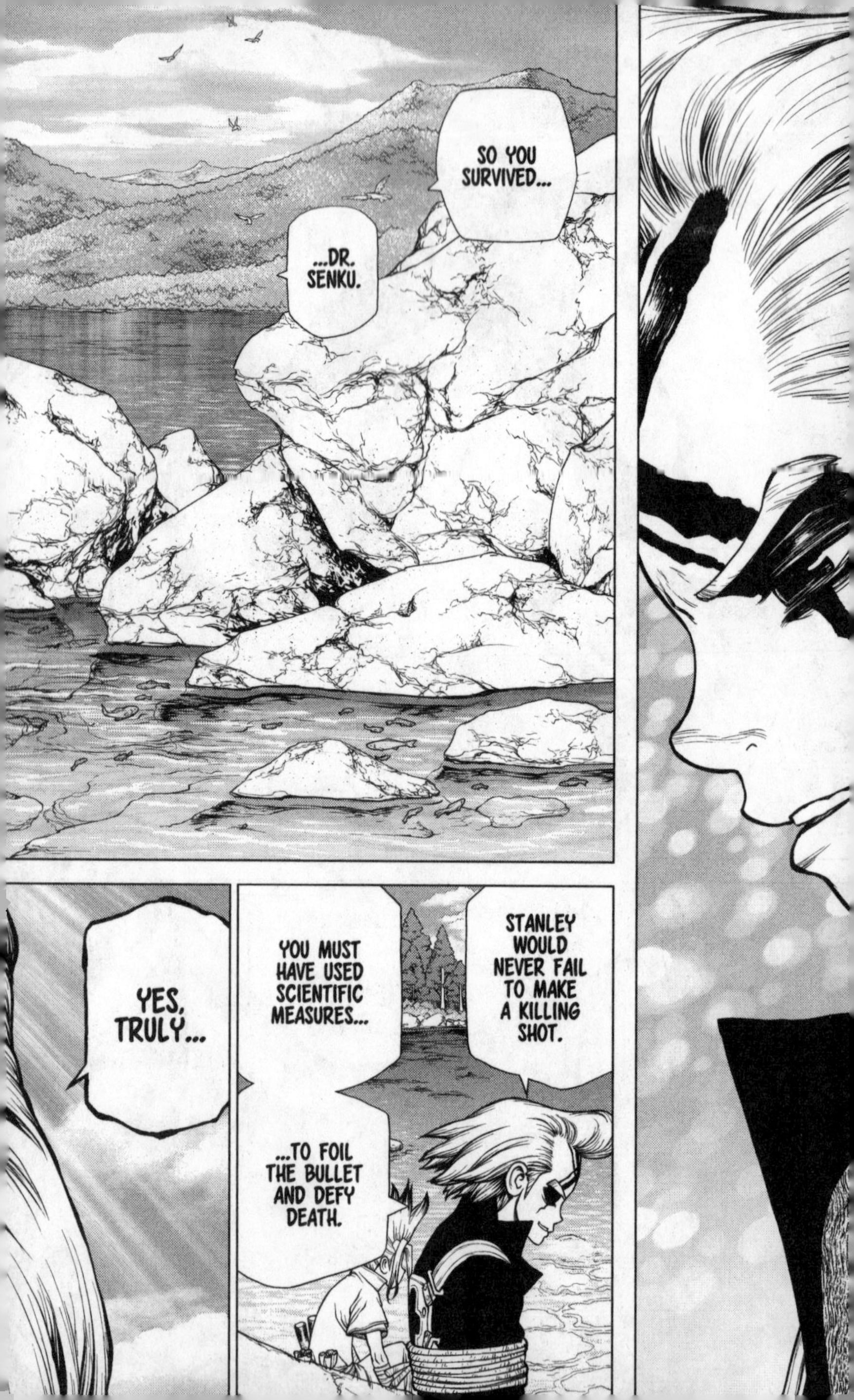
SO YOU SURVIVED...
...DR. SENKU.
STANLEY WOULD NEVER FAIL TO MAKE A KILLING SHOT.
YOU MUST HAVE USED SCIENTIFIC MEASURES...
...TO FOIL THE BULLET AND DEFY DEATH.
YES, TRULY...

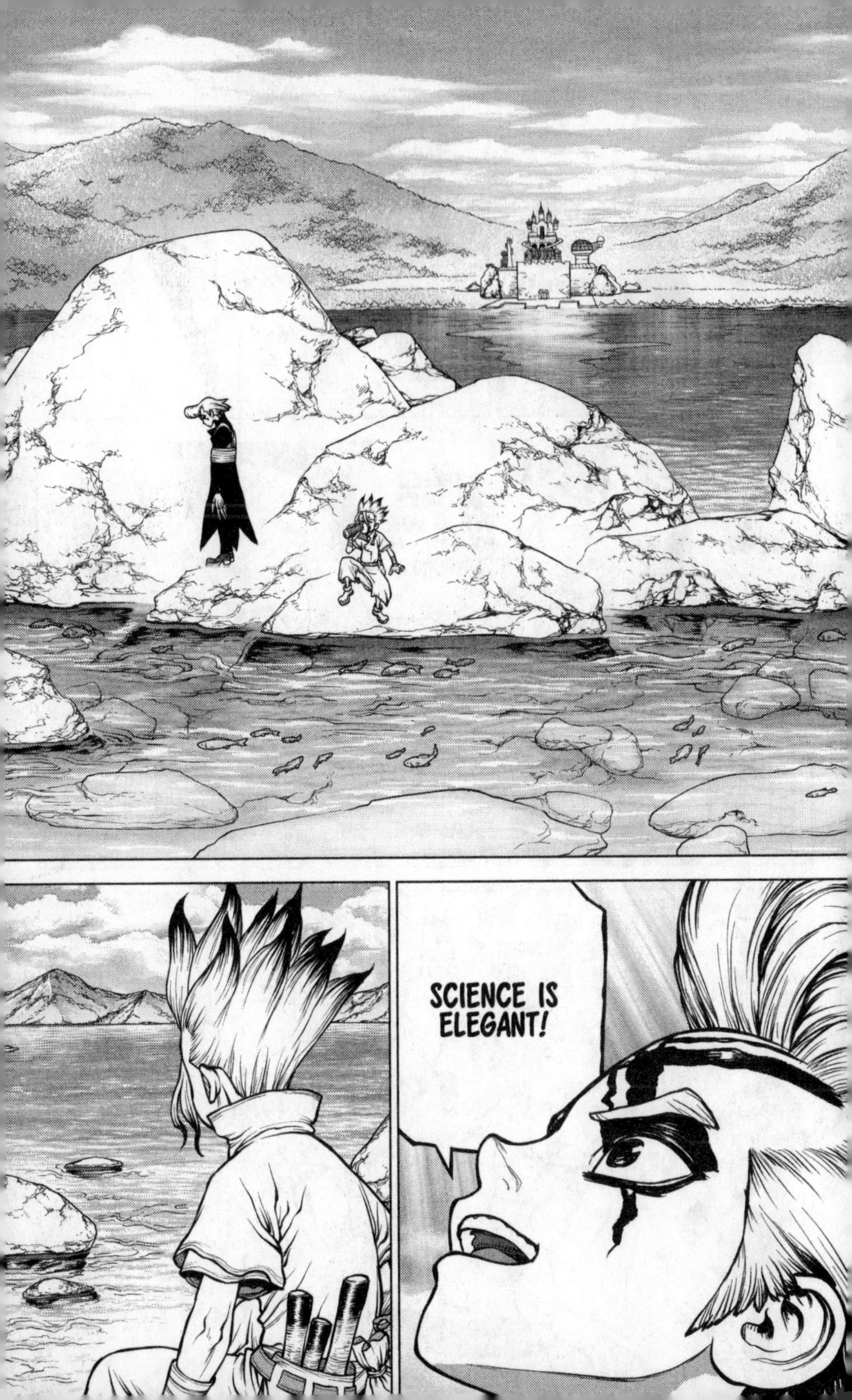
SCIENCE IS ELEGANT!

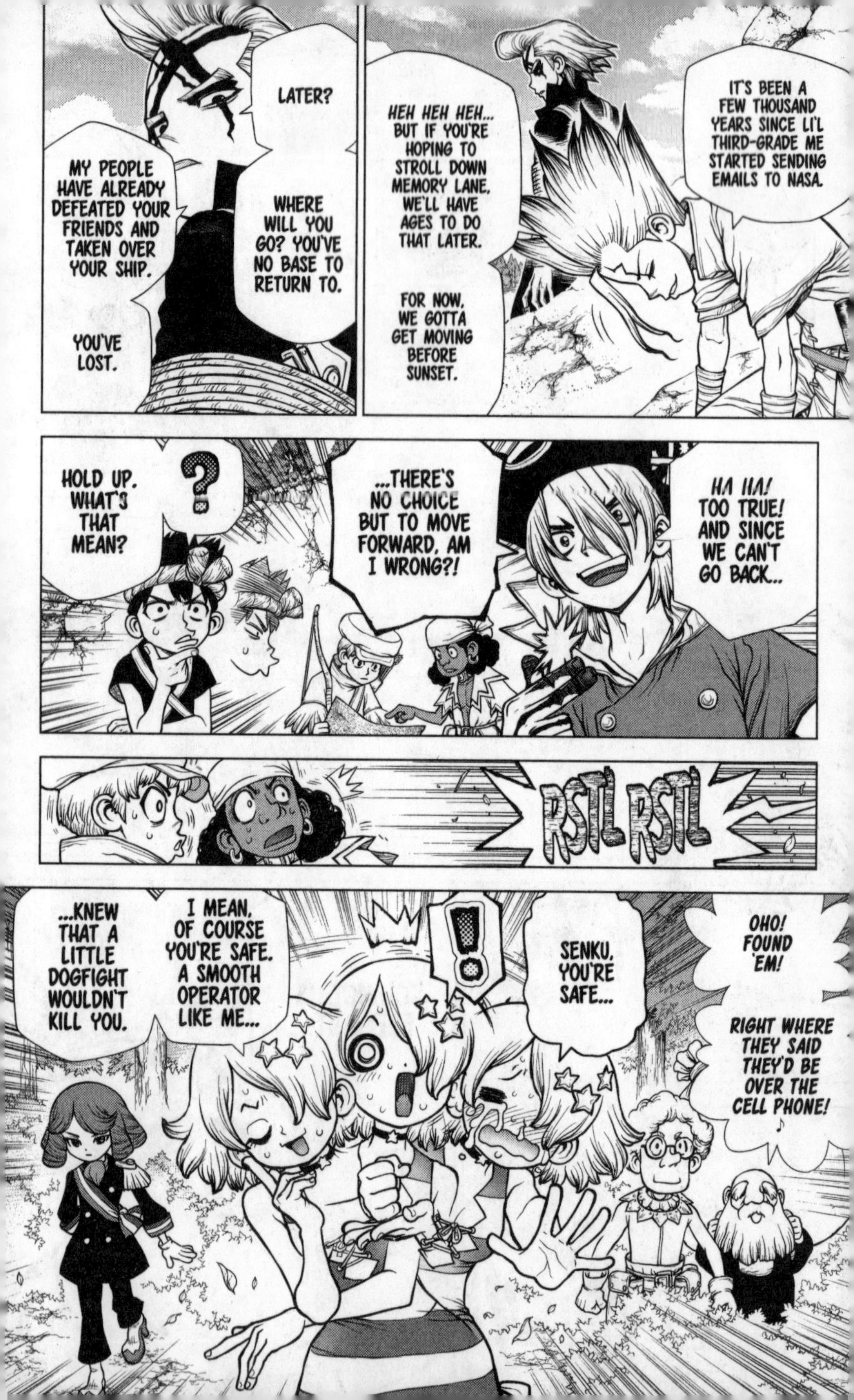
IT'S BEEN A FEW THOUSAND YEARS SINCE LI'L THIRD-GRADE ME STARTED SENDING EMAILS TO NASA.
HEH HEH HEH... BUT IF YOU'RE HOPING TO STROLL DOWN MEMORY LANE, WE'LL HAVE AGES TO DO THAT LATER.
FOR NOW, WE GOTTA GET MOVING BEFORE SUNSET.
LATER?
WHERE WILL YOU GO? YOU'VE NO BASE TO RETURN TO.
MY PEOPLE HAVE ALREADY DEFEATED YOUR FRIENDS AND TAKEN OVER YOUR SHIP.
YOU'VE LOST.
HA HA! TOO TRUE! AND SINCE WE CAN'T GO BACK...
...THERE'S NO CHOICE BUT TO MOVE FORWARD, AM I WRONG?!
?
HOLD UP. WHAT'S THAT MEAN?
RSTL RSTL
OHO! FOUND 'EM!
RIGHT WHERE THEY SAID THEY'D BE OVER THE CELL PHONE! ♪
!
SENKU, YOU'RE SAFE...
I MEAN, OF COURSE YOU'RE SAFE. A SMOOTH OPERATOR LIKE ME...
...KNEW THAT A LITTLE DOGFIGHT WOULDN'T KILL YOU.

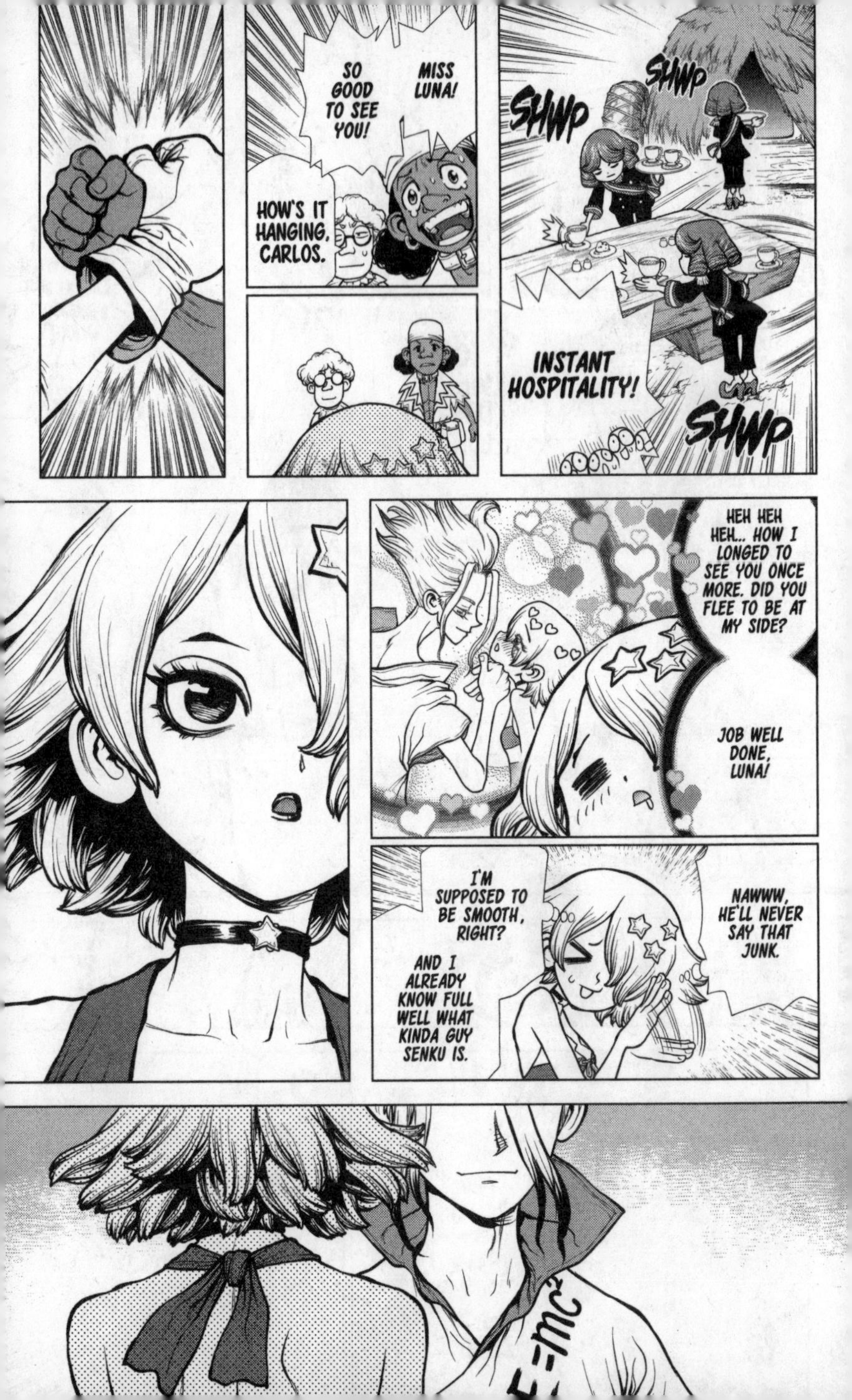
SHWP
SHWP
INSTANT HOSPITALITY!
SHWP
MISS LUNA!
SO GOOD TO SEE YOU!
HOW'S IT HANGING, CARLOS.
HEH HEH HEH... HOW I LONGED TO SEE YOU ONCE MORE. DID YOU FLEE TO BE AT MY SIDE?
JOB WELL DONE, LUNA!
NAWWW, HE'LL NEVER SAY THAT JUNK.
I'M SUPPOSED TO BE SMOOTH, RIGHT?
AND I ALREADY KNOW FULL WELL WHAT KINDA GUY SENKU IS.
E=mc²

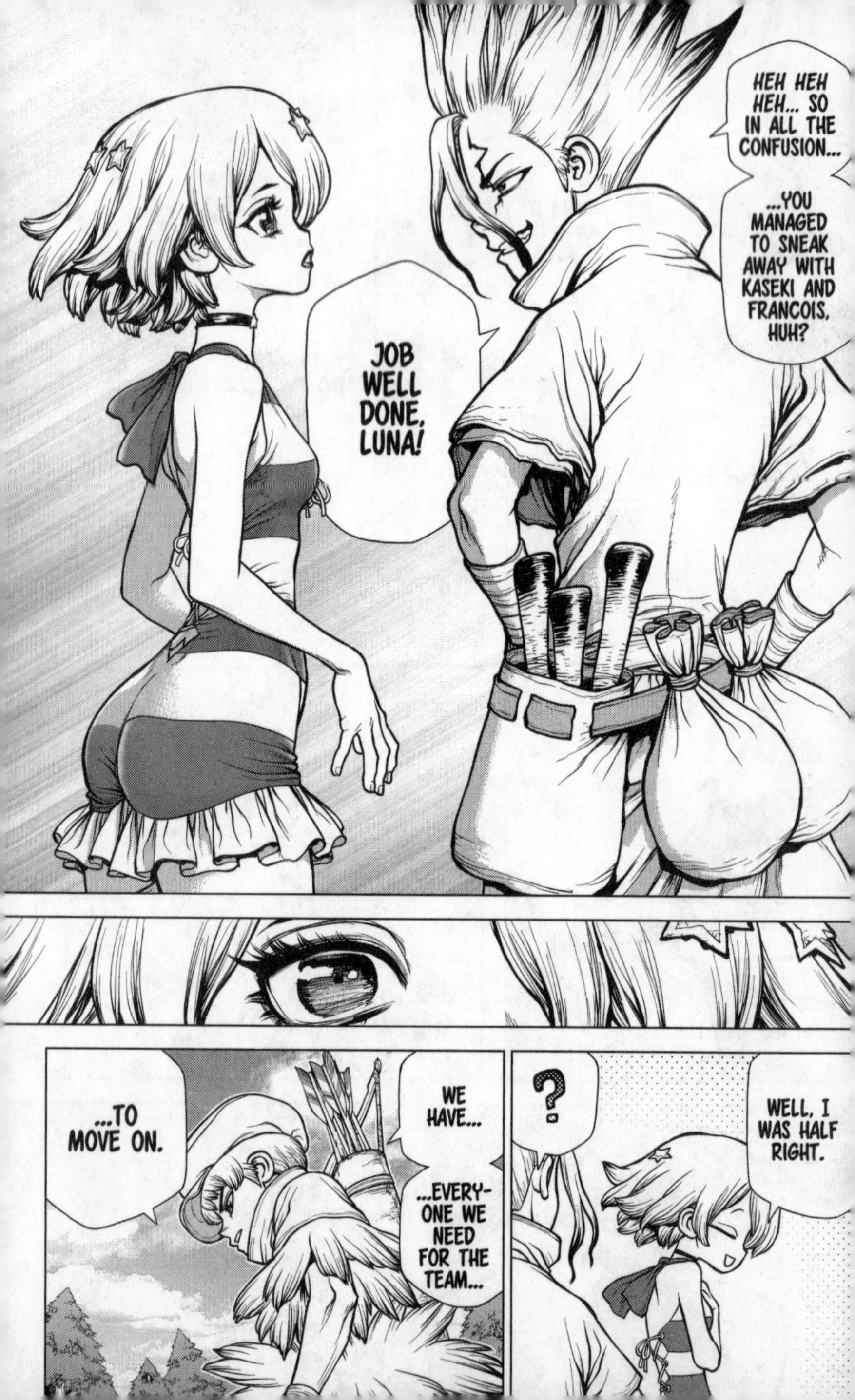
HEH HEH HEH... SO IN ALL THE CONFUSION...
...YOU MANAGED TO SNEAK AWAY WITH KASEKI AND FRANCOIS, HUH?
JOB WELL DONE, LUNA!
WELL, I WAS HALF RIGHT.
?
WE HAVE...
...EVERY-ONE WE NEED FOR THE TEAM...
...TO MOVE ON.

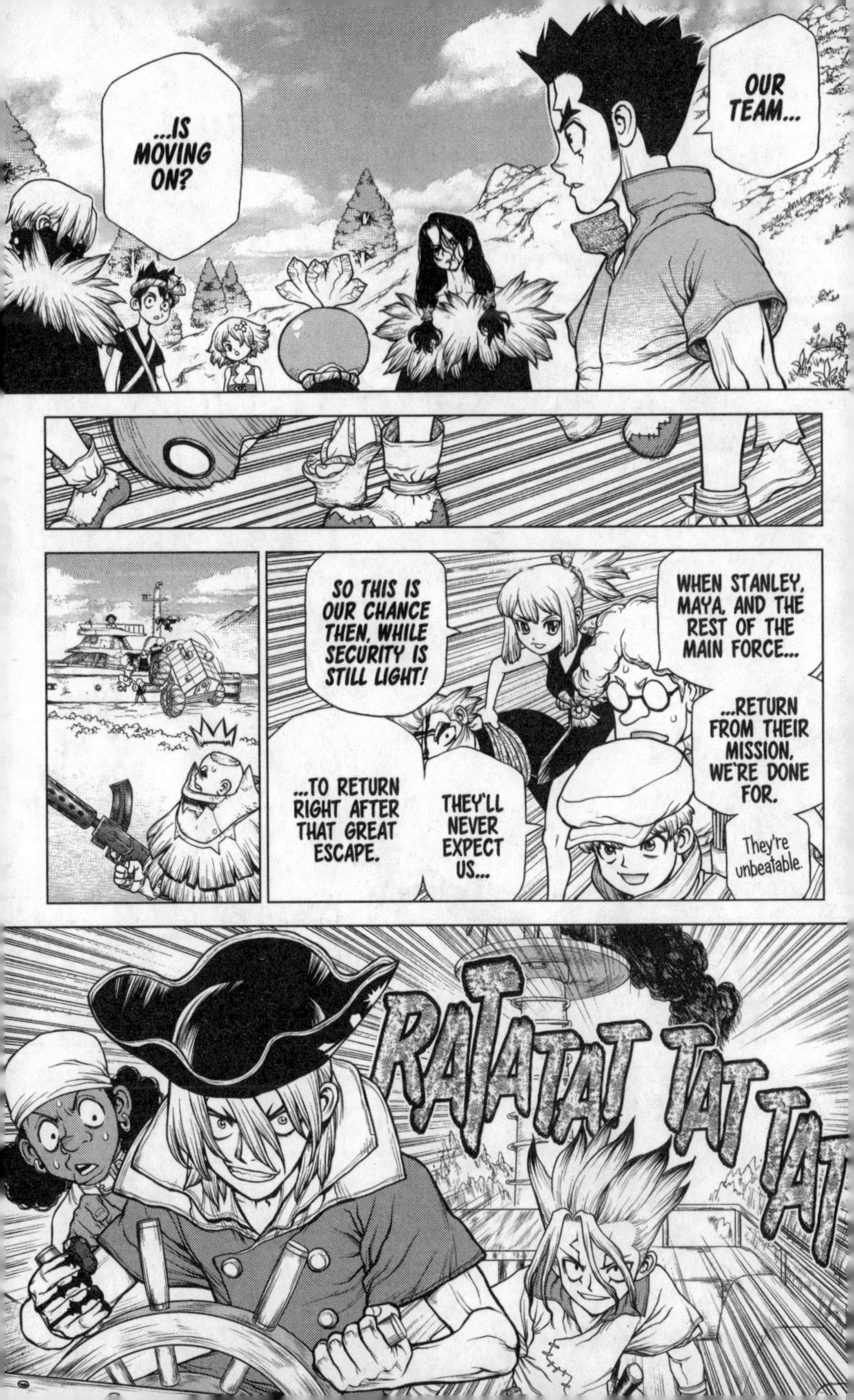

OUR TEAM...
...IS MOVING ON?
WHEN STANLEY, MAYA, AND THE REST OF THE MAIN FORCE...
...RETURN FROM THEIR MISSION, WE'RE DONE FOR.
They're unbeatable.
SO THIS IS OUR CHANCE THEN, WHILE SECURITY IS STILL LIGHT!
THEY'LL NEVER EXPECT US...
...TO RETURN RIGHT AFTER THAT GREAT ESCAPE.
RATATAT TAT TAT

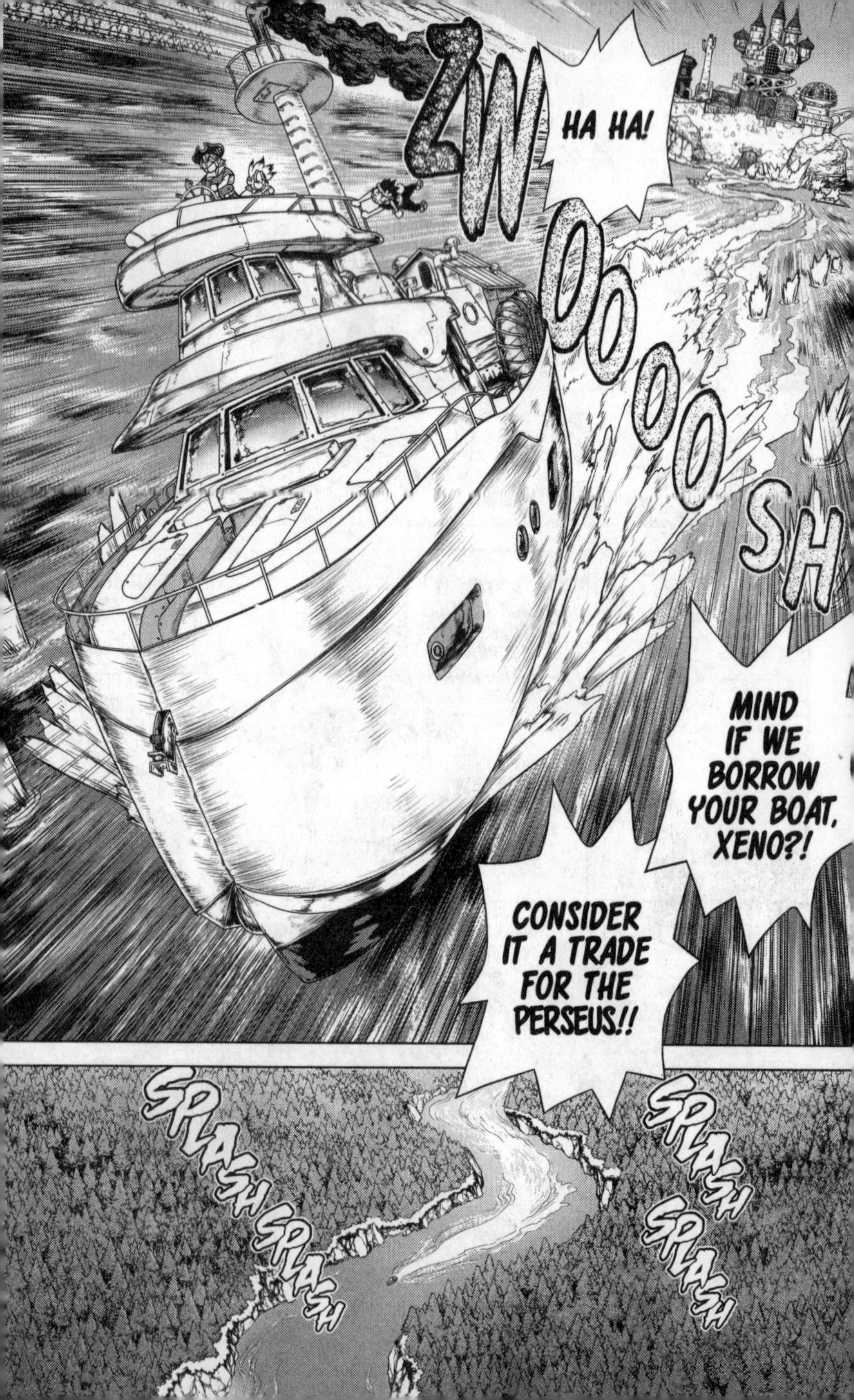
ZWOOOOOSH
HA HA!
MIND IF WE BORROW YOUR BOAT, XENO?!
CONSIDER IT A TRADE FOR THE PERSEUS!!
SPLASH SPLASH
SPLASH SPLASH

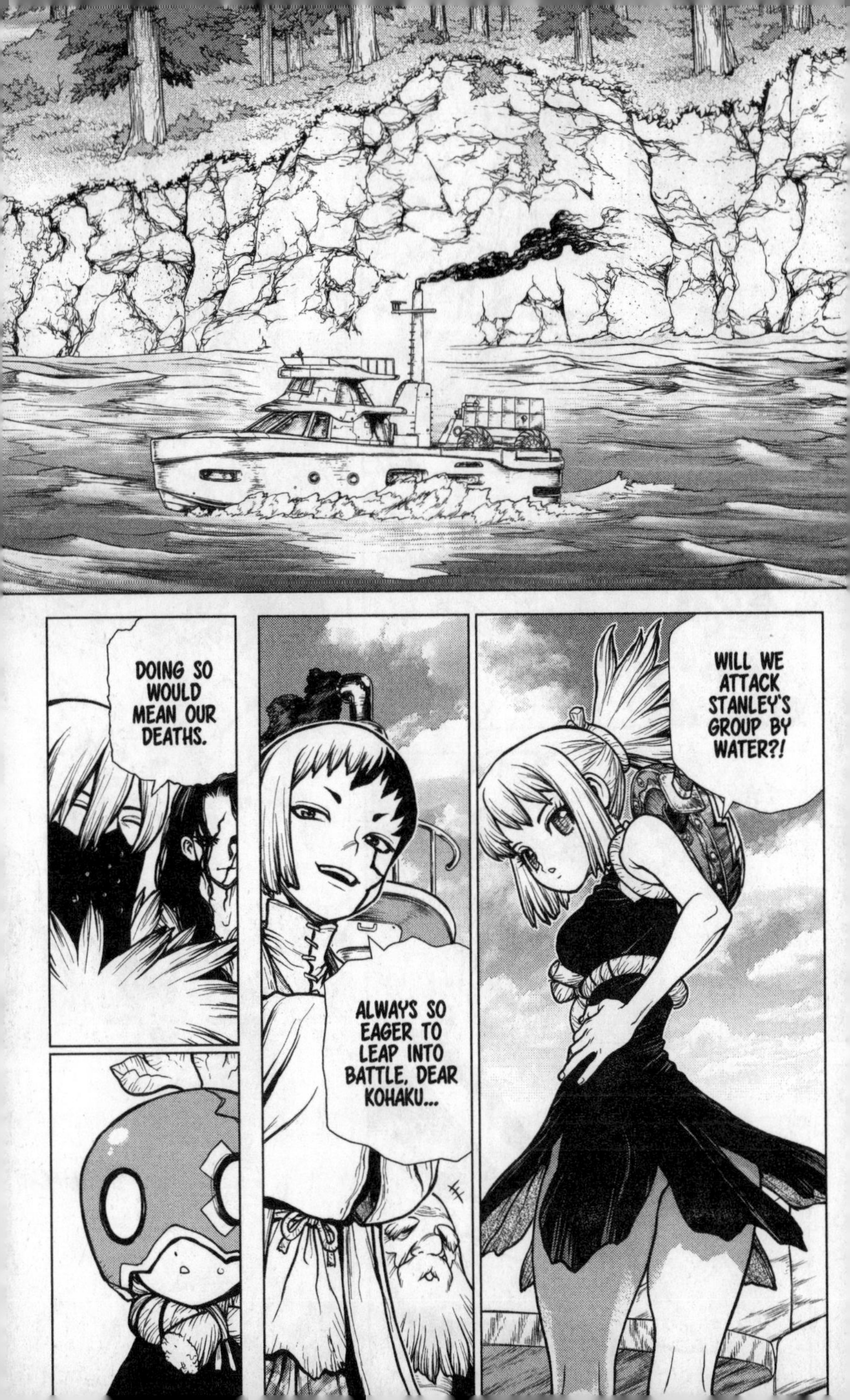
WILL WE ATTACK STANLEY'S GROUP BY WATER?!
ALWAYS SO EAGER TO LEAP INTO BATTLE, DEAR KOHAKU...
DOING SO WOULD MEAN OUR DEATHS.

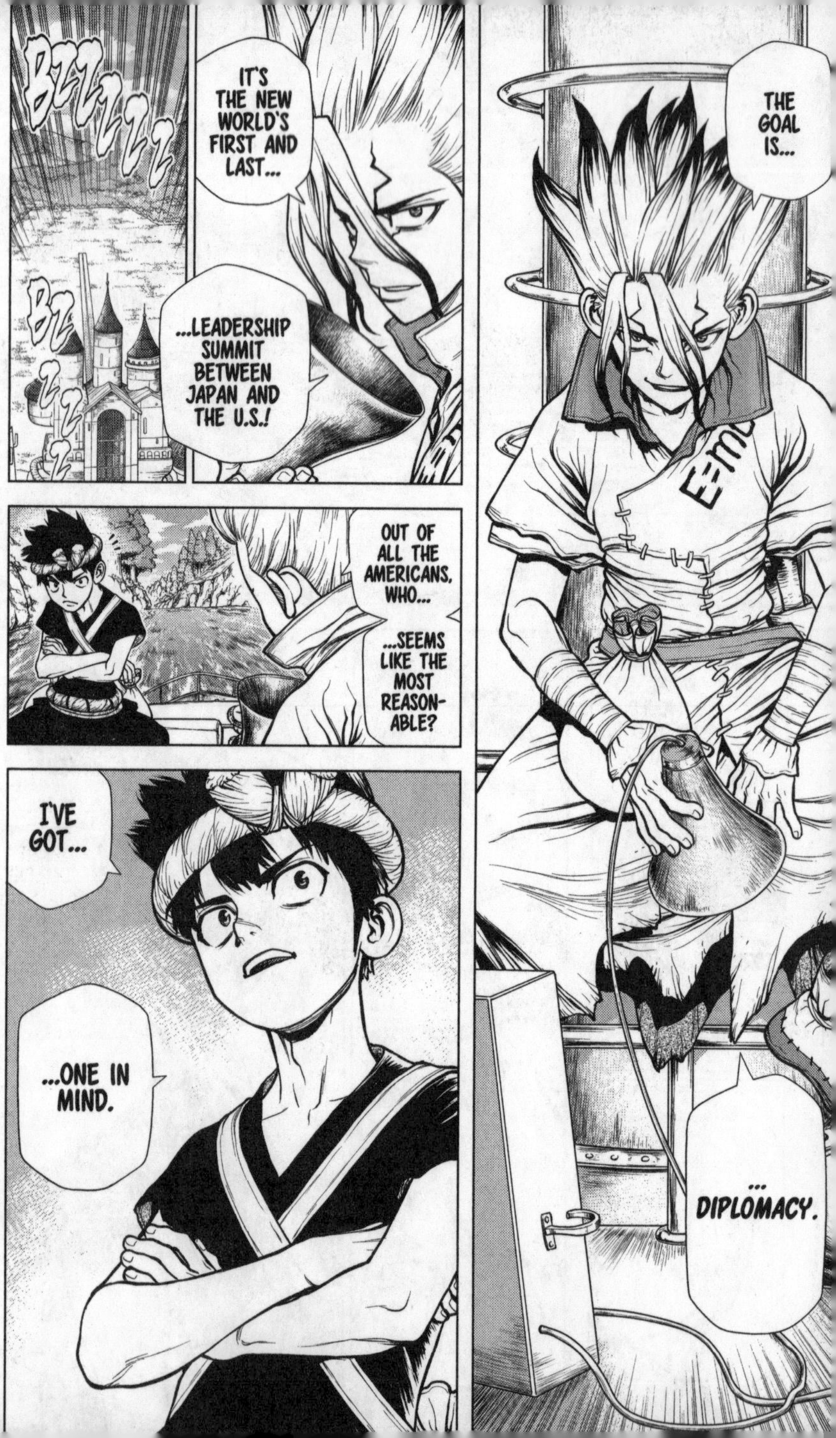
THE GOAL IS...
... DIPLOMACY.
IT'S THE NEW WORLD'S FIRST AND LAST...
...LEADERSHIP SUMMIT BETWEEN JAPAN AND THE U.S.!
BZZZZZZ
BZZZZ
OUT OF ALL THE AMERICANS, WHO...
...SEEMS LIKE THE MOST REASON-ABLE?
I'VE GOT...
...ONE IN MIND.

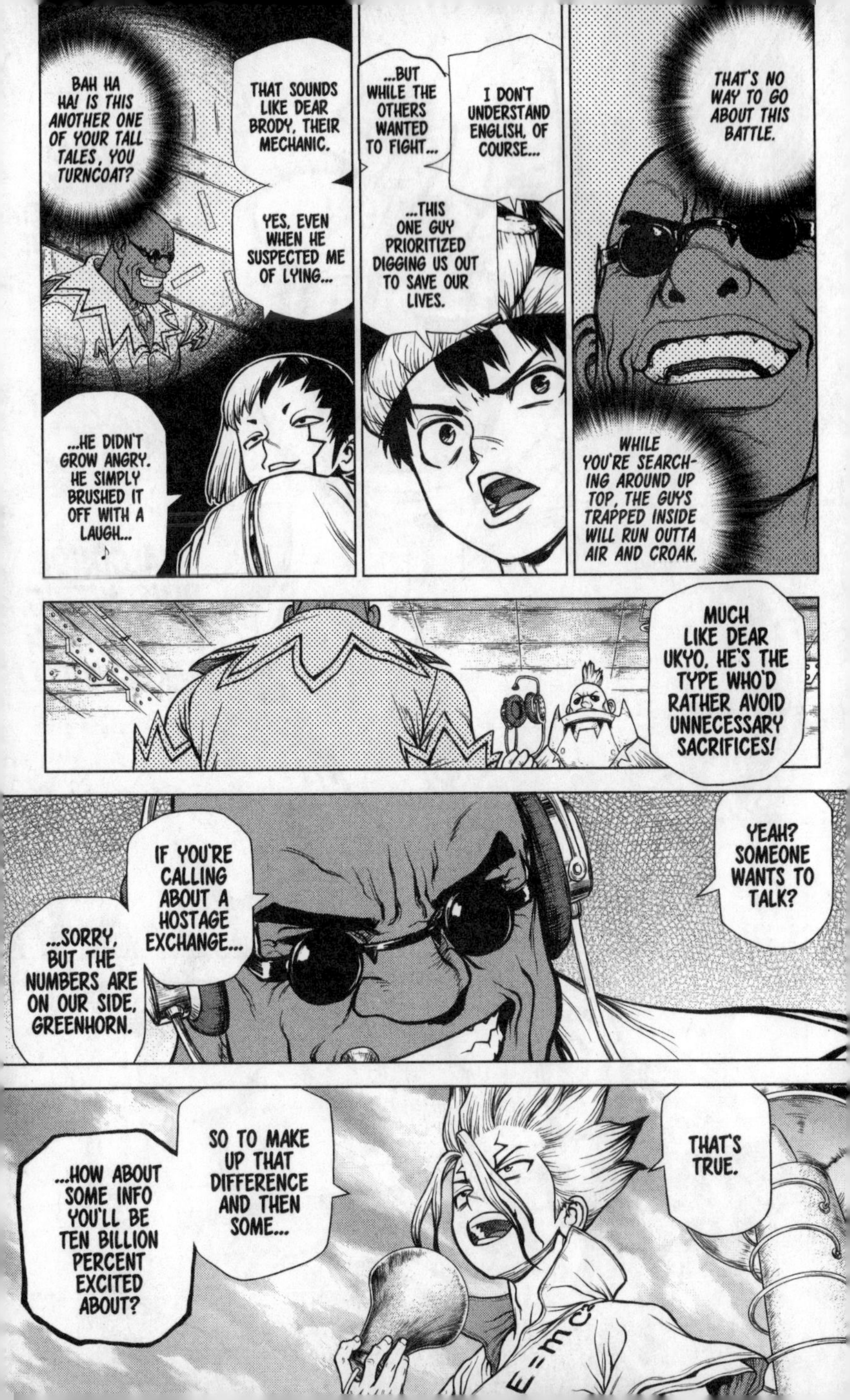
THAT'S NO WAY TO GO ABOUT THIS BATTLE.
WHILE YOU'RE SEARCHING AROUND UP TOP, THE GUYS TRAPPED INSIDE WILL RUN OUTTA AIR AND CROAK.
I DON'T UNDERSTAND ENGLISH, OF COURSE...
...BUT WHILE THE OTHERS WANTED TO FIGHT...
...THIS ONE GUY PRIORITIZED DIGGING US OUT TO SAVE OUR LIVES.
THAT SOUNDS LIKE DEAR BRODY, THEIR MECHANIC.
BAH HA HA! IS THIS ANOTHER ONE OF YOUR TALL TALES, YOU TURNCOAT?
YES, EVEN WHEN HE SUSPECTED ME OF LYING...
...HE DIDN'T GROW ANGRY. HE SIMPLY BRUSHED IT OFF WITH A LAUGH... ♪
MUCH LIKE DEAR UKYO, HE'S THE TYPE WHO'D RATHER AVOID UNNECESSARY SACRIFICES!
YEAH? SOMEONE WANTS TO TALK?
IF YOU'RE CALLING ABOUT A HOSTAGE EXCHANGE...
...SORRY, BUT THE NUMBERS ARE ON OUR SIDE, GREENHORN.
THAT'S TRUE.
SO TO MAKE UP THAT DIFFERENCE AND THEN SOME...
...HOW ABOUT SOME INFO YOU'LL BE TEN BILLION PERCENT EXCITED ABOUT?

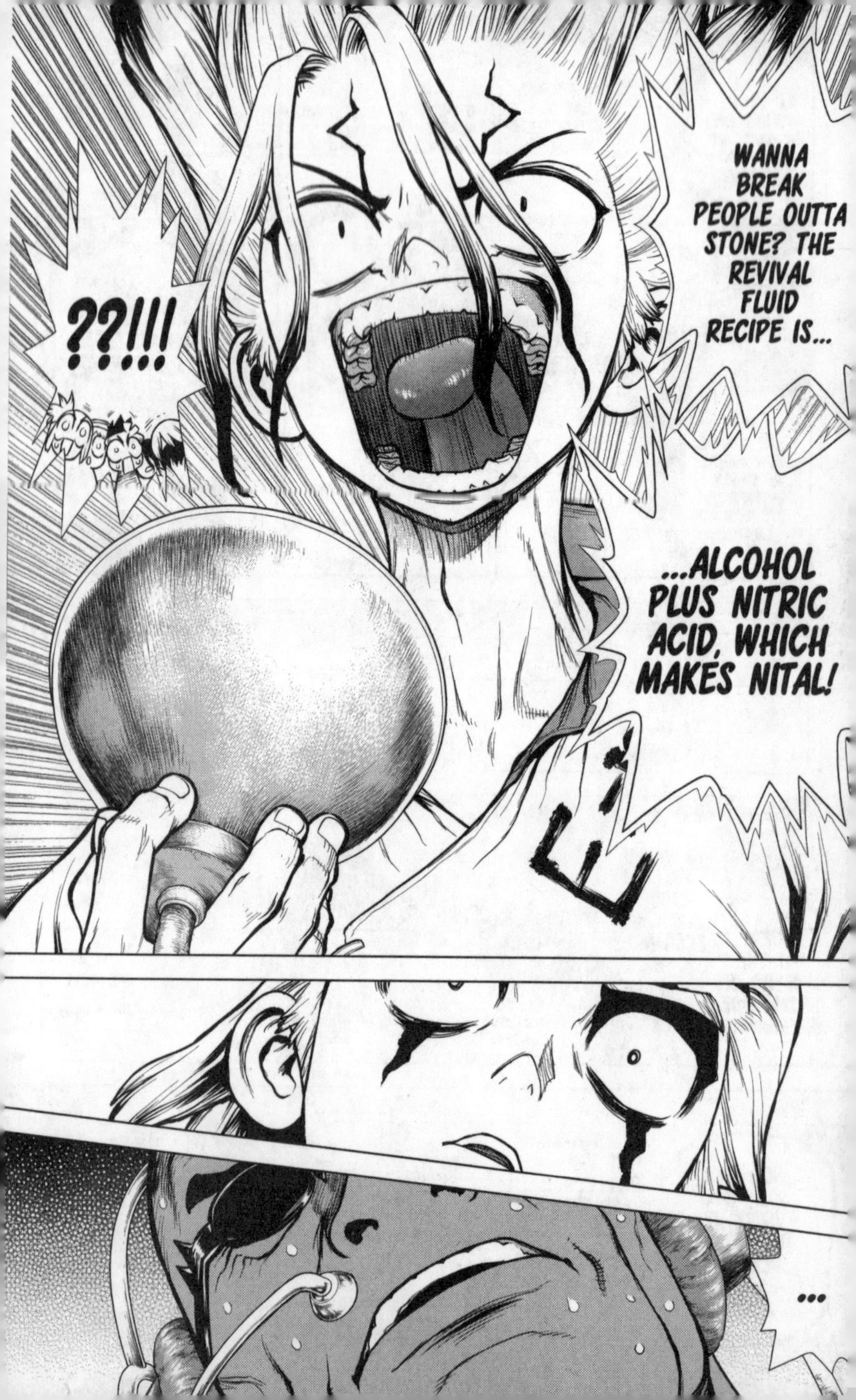
WANNA BREAK PEOPLE OUTTA STONE? THE REVIVAL FLUID RECIPE IS...
??!!!
...ALCOHOL PLUS NITRIC ACID, WHICH MAKES NITAL!
...

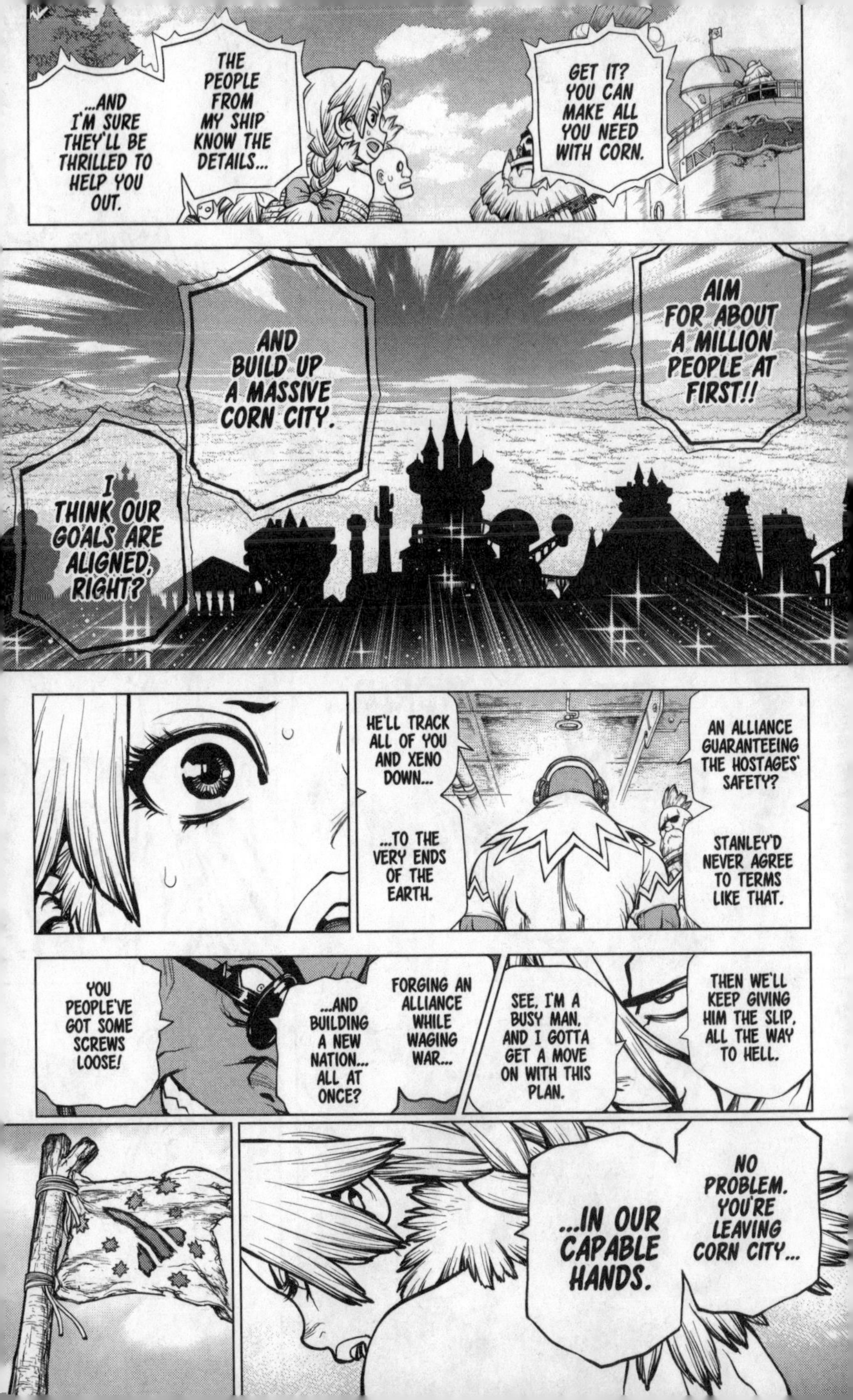
GET IT? YOU CAN MAKE ALL YOU NEED WITH CORN.
THE PEOPLE FROM MY SHIP KNOW THE DETAILS...
...AND I'M SURE THEY'LL BE THRILLED TO HELP YOU OUT.
AIM FOR ABOUT A MILLION PEOPLE AT FIRST!!
AND BUILD UP A MASSIVE CORN CITY.
I THINK OUR GOALS ARE ALIGNED, RIGHT?
AN ALLIANCE GUARANTEEING THE HOSTAGES' SAFETY?
STANLEY'D NEVER AGREE TO TERMS LIKE THAT.
HE'LL TRACK ALL OF YOU AND XENO DOWN...
...TO THE VERY ENDS OF THE EARTH.
THEN WE'LL KEEP GIVING HIM THE SLIP, ALL THE WAY TO HELL.
SEE, I'M A BUSY MAN, AND I GOTTA GET A MOVE ON WITH THIS PLAN.
FORGING AN ALLIANCE WHILE WAGING WAR...
...AND BUILDING A NEW NATION... ALL AT ONCE?
YOU PEOPLE'VE GOT SOME SCREWS LOOSE!
NO PROBLEM. YOU'RE LEAVING CORN CITY...
...IN OUR CAPABLE HANDS.

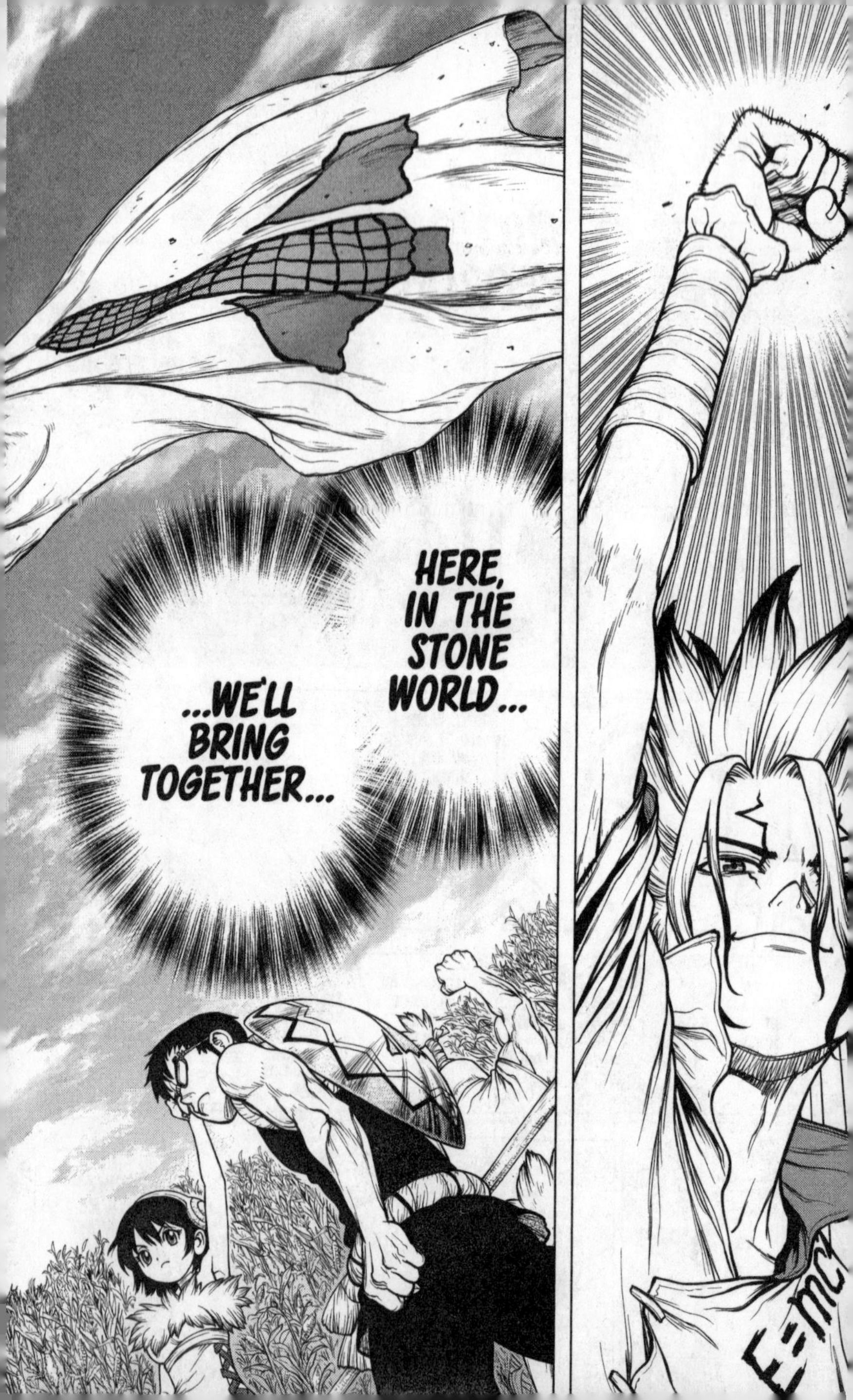
E=mc
HERE, IN THE STONE WORLD...
...WE'LL BRING TOGETHER...

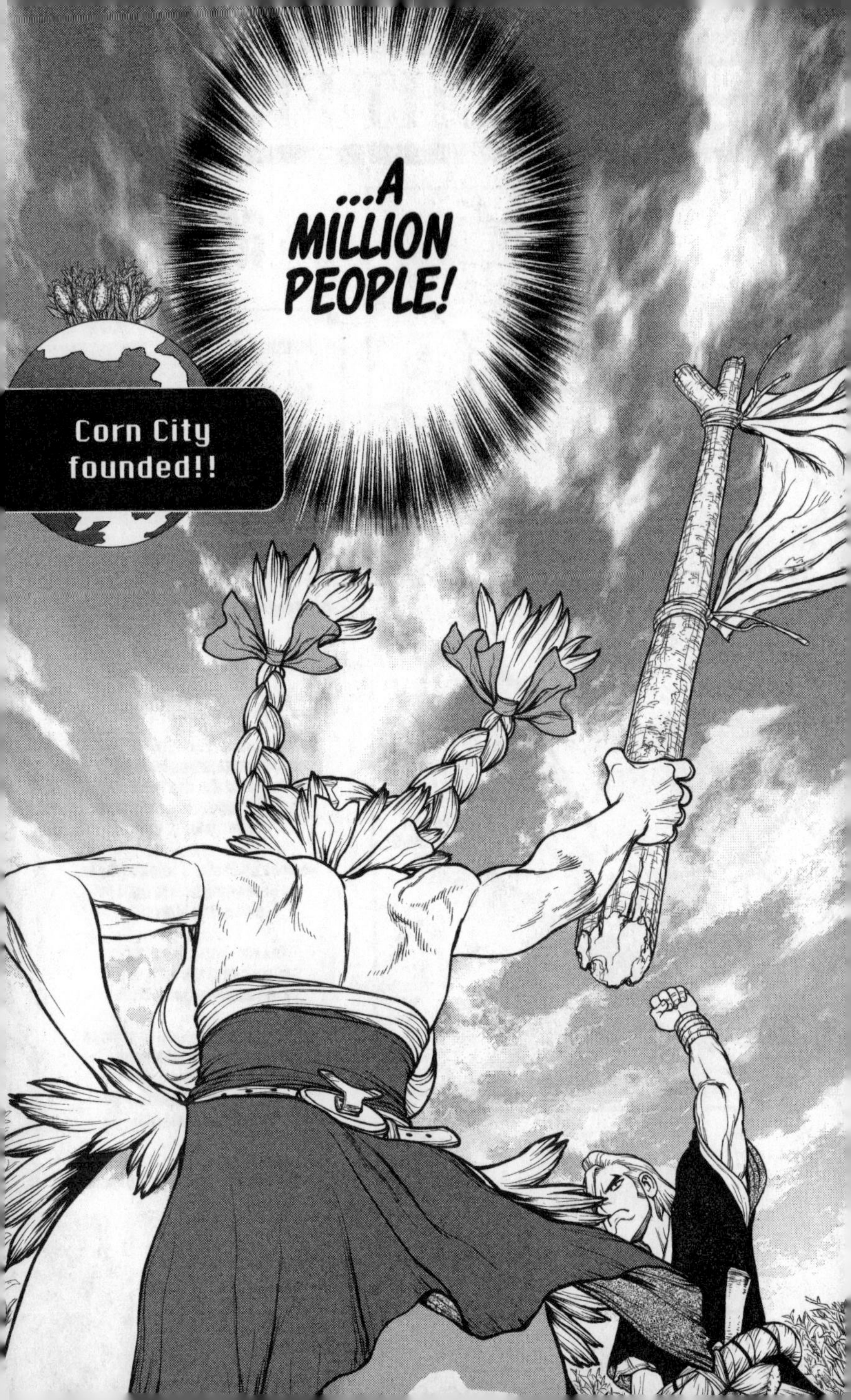
...A MILLION PEOPLE!
Corn City founded!!

Xeno's Science Kingdom

KNIGHT FILE 6

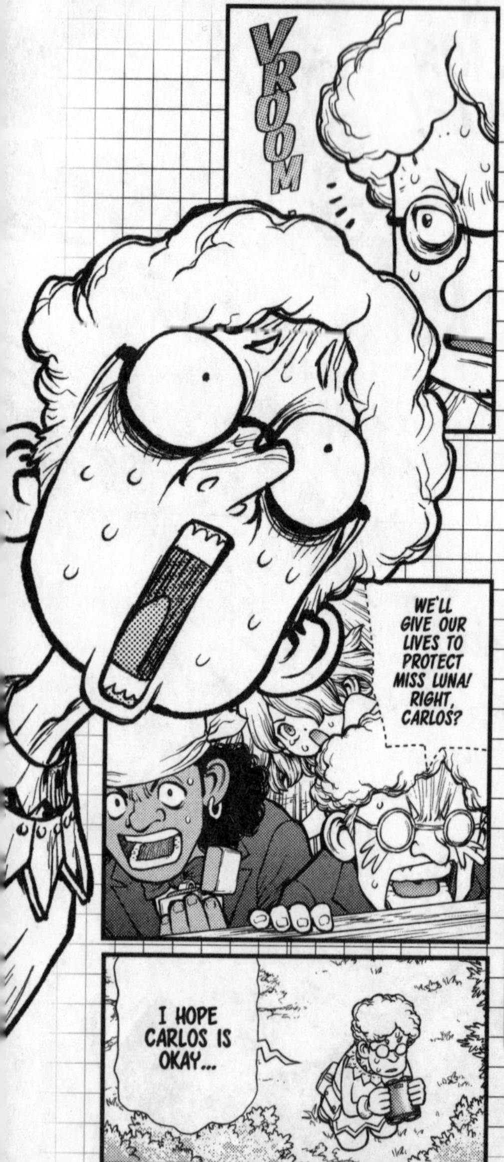
VROOM
WE'LL GIVE OUR LIVES TO PROTECT MISS LUNA! RIGHT, CARLOS?
I HOPE CARLOS IS OKAY...

Max

Power	★★
Speed	★★★★
Technique	★★★★

■ Full Name: Max Adomc

■ Height: 160 cm

■ Profession: Hunter/Farmer

Max's short stature isn't a disadvantage, since he takes full advantage of his size to maneuver around opponents quickly to get the drop on them.

He grew up in a bad neighborhood, so he learned how to fight by defending himself.

Max was hired to be Luna's bodyguard at the suggestion of his acquaintance, Carlos.

He somehow managed to provide the young miss with ample protection without being too suffocating or preventing her from living her life!

Max views his (lack of) height as the ultimate gift from the heavens.

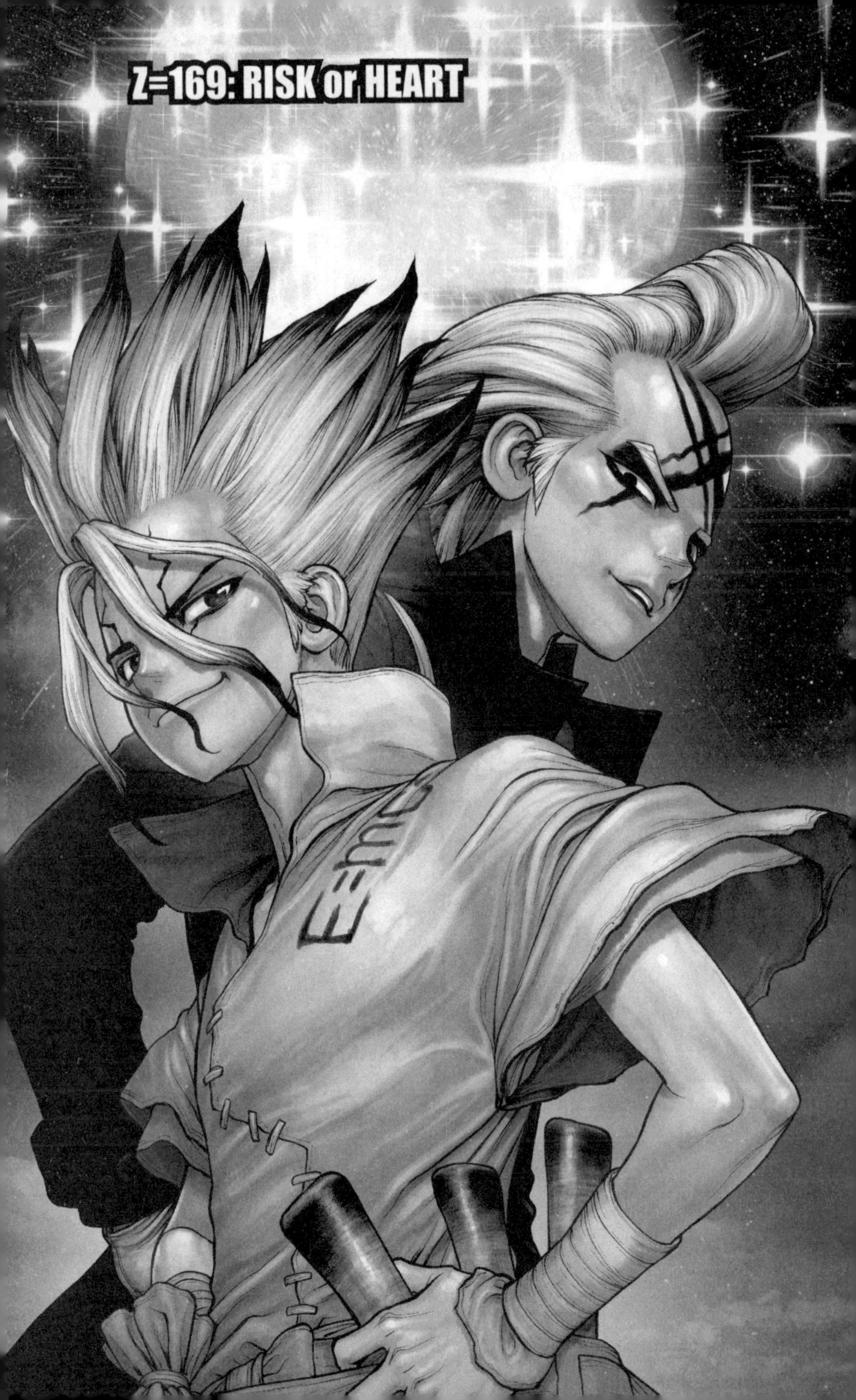
Z=169: RISK or HEART

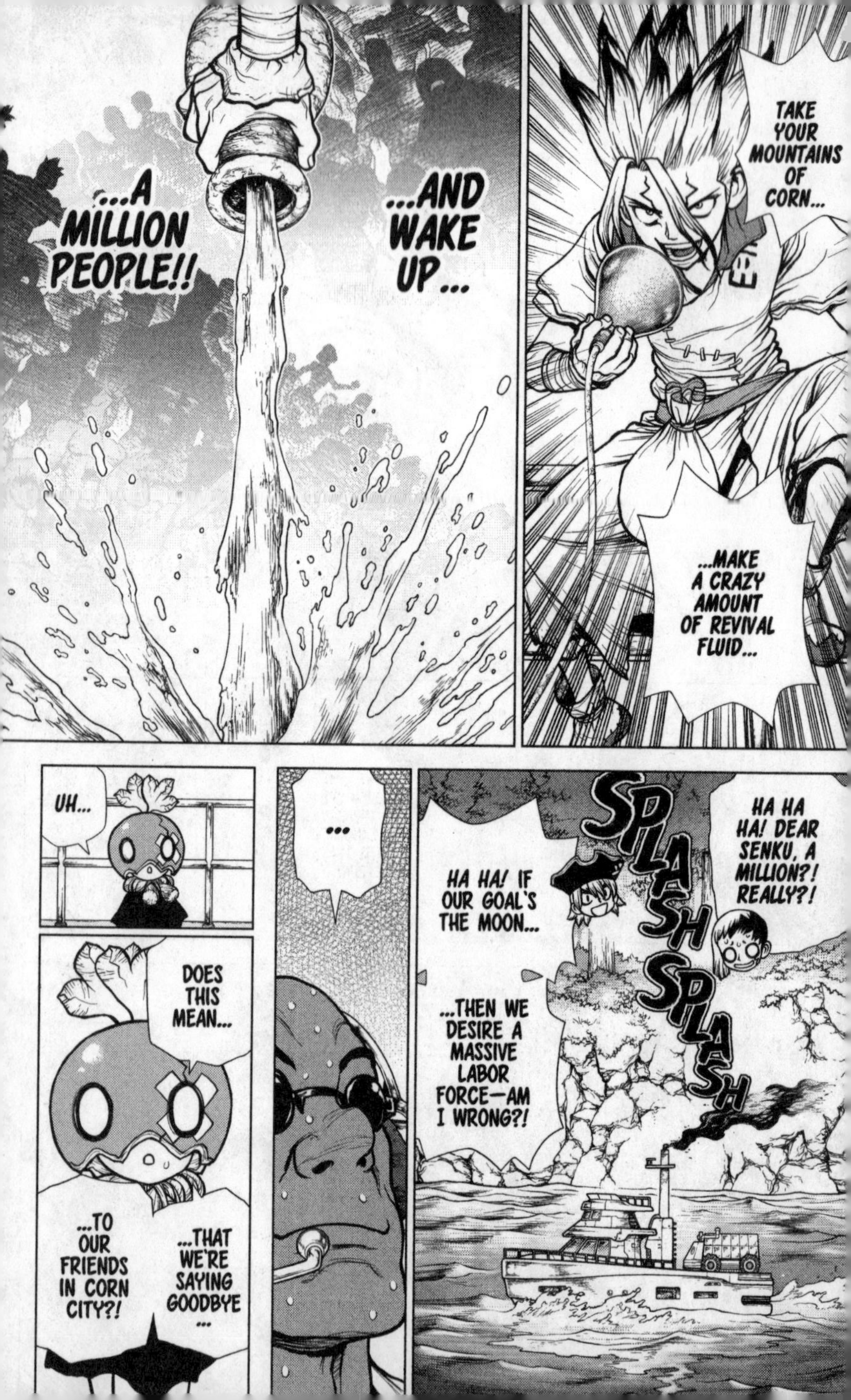
TAKE YOUR MOUNTAINS OF CORN...
...MAKE A CRAZY AMOUNT OF REVIVAL FLUID...
...AND WAKE UP...
...A MILLION PEOPLE!!
HA HA HA! DEAR SENKU, A MILLION?! REALLY?!
SPLASH
SPLASH
HA HA! IF OUR GOAL'S THE MOON...
...THEN WE DESIRE A MASSIVE LABOR FORCE—AM I WRONG?!
...
UH...
DOES THIS MEAN...
...THAT WE'RE SAYING GOODBYE...
...TO OUR FRIENDS IN CORN CITY?!

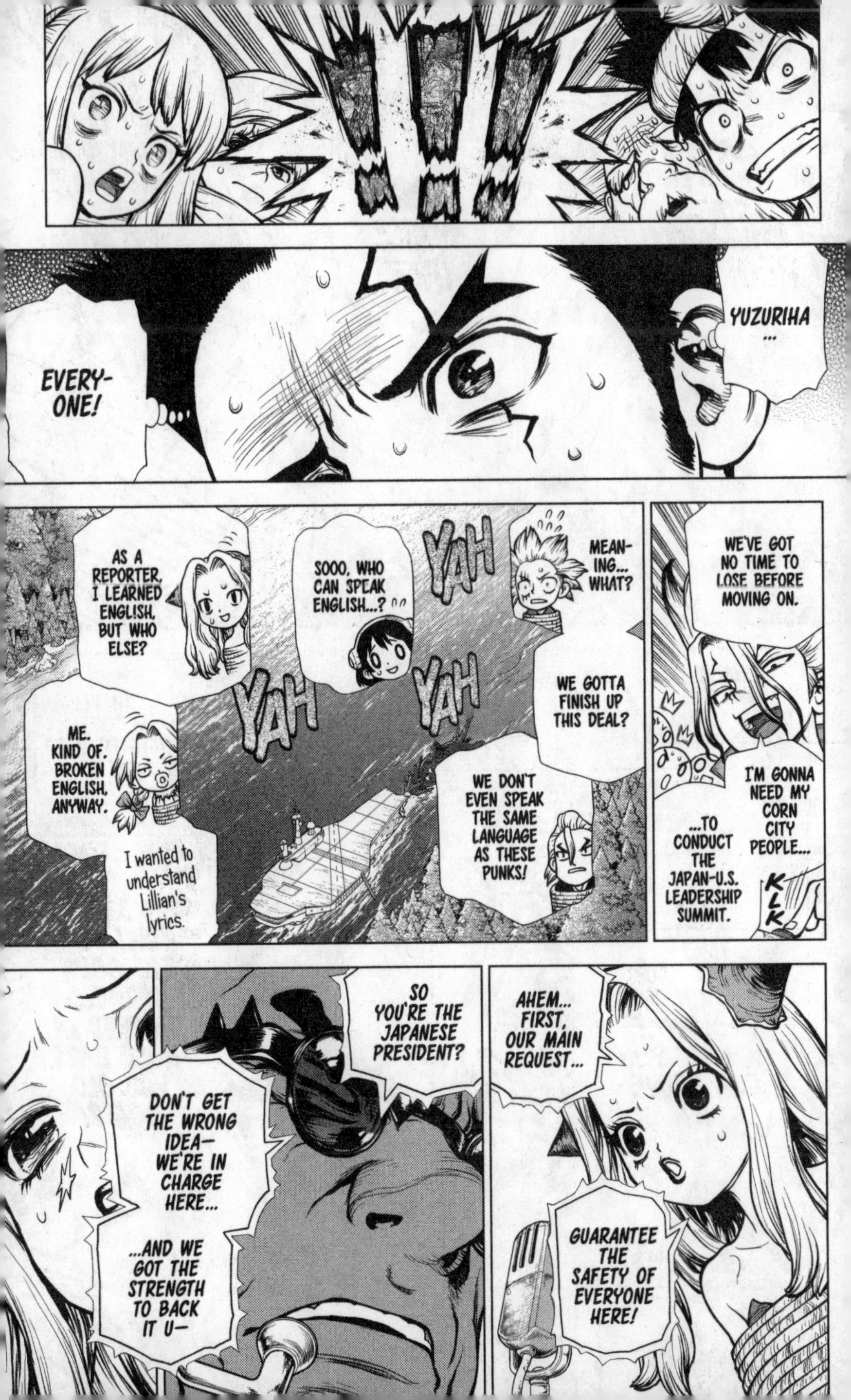
YUZURIHA ...
EVERY-ONE!
WE'VE GOT NO TIME TO LOSE BEFORE MOVING ON.
I'M GONNA NEED MY CORN CITY PEOPLE...
...TO CONDUCT THE JAPAN-U.S. LEADERSHIP SUMMIT.
KLK
MEAN-ING... WHAT?
YAH
SOOO, WHO CAN SPEAK ENGLISH...?
AS A REPORTER, I LEARNED ENGLISH, BUT WHO ELSE?
WE GOTTA FINISH UP THIS DEAL?
YAH
YAH
WE DON'T EVEN SPEAK THE SAME LANGUAGE AS THESE PUNKS!
ME. KIND OF. BROKEN ENGLISH, ANYWAY.
I wanted to understand Lillian's lyrics.
AHEM... FIRST, OUR MAIN REQUEST...
GUARANTEE THE SAFETY OF EVERYONE HERE!
SO YOU'RE THE JAPANESE PRESIDENT?
DON'T GET THE WRONG IDEA— WE'RE IN CHARGE HERE...
...AND WE GOT THE STRENGTH TO BACK IT U—

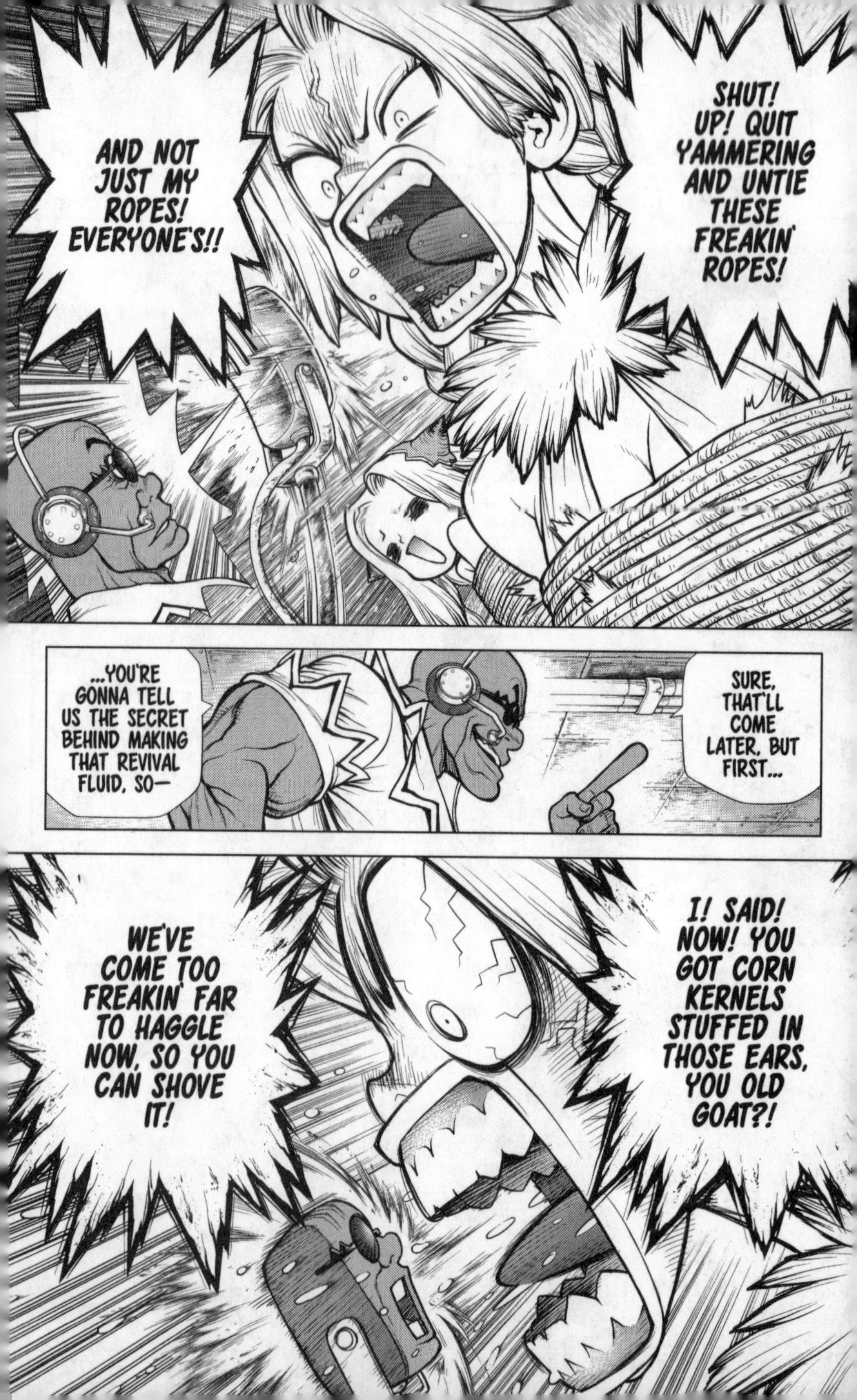
SHUT! UP! QUIT YAMMERING AND UNTIE THESE FREAKIN' ROPES!
AND NOT JUST MY ROPES! EVERYONE'S!!
SURE, THAT'LL COME LATER, BUT FIRST...
...YOU'RE GONNA TELL US THE SECRET BEHIND MAKING THAT REVIVAL FLUID, SO—
I! SAID! NOW! YOU GOT CORN KERNELS STUFFED IN THOSE EARS, YOU OLD GOAT?!
WE'VE COME TOO FREAKIN' FAR TO HAGGLE NOW, SO YOU CAN SHOVE IT!

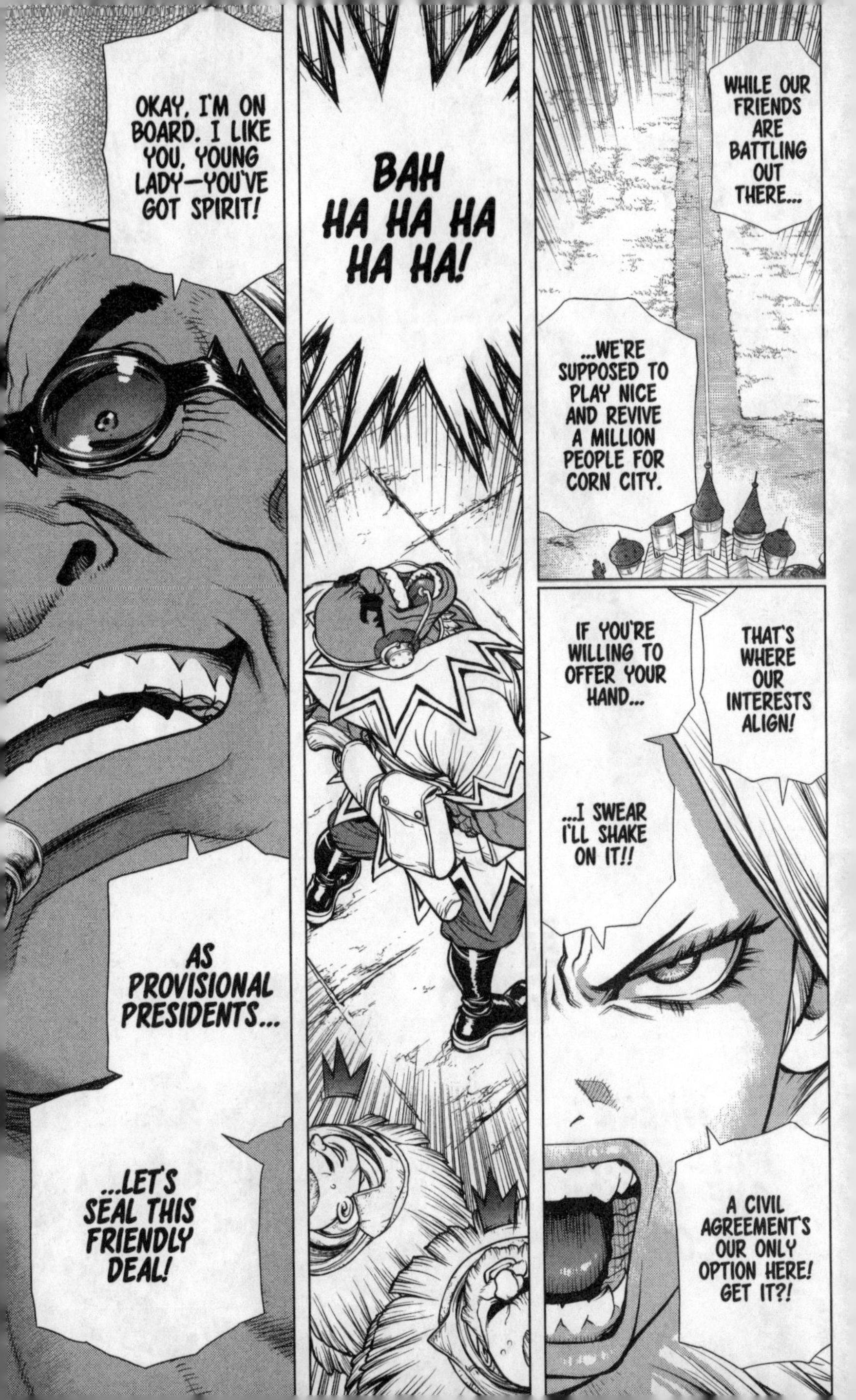
WHILE OUR FRIENDS ARE BATTLING OUT THERE...
...WE'RE SUPPOSED TO PLAY NICE AND REVIVE A MILLION PEOPLE FOR CORN CITY.
THAT'S WHERE OUR INTERESTS ALIGN!
IF YOU'RE WILLING TO OFFER YOUR HAND...
...I SWEAR I'LL SHAKE ON IT!!
A CIVIL AGREEMENT'S OUR ONLY OPTION HERE! GET IT?!
BAH HA HA HA HA HA!
OKAY, I'M ON BOARD. I LIKE YOU, YOUNG LADY—YOU'VE GOT SPIRIT!
AS PROVISIONAL PRESIDENTS...
...LET'S SEAL THIS FRIENDLY DEAL!

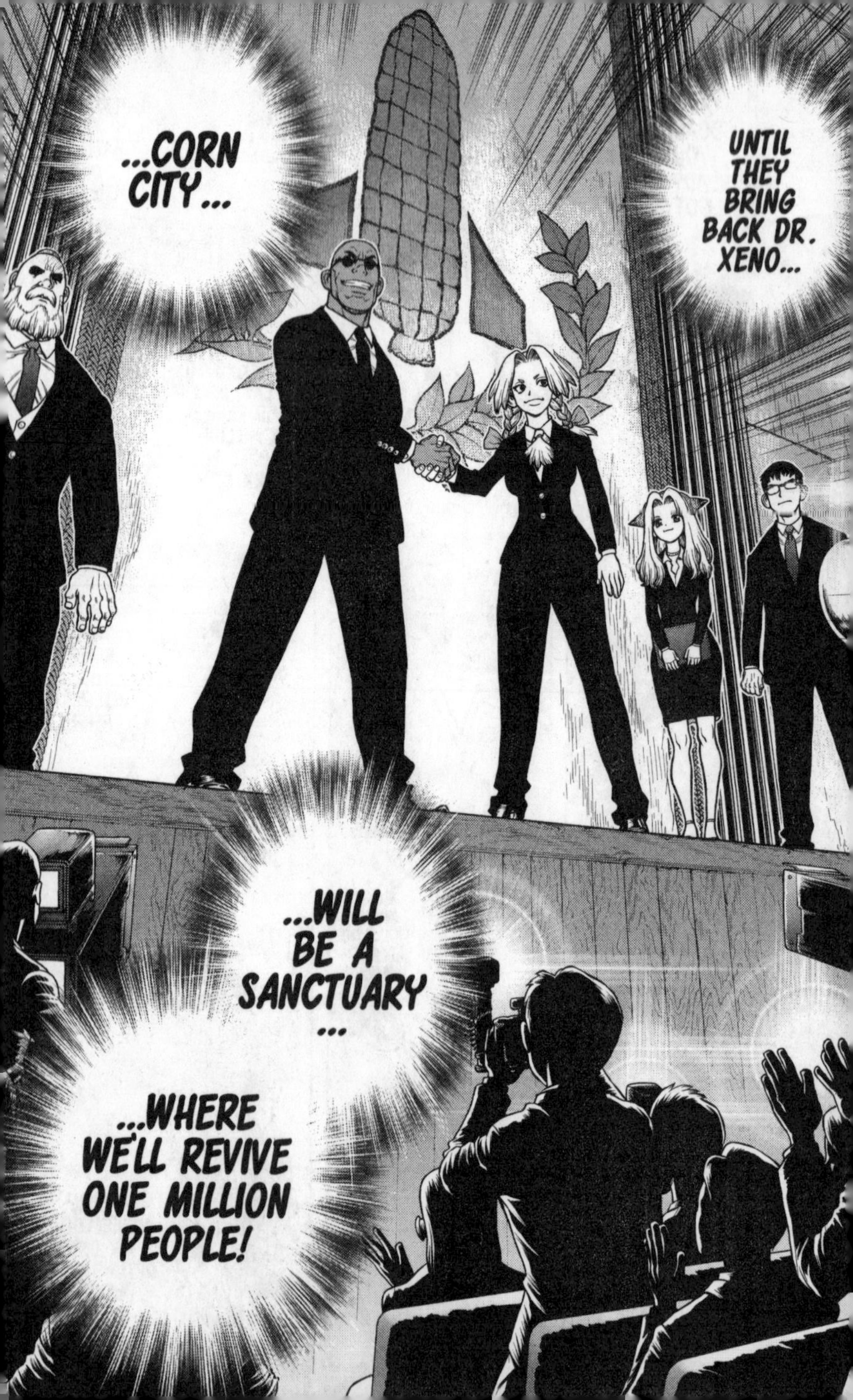
UNTIL THEY BRING BACK DR. XENO...
...CORN CITY...
...WILL BE A SANCTUARY ...
...WHERE WE'LL REVIVE ONE MILLION PEOPLE!

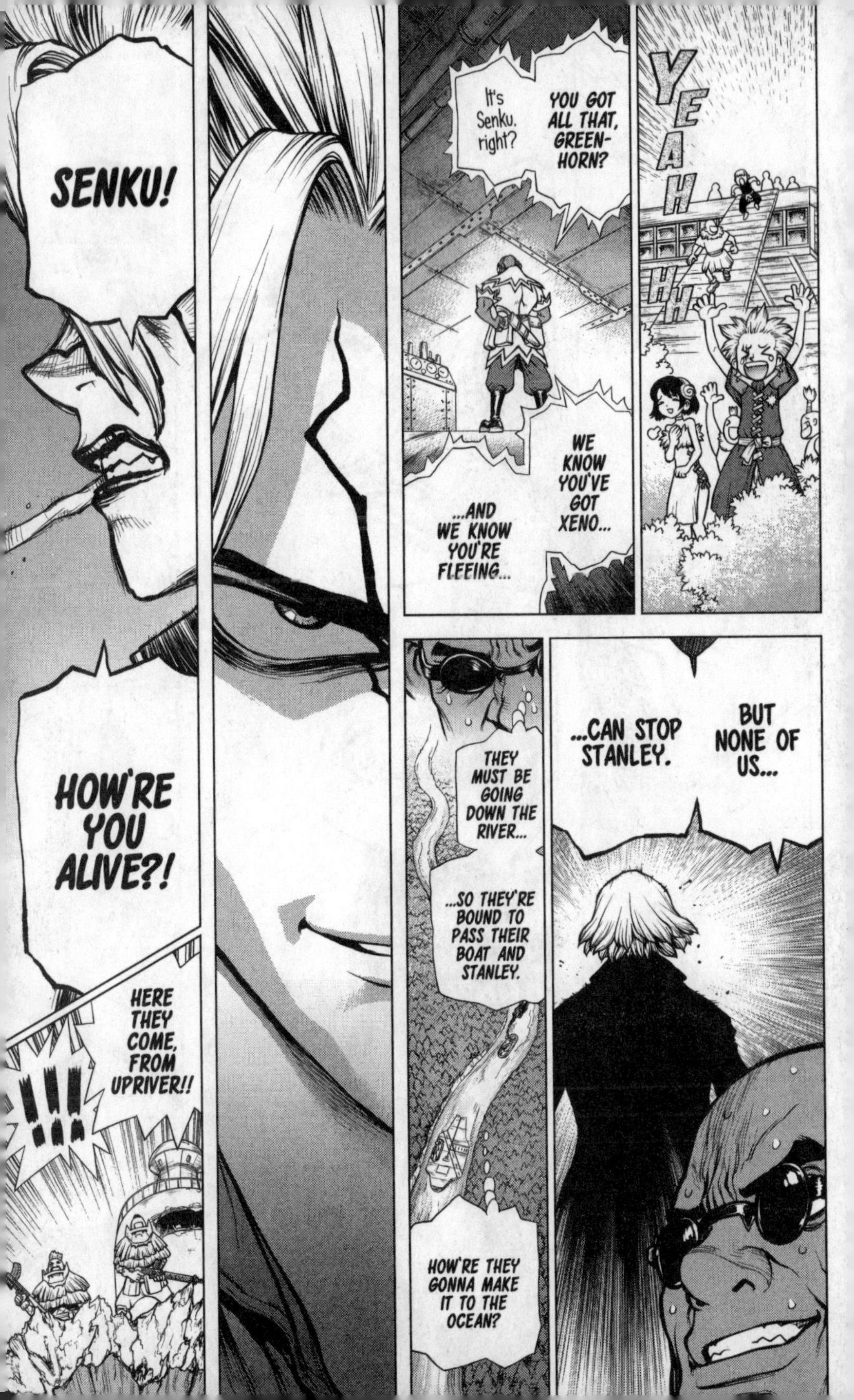
YEAHHH
YOU GOT ALL THAT, GREENHORN?
It's Senku, right?
WE KNOW YOU'VE GOT XENO...
...AND WE KNOW YOU'RE FLEEING...
BUT NONE OF US...
...CAN STOP STANLEY.
THEY MUST BE GOING DOWN THE RIVER...
...SO THEY'RE BOUND TO PASS THEIR BOAT AND STANLEY.
HOW'RE THEY GONNA MAKE IT TO THE OCEAN?
SENKU!
HOW'RE YOU ALIVE?!
HERE THEY COME, FROM UPRIVER!!
!!!

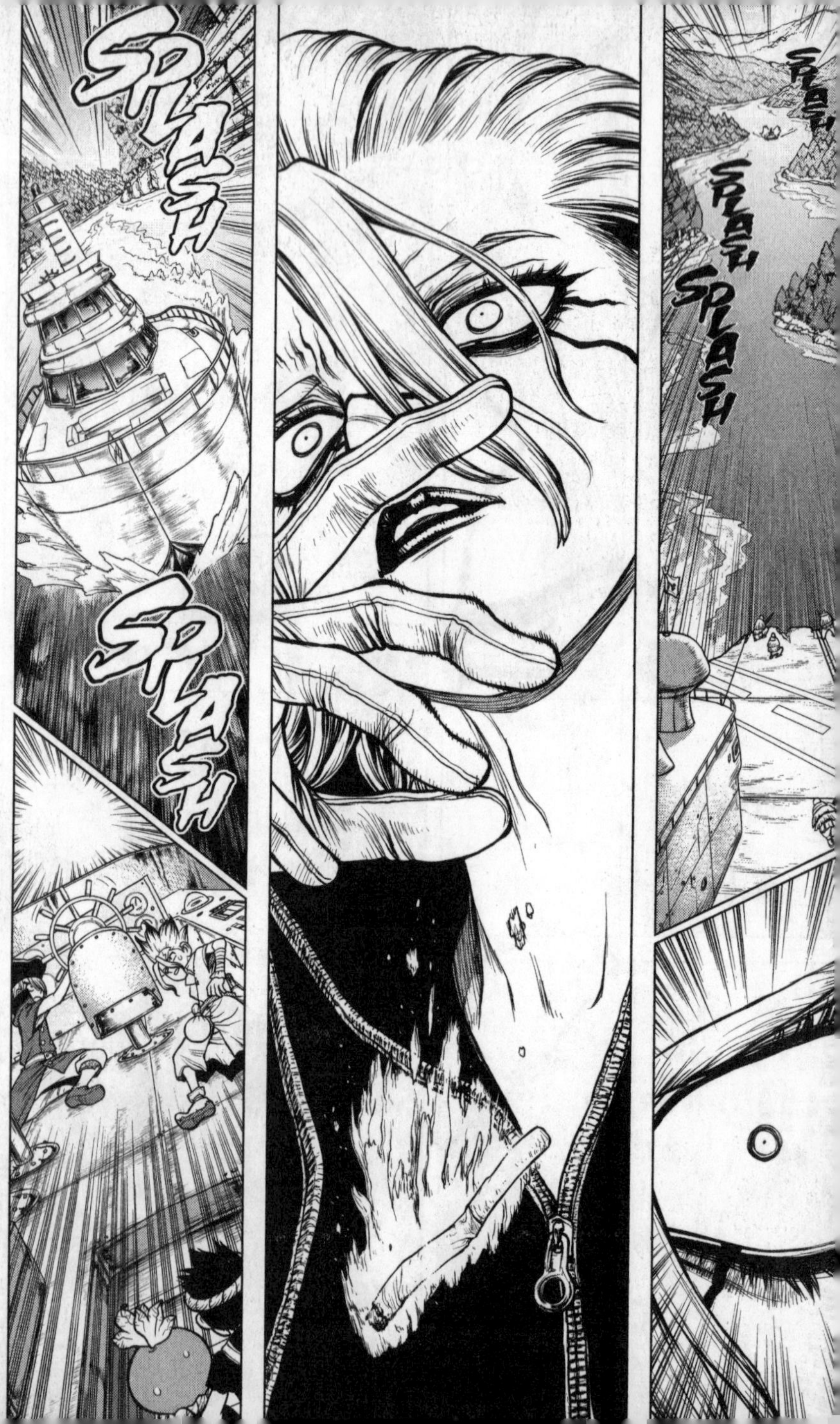
SPLASH
SPLASH
SPLASH
SPLASH
SPLASH

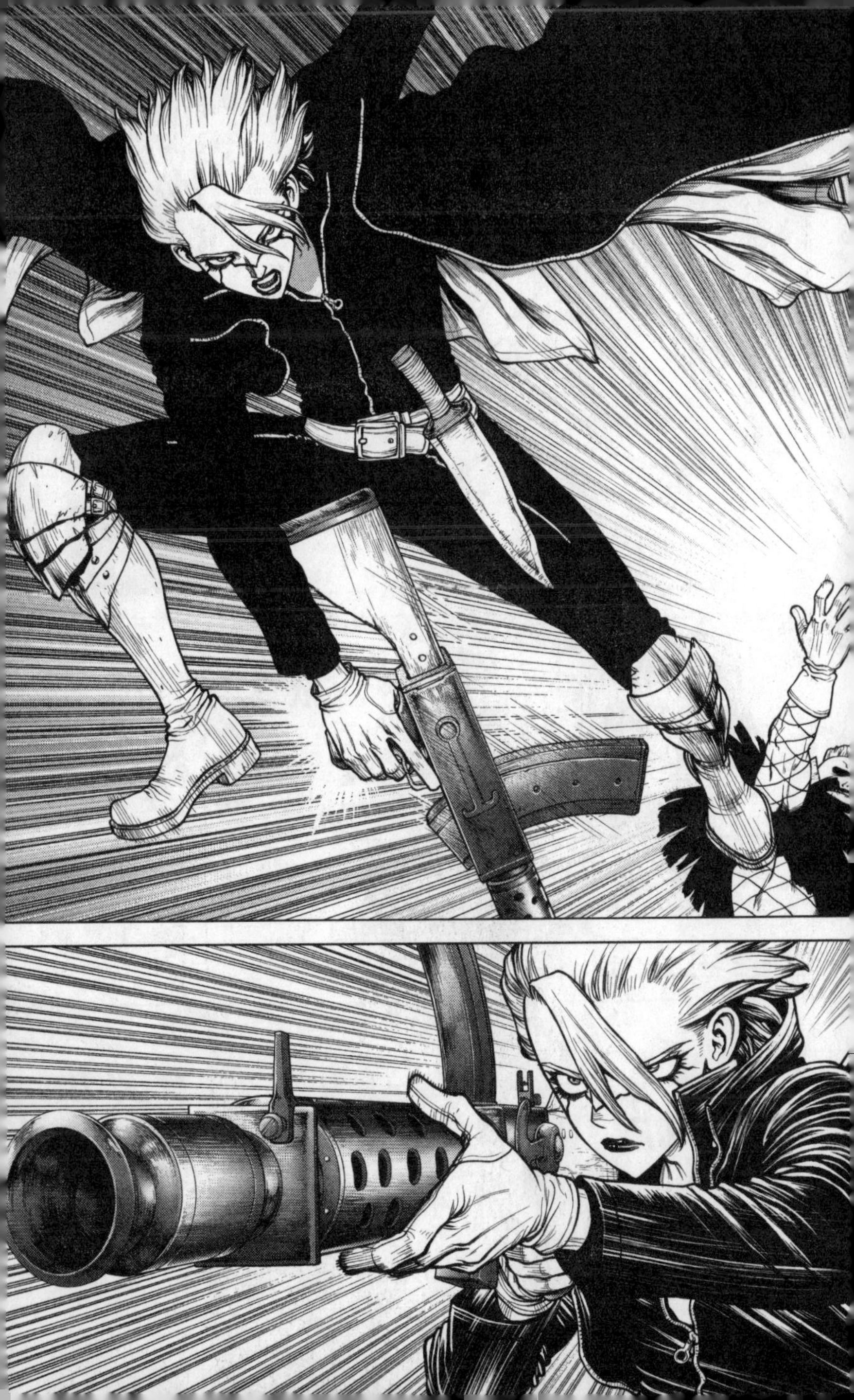

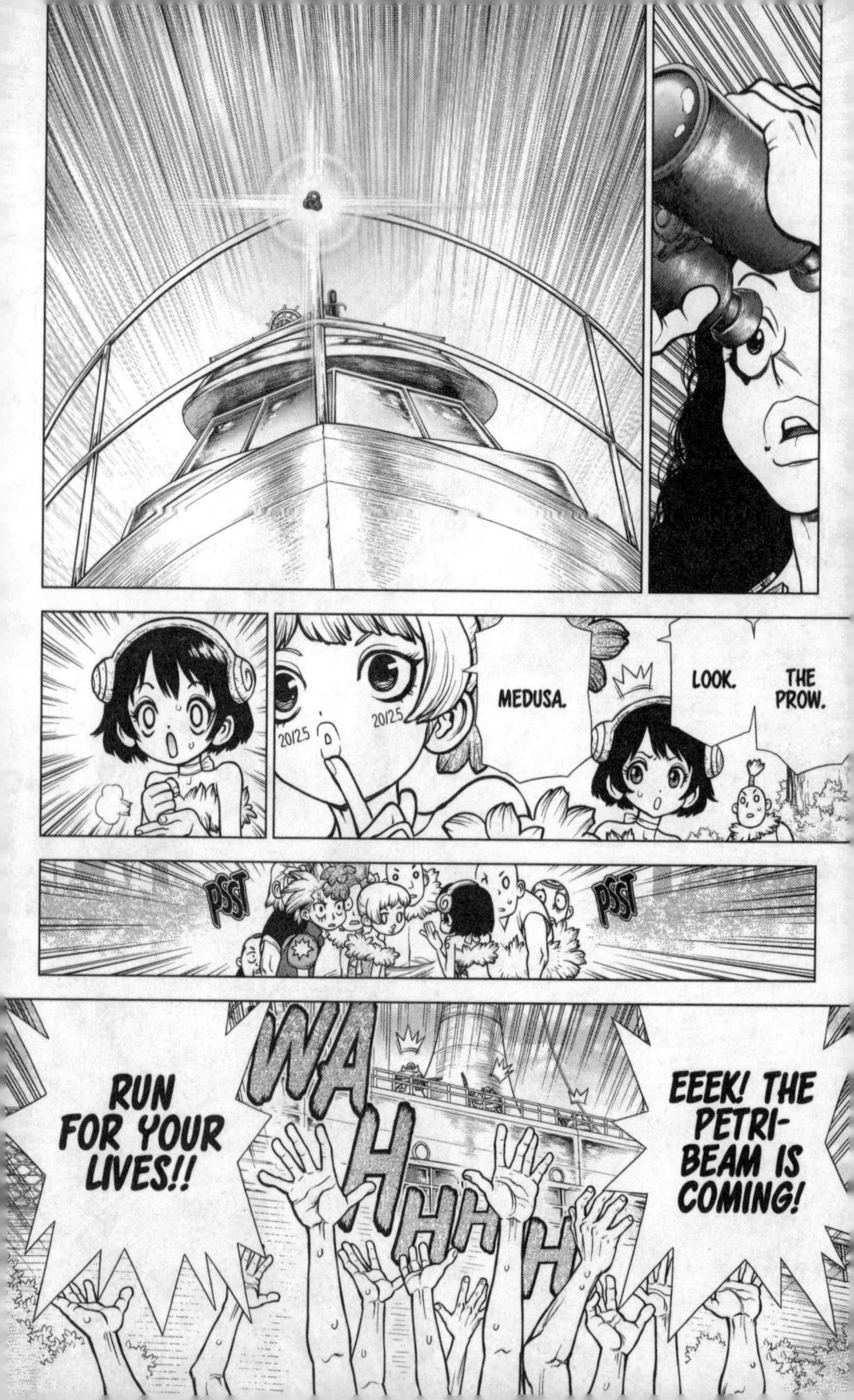
LOOK. THE PROW.
MEDUSA.
PSST
PSST
EEEK! THE PETRI-BEAM IS COMING!
WAHHHHH
RUN FOR YOUR LIVES!!

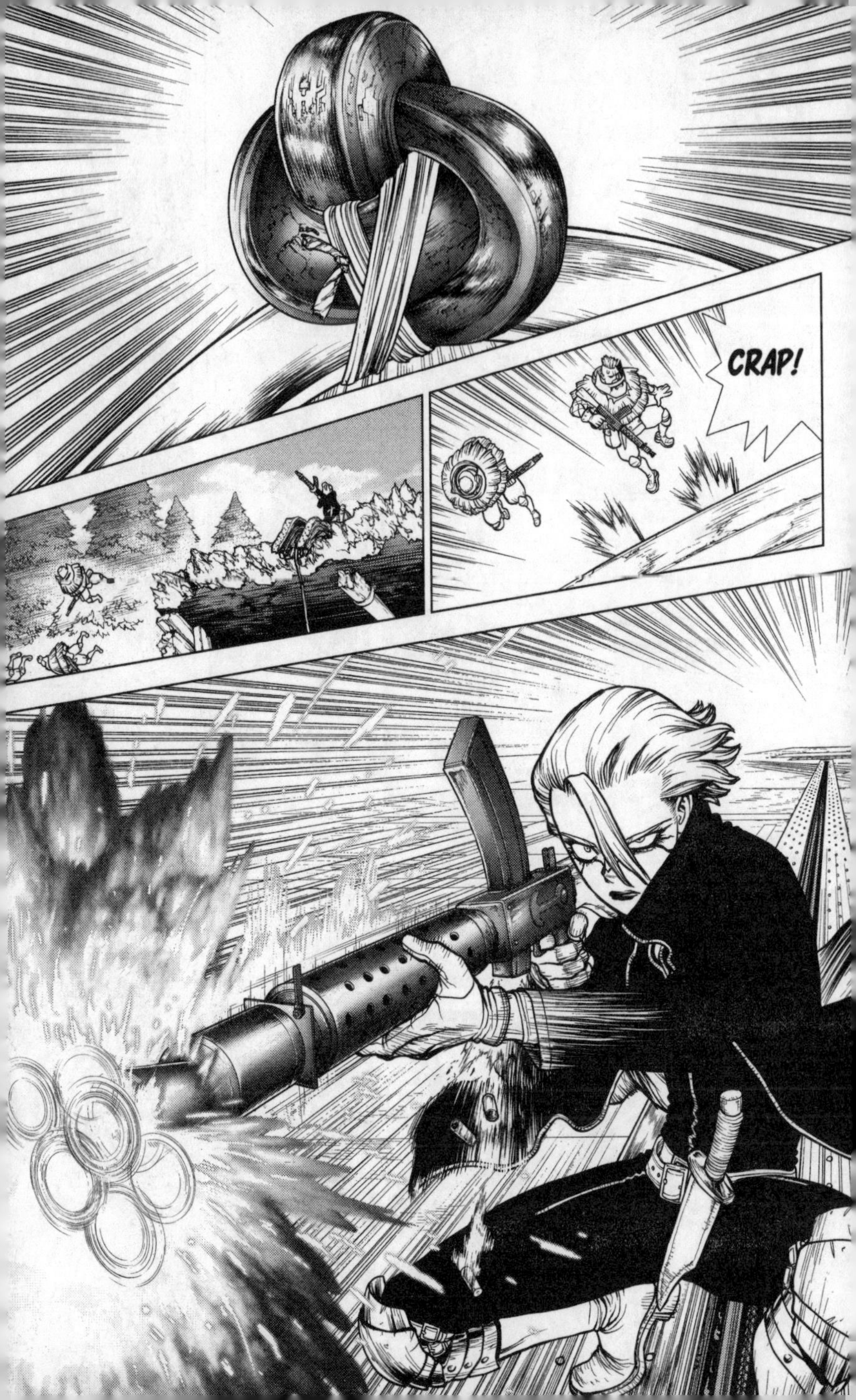
CRAP!

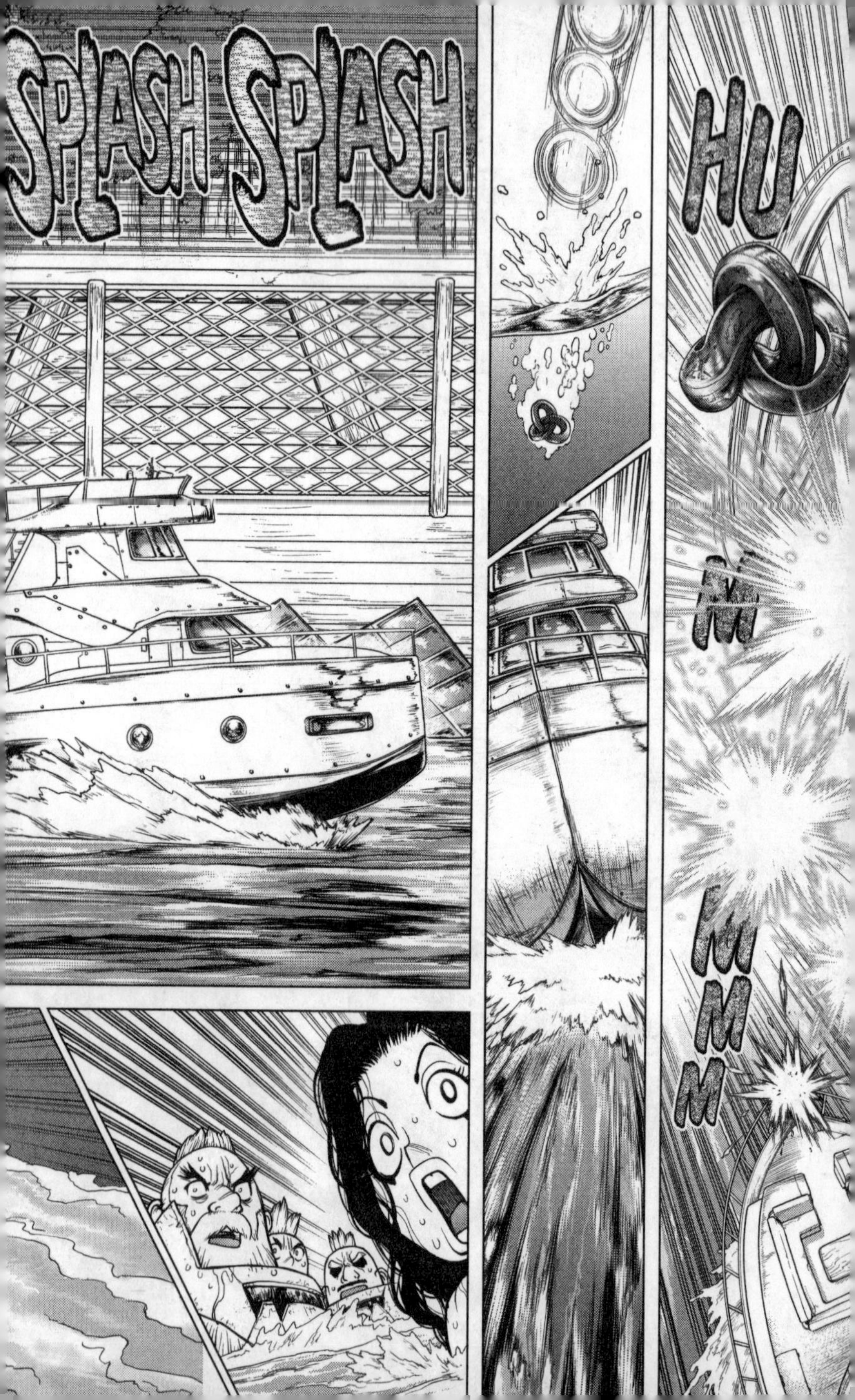
HUMMMM
SPLASH SPLASH

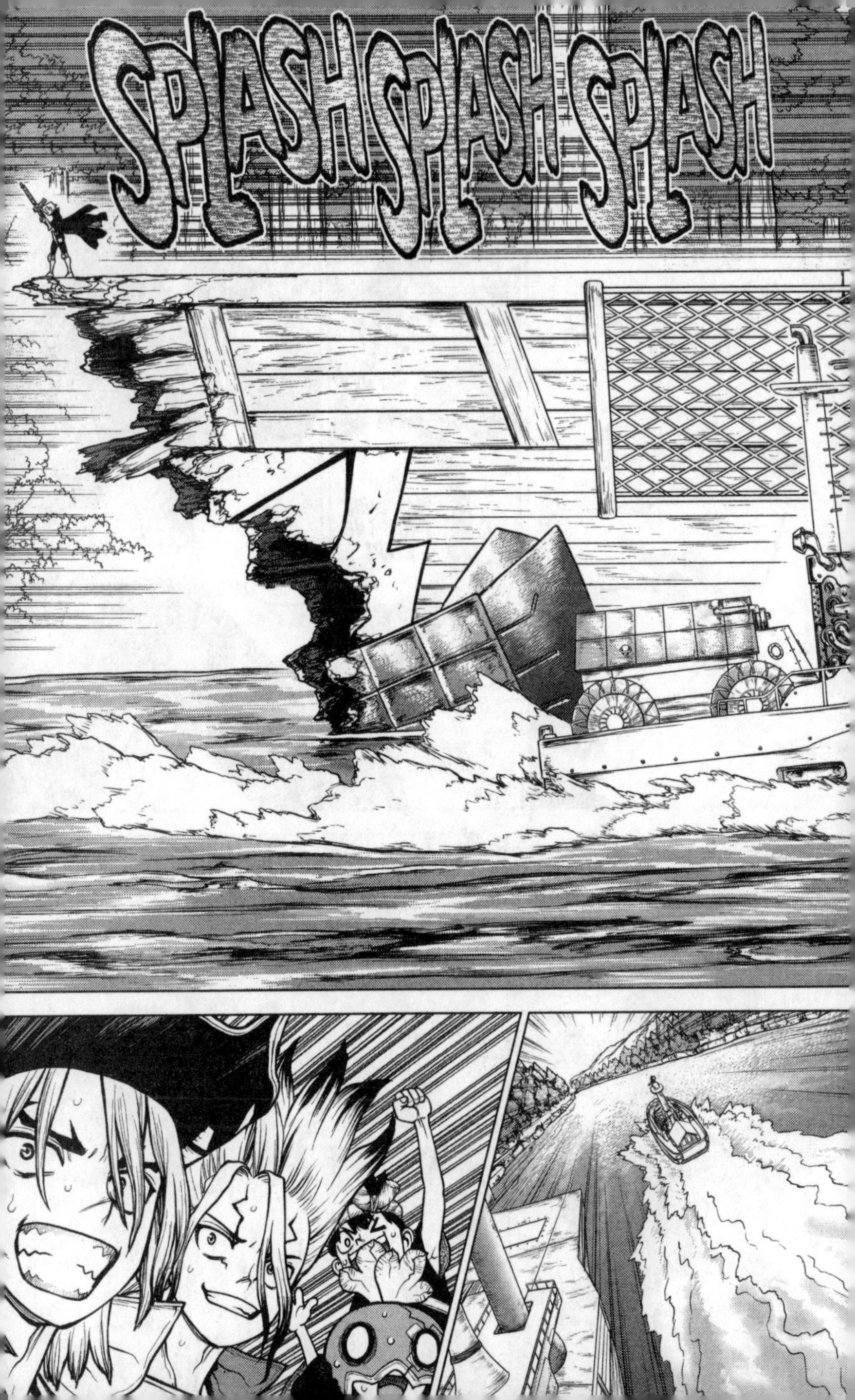
SPLASH SPLASH SPLASH

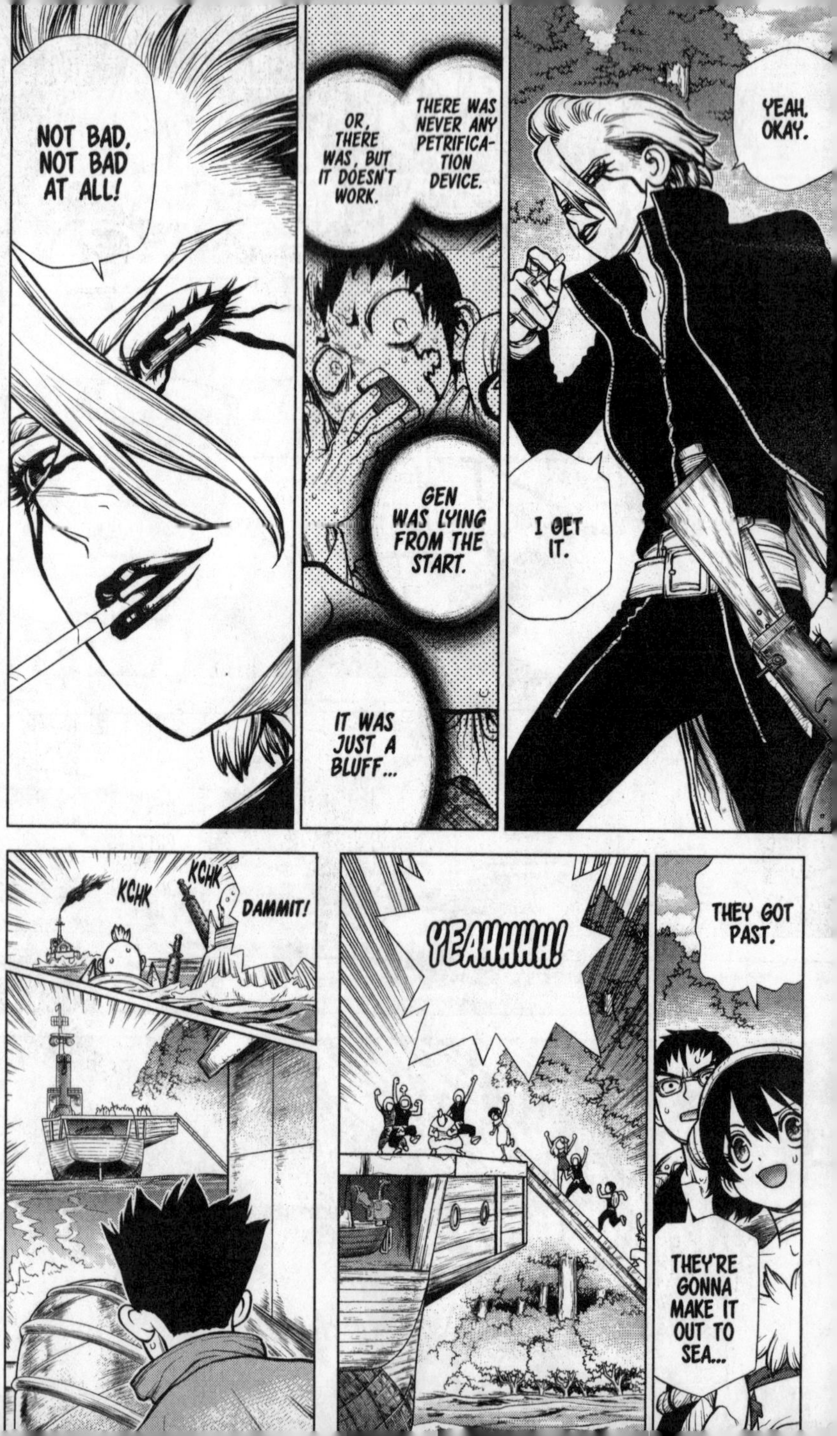
YEAH, OKAY.
I GET IT.
THERE WAS NEVER ANY PETRIFICATION DEVICE.
OR, THERE WAS, BUT IT DOESN'T WORK.
GEN WAS LYING FROM THE START.
IT WAS JUST A BLUFF...
NOT BAD, NOT BAD AT ALL!
THEY GOT PAST.
THEY'RE GONNA MAKE IT OUT TO SEA...
YEAHHHH!
KCHK
DAMMIT!
KCHK

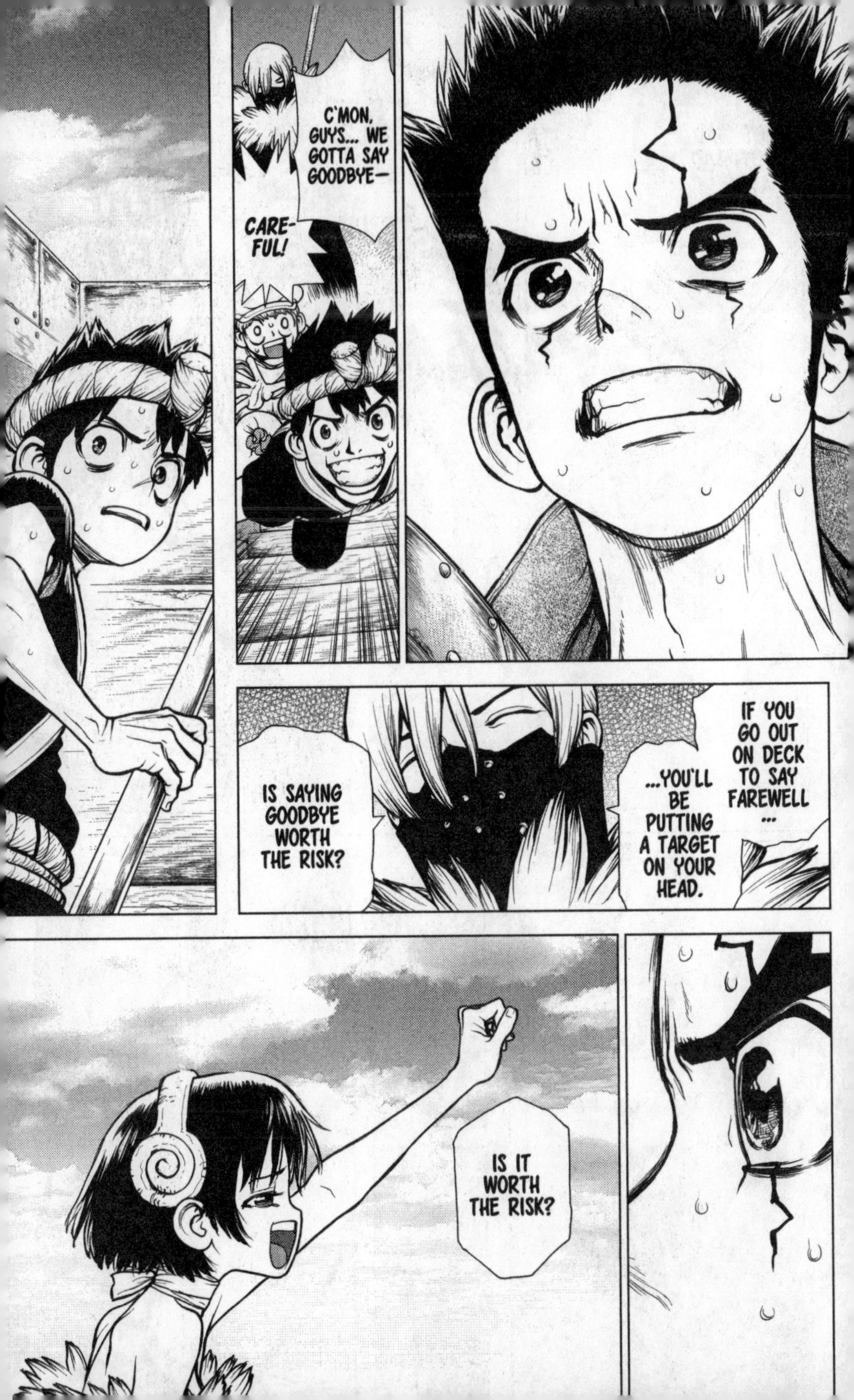
C'MON, GUYS... WE GOTTA SAY GOODBYE—
CARE-FUL!
IF YOU GO OUT ON DECK TO SAY FAREWELL ...
...YOU'LL BE PUTTING A TARGET ON YOUR HEAD.
IS SAYING GOODBYE WORTH THE RISK?
IS IT WORTH THE RISK?

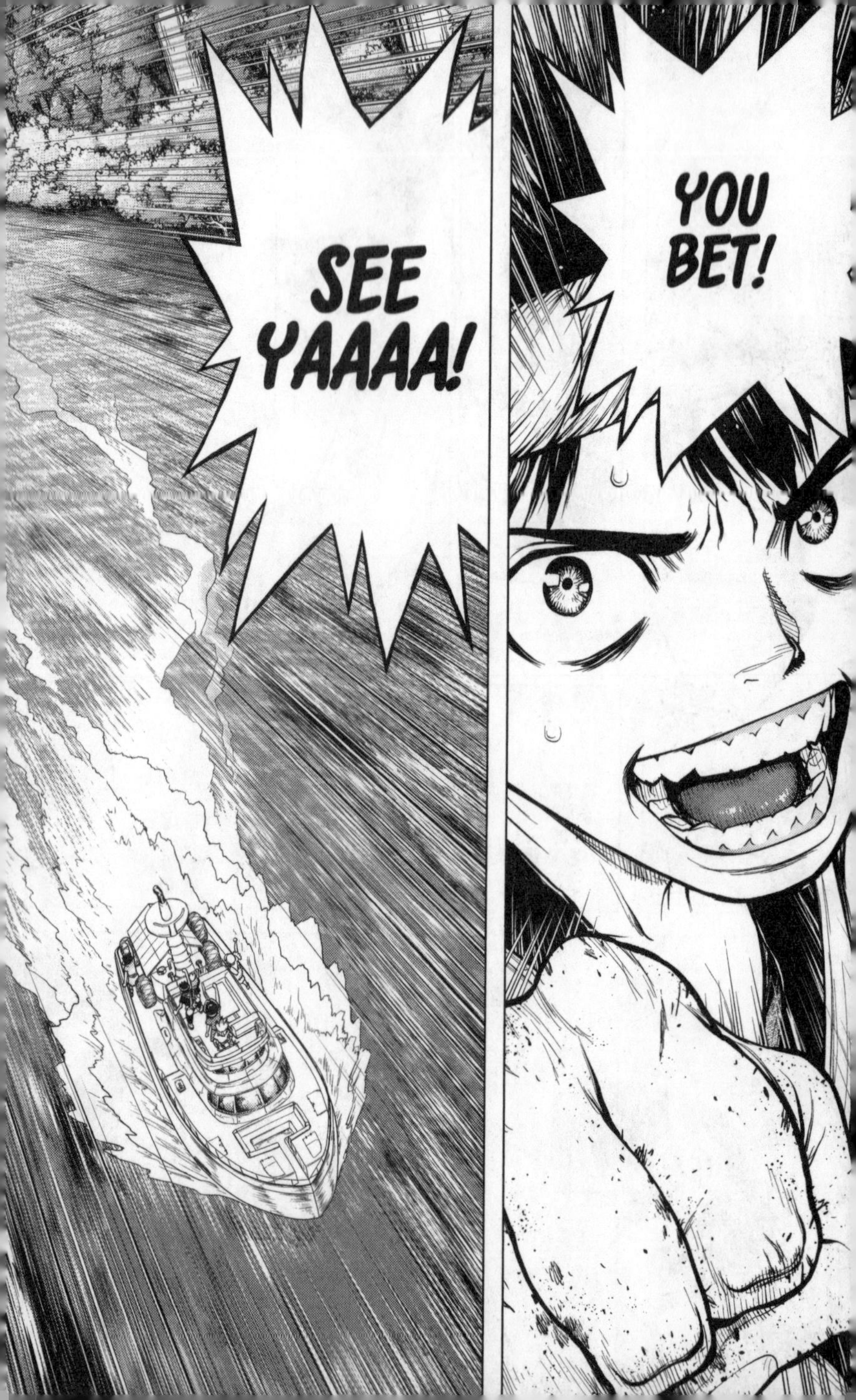
YOU BET!
SEE YAAAA!

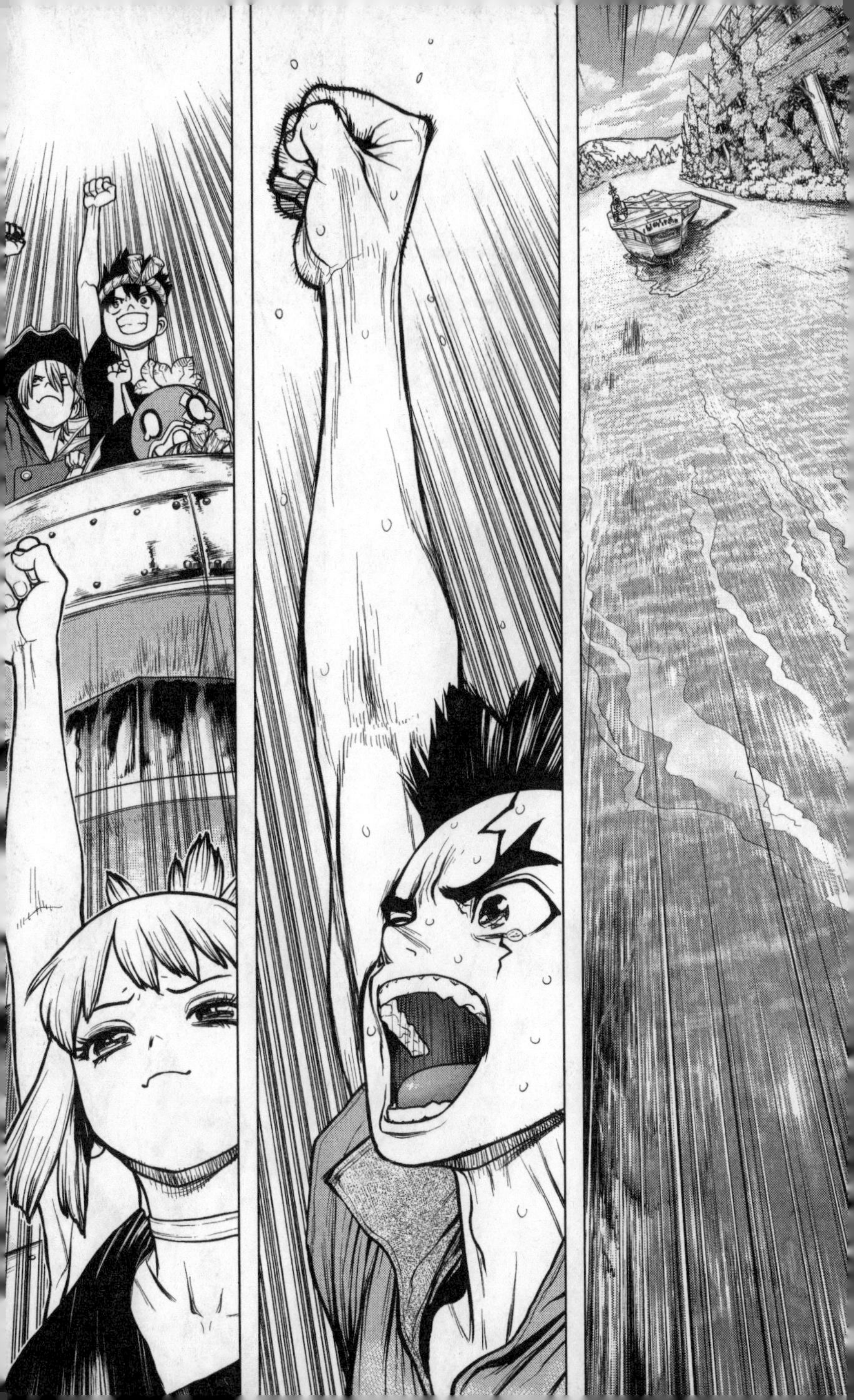

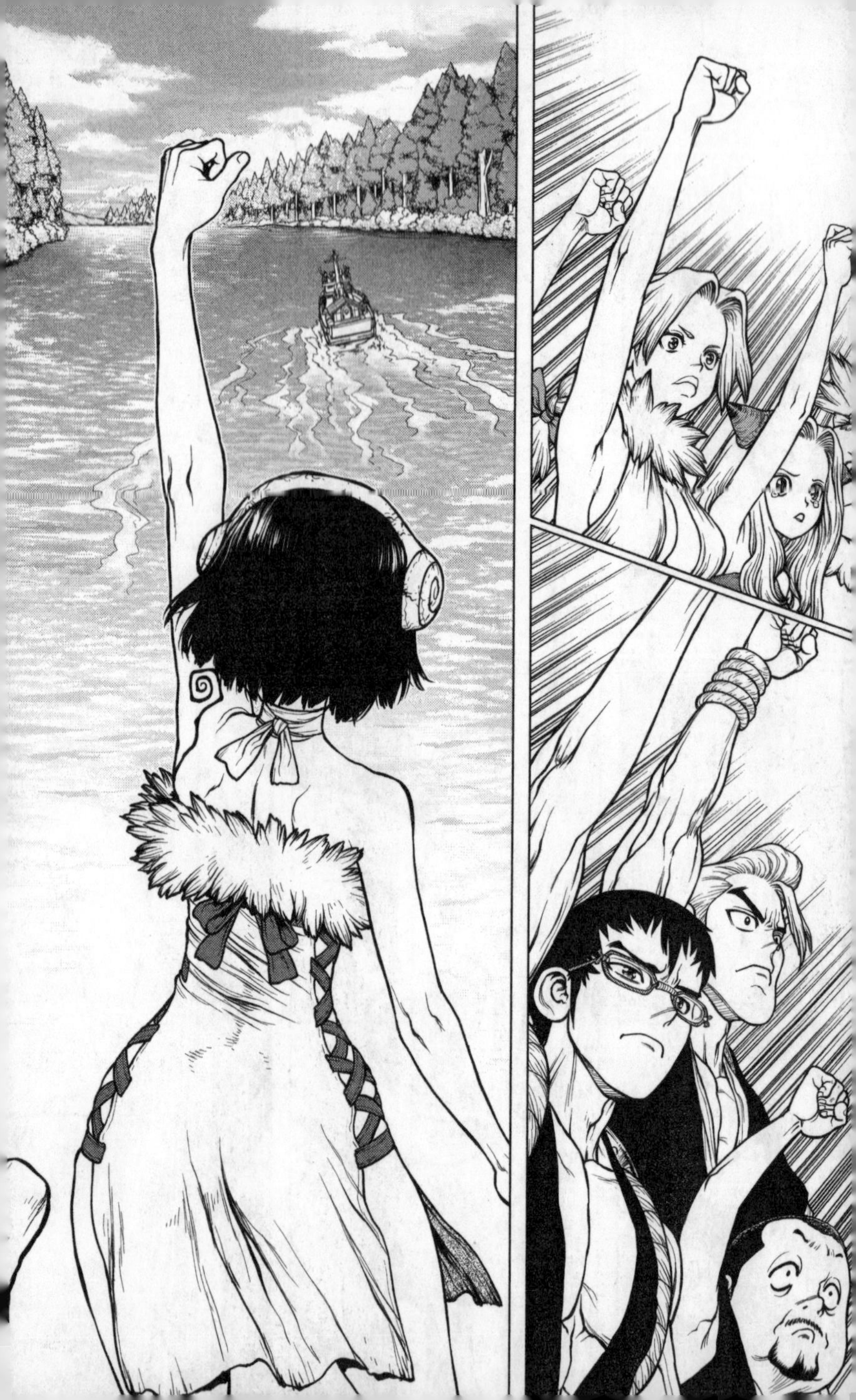

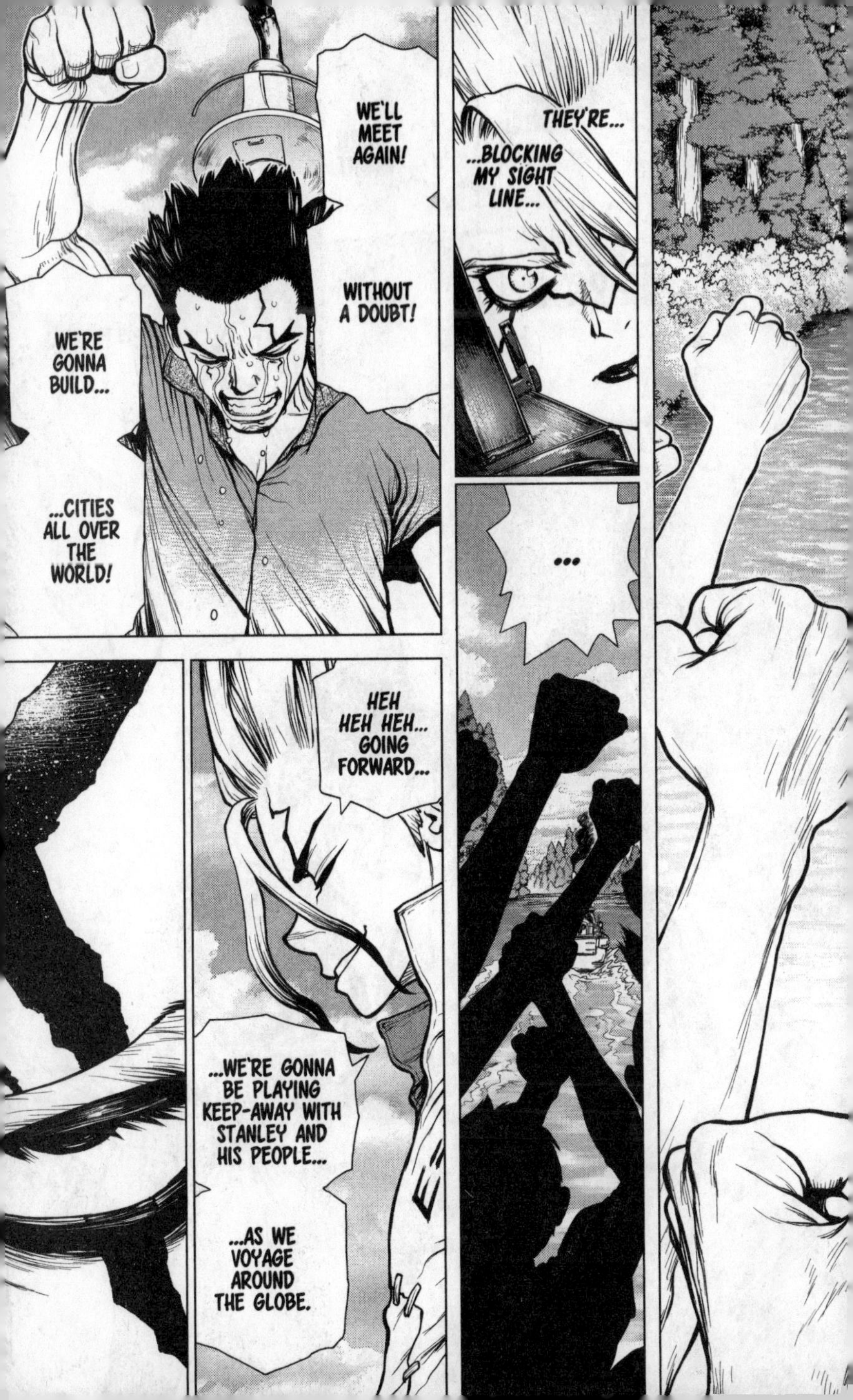
THEY'RE...
...BLOCKING MY SIGHT LINE...
WE'LL MEET AGAIN!
WITHOUT A DOUBT!
WE'RE GONNA BUILD...
...CITIES ALL OVER THE WORLD!
...
HEH HEH HEH... GOING FORWARD...
...WE'RE GONNA BE PLAYING KEEP-AWAY WITH STANLEY AND HIS PEOPLE...
...AS WE VOYAGE AROUND THE GLOBE.

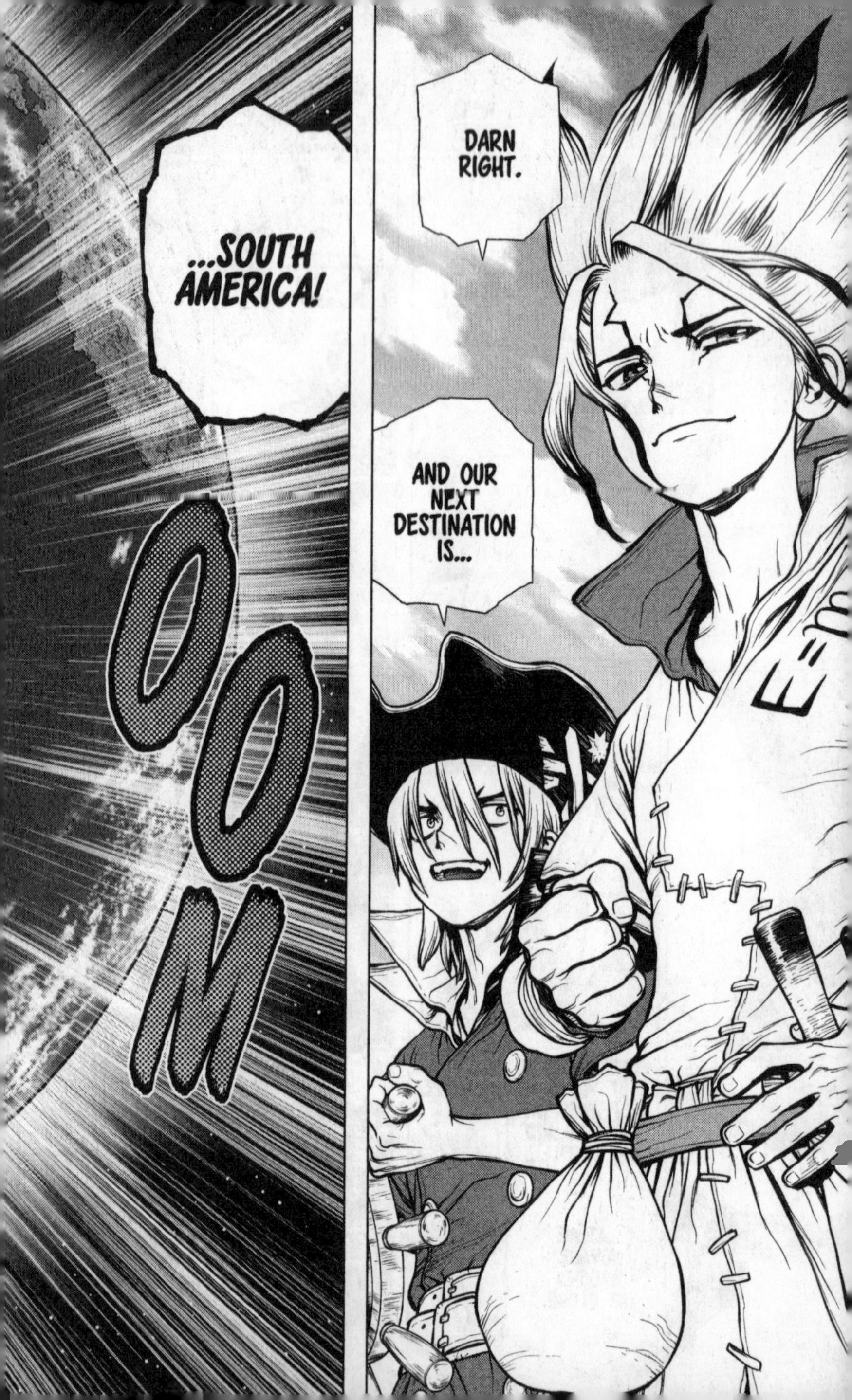
DARN RIGHT.
AND OUR NEXT DESTINATION IS...
...SOUTH AMERICA!
OOOM

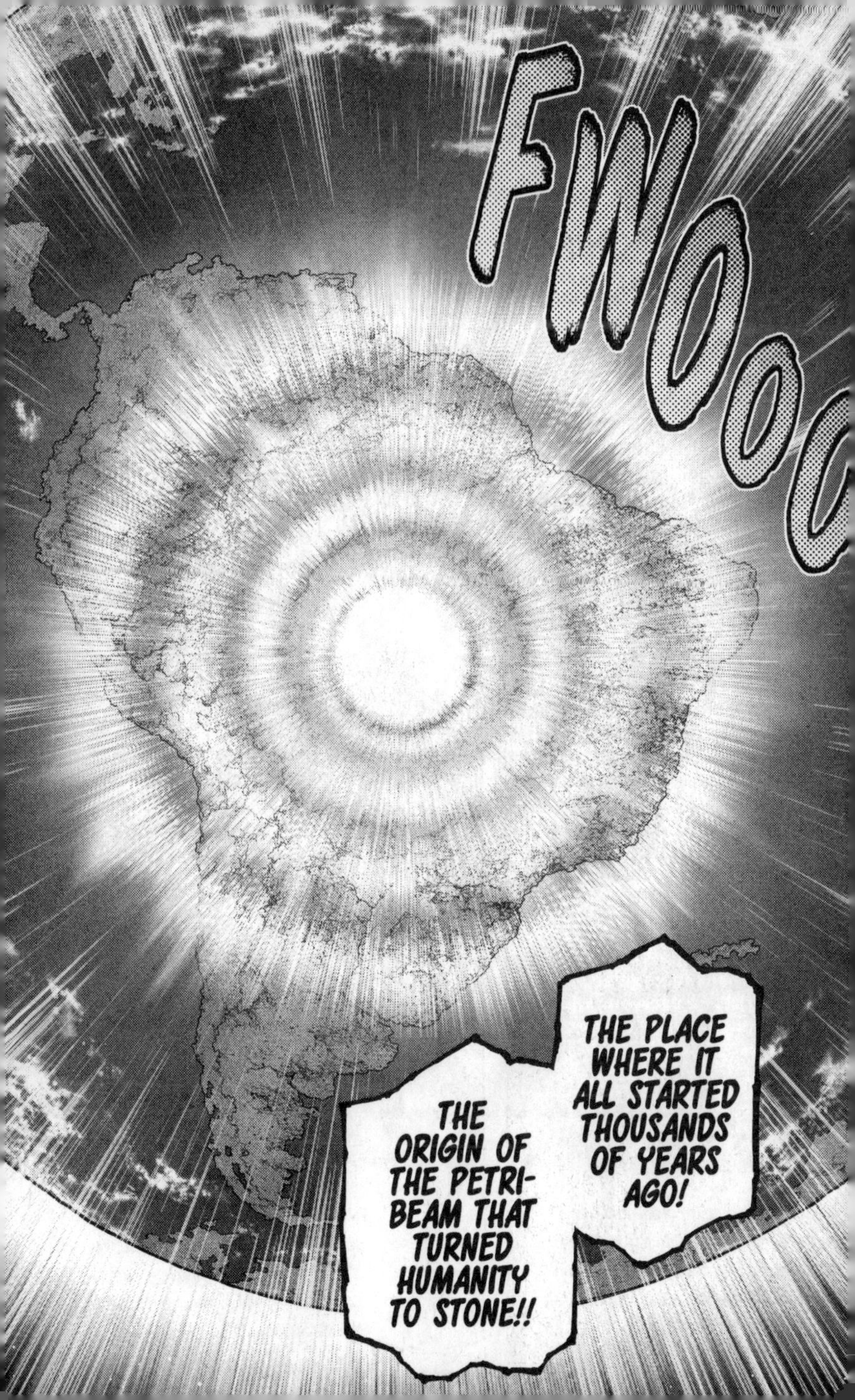
FWOOO
THE PLACE WHERE IT ALL STARTED THOUSANDS OF YEARS AGO!
THE ORIGIN OF THE PETRI-BEAM THAT TURNED HUMANITY TO STONE!!

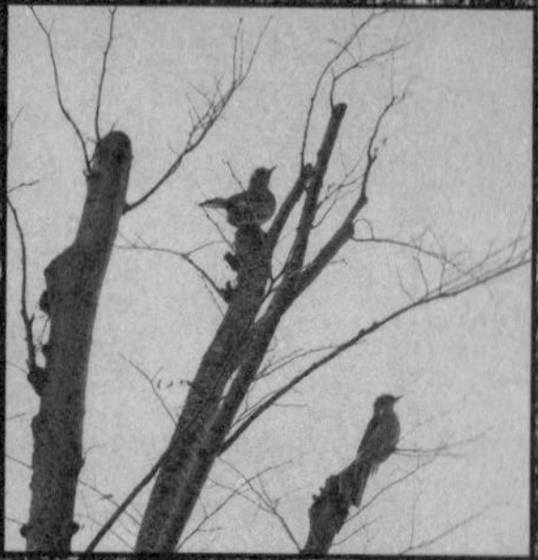

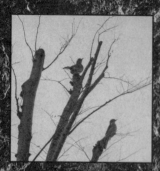

BOICHI

What exactly does it mean to be a pioneer, breaching unknown territory?

In theory, people should admire such attempts and see the value in them. But in practice, it can be almost too difficult to put into words. One will encounter fewer people willing to help than those who stand in opposition. It can be a lonely path with very few earnest supporters.

Sometimes, a lack of know-how can lead to mistakes that break the spirit and destroy one's life. Not many can comprehend that sort of pain and solitude. Despite all this, there will always be new pioneers emerging. Why? Because humans are always willing to break new ground. Today, tomorrow, and the day after.

From the bottom of my heart, I'm throwing my support behind the overseas challengers selected for the Tezuka Prize. To everyone who took up this challenge, I want to say, "You have all my love."

Every last one of you is like Senku, standing strong upon your own piece of this world.

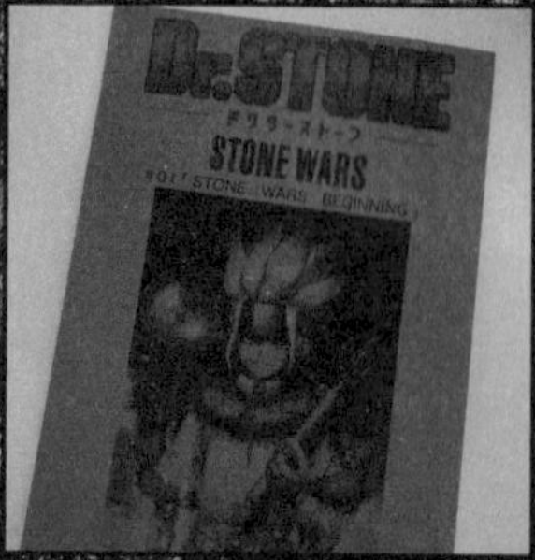
Dr.STONE
STONE WARS

RIICHIRO INAGAKI

SEASON 2 OF THE ANIME!!!

Season 2 of the *Dr. Stone* anime started airing in January 2021! You can check it out on a number of channels and streaming services!

Boichi is a Korean-born artist currently living and working in Japan. His previous works include *Sun-Ken Rock* and *Terra Formars Asimov*.

Riichiro Inagaki is a Japanese manga writer from Tokyo. He is the writer for the sports manga series *Eyeshield 21*, which was serialized in *Weekly Shonen Jump*.

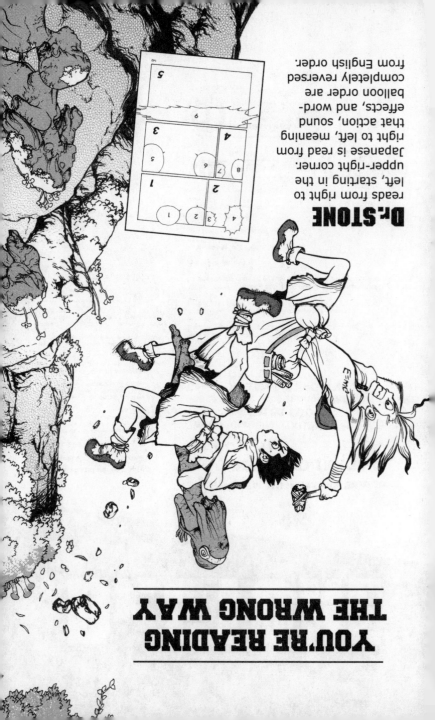

YOU'RE READING THE WRONG WAY

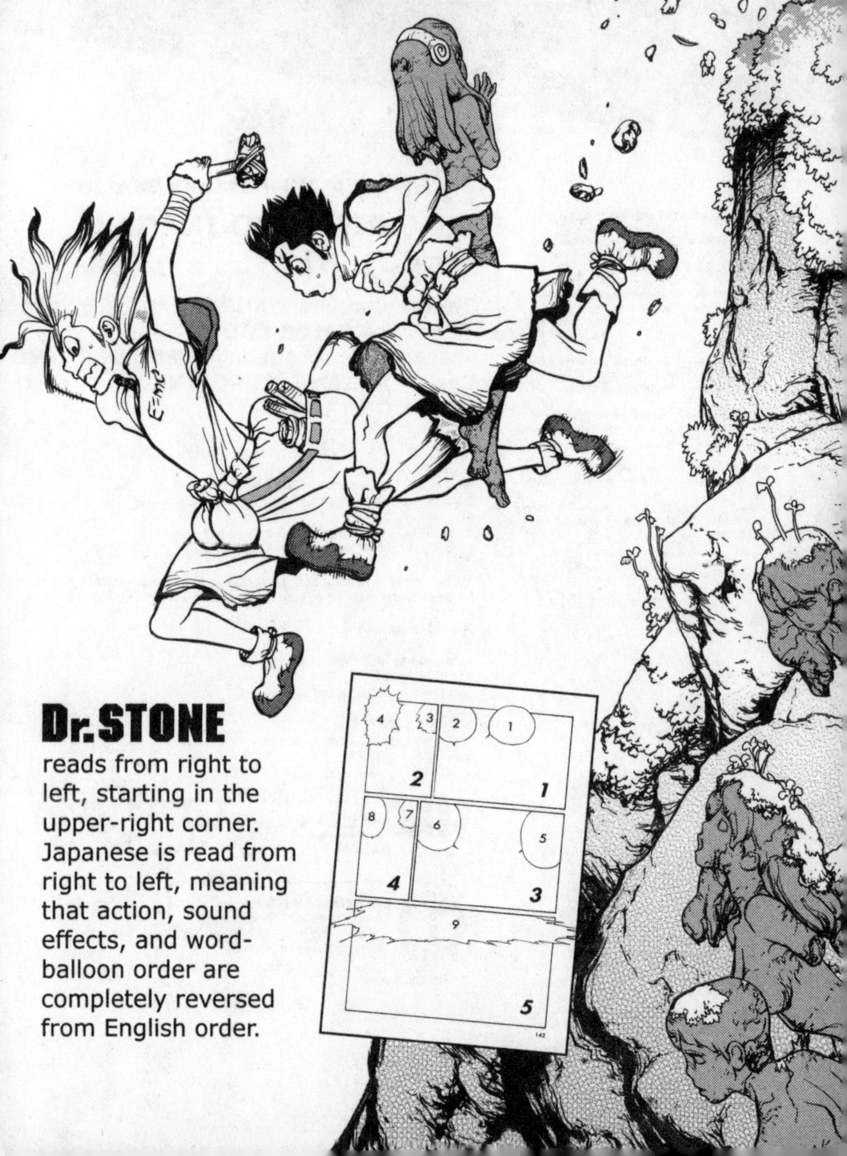

Dr.STONE

reads from right to left, starting in the upper-right corner. Japanese is read from right to left, meaning that action, sound effects, and word-balloon order are completely reversed from English order.

Dr.STONE

19

SHONEN JUMP Manga Edition

Story **RIICHIRO INAGAKI**
Art **BOICHI**

Science Consultant/**KURARE** **with Yakuri Classroom of Doo Aruma Zirou, Cyrano, POKA**
Translation/**CALEB COOK**
Touch-Up Art & Lettering/**STEPHEN DUTRO**
Design/**JULIAN [JR] ROBINSON**
Editor/**JOHN BAE**

Printed in Canada

Published by VIZ Media, LLC
P.O. Box 77010
San Francisco, CA 94107

10 9 8 7 6 5 4 3 2 1
First printing, November 2021

VIZ MEDIA
viz.com

SHONEN JUMP

Consulted Works:

- Asari, Yoshito, *Uchu e Ikitakute Ekitainenryo Rocket wo DIY Shite Mita (Gakken Rigaku Sensho)*, Gakken Plus, 2013
- Dartnell, Lewis, *The Knowledge: How to Rebuild Civilization in the Aftermath of a Cataclysm* Translated by Erika Togo, Kawade Shobo Shinsha, 2015
- Diamond, Jared, *Guns, Germs, and Steel: The Fates of Human Societies* Translated by Akira Kurahone, Soshisha Publishing Co., 2012
- Harari, Yuval Noah, *Sapiens: A Brief History of Humankind* Translated by Hiroyuki Shibata, Kawade Shobo Shinsha, 2016
- Weisman, Alan, *The World Without Us* Translated by Shinobu Onizawa, Hayakawa Publishing, 2009
- Akatsuka, Satoshi. *Dogfight Science: The Secrets Behind Mid-Air Combat*, Revised Edition. Science-i Shinsho, 2018